A History of Prussia

First published by Longman Group Limited, 1978

This edition published by Dorset Press,
a division of Marboro Books Corporation,
by arrangement with Longman Group Limited
1987 Dorset Press

ISBN 0-88029-158-3

Printed in the United States of America

M 9 8 7 6 5 4 3 2

A History of Prussia

H. W. Koch

Dorset Press
New York

Preface

The primary intention of this book is to provide the general reader and the student with a reasonably comprehensive history of the Prussian *state*, to fill a gap in the existing literature on Prussia, at least of English-speaking countries. Until now, after reading F. L. Carsten's excellent *Origins of Prussia*, the reader in order to enrich and expand his knowledge of Prussia had to turn to biographies or extract information from general histories of Germany. Yet even in the realm of the political biography Prussia is not particularly well served. Even in German there exists no satisfactory biography of so crucial a personality as was the soldier king Frederick William I; C. Hinrich's masterpiece has remained incomplete and takes us only to the point of Frederick William's accession to the throne. Only his son Frederick the Great and later Bismarck have received extensive treatment by historians; whether satisfactorily is another matter. Bismarck apart, only Stein seems to have captured the imagination of an English biographer. But Seeley's three-volume biography so rich in material, seems to have been largely forgotten.

Given the decisive role Prussia played in German and European history, a history of Prussia is rather more important than say that of Bavaria although a Bavarian might well vociferously object to this. Since the author is himself German, born in Bavaria, of Prussian-Huguenot descent, he would reject any charge of writing from a specifically Prussian point of view, although he has taken account of the merits of that point of view.

There is no point in trying to disguise the fact that in its own way this history of Prussia is 'revisionist' in its approach. But it should never be the task of the historian to tread in the well-trodden footsteps of the past seven decades, to do no more than touch up old clichés, themselves the product of feverish and sometimes rightly embittered minds. On the other hand little purpose would be served by replacing unsound opinions and judgements by their distorted opposites. The task this author has set himself is to look at Prussia's history in its own terms and context, rejecting outright the approach which views German history and that of Prussia within it against the background of the Wilhelmine era, or even that of the atrocities of the Third Reich.

One of the many problems when dealing with the Prussian state is to decide when it came to an end. Should it be 1871 when Germany was reunified and Prussia merged into the Reich; should it be 1918 when the Hohenzollern dynasty abdicated; or 1932 when Chancellor von Papen put an end to the last Prussian government; or 1947 when the victors of the Second World War formally dissolved Prussia? This author, for reasons mentioned in the last two chapters of the book, decided on 1871. Therefore the political developments in Prussia after 1871 have been indicated in outline only.

A work of this nature is deeply indebted to other historians who in their work have provided the new materials and insights on which this book is based. More detailed reference to these will be found in the bibliography. However, the author is also deeply in debt to the Inter-Library Loan Service of the Morell Library of the University of York and its staff, without the aid of whom many of the works used would have been inaccessible. Needless to say he is also in debt to many individuals, foremost among them Frau Magdalena Sailer, Kirchdorf bei Haag/obb, Frau Karla Zapf, Munich, Frau Franziska Henning, Berlin-Dahlem who provided the atmosphere of calm and quiet in which this book was written.

H. W. Koch
York and Munich, 1977

Chapter 1

The Teutonic Order

Ruthlessness, romantic idealism and other similar characteristics are attributed to the *Deutschritter Orden*, the Teutonic Knights. Yet the story of this order is less colourful than that of similar orders such as the Templars. Most of them claimed – not always quite correctly – that their origins dated back to St Bernard of Clairvaux, who had issued the Rule of the Templars to two knights, Hugo of Payens and Godfrey of St Omer; rules closely modelled on St Bernard's own order, in a spirit of profound Christian devotion and strict asceticism. At the time of the second crusade, St Bernard himself called for recruits for the Templars, and in a tract issued for this purpose he wrote:

The warriors are gentler than lambs and fiercer than lions, wedding the mildness of the monk to the valour of the knight, so that it is difficult to decide which to call them: men who adorn the Temple of Solomon with weapons instead of gems, with shields instead of crowns of gold, with saddles and bridles instead of candelabra; eager for victory not for fame; for battle not for pomp; who abhor useless speech, unnecessary action, unmeasured laughter, gossip and chatter, as they despise all vain things; who, in spite of their being many, live in one house according to one rule, with one soul and one heart. (Ernst Kantorowicz)

St Bernard's foundation did not put an end to the hero of the 'age of chivalry' and his courtly pursuits, but countered the 'restless, vacillating secular knight errant, who flew from adventure to adventure, or sacrificed himself in the service of his lady-love, leading his own individual life and entirely destructive to the firm fabric of the state' with a closed, rigidly disciplined corporation, dedicated, as in the case of the Templars, to the service of Christ, their spiritual head. They were monks, actively serving a common purpose with the New Testament and the sword, men who subordinated themselves to a common master. In modern terminology: they were activists of the word and the sword, recognizable by the uniformity of their dress, the mantle with the cross, and style of life.

But as with all human institutions, the original idealism could not be sustained indefinitely. By the end of the twelfth century, spiritual knighthood seemed almost extinct. The institutions of the Knights of the Templars, whose members were mainly French, and the Knights of St John, composed largely of English and Italian members, seemed on the wane, perhaps even on the point of disintegration. Yet precisely at this point in time, in 1190, a new order made its appearance, one which was to be called the Teutonic Order. The initiative for it, however, did not come from the clergy, nor for that matter from German knights, but from German burghers, merchants from Bremen and Lübeck, the old cities of the Hanseatic League.

Disease had badly affected the army of crusaders camping on Mount Turon outside the city of Acre. Merchants from the two German cities showed compassion for their helpless fellow countrymen. They removed the sails from their boats, and from them made large tents which they provided with beds and hospital equipment. Above all, they supplied the finance with which to maintain them. In these hospital beds, dedicated to the Virgin Mary, sick German knights were cared for by the merchants. Their leader, a German merchant by the name of Siebrand, obtained from King Guy, then King of Jerusalem, a grant of a plot of land and a street in Acre, once the city had been conquered. Here the new foundation was to find a more permanent home. When Siebrand and the merchants returned to Germany, they put the administration of the foundation into the hands of the chaplain, Conrad, and the chamberlain, Burkhard, who had arrived at Acre in October 1190 with Frederick of Swabia, a son of Frederick Barbarossa. Burkhard and Conrad administered the foundation according to the rules of the Order of St John. Once Acre had been taken, the grant of land made to their predecessors was appropriated. On this land they built a church and a hospital, as well as dormitories for the members. They then applied for recognition as a spiritual corporation of the Brothers of the Hospital of St Mary of the German Nation. This recognition was duly granted by Pope Celestine III in 1196, and confirmed by Pope Innocent in 1199. The latter, however, insisted that the corporation become a knightly order which would take its knightly rules from the Templars, while its hospital rules were to come from the Order of St John.

This new order of German knights never distinguished itself in the Holy Land; it fought no famous battles there, nor did it enjoy that abundant wealth which had been the cause of the corruption and decay of the older orders. It was, and remained, a purely Germanic movement, one of the most significant features of which, particularly in the context of its long-term development in the colonization of the German east, was its close association with the German burghers. As a founder of cities and towns, and as a protector of and participator in the trading ventures of north-eastern Europe, it established its reputation. But once the interests of the cities and traders on one hand, and of the Teutonic Knights on the other began to diverge, the order declined. Throughout its duration the Teutonic Order consisted of three main branches. Firstly, there was the German branch, concentrated primarily in southern and south-western Germany, including Alsace, with possessions also in Burgundy. Secondly, there was the branch in Livonia

Contents

List of maps and genealogical tables

For Verona

and thirdly, the Prussian branch with its centre at the Marienburg. After the residence of the Grand Master was transferred to this castle, it became the centre of the order as a whole.

The Servants of St Mary of the German House, as the Teutonic Knights were called in their oldest set of rules, were to be dedicated men of our Lord Jesus Christ. They were exempted from secular justice, and were to preserve a state of chastity, renounce freedom of personal will and the possession of personal property. Only the order was to possess land and buildings, men and women, and to receive financial income. In acknowledgement of the fact that a hospital rather than knighthood represented the origin of the order, it was dedicated to maintaining hospitals in perpetuity. The sick and ailing accepted into the hospital had first to confess; then, throughout their stay, they were to be fed before the brothers of the order ate and the order was to provide doctors for them. The sick were to be served humbly and faithfully. To cover the not inconsiderable expenses of the hospital the Grand Master was allowed to send brothers far and wide to beg for alms.

The inner core of the order consisted of clergy and laymen. Both were dutifully to attend mass and other church services, and take holy communion seven times a year. The rules laid down that when a brother died, his best clothes, as well as his food and drink for 40 days, should be distributed to the poor. Of the lay brothers only the knights were to wear white mantles; apart from this there was to be no difference between them and the other lay brothers. The white mantle was to bear a black cross. Every man was to wear his hair closely cropped; the clergy a tonsure, and the lay brothers beards of moderate length. In contrast to knightly fashion the full beard became the characteristic feature of the brothers, earning them the nickname 'the bearded ones'.

At mealtimes the priests were to bless the food; this was to be followed by the Lord's Prayer and a Hail Mary, spoken by the lay members. On three days of the week meat was to form part of the meal; on three other days there was dairy produce and eggs. Friday was the fast day. However, for the weak and sick the meal could be improved according to need. At the meal two brothers were to share a bowl; only drink could be taken from individual cups.

Generally each house of the order consisted of a convent of 12 brothers – the number of Christ's disciples. They were headed by a *Komtur*, a bailiff, who was to read the lesson. The brothers had to remain silent at table unless the *Komtur* granted an exception, usually when there were guests from outside. Bread left on the table uneaten was to be given to the poor, in addition to one-tenth of all the bread baked in the house. All the brothers were to sleep in one room, clothed in a shirt, trousers and stockings. A light was to burn in the room throughout the night.

A brother was to have neither his own seal nor a coat of arms. Nor was he to write, send or read letters without the permission of the Superior, who could demand that the content of a letter be read aloud.

The brothers could exchange or give away wooden arms which they had
made themselves, such as crossbows, spears and arrows. No chest or
cupboard was to have a lock. Whatever was necessary for a brother in
fulfilling his role as a warrior – such as horses, weapons and servants –
he could have in his possession, but not actually own. His shield, saddle
and bridle were to bear neither secular colours nor gold or silver. Horses
and weapons presented to one brother had to be handed over to another
upon instruction from the Superior, an instruction against which no
objection could be raised. A brother was forbidden to participate in, or
take any interest in, the hunt. Where hunters could be useful the order
could keep them, and the brothers accompany them for their
protection, but all they were allowed to kill were wild animals, without
the aid of dogs. Birds could be shot only as archery practice.

In their relationships with one another, the rules decreed that if one
brother had given offence to another he was to ask for forgiveness
before the sun set. When decisions had to be taken, such as appointments within the order or the sale or purchase of land, the brothers
were to assemble and offer their advice, but it was up to the Superior to
decide which recommendation was best and should be followed. In
journeys across the land they were to set a good example at all times.
Wedding celebrations were to be avoided, likewise the company of
secular knights and worldly games. Wherever this might give grounds
for scandal, they were to avoid talking to women, especially young ones.
They were not allowed to kiss women, not even their own mothers or
sisters. No boy could be admitted to the order before reaching the age of
14; nor might any women be admitted to any ceremony since their
presence would impair the virility of the order. The only employment
suitable for women was to be the care of the sick and animals. They also
had to occupy a house separate from that of the brothers.

Secular applicants could be admitted to the order, whether they were
married or single, provided that they were considered worthy and
would surrender their worldly possessions to the order. The Superior
was to be the support of the weak and the persecutor of the disobedient.
Hence he was to carry a rod and staff in his hands. It was within his
power to grant dispensations from any rules of the order except those of
chastity, poverty and obedience.

Whoever was accepted into the order as a brother had first to be
instructed by another brother in the ceremonies that preceded his
admission. On being introduced he had to kneel down in front of the
entire chapter of brothers and beg to be admitted to the order for the
sake of his soul. The Superior then asked whether he had any liabilities,
or whether he were burdened with any guilt that might affect the order.
If the applicant could reply in the negative, he would then solemnly vow
to serve the sick, to protect the Holy Land and any other land belonging
to the order, and not to leave the order without permission. Thereupon
he was accepted on probation. The order, in its turn, vowed to the
applicant that it would supply him with water, bread and old clothes.

Applicants were expected to know the Creed and the Lord's Prayer; if they did not then they were to be instructed by the priests during the first six months of their stay.

When a Grand Master died, his deputy convened all the *Komturs* of Germany, Prussia and Livonia, as well as Apulia. Their function was to elect 13 members who in turn would elect the new Grand Master. Among the qualifications for this office were to have been born in wedlock, never to have offended against the laws of chastity, nor committed theft.

Throughout its duration the Teutonic Order was never an aristocratic order, nor did it accept only people of knightly origin, or those who had been made knights by the Grand Master. As a rule the condition for joining was to be a freeman, yet that Grand Master whose personality determined to a large extent the early fortunes of the order, had probably risen to his high rank from that of a *Ministeriale*, a chancery official of unfree origin, at the court of Emperor Henry VI and his son Frederick II, the greatest of the Hohenstaufen emperors. The first Grand Masters of the order were burghers of the city of Bremen. But in 1216 Pope Honorius III insisted that the Grand Master of the order should be of knightly origin, or of honest birth to ensure that he could be made a knight. Thus the illegitimate sons of the princes, or for that matter even those of the Grand Master himself, were prevented from turning the office into a hereditary property.

Nevertheless, knightly ethics determined the institutions, attitudes and behaviour of the order. Its highest representative was the Grand Master. Although obliged in all important matters to take counsel from experienced brothers and to take into consideration the decision of the chapter of the order, he was, during the order's heyday, an extremely powerful man, and only during the final stages of its disintegration did the Grand Master's rule degenerate into a joint government consisting of other officers of the order.

Below the Grand Master were the offices of the central administration: the *Grosskomtur*, the *Ordensmarschall* or *Grossmarschall*, the *Spittler* (hospitaller), the *Tressler* (treasurer) and the *Trapier* (quartermaster). Following the occupation of Prussia, the office of *Grossschäffer* gained in significance since he acted as a Minister of Trade, establishing the continually expanding commercial relations of the Teutonic Order. The territory of the order was divided into *Komtureis*, each headed by a *Komtur*; smaller territorial subdivisions were headed by *Vogts* or caretakers.

During the first decades of the order's existence ecclesiastical brothers were few, monks from mendicant orders frequently attending to its spiritual affairs. This prevented powerful bishops from gaining influence within the order. But throughout its history there is discernible a policy of keeping the influence of the order's clergy within narrow limits; after all, one of the explicit purposes of the order was to train skilled warriors, not comfortable and complacent monks. The clergy wore the white mantle with the black cross.

The lay members, warriors and workers came from all walks of life. They made their monastic vows, all received the same food and lodgings, all participated equally in the affairs of the chapter, and in principle possessed the same political rights, such as active and passive franchise. They also bore the cross on their mantle, though secular members, such as married men or those who had not taken the three vows, bore a cross the upper part of which was omitted and thus resembled the letter T. Among the lay members it was the knights who represented the aristocracy although, except for the white of their mantle, they were denied knightly decorations. Their role in warfare was that of a heavy cavalry, since they had more horses than the other warriors. It was the Grand Master's right to promote brothers of the order, or those who wanted to join the knighthood, and hand them the knight's sword. In spite of the fact that the order was a specifically Germanic institution, it did accept foreigners into its ranks, particularly Poles, as well as other Slavs.

In its early years there were few signs of the historic role which the order was destined to play. It led a relatively insignificant life on the periphery of medieval Europe's political and military concerns. It is true that Emperor Henry VI, the son of Frederick Barbarossa, had turned his attention to the order while planning a crusade, but this development was cut short by his death. Its actual rise was closely linked to the rule and reign of his son Frederick II. Frederick was quick to recognize the potential of this relatively new and unknown order. Unlike other similar orders, this one, free from both feudal ties and the influence of temporal and spiritual lords, was still capable of being turned into an elite body for the Emperor's purposes. Frederick envisaged it as a body unconditionally loyal to the Emperor. On behalf of the order he had the Papacy grant charters for it; he recruited prominent members, and even went as far as persuading members of other orders to join it. In the Holy Land he relied upon it almost exclusively whenever he required for a certain task men in whom he could place his trust. To its knights he entrusted the administration of entire territories, such as Alsace. He accorded to the order the privilege that its Grand Master, when attending court, should be part of the royal household, and belong to the inner circle of the Emperor's advisers. Two brethren of the order were to be in permanent attendance at the imperial court.

Indeed, Frederick's greatest confidant was the first Grand Master of stature, Hermann von Salza. For over two decades Hermann was his counsellor and closest friend; not, of course, because he was the Grand Master of the Teutonic Order, but rather on account of his personal qualities which combined unflinching loyalty to Frederick with stable judgement and political good sense. These qualities enabled him to act time and again as a mediator between Frederick and the Papacy, without losing the respect and high esteem of either.

It was Frederick's court and his administration which imprinted themselves upon the structure of the Teutonic Order. The history of medieval Europe seems still to be written far too much in European terms without giving more than scant attention to the influence of the Arab world, particularly in the field of public administration. Frederick II was, in Jakob Burckhardt's words,

The first ruler of the modern type who sat upon a throne, had early accustomed himself to a thoroughly objective treatment of affairs. His acquaintance with the internal condition and administration of the Saracenic States was close and intimate; and the mortal struggle in which he was engaged with the Papacy compelled him, no less than his adversaries, to bring into the field all the resources at his command . . . He centralized, in a manner hitherto unknown in the West, the whole judicial and political administration . . .

Frederick's introduction of a centralized administration gave Hermann von Salza a model for the structural reorganization of the Teutonic Order, though of course not without considerable modifications. For example Frederick had virtually abolished the elective principle in southern Italy, but such a policy in the order would most likely have resulted in complete revolt.

This structural reorganization unwittingly prepared the order for its main task in north-eastern Germany. The centre of the order's missionary activity was always considered to be the Holy Land, but as the practicability of that venture began to recede more and more into the realm of pious hopes and intentions, the order began to envisage firm settlement combined with missionary activity in eastern central Europe. Around 1222 the order had attempted to gain a foothold in the Transylvanian Burzenland in Hungary, which King Andrew of Hungary had, somewhat reluctantly, presented to the order, and which the Pope had declared as a fief of the Papacy. The order did manage to build five castles in the region, but the resistance of the combined forces of the Hungarians and Germans who had settled there compelled it to give up any attempts to impose its own rule. Just at the time when the order's failure in Hungary became apparent, Conrad of Masovia, Duke of Poland, found himself similarly unable to repulse the heathen Prussians. And so he turned to the Teutonic Knights for help, and provisionally gave a verbal undertaking that, in return for their services, he would reward them with the territories of Kulm along the river Vistula.

Hermann von Salza immediately recognized the opportunity. With the full support of Emperor Frederick, who was prepared to grant considerable privileges to the order, Hermann took the matter up with the Papacy. The Pope also held Hermann in high esteem, and as a result granted the Golden Bull of Rimini in 1226. This laid down the future tasks of the Teutonic Order, as well as setting out in minute detail the constitution of the future state for the order in north-eastern central Europe. In fact the Bull was completed before the negotiations with Conrad of Masovia had been concluded, and before a single knight bearing the white mantle with the black cross had reached the west bank of the Vistula.

At first sight it seems that in actual fact neither Emperor nor Pope gave anything away since, after all, the land had yet to be conquered But over the long term the charter made grants of a size and significance almost unprecedented, bestowing privileges which were to determine the development of the order for nearly two centuries. '. . . All gifts and conquests are to be the free property of the order, which is to exercise full territorial rights and be responsible to none. The Grand Master is to enjoy all the privileges that pertain to a prince of the Empire, including all royal privileges, and in Prussia the order shall be free from all imperial taxes, burdens and services.' The future territory of the Teutonic Order was to be 'an integral part of the monarchy of the Empire'. Frederick considered that missionary activity was primarily the task of the Empire, and only secondarily that of the church: '. . . let us therefore turn our minds to the conquest, no less than to the conversion, of the heathen peoples'. By stating the imperial mission of the heathen conquest, and by announcing his intention of turning the territories to be conquered into a part of the Empire, Frederick countered the papal move according to which any new converts were to owe obedience to none except Christ and the Roman church.

Obviously the importance which the undertaking was to acquire could not have been foreseen in 1226, but the position of the order and its future were assured by the charter. Besides the Teutonic Knights, another order was and had been active in the conversion of the heathens of the north-east, namely the Cistercian monks. Hermann von Salza was able to make allies of these also, and the two orders together represented the main pillars of missionary activity in the north-east. It is one of those subtle ironies of history that while Hermann von Salza was one close friend of Frederick II, the young Rudolph von Hapsburg was another. Hence, unwittingly, Frederick II stood at the cradle of two German states whose rivalry and antagonisms were to determine the fate of Germany as a whole.

The heathens who occupied the coastal plains of the Baltic Sea from the Vistula to the river Memel, had already been subjected to earlier, unsuccesful attempts at conversion. Divided into various tribes, frequently engaged in feuds one with another, they are believed to have descended from the Lithuanians. But their customs were in contrast to those of most of their Slav neighbours. They were renowned for their generous hospitality, their excessive drinking, their holy shrines, their barbaric custom that a widow should not survive her husband, and the practice of burning a deceased warrior together with his slaves, dogs and falcons. In other words their customs were not very far removed from those of the ancient Germans. But unlike them they showed, in spite of their feuds, little ambition for territorial expansion, being content to live where they had settled. They were fairly populous and lived in groups in villages and castles. The rivers flowing into the Baltic gave access to the interior, and on land the territory was traversed by traders making their way to Poland and even as far as Novgorod. The territory around Kulm and Löbau had become Polish but, like the entire region between the Vistula and the Memel, was not exclusively inhabited by Prussians but by numerous other tribes as well. Even before the Teutonic Knights began their venture, German colonists brought in by the bishops of Kulm posed a threat to them from the west and south; furthermore, Christian Germans had settled along the Baltic coast under the protection of the bishops of Livonia. These traded mainly with the interior, protected by a knightly order founded by the Bishop of Riga and modelled on the order of the Templars, and were instrumental in spreading German rule, language and culture across Courland, Latvia and Estonia.

Thus, the Teutonic Knights came fairly late on the scene. Indeed, in the context of the thirteenth century, they can be considered almost an anachronism at a time which saw the beginning of the decline of medieval knighthood. Inside Germany the nobles time and again refused to support the Empire; increasingly the journey to Rome to receive the imperial crown was considered a pointless and tedious duty rather than a vital aspect of the politics of the Holy Roman Empire of the German Nation. Poetry inspired by courtly chivalry was on the decline; no further epics were forthcoming: no *Chanson de Roland*, no *Parsifal*, no *Nibelungenlied*. Louis the Pious of France represented the swan-song of European knighthood; a new order was on the threshold of power, whether represented by France in Phillip the Fair and his *Realpolitik*, or by England in the form of the House of Commons. The decline of European knighthood is also illustrated by changing military tactics which questioned the very *raison d'être* of knighthood. The English long bows at Crecy had given an early indication of this, and when Austria's knighthood was defeated by the Swiss foot levies at Sempach in 1386, it showed that the days of chivalrous individual combat were gone forever. In Prussia and Livonia the Teutonic Order could still uphold the old traditions longer than elsewhere, but it was clear that it lived on borrowed time.

During that epoch the Teutonic Knights set about creating a new state of their own, thus taking the last step in the process of colonization. Within a matter of a few years the lands around Kulm and Löbau had been converted by the Germanic order, and by 1230 Conrad of Masovia had handed over the land to the order. Hermann von Salza, in order to have the new possessions also sanctioned by the church, and thus avoid their becoming a pawn in the struggle between Papacy and Empire, had the territory declared the property of St Peter, a decision of fateful long-term consequences for the order. And, inevitably, the Teutonic Knights were considered by many as unwelcome rivals. The bishops in the east resented the order's direct access to the Pope as well as to the Emperor. The nobility, especially the Polish nobility which had summoned the order in the first place, was bound to consider the creation of a German state as a potential threat. The common interest of the religious cause stopped at the point where practical political conflicts of interest began to emerge.

Yet during its early years, around 1230, the brothers of the Teutonic Order showed little inclination to carry out their missionary activity by force of arms, since their initial numbers were rather small. Moreover, until 1230 the order's economic position was very weak, and it was only after this time that its economic growth and consolidation began. This was firstly the result of several major grants of land which Frederick made to the order in Sicily and southern Italy – land taken from the Templars and the Order of St John. Secondly there were increasing gains of land in Prussia as the result of its colonization. In one report, the membership of the order in the days of Hermann von Salza is listed as being approximately 600, while by the late 1270s the membership had increased to about 2,000. Consequently, it was not the brothers of the Teutonic Order themselves who conquered and settled the new land, but crusaders recruited by the brothers throughout the German Empire on the promise that whoever participated in the crusade against the heathen Prussians would be relieved of penance for past wrong-doings. The preaching of the crusade must have fallen on ready ears, for in 1231 the Master, Hermann Balke, sent by Hermann von Salza, together with seven brothers of the order, headed a crusading army and crossed the Vistula. As soon as they gained a foothold, German boats sailed up the Vistula with supplies and building materials, and the first castles of the Teutonic Order began to raise their powerful and arrogant silhouettes against the eastern skyline: Thorun, Kulm and Marienwerder, bases from which further territorial expansion could be undertaken, and the centres upon which the attacks of the natives were concentrated.

But the Prussians and other tribes in the region were at first totally unaware of the threat confronting them; they did not even obstruct the building of the castles. Undoubtedly in the majority *vis-à-vis* the invading Germans, politically they were too divided among themselves to rally together and eliminate the new threat. When they did take the first steps in this direction, they had to give way to a German minority far more effectively organized in military terms. Relentlessly the Germans drove forward into the wilderness, secured the Vistula by building the fortress at Elbing, destroyed the heathen shrines, and subdued and converted the natives at the point of the sword. In 1237 the Sword Order of the Bishop of Riga combined with the Teutonic Order. Two years later Hermann von Salza, who had never set foot upon the new colonial territory himself, could die in the knowledge that the order controlled more than 150 kilometres of the Baltic coast from which it could expand inland. Less than two decades later, in 1255, Otakar the King of Bohemia joined the crusade in Prussia, and there in the Samland, in his honour, a new fortress was built by the name of Königsberg, displaying on its arms a knight with a crowned helmet.

It would, however, be a serious error to equate the crusades in the Holy Land with those in north-eastern Europe. In the former, the territories conquered were exploited; the majority of the crusaders returned home after a year or more of service in the Holy Land. It was essentially a knightly venture. In Prussia, by comparison, the ties between knights and burghers were inseparable, and the newly founded settlements were established with a view to permanency. The settlers came from all parts of north and north-western Germany and from the south-west. Once again this Flemish song enjoyed popularity:

> Naer Oostland wille wij rijden,
> Daer isser een betere stee.

> *To the Eastland we want to go,*
> *There is a better life.*

The initially low number of brothers of the order and crusaders determined, of course, the kind of warfare, as well as the relationship between the order and the natives. Since they were few in number it was hardly advisable to provoke hostility. But as their numbers, and their castles, increased and they steadily advanced eastwards, their ultimate intentions could no longer be hidden. In addition, the contradiction between the religious motivation of the crusade and the political realities emerged. The Germans subjecting the Prussians were in the minority but were determined to maintain their dominance. Consequently they considered it politically unwise to convert the Prussians in excessive numbers, for that would have given the Prussians almost equal rights with the Germans, and threatened the political position of the latter. As early as 1237 the Papacy had found it necessary to intervene against the order on behalf of the Prussians, but until 1241 the progress of the Teutonic Order continued relatively unimpeded. Then during the next 11 years, uncoordinated uprisings against the foreign invaders took place, though the Germans maintained the upper hand. By 1260 it seemed that the order's hold on Prussia had been secured.

Yet that picture was deceptive. Hardly any of the order, lay or clergy, troubled to acquire any knowledge of the language of the natives. The priests arrogantly destroyed ancient shrines, imposing the symbols of the new religion by force rather than persuasion. A people of peasants and shepherds was forced to bear the heavy burdens placed on them by the order, build castles and carry out other services. Mutual suspicion was rife, so much so that no Prussian might offer a German a mug of mead unless he himself had taken the first sip.

Moreover, what happened in Germany almost at the beginning of the Christian era, when Arminius the Cheruskan, educated and trained in Rome by the Romans, vanquished the Roman legions in the depths of the Teutoburg Forest, was very nearly repeated in 1261, when Prussian noblemen, educated in German convent schools, were ready to beat their masters with their own weapons. The imminent danger was recognized by one German knight, who invited the Prussian nobles to his castle and then burnt it down over their heads. But the flames of the Castle of Lenzenberg became the signal for a general uprising against the Germans, lasting 10 dreadful years during which German rule in Prussia was almost at the point of disappearing. Only in 1271, under the Land Marshal of the order Konrad von Thierberg, did the tide turn again in favour of the Teutonic Knights. But another decade had to pass before German rule was once again established and consolidated.

The uprising marked a turning point in the attitude of the Teutonic Knights towards the natives. Whereas so far, in spite of their arrogance and occasional excesses, they had been prepared to deal with the individual tribes, conclude treaties and end feuds by elaborate peace agreements, they now demanded complete submission, granting mercy and pardon only in accordance with the degree of guilt. A large part of the Prussian nobility was reduced to the status of serfs, men no longer free, while potentially dangerous communities were deported from their native villages and resettled in areas where their activities were considered less harmful. Feudal obligations were imposed upon the native population in their full severity. The system of centralized administration on the Saracen pattern, first introduced into Europe by Emperor Frederick II and adapted by the Teutonic Knights, was now put into operation in its entirety in Prussia. The duties of the natives were strictly and uniformly regulated throughout the colonial territory, and the Teutonic Order established itself as the sole proprietor of all the land. Only rights of possession were granted, ensuring that awareness of the supremacy of the order was forever present. Yet at the same time, in order to attract the immigration of more Germans from the Reich, the order pursued a positive policy in encouraging the growth of the towns. The charters of such cities as Lübeck and Magdeburg were repeated in the new German east. The very character of the order, with its integration of clergy and laymen, ensured that the rivalry between state and church, a rivalry which had been a prominent feature in the history of the relationship between Empire and Papacy, barely existed. In Prussia, the church represented an essential element in the system of the state; it was virtually an established church. This integration, combined with an increasing immigration of German farmers, traders and burghers, led, towards the end of the thirteenth century, to the rapid Germanization of Prussia. There were indeed few signs of the Prussians integrating with the Germans; rather one may speak of their absorption, by force or by other means. By the beginning of the fourteenth century the German language clearly dominated; Germans were forbidden to converse with their Prussian serfs in Prussian. Even for the converted Prussians no allowance was made for preaching in Prussian. The sermon was read in German and then translated by an interpreter for those who could not understand.

This policy of Germanization in its most rigorous form was implemented in Prussia alone, particularly in those regions which had previously revolted. In the Baltic regions of Courland, Livonia and

Estonia, by comparison, a German upper class dominated over the native masses although the process of integration here was far less intense. Germans ruled over the land, but except in the towns and cities, which were largely their creation, they were unable to Germanize it.

Prussia comprised a colony of the Reich as a whole; the lines of communication to the homeland were direct and relatively uncomplicated. In the process of eastward expansion new villages and towns were modelled on those already existing in the west – a process to be repeated centuries later on the North American continent. Frontier life was precarious; survival depended upon good communications and further expansion. Hence, hardly had Prussia been conquered than the order began to turn its sights to the lands west of the Vistula, the Polish-owned Pomerelia. The Vistula was no longer what it once had been, namely a natural frontier, but was now a vital line of communication with Germany. The order's policy of expansion, however, did not remain uncontested, since the neighbours to the west, the Margraves of Brandenburg, following the extinction of the Pomerellian dukes considered themselves the rightful heirs and occupied Danzig. As a result King Vladislav of Poland called upon the Teutonic Order to assist him in expelling the Askanian Brandenburgers, a request which, in 1308, the order gladly carried out. Then, having made their assessment of the situation, the order demanded from Poland compensation of a magnitude which it well knew Poland could not afford. It therefore declared itself content to maintain the hold on Danzig, while at the same time appeasing the Brandenburgers by paying them compensation for their claims to the Pomerelia. The Polish monarchy was unwilling to accept the change in political fortunes; nevertheless, its forces were expelled by the order. The peasants, moreover, were reconciled to the new situation by a considerable lightening of their feudal obligations. Thus the Teutonic Order acquired, besides Thorun, Kulm and Elbing, the city of Danzig, and with it control over the Vistula estuary. But the hostility which was thus created between Poland and the Teutonic Order was more serious because the heathen Lithuanians, whose rule in those days extended as far as Kiev, resented the expansion of the order. The spectre of a Polish–Lithuanian alliance directed against the order began to loom on the horizon.

In the meantime the order had transferred its headquarters from Venice, to which city it had moved from Acre, to Prussia. The Grand Master took up residence in the Marienburg, situated midway between Königsberg and Thorun. The first Grand Master to reside in the Marienburg, Siegfried von Feuchtwangen, in 1309, placed great emphasis on further consolidating and expanding the order's colonial territory, while at the same time rejecting all notions of the crusading fervour of the past. This was all the more necessary since King Casimir of Poland had married the only daughter of the King of Lithuania. Being favourably disposed towards the Germans, the king at first resisted the pressure put on him by his nobles to take agressive action against them and wrest from the order the control of the Vistula. Ultimately he was compelled to yield to his nobles, although for almost three decades there was sporadic warfare between Poles and Lithuanians on the one hand, and the knights of the Teutonic Order on the other, until, in the Peace of Kalisch in 1343, the Poles finally renounced their claims to Pomerelia. The conflict was of further significance because it provided the first major indication of an estrangement between the order and the Papacy. Rome supported the Poles, while for some time the conflict tied the order more closely to the Reich. This was of some help to Emperor Ludwig of Bavaria during his conflict with the church.

After the victory over the Poles, the threat from the Lithuanians diminished in significance, and the order was able to resume its policy of expansion. During the period between 1329 and 1382, a period in which the order reached the zenith of its secular power, it was a particular point of pride, an ambition even, to become a knight in Prussia. This applied not only to Germans but to many members of Europe's nobility, for example Henry Bolingbroke and Jean Boucicaut.

The Lithuanian problem, although reduced, continued to pose a permanent threat to the security of the order, and one of the order's main aims was its complete elimination. But the order's warlike engagements should not obscure the fact that it had for a long time been actively engaged in trade, more often than not in association with the Hanseatic League. It was the policy for the order to obtain the maximum economic return from its territories. Rising prices made corn particularly attractive, and provided a powerful incentive for increased cultivation of the land and further territorial expansion. A start was also made in exploiting available mineral resources. In consequence, within the strictly centralized administration of the order in the Marienburg, the office of the *Tressler* gained in importance in a way not originally envisaged. The order introduced a principle hitherto unknown in the financial practice of the European states, namely the separation of the budget of the state from that of its leaders. The latter had to finance their personal expenses out of the returns from the lands they held. No wonder the *Ordensstaat* (The State of the Order) prospered, unaffected by the disruptive practices prevalent in the Reich at the time, such as the right to feud, or what amounted to blatant highway robbery planned and executed by a nobility no longer prepared to acknowledge any law or right other than those which suited them.

With the growing importance of the cash nexus which the order had early and quickly recognized, it was quite prepared to allow feudal services to be commuted into monetary payments of a modest size. This applied to farmers as well as to monasteries, which remained under the control of the order throughout. Members of mendicant orders were allowed to carry on their practice only with the explicit permission of the order, permission usually given only in return for part of the yield made by the friar on his journeys through Prussia. Besides being the head of the *Komturei* and the house, the *Komtur* of every castle was at the same time the head of the administration of the surrounding country; he chaired the *Thing*, the popular assembly, and even towns and cities had to obey him. It was the Grand Master who issued common rules for the cities, who admitted foreigners and regulated trade. It was through the authority of his office that uniform weights and measures were introduced in Prussia. Yet, in spite of his apparent omnipotence, the Hanseatic cities of Prussia, Kulm, Elbing, Königsberg, Braunsberg and Danzig maintained their separate and independent powers. These powers included the decision to go to war, often against territories and their rulers with which the order itself lived in peace. The close ties existing between the order and the burghers demonstrate that the relationship was not one of subordination of the latter to the former, but rather one established in the common recognition of an identity of interests – which of course pointed also to the possibility that one day this identity might collapse. So far that identity had been based on, among other things, the awareness that members of the Hanseatic League, as well as the brothers of the order, were dependent upon one another for survival in an essentially hostile territory. Indeed, the towns could not prosper without the protection of the order. The degree of independence enjoyed by the Hanseatic cities also made them useful mediators in the conflicts between the order and its neighbours. Control of the Vistula and a large part of the Baltic coast inevitably turned the order into a sea power. It created its own fleet and, supported by that of the Hanseatic cities, pacified, in 1398, the Baltic Sea, conquered Gotland and eliminated piracy along these vital arteries of commerce.

But prosperity and political dominance bore within them the seeds of decay. The vows of obedience, poverty and chastity, although still taken in the latter part of the fourteenth century, had in many cases become mere lip service. The hard-headed *Komturs* had become men of the world who relished the pleasures which a comfortable life had to offer. The charge of tyranny was increasingly levelled against them, especially by the towns and land-owners who complained that the order was restricting them in the exercise of their economic freedom and thus retarding their economic development. The major factor which had held all of them together had been the heathen threat, especially from the Lithuanians. But once they had adopted Christianity there was little to keep Poles and Lithuanians apart, or, for that matter, to prevent the burghers of the Prussian cities from seeking support for the redress of their grievances from Poles or Lithuanians, or both.

The intellectual development of the order during the fourteenth century is hardly worth speaking of. There were Grand Masters who could neither read nor write. A law school in the Marienburg soon withered away into obscurity. The idea of founding a university at Kulm was never realized. Indeed, monks belonging to orders of intellectual distinction such as the Benedictines were not tolerated on the territory of the order at all. The Cistercian monasteries were only tolerated on account of the part they had played, in collaboration with the order, in missionary activities, or because they had been foundations established by the Pomeranian nobility. On the whole the order preferred members from the mendicant orders, whose reputation for dullness of intellect was not inconsiderable. Nor did knightly poetry flourish in the order's environment. The single lasting expression of the arts was the order's architecture, which included its castles and in particular the Marienburg, completed under Grand Master Winrich von Kniprode. This vast gothic brick structure is symbolic of the entire architecture of the order; its stylistic severity exudes the spirit of a military state, gothic architecture devoid of the more light-hearted refinements which the style managed to achieve in France and England. If anything characterized it then, it was the spirit of the functional, a characteristic of all the castles of the order. If contrasts in attitude are expressed in architectural styles, then one need only look at the Hermannsburg on the west bank of the Narva and the Ivangorod on the east bank. The one is challenging, aggressive and symbolic of the advance of western Christian culture; the other of low structure, essentially defensive in appearance, nestling into the countryside rather than dominating it.

The Teutonic Order had conquered, but it had also begun to rest upon its laurels. It no longer encouraged the identity of interests that had once existed between the order and the immigrants who had settled and cultivated the country. The order consisting of celibate monks had institutional but not personal roots in the land. The members of the order became estranged from their own people, in particular those living in the cities. Even members of the landed gentry who were not members of the order believed themselves to be living under a harsh regime; peasants saw their path of economic development blocked by what were taken to be the order's restrictive policies.

In this atmosphere of economic and social discontent, which was not simply restricted to Prussia but affected many areas of Germany, France and England, the Slavs, for so long if not the victims of Germanic expansion then at least its objects, began to reassert their national and political identity. The greatest and most far-reaching movement was that of the Hussites in Bohemia, where the combination of national, economic, social and religious grievances led to an uprising which was to become an important precedent for all Slavs for centuries to follow. The uprising was never defeated by the Empire and much of the self-confidence which the Slavs had lost during centuries of German domination, was restored.

The marriage of Prince Jagiello of Lithuania to the heiress of the crown of Poland in 1386, and his subsequent policy of forceful conversion to Christianity of all Lithuanians, deprived the Teutonic Order of its missionary *raison d'être*. There were no longer any crusades to the east, but only secular wars. What had been feared for almost a century had come true at last : the union of Poland and Lithuania. As a result, Catholic powers now confronted the order, exploiting the accumulated grievances of the population under its rule, and hardly disguising their ultimate aim of subjecting it to themselves. The Hanseatic cities in Prussia began to contest the privileges enjoyed by the city of Lübeck; they were weakened by internal feuds between the guilds, while at the same time, to the north, a strong Denmark emerged, strong enough to persuade the Teutonic Order to cede Gothland to the Danes in 1408. But the order failed to realize the need for reform, the need to turn a closed corporation into an open one by drawing into its ranks urban and more democratic elements. The threat from Scandinavia in the north, and from Lithuania and Poland to the east and south, put an end to one of the prevailing principles of the order's policies in the past: divide and rule. As the result of the process of consolidation around them, there was precariously little remaining for the order to divide. Even the clergy in Livonia asked the Poles for assistance, as did the landed nobility within Prussia, while in the rear of the order, in Pomerania, the same development was afoot. The territory of the Order of the Teutonic Knights was about to be cut off from its hinterland, and thus from its lines of communication with the Reich.

Not that the Reich was much concerned with the problems confronting the order. Prussia was far away; there were problems enough without it. But to tackle the impending danger, to take, so to speak, the bull by the horns, the Grand Master Ulrich von Jungingen, in 1410, staked all on one card. He raised an army the size of which the order had never seen before. It numbered almost 50,000 men, one-third of whom were knights on horseback, and was supported by artillery[1], the weapon which in the final analysis rendered obsolete the basic function of knighthood. He confronted the Poles and Lithuanians on 15 July 1410, at the battle of Tannenberg, and sustained a resounding defeat at the hands of an enemy numerically twice his size. But the battle was lost more by the Order's adherence to traditional tactics of heavy armour and slow horses than inferiority of numbers.

Tannenberg highlighted a crisis which had its parallel in the economic field. The agrarian crisis which occurred in Germany during the middle of the fourteenth century and lasted for more than a hundred years, caused a serious decline in the price of wheat, while at the same time wages and prices of manufactured goods increased. The lower ranks of the nobility were the most seriously affected, in so far as this group gained its livelihood from the rents of the tenant farmers. A strong inflationary tendency made it, on the one hand, easy for peasants to pay their dues, on the other hand more difficult for the nobility to live off fixed rents. The Teutonic Order suffered badly, and in Prussia, where its economic base lay in the export of wheat, it became rapidly impoverished, whilst for similar reasons its other branches were unable to give financial aid to their brothers in Prussia.

That, in actual fact, the order was given another opportunity to rally its forces, under Heinrich von Plauen, was due less to any forces of regeneration within the order than to internal divisions among the Slavs. Furthermore, the possibility that King Sigmund of Hungary would invade Poland was a sufficient threat to persuade King Vladislav of Poland to conclude the Peace of Thorun with the Teutonic Order in 1411. It now seemed that under Heinrich von Plauen the order was again lord over most of the domains which it had held before 1410. But relations with the Poles remained hostile, nor was Heinrich von Plauen the type of man to go out of his way to change that. However, he did realize that for the sake of stability internal reforms were necessary, even if this meant contravening the rules and statutes of the order. Although these rules forbade the participation of secular members in the affairs and councils of the order, Heinrich von Plauen founded the *Landesrat*, an assembly of the estates, in 1412. The need for such an assembly arose primarily from a stipulation of the Peace of Thorun which required the Teutonic Order to make a considerable money payment to the Poles. The order could not raise it from its own treasure, hence it had to be raised by taxation. The assembly was composed of representatives of the cities and the landed nobility which met for the purpose of granting taxes and giving advice in various matters affecting the territory of the order as a whole. Prussia's internal development was henceforth characterized by the conflicts between the order and the estates. But these piecemeal reforms failed to halt the decay of the order, and internal dissension continued; indeed, such reforms as were carried out provided grounds for those who accused the Grand Master of betraying the principles of the order. King Vladislav recognized his opportunity too, and although war had not been formally declared, marauding bands of Lithuanians and Poles entered Prussia. Heinrich von Plauen asked the King of Hungary to mediate. The attempt failed and consequently, in 1413, the Grand Master decided to take the military initiative. This failed abysmally, not because of the superior strength of his Slav opponents, but because of the divided counsels within the order, counsels of knights whom Heinrich had decided to ignore. His own brother apparently opposed him and had dealings with the Poles.

From that point onwards the divisions within the Teutonic Order became endemic. Knights from Northern Germany opposed those from the south and south-west, from Bavaria, Swabia and Franconia. Seemingly endless wars and feuds eroded the prosperity not only of the order as such, but of Prussia as a whole, further assisted by a series of extremely bad harvests.

To counteract the order's increasing political impotence, members of the cities and the landed nobility founded in 1440 at Marienwerder the Prussian League. This, in effect, was to constitute an alternative government to that of the Teutonic Order. In less than 15 years the league rejected outright the government of the order, and attacked and set on fire its castles, among them the very first castle of the order, that of Kulm. They then offered their submission to the crown of Poland, for there was no-one in Germany who could have offered them protection. Here and there the Teutonic Knights endeavoured to make a last stand, but on Whitsunday 1457, the Grand Master was expelled from the Marienburg by Bohemian mercenaries. He just managed to escape to Königsberg where the magistrate of the city, suddenly overwhelmed by compassion, presented him with a barrel of beer.

Finally, by the Peace of Thorun on 19 October 1466 – like many of the peace treaties of the time, bearing the adjective 'eternal' – all territory west of the Vistula and the Nogat was ceded to Poland, in addition to Kulm, Marienburg, Elbing and some bishoprics. Poland had thus again wrested control of the Vistula from the Germans. Prussia was given as a fief of the Polish crown to the Teutonic Knights, and the Grand Master swore the oath of fealty to the King of Poland, allegedly in rags and tears.

Some powers of resistance still remained in the Teutonic Order. As a its colonial territory in the north-eastern corner of the Reich. Only the Elector of Brandenburg, Frederick II, entertained ambitions of expanding his control of the Baltic coast by eventually making himself master of Prussia. But his power and financial strength were sufficient only for the purchase of Neumark from Prussia in 1454.

Some powers of resistance still remained in the Teutronic Order. As a countermove against the tendency of uniting the Grand Mastership with the Polish crown the order elected, in 1498, Duke Frederick of Saxony to this office. He was followed in 1511 by the first Grand Master to come from Brandenburg, Margrave Albrecht of Brandenburg-Ansbach. Under Albrecht, and as a result of the Reformation, the order became a secularized institution, and Prussia a secularized state. The black cross disappeared from the mantle and shield. What remained, until 1945, was the University of Königsberg, the Albertina, which Albrecht founded. The State of the Order of the Teutonic Knights was irretrievably at an end.

Still, the picture of the order and its policy is coloured not only by the impact of two world wars in our own century, but also by the Germanizing policy of the German Empire after 1871, and to an equal if not greater extent by the *Feindbild* of the Slav nations, which, as in every process of national consolidation, is necessary for achieving a sense of national identity. According to that picture the Teutonic Knights were little less than the scourge of the peace-loving Slavs, precursors of that policy of extermination and annihilation practised in our own age under the aegis of the runes and the swastika. Yet most recent research produces a considerably more varied picture. Firstly, the Teutonic Order did not apply identical policies to all natives. There were considerable differences in its attitude towards, and treatment of, Prussians, Poles, Pomeranians, Courlanders and Lithuanians. Secondly, its attitude was also determined by that of the natives towards the order. Thirdly, its attitudes towards these groups were subject to several changes in the course of time. The Prussians were the most populous group the order had to deal with, and obviously the areas of conflict were many. The question of the tithe, recognized since the days of Alcuin as a major problem in missionary ventures, caused serious misgiving among the natives upon whom it was imposed; likewise duties such as the building of castles, and the military service of the newly baptized. Factors such as these led to uprisings and their suppression, both conducted with the cruelty typical of the period. Yet the aim of the order was not extermination but subjugation, the fixing of respective rights and duties by treaties. The first uprising against the order in 1242 was brought to an end seven years later by papal mediation and a treaty which listed mutual rights and duties down to the minutest detail, though it was only applicable to the free natives which represented a quarter to a third of the total population. Moreover, the order tried to gain support from the various factions among the Prussians by playing off one against the other, and it was successful in attracting large parts of the native aristocracy, whose scions were at that time educated in Germany – not always, as it has been seen, with the desired results. But native Prussian nobles could become German knights as early as the thirteenth century.

The free Prussian peasants had their privileges too, especially in the reduction of the tithe due. The heaviest burden was borne, of course, in Prussia as elsewhere, by the unfree. They also constituted the core of rebellion and were the least susceptible to conversion.

Certainly, in the fourteenth century Prussians could still enter the Teutonic Order; in other words, the condition of German birth was not fully enforced until very much later, when, to some extent, the order developed into a welfare institution for the lower German nobility. Several Prussians rose to the position of *Komtur* in the order. But apart from the high offices, numerous other lower offices were open to the natives, such as interpreters, scribes, and offices carrying out economic, military and policing functions. By serving in the castles of the order, a young son of the Prussian nobility obtained the same rights as those enjoyed by native Germans. Actually the majority of the Prussian land-owners not only survived but managed to extend their possessions. And many of those who were not free could, through the exercise of particular skills in the service of the order, become freemen.

However, the question remains to what extent German settlement affected existing Prussian settlement. The inevitable answer is that, it was bound to affect the natives adversely. Castles and new towns could not be built without someone being deprived of his property, without some communities being displaced. But, nevertheless, figures show that the birthrate of the native population was rising, and that outside the main centres of the order property relations remained relatively untouched. It was among the peasantry settled on territory in close proximity to the order where interference was noticeable, the peasants effectively being reduced to the status of the unfree. Individual village communities were combined to form larger, economically more efficient agricultural units. The field system which then prevailed in Germany, where land was systematically parcelled out and economically filled, was introduced, or rather imposed, in Prussia. But this does not mean that the natives lost any substantial amount of land in terms of the size of their holdings. Their landholdings were smaller than those of German immigrants, but not insignificant. Since the German immigrants brought the laws and jurisdiction from the regions in Germany from which they originated, these laws and customs were bound to clash with those of the native Prussians. From the point of view of the Teutonic Order this proved an advantage, since it ensured its role as arbitrator as well as the supreme authority of justice over the native Prussians.

Prussians, especially freemen, also participated in the movement of colonial expansion, in the opening up and settling of new land, soon realizing that new settlement according to German terms was proving more advantageous than that according to Prussian terms. This is particularly noticeable after 1320, when the Teutonic Order began opening up and expanding into the wilderness on a large scale. The general change to the cash nexus also transformed the duties and payments of the natives. Whereas many of the free peasants had at first the additional duty of providing the light cavalry in any military expedition of the order, during the course of the fourteenth century the increase of the economic yield of the peasants became more and more important. Hence services could be commuted into monetary payments, which in turn enabled the hiring of mercenary forces.

In contrast to the knights, the minor freemen were allowed to speak their native language, and even during the final phase of the order in the fifteenth century one notices that the native Prussians supported the order rather than the Prussian League, since from the former they had received, and could expect to receive, a greater degree of justice and protection than from the burghers of the cities or the landed nobility. Against the ambition of the latter to enlarge their estates at the expense of the natives, the Teutonic Order provided the only check.

All in all the image of the policy of the Teutonic Order as being one of extermination is a cliché no longer tenable, and requires considerable qualification and, for that reason, revision.

What, then, was the relationship between the Teutonic Order and the future Prussian state? Certainly, the Teutonic Order had no influence in the formation of the state of Brandenburg-Prussia. Yet, like all frontier existence, that in Prussia imposed sobriety, duty, precision and clarity of purpose, for only these qualities could ensure survival. Indeed, to the lack of some of them may be attributed the downfall of the order. It was, and remained, a hard environment. Little wonder, therefore, that this territory failed to produce even the palest imitation of the Renaissance; little wonder, also, that it produced Immanuel Kant.

But the most important and enduring legacy of the state of the Teutonic Knights, apart from the name Prussia itself, was its economic system based on large-scale agricultural production. No region within Germany could equal it, and in the centuries to come it gave Prussia a strong economic base which allowed its nobility to exert profound political influence, first upon the kingdom itself and then upon Germany as a whole.

Notes
1. This proved to be of little use as the rain ruined the gunpowder.

Chapter 2

Brandenburg and Prussia

The settlement of Prussia by the Teutonic Order was by no means the only venture of German colonization in the east. Charlemagne's successful subjugation of the Saxons may be considered one of the earliest moves of eastern expansion. This took the Germans to the river Elbe, an ideal position from which to penetrate further eastward. There were several marches of the Reich, established for protection against the heathens such as the Wends and the Slavs. The marcher territory of Brandenburg, the Mark Brandenburg, was one of these, its origin lying in the period of Charlemagne's reign. It was subdivided into various parts, the most important of which, almost coinciding in terms of territory with the later Mark Brandenburg, was the Nordmark. This consisted of all the German-colonized territories on the west bank of the river Elbe, later to be called the Altmark. From the Altmark trade developed with the Wendish neighbours; it formed the base of power and supplies for war with them, as well as missionary activity. Already in the tenth century, under Otto the Great, two dioceses were established in Havelberg and Brandenburg, supervised by the bishopric of Magdeburg which had been founded in 968. An uprising of the Wends against their new masters and new religion had put a temporary end to these dioceses, and it was only in the twelfth century, as part of the general crusading fervour and the beginnings of a further German movement eastwards in which the Teutonic Knights were later to take part, that German settlement east of the Elbe was firmly re-established. This process of colonization of the east had basically little to do with imperial policy, whose focus of political and military attention lay to the south of Germany, in Italy. Rather it was the policy of several of the German territorial princes, notably Henry the Lion, who, as vassal of Frederick Barbarossa, fell out with him when he refused to support the crusade to the Holy Land, seeing his primary mission within Germany and its eastern expansion.

This eastern territorial expansion aimed at enlarging land possessions with an eye mainly to their economic development. But the rulers had spiritual as well as temporal interests; they also desired the conversion of the native heathen population. The character of the colonization varied from region to region. Often it was military, as in the case of the Teutonic Knights or the expeditions of Henry the Lion in Mecklenburg and Holstein. But in other areas, for example Magdeburg, colonization proceeded very peacefully. The religious orders, such as the Premonstratensians in the twelfth century and the Cistercian monks in the twelfth and thirteenth centuries, provided exemplary models of expansionist economic and agricultural organization. Poland, the predominant power in the east, under the rule of King Boleslav III, gave, in the twelfth century, vital support to the missionary activity of Bishop Otto of Bamberg. In such territories as Pomerania and Silesia it was the native nobility who called in the Germans to colonize the region, to establish towns and villages and introduce trade. There, the general policy followed was neither one of exterminating the native population nor of replacing it with German colonists. No doubt isolated instances of brutality can be found, especially as the result of misdirected crusading zeal, but on the whole Wendish and German populations gradually integrated. It was a melting pot, intermingling not only Germans and Wends, but also other immigrant groups such as Flemings, Walloons, northern French, Englishmen and Piedmontese. The colonists, who from the very beginning had the superior military and economic organization, naturally assumed political leadership.

In Brandenburg it was the House of the Askanians, of Saxon origin, which led the colonization. Albrecht von Ballenstedt, called the Bear, was given the Nordmark as a fief by Emperor Lothar in 1134, for services rendered in Germany and Italy. This territory was later to be transferred to Henry the Lion. In neighbouring Pomerania, Bishop Otto of Bamberg had already managed to extend the church's influence to the heathens on the Nordmark's northern frontier. Albrecht enjoyed good relations with Bishop Otto, as indeed he did with the Premonstratensian order in Magdeburg, which had founded several settlements and monasteries in Brandenburg.

When Bernard of Clairvaux preached his Slav crusade in 1147, Albrecht immediately participated, though it did not gain him any territory. In fact, a Wendish uprising led again to the temporary loss of Brandenburg, and only from 1157 can one speak of the systematic and extensive colonization of Brandenburg by Albrecht, who brought settlers into the new territory from all parts of Germany as well as the Low Countries.

The rule of Henry the Lion in the north of Germany prevented to some extent the development of regions held by less powerful rulers. But after his fall, the Margraves of Brandenburg had greater scope to pursue their political ambitions, one of which was to take Pomerania and thus gain access to the Baltic Sea. This brought them into conflict with the Danes, who for some time had the upper hand, and it was only after the battle of Bornhoeved in 1227 in which the Danes were defeated that the Askanians were able to gain a significant foothold in Pomerania, land which they had held in fief from Emperor Frederick II since 1231. By 1250 they had also obtained Pomerania-Stettin, as well as the Uckermark, the border territory of Pomerania. During the same period the Lebus territory was acquired, and thus the river Oder reached. With that the territory of the new marches, the Neumark, had been consolidated, and together with the Nordmark, was now called the Altmark. The lands beyond the river Oder, to which, after the middle of the fifteenth century, the name Neumark was given, were obtained piecemeal, partly by purchase, marriage contracts, or in reward for services rendered to the Polish Piast dynasty.

With the acquisition of the Lebus territory, the bulk of the territory of Brandenburg had been created. During the course of the thirteenth century a series of settlements was founded or expanded into townships there, such as Stendal, Spandau and Brandenburg-Altstadt. The founding of the last two actually goes back to the twelfth century. This was followed in 1232 by Cöln-Spree, in 1242 by Berlin, and in 1253 by Frankfurt-an-der-Oder. Four years later came Landsberg-an-der-Warthe. In contrast to the process of colonial expansion in Prussia, where new gains were always consolidated by the building of castles and fortresses, military protection in the territories of Brandenburg was provided by the Askanians, who settled knights and warriors in open villages. At first there were no knights concentrated in castles, these only making their appearance in the Neumark and there mainly for protection against the Polish neighbours. It was not until the fourteenth century, when there was a decline of imperial central power, that many castles were built. In some cases the knights felt sufficiently independent to build these themselves; alternatively they were transferred into the hands of the knights once they had been built.

At first, the knight lived as a neighbour to the farmer in settlements built along the road or in 'roundlings', so called on account of their circular lay-out which was ideal for defence. Road and roundling settlements were planned, but whenever the new settlers were left to themselves they tended to ignore military considerations and build houses and farms wherever and however it suited them. Yet on the whole the colonists were wise enough not to settle in isolated farms. In the newly founded towns the aim was to include the greatest possible number of houses within the protective wall. The centre of each town was the market, around which blocks of houses were grouped.

But Brandenburg could hardly have been called an agriculturally rich region, and not without reason was it later known as the Holy Roman Empire's sand-box. To transform sandy soil and vast forests into arable land demanded supreme effort from the colonists. Yet to this day the area is not without its great charms – its quiet rivers and frequently hidden lakes, and the peace of the landscape which no-one has portrayed better than Theodor Fontane.

Primogeniture did not exist in Brandenburg any more than elsewhere in the Reich. All the sons of a margrave were enfeoffed with the territory, though only the eldest represented the territory at the court of the Emperor. There, within the Empire, the Margraves of Brandenburg played an important role. Frederick Barbarossa, for instance, appointed Margrave Otto I of Brandenburg to the important office of

Reich Chamberlain, and during the course of the thirteenth century they were elevated to the electoral college which elected the Emperor. The political ambitions of the Askanians were extensive. They had cast an eye on Danzig, but were compelled to give way to the Teutonic Order. They also tried to obtain Lübeck, which Henry the Lion had founded, though only with short-lived success. Their ambitions in the coastal regions of the Baltic Sea involved them again in conflict with the Danes, at whose hands they were defeated. In 1320 the House of the Askanians became extinct.

Several interim dynasties of the Bavarian House of Wittelsbach and the House of Luxembourg followed, all of them generally strong enough to maintain Brandenburg in the face of external powers but not strong enough to counteract the increasingly powerful local rulers. In 1411 the last ruler of the House of Luxembourg died, and the internal situation in Brandenburg had deteriorated to such an extent that the deputies of the cities requested the Emperor to send a man capable of restoring peace and order. The man he sent as the new margrave was the Burgraf Frederick of Nuremberg of the Swabian House of Hohenzollern.

In terms of constitutional and administrative development in Brandenburg, the twelfth and thirteenth centuries are marked by rapid growth, the fourteenth by decay.

Throughout the period of colonization the pattern was generally the same. The process began when a nobleman was enfeoffed with a piece of land for which he in turn selected *Locator*, a type of entrepreneur who in return for part of the land undertook to settle it with German farmers. The unit of area, or *Hufe*, was not a uniform measure but varied from region to region. A *Hufe* in Magdeburg was generally slightly smaller than one in Silesia; in Brandenburg it was somewhere in between. The *Locator* would receive two to four *Hufe* for his troubles; two were automatically allocated to the church. Once the *Locator* had established the village he usually became the head of the community for administrative purposes, the *Schulze*. The land he held was free except for the supply of horses for the noblemen, but the rest of the farmers had to pay tax on the ground they held, though exemptions were frequent especially in areas where considerable sweat and toil were required to cultivate the soil.

Towns were generally founded in a similar way but on a larger scale. To begin with the area was larger, so settlement was put in the hands of a group of *locators* rather than one only. These often included members of the nobility. Jurisdiction, which in principle was in the hands of the nobility, was delegated to a deputy, the *Schultheiss*. A *Locator* of a town, unlike those of the villages, had to pay tax, which was assessed on the type of house he owned. Especially in regions where land distribution was complex it was customary to work all the fields communally, a practice understandable enough in an environment where, if for no other purpose than survival, people had to be able to depend upon one another. The three-field crop rotation system was also practised. And of course there was common forest, water and grazing land for the use of the whole of the village. More systematic divisions of land tended to be practised by the Flemings and Dutch, but these were in the minority.

Apart from the peasants, knights were also settled in the villages, though whether simply as neighbours or as land-owners from the very beginning is by no means certain. However, evidence that knights were land-owners exists only from the late fourteenth century onwards, and the estates of the nobility were a product of the fifteenth century. Evidence of specific services which the farmers owed to the knights, the establishment of their vassalage, exists from the end of the thirteenth century. One can assume with reasonable certainty that during the period of colonization conditions must have been favourable for the peasants, for otherwise they would not have come in the first place. Only once erstwhile colonial territory ceased to be frontier territory, as social and economic stratifications hardened, did the nobility endeavour to extend its powers over its landed subjects and increase their economic and financial burdens. Because of its near monopoly of arms the nobility was in a position to do this, particularly in times when the central authority grew weaker as was the case after the extinction of the House of the Askanians.

During the course of the thirteenth century, administrative and executive power was delegated to the *advocati* appointed by the Margrave. In his name they administered the surrounding district from a town or castle. The *advocati* were not necessarily men with legal and administrative training, and were very often knights, who were noble servants of the Margrave or *ministeriales*. They could be appointed and dismissed by the Margrave at will; in return for their efforts they took a share of the fines or taxation. Their functions were fairly extensive, ranging from the conduct of war and preservation of the peace to judicial, financial and excise administration. What developed fairly early on was a distinction between court officials and land officials, though during the thirteenth century the degree of interchange between these two types of officials was still very high and the name *ministeriales* could be applied to both. They represent the basis on which a civil service was later to develop.

Courts soon developed into two types: the High Court of the Margrave, and the Lower Court of the *advocatus*, or *Vogt* as he was called ultimately. The former had jurisdiction over members of the nobility, the latter over the rest of the population. But since it was not uncommon for legal feuds to be carried on between burghers and nobility, mainly over debts, the High Court of the Margrave for some time had no firm place of residence but moved around Brandenburg, making it necessary to establish branches of the High Court in the various districts.

The towns were of course also subject to the power of the Margrave.

But in the town communities a sense of unity among the burghers was not slow in developing. Since the thirteenth and fourteenth centuries towns had begun to acquire more powers by purchasing privileges from the Margrave, including the right to their own jurisdiction. Thus the *Schulze* became the town judge, and the entire judiciary of a town became municipal. On the other hand as a result of the growing ascendancy of the nobility, judiciary rights of the towns were also sold to noblemen.

The administration of the towns in Brandenburg was carried out by the town councils whose members were probably also members of town courts. As towns acquired their communal independence, the council also assumed responsibility for the administration of the town's finance and police. However, it was only a question of time before the individual councillors had to draw in additional personnel to look after day-to-day affairs, people who in time were to become experts in their own field. This led ultimately to the separation of the town's judiciary from its administrative council.

As the power of the Margrave began to deteriorate, the towns acquired the power of granting supplies – or refusing them – to the Margrave. The Margrave in turn was compelled to grant privileges which, if he infringed them, entitled the towns to take up arms against him. A Commission of six, to be elected annually, had no other task than to examine whether any action of the Margrave infringed any of the rights of the town. Naturally enough this development did not take place without resistance from the Margraves, who at first tried to enlist the support of the nobility against the towns in order to isolate them. But the interests of nobility and Margrave were not always identical. Consequently internal strife in Brandenburg was not uncommon.

Neither Bohemia nor Poland were averse to taking advantage of the internal dissensions in Brandenburg, particularly after the Poles had subdued the Teutonic Order. In the Peace of Thorun of 1466, the order had acknowledged the supremacy of the Polish crown and ceded Western Prussia with the mouth of the Vistula. Now completely separated from Germany, East Prussia lost a considerable amount of its political significance.

When Margrave Frederick of Nuremberg assumed control, his task was fraught with difficulties. The nobility was virtually in uproar against him, a situation which culminated in open warfare. However in 1414, as he gathered his resources, he was in a position systematically to reduce the castles of his opponents to rubble – by the use of artillery. One of the largest pieces on loan to him came from one of his relations, Frederick of Zollern who was *Grosskomtur* of the Teutonic Order. Castle walls previously thought impenetrable were reduced to dust, and the Quitzow family, perhaps the most obstinate of his opponents, was subjugated one by one. Medieval knighthood and the method of warfare associated with it had outlived itself. Horse and shining armour were unable to resist clumsy but effective siege guns.

At the general assembly at Tangermünde on 20 March 1414, Frederick held court over the rebels. Some of them had all their property confiscated. All estates of the land, nobility, clergy and burghers, proclaimed their allegiance to the Margrave, and the regular function of all courts was restored.

A little later Frederick was also given the suzerainty over Pomerania, which involved him in extensive warfare with Pomerania, Mecklenberg, and especially, Poland. Poland was the conqueror of the Teutonic Order and was not to be underestimated. Frederick's plan was to establish close family ties between the Hohenzollerns and the Polish crown, and so his second son was engaged to the daughter of King Vladislav of Poland, whose own marriage had not been blessed with any male successors. This, however, brought Frederick into conflict with the man to whom he had so far owed his rise to power, Emperor Sigismund. The Emperor clashed with the Poles over the future of Bohemia, where he pressed his own succession against the Hussites, and Sigismund's unsuccessful campaign against them was in his mind associated mainly with Frederick's failure to aid him successfully in his hour of need. Revenge was not slow in coming. He showed it first by supporting the Margrave of Saxony on various issues and then by throwing his full support behind Brandenburg's northern opponents, especially the Dukes of Pomerania. He granted them the right to the Uckermark, so far successfully held by Frederick. War broke out in the spring of 1425. Ranged against Brandenburg were Pomerania, Mecklenburg, the Teutonic Order and even Poland, which had left him in the lurch despite the betrothal of his son to Vladislav's daughter.

To all intents and purposes Frederick was defeated. He handed over power of regency to his son John. A year later reconciliation with Sigismund took place while in 1427 peace with Pomerania and with Mecklenburg was concluded, which left Brandenburg essentially in possession of the Uckermark. Frederick himself, however, never returned to Brandenburg again, but turned his attention to his possessions in Franconia. He died there as Elector in 1440.

His eldest son, Margrave John, did not have anything like the ability of his father, and his lack of resoluteness very nearly led to a return of the conditions which Frederick had found on coming to Brandenburg. The nobility once again raised its head in defiance. Without previous consultation Berlin and Cölln merged into one urban community in 1432. For the sake of peace John had to avoid Berlin altogether, the nearest place to which he could venture being Spandau. Frederick was still alive, and recognizing the problems divided up his property accordingly. Brandenburg was given to his second son Frederick, who took over its administration in 1437. However he had to promise to rule jointly with his youngest brother, Frederick the Fat, for 16 years and then divide the territory with him. This division actually took place in 1447 when Frederick the Fat received part of the Altmark, but since he died without issue the territory reverted to Frederick II.

Frederick II, being betrothed to a Polish princess, had been raised at the Polish court in Cracow, but his fiancée had died. He followed very much in the line of his father's policy, reasserting his rights over his domains and subduing the feuding nobility, particularly the robber barons who threatened Brandenburg's commerce. He treated the towns similarly. Significant in this context was his conflict with Berlin and Cölln, for they represented the example to the other towns. He decided to curb the freedom which they had acquired in the absence of a strong ruler in Brandenburg and to demonstrate his firmness of purpose dissolved the union between them, appointed new town councillors and reserved the right of appointment for himself. He also assumed all rights of jurisdiction. Then the towns were compelled to give free transit to commerce – en route to Mecklenburg for example. He took possession of the land between the two towns in order to build on it his own residence.

The Berlin burghers quite rightly considered this as threatening their liberties and in 1442 there was an uprising with the aim of restoring Berlin and Cölln's autonomy. It proved unsuccessful and finally the towns submitted to Frederick. Their rights of establishing alliances with other towns were completely removed, particularly their connection with the Hanseatic League. But in view of the declining importance of the Hanseatic League, that connection was becoming of only symbolic value anyway. The church in Brandenburg too was made to obey Frederick. He insisted upon, and obtained, the right of nomination of bishops within his territory, and assured the predominance of his secular justice over ecclesiastical jurisdiction.

Administratively he operated through his own chancellery, where clerical members were, by and by, replaced by secular officials. If his internal policy assured him of supremacy within his own territory, his external policy proved rather costly, at least in financial terms. His aim was to recover all the territories which had once been Brandenburg's but had been lost as the result of his father's conflict with Emperor Sigismund. This involved him in a successful war with Mecklenburg, and he also obtained the lower Lausitz and other smaller territories. But the most significant gain was that of the Neumark which had become the property of the Teutonic Order – significant because it was on the point of becoming Polish property. Frederick made the decisive move and repurchased the area from the Grand Master Ludwig von Erlichhausen. The ultimate goal of his territorial ambition, however, was the acquisition of Pomerania, which would have turned Brandenburg into the dominant power in north-eastern Germany. Once again this led to a war in which he could obtain only part of what he desired. These efforts emptied the coffers of his treasury and he ended his reign with considerable debts. His only son had died in 1467 and so the succession in Brandenburg was transferred to Frederick's brother Albrecht Achilles.

Albrecht Achilles had been raised in Brandenburg, then at the age of

15 became a page at the court of King Sigmund at Bratislava, participated in the Hussite wars and was involved in extensive feuds over his Franconian territories, particularly with the city of Nuremberg.

Upon taking up residence in Brandenburg he concluded a peace with Pomerania that left him in possession of those lands conquered by his brother. Nevertheless it did not take long for war between Brandenburg and Pomerania to break out again, essentially over some minor territories which by 1470 he obtained.

By comparison with the reign of his brother Frederick, Albrecht left well-ordered finances and well-stocked stores of agricultural produce. Equally important for Brandenburg's future was his determination that it should not be divided by the succession. He did not formally introduce primogeniture but apportioned his possessions in a way which left his sons to rule over relatively compact territories. He was also the last Hohenzollern prince who reigned simultaneously over Brandenburg and his Franconian territories. His successor John (1486–1499) directed his attention less to territorial aggrandisement than to internal consolidation. Nor did he show any ambitions in the politics of the imperial court.

But his reign also showed the first major signs of the growing suppression of the peasantry by the nobility. For instance the nobility of the Altmark succeeded in making it an offence to harbour or settle peasants who had left of their own accord the estate of any nobleman in the region. In view of the rising demand for corn and its increasing price the nobility had a particular interest in maximizing output, which led to greater rationalization in the estates and their enlargement by, among other things, reducing even formerly free peasants to a state of servitude. Elector John firmly took the side of his nobility, since in the final analysis his economic interests were identical with theirs.

His reign was also notable for the replacement of the councillors and administrators, who in previous reigns had usually been imported from the Franconian territories, by native talent from Brandenburg. For the first time names like Bülow, Alvensleben and Schlabrendorff begin to gain prominence in the court. Brandenburg provides an excellent example of the rise of the modern state – the product of the centralizing forces of absolutism which in turn were the product of the conflict of the ruling princes with two primary forces. Firstly the princes had to acquire unrestricted access to financial resources. In Brandenburg this meant that they had to maximize their successful economic activity. In the final analysis they could no more than the Hapsburgs, rely on the resources in the possession of the holders of private financial monopoly. Those monopoly holders, families like the Fuggers and the Welsers in whose hands economic power was concentrated, could bridge, if it lay in their interest, the endemic gap between the declining financial and feudal revenues of the prince and his actual requirements. Jakob Fugger had no qualms in writing blandly to Emperor Charles V: 'Without my aid Your Imperial Majesty would hardly have obtained the Roman crown.' They could bridge the gap but they could not fill it. The second conflict was with the estates of the realm, with the nobility, the church, the towns. In many cases the estates had succeeded in twisting medieval feudal traditions into something akin to democracy, insisting that public power resided in the hands of those strata of society which in fact produced the necessities for the state. What the nascent absolutist prince had to achieve and in most cases did achieve was the transfer of all power into his own hands, by turning power held by the traditional medieval institutions such as the church and the guilds, as well as that of the estates, into his personal private 'property'. Previously this 'property' had been more of less run by the estates of the realm, the holders of financial monopoly and the princes.

This successful transfer of power required changes in several directions. For one thing it affected the system of administration, in particular the bureaucracy. The roots of modern bureaucracy, in spite of tentative beginnings in the Middle Ages and the Renaissance, are really deeply buried in the Age of Absolutism. A policy aimed at the concentration of maximum power in the hands of a prince was in need of effective centralization. With the growing complexity of all forms of social and economic life, it was no longer enough to have a scribe as an administrator; what was increasingly needed was the specialized expert. However, absolute monarchy and the institution of bureaucracy are, provided something more is understood by bureaucracy than the transaction of day-to-day business by underlings, not compatible but in the long term mutually exclusive. The growing acquisition of expertise which can hardly be mastered and supervised by one man, the prince, inevitably leads to claims of greater independence, and to resentment or for that matter even outright rejection of interference by the prince. Hence the only countervailing power against this tendency was the recruitment, or the re-enlistment, of the nobility directly into the prince's services, that is to say into the bureaucracy. But not in the bureaucracy only.

Another change took place in the field of warfare. Here after the decay of chivalry and the rise of mercenary armies absolutism produced, in the jargon of our own day and age, the nationalization of the armies: in other words the professional army. Their ownership changed from the private possession of some colonel into the hands of the prince. Wallenstein was the first to demonstrate that change dramatically.

The people, especially the unfree, were subjected to increasing severities, since of course one of the compromises upon which the integration of the nobility into the absolutist state rested was the prince's consent to increasing the burdens of the peasants. To remove himself from the necessity of requesting and accepting loans from private bankers he depended upon the full exploitation of all economic resources in his territory. And for that, peasants apart, he needed again a highly efficient administration.

The beginnings of all these changes which were to mark an age are clearly visible in Brandenburg in the fifteenth and sixteenth centuries. But on the surface this development seemed overshadowed by the impact of the Reformation. The Reformation first affected the territory of the Teutonic Order. Their state seemed to be in a condition of utter decay and it was highly questionable whether it could survive at all. The pressure from Poland seemed irresistible: within the state the Reformation first affected Danzig, then Königsberg where the Bishop of Samland, Georg von Polentz, also a member of the Teutonic Order, gave a famous sermon in favour of the new teachings at Christmas 1525. The Grand Master of the Order, Margrave Albrecht of Brandenburg-Ansbach, was very much in sympathy with Luther and in view of the condition of his order could see the only avenue of salvation in its secularization.

By concluding a treaty with the King of Poland he divested himself of the office of Grand Master and entrusted the state of the Teutonic Order to the crown of Poland. In return he received from Poland Prussia in fief as a secular duchy. Albrecht had now become a Polish duke, but not a duke of the Reich, and Prussia a duchy.

To what extent Albrecht had consulted his fellow members of the order is unknown. In justification of his action Albrecht himself referred to the need for the secularization of all religious orders as demanded by Luther. Immediately after returning to Königsberg, Albrecht publicly announced his conversion to Lutheranism and his new dignity, if such it can be called, as Duke of Prussia by the grace of the King of Poland. He revoked the vows of the Teutonic Order and married Princess Dorothea of Denmark. If Catholicism had perhaps been severe, Lutheranism as far as the Prussian subjects were concerned was even more so. Regular visitations endeavoured to ensure that the new religious teachings were observed everywhere and severe penalties were imposed on offenders.

Albrecht's university at Königsberg was for more than two centuries an exclusively Protestant institution. The first 200 students came from throughout the Duchy of Prussia, from Elbing and Danzig as well as from Poland and Lithuania. And since Luther had insisted that the teachings of the Bible be communicated to everyone in his own native language, the university soon established a Polish and a Lithuanian Seminar within the theological faculty. Religious texts were translated into the various languages spoken by the native population.

There exists no evidence pointing to any resistance by the population to the new religion, perhaps an indication of how much the old had discredited itself in the course of time. But the fact that it was the Teutonic Order, the very institution which had represented Catholic power, that was instrumental in spreading Protestantism may also have made the break in continuity less harsh than it otherwise might have been. But if any resurgence of Catholicism was hardly noticeable, what surprisingly did reappear were heathen customs, particularly in the area in which the Prussian native population was still in the majority. Although the year 1525 has entered the annals of history as the year of the Peasant Rebellion in Germany, these risings were restricted to the regions of south-western Germany and Thuringia. East of the river Elbe there were no risings except in the Samland in Prussia. While the estates swore allegiance to the new Duke, the peasants too were ready to do so but only to the person of the Duke alone and in return for the abolition of all the special privileges which the land-owning nobility had acquired since the beginning of the decline of the Teutonic Order, privileges which of course had meant greater burdens of servitude for the peasants.

The peasants assembled before the gates of Königsberg, where Albrecht and his troops compelled them to lay down their arms and then executed several of the leaders. Although the main impetus of the rebellion had been broken, never to lift its head again, currents of resistance, often expressed in religious form, were frequent and Prussia became quite renowned as a breeding ground for Protestant sectarianism – so much so that Luther himself found it necessary to warn Albrecht to maintain the unity of the faith. On the other hand Albrecht was aware that the successful development of Prussia depended very much on attracting new immigrants and that therefore a degree of toleration towards religious beliefs was necessary as long as the principle of the Reformation as such was not put to question.

In his external policy Albrecht aimed at the consolidation of the new duchy and its general acceptance by its neighbours and by Europe as a whole. However, within the Holy Roman Empire of the German Nation he had a difficult stand, the very act of turning to the Polish crown being considered an act of betrayal of former German colonial territory to foreigners. In 1532 Albrecht was banned by the highest court of the Empire after the Roman Catholic church had done the same. This ban was extended over all Prussian subjects. That no serious consequences emerged from this for Prussia can in the main be ascribed to the success of the Reformation as a whole. Also the attitude of Poland was of decisive importance. The Reformation left its marks in Poland too, but in spite of temporary strong Calvinist influences and occasionally strained relations with the Papacy the country remained basically true to the Roman Catholic faith. Thus the seeming contradiction occurs that the major Catholic power on Prussia's border took great pains to assist the survival of its new Protestant neighbour, an attitude explained only in terms of Poland's policy towards the Reich, whose north-eastern colony it had felt as a threat to its own security. The same motives that caused Richelieu to support Gustavus Adolphus were at the roots of Poland's support of Albrecht of Prussia.

Internally the rule of Albrecht is characterized by a development in which the estates gained the upper hand politically. From the point of view of domestic politics, the land-owning nobility moved more and more to the fore. Given the geography of Prussia, with its vast arable potential, then the development towards greater arable areas, estates of a larger size and a different type of economic organization to that in other parts of Germany, seems natural.

Its basically simple and uncomplicated political organization was primarily a legacy of the Teutonic Order. The administration of the territory and its effective economic organization had to be transferred onto capable shoulders. But not onto too many, to avoid proliferation and with it excessive exercise of power. The organization of Prussia into large landed estates administered by the nobility is a product of this policy, which, as can be expected, was carried on the backs of the peasants. The territorial divisions, and subdivisions, and subdivisions of subdivisions which are so typical of the land-holding pattern of southern Germany were avoided. Estates were aggrandized, consolidated, peasants forcibly dispossessed, reduced from freemen to a state of servitude, and entire sections of a peasant population deprived of their rights. The sixteenth century in Prussia is the period in which the nobility established its strong economic position which for more than three centuries was to make its political influence felt in Brandenburg-Prussia.

Albrecht, after all, could not consider his own position as fully consolidated. He had to lean for support on someone. The peasant rising in Samland did not make it advisable to rest his rule, like his Swedish neighbour, upon a free peasantry. The land-owning nobility was therefore, so he believed, the only prop upon which he could rely. On the other hand the nobility had become not only a class of agricultural entrepreneurs but also exercised judicial and policing power over their serfs and often dominated their local churches, the end result being the erosion of the authority of the state as well a serious weakening in the social and economic position of a peasantry. Ironically these same peasants were the descendants of many of those who had entered the country in response to the call for eastern colonization, the spreading of the mission of Christianity and the expansion of the area of Christian influence.

Yet the land-owning nobility of East Prussia differed in one vital respect from similar classes in other parts of Germany, or in Europe, where in the main the land was rented out or put into the hands of bailiffs, or simply managed by others. The Prussian land-owning nobility managed its own estates. The Prussian land-owning noble was a farmer, plain and simple. The suitability of Prussia's soil for the large-scale production of wheat had been one of the close bonds in the relationship between the Hanseatic League and the Teutonic Order. North-eastern Europe including Prussia was the corn chamber of Western Europe, wheat the factor which in the first place gave cities like Stettin in Pomerania, Danzig in West Prussia, Riga in Livonia, Königsberg and Memel, their prominence as exporting harbours. Wheat lay at the very roots of their rapid urban growth and flourishing urban culture.

Such economic power was bound to develop the dynamics necessary for its transformation into political power. The *Landtag*, the assembly of the estates, had to give its agreement to requests for grants of revenue, for the levying of taxation. The *Landtag* was composed of the three estates, the first being essentially members of the nobility originating from the Reich, the second the local nobility and the third the deputies of the towns. There are no signs to indicate that Albrecht ever attempted to rely upon the first and the third in order to contain the local nobility. On the whole the *Landtag* left Albrecht in peace, since they were aware that his policy of protecting Prussia from a possible Catholic reaction coincided with their interests. But they did not tolerate any interference with their own economic interests. The centralizing tendencies so characteristic of the German principalities, of Brandenburg during the sixteenth century for instance, were at that time still in their infancy in that corner of north-eastern central Europe. The estates managed to secure for themselves a dominant influence in the government apparatus and in the administration. This apparatus was in the main collegiate in character and essentially adapted from the administrative apparatus of the Teutonic Order. It was the administration which determined the selection of new recruits for itself while Albrecht was left very little say in the matter. The nobility selected its own; it legislated in its own interest.

Late in the day Albrecht seems to have noticed the immense power which the estates had acquired, with the result that he tried to change course and to introduce a more absolutist regime. The estates were incensed and as a warning, as happened similarly a century later to Thomas Wentworth, they tried and executed several of the Duke's councillors.

The estates secured for themselves further prerogatives, for example acting as the Duke's representative in case of his absence or even death. Albrecht died in 1568 and he left his son Albrecht II as his successor. However he soon proved to be mentally ill and Elector Joachim Frederick of Brandenburg was appointed as regent of Prussia in 1605.

In the meantime the Reformation had also succeeded in Brandenburg. Elector Joachim I, who came to power in 1499, though still devout to the Catholic church allowed the humanist currents of the late fifteenth century free flow and founded the University of Frankfurt-an-der-Oder which, endowed with papal and imperial privileges, opened its doors in 1506. Dietrich von Bülow, the Bishop of Lebus, was its first chancellor. Joachim also founded the Stiftskirche in Halle which he decorated with works by Dürer and Peter Vischer. He was a friend of Ulrich von Hutten and Erasmus of Rotterdam.

The House of Brandenburg was able to wield considerable influence in the politics of the Reich, influence which could have been greater had the family been of one mind. These differences crystallized and came to the fore in the imperial elections of 1519 in which the contestants were the grandson of Emperor Maximilian I, Charles of Spain, and Francis I of France. Joachim's cousin, John Albrecht, the brother of the Grand

Master of the Teutonic Order, supported Charles from the very beginning; Joachim on the other hand tried to keep his options open to see which of the two candidates had the most to offer him. Ultimately, though only under strong military pressure from Charles's forces, Joachim finally committed himself to the Hapsburg side and Charles V became Emperor on 28 May 1519.

In spite of his humanist leanings Joachim opposed the rise of Luther, in contrast to his brother, the Elector of Mainz, and in return the church granted him the privilege of nominating the bishops for his own bishoprics in Brandenburg. Charles V showed little interest in equally rewarding Joachim's services and much to the latter's chagrin he enfeoffed the Duke of Pomerania although that territory had previously been acknowledged by Charles as a fief of Brandenburg. Marriage projects with the Hapsburgs failed as indeed they did with France. Instead Joachim's son married, in 1524, Magdalene, the daughter of Duke George of Saxony, which led to closer ties between the cousins of Brandenburg and Prussia. But Charles V's successful battle at Pavia and the acquisition by the House of Hapsburg of Bohemia and Hungary gave him such power as to dismiss any doubts in Joachim's mind about continuing to support him. Nevertheless Joachim's wife Elizabeth became a Lutheran, despite all his efforts to prevent her. He prohibited her from participating in Lutheran communion rites and she therefore found it necessary to escape to Saxony.

At the imperial diet in Augsburg in 1530 Joachim was the leader of the Catholic struggle against the Protestant cause, and he also supported the election of Charles V's son Ferdinand as King of the Romans. When he died in his Palace in Berlin in July 1535, he left the Neumark to his younger son John of Küstrin and the Kurmark, the core of the territory, to his elder son Joachim. Until 1570 both governed in their own part of Brandenburg. Joachim II had none of the political ambitions of his father and was a relatively mild-mannered man. John, on the other hand, was more like his father; he also believed there were definite advantages to be gained by supporting the Reformation. Whereas Joachim liked the show of wealth and lived in truly princely style, John was rather more economically minded, and was not averse to lending out money at high interest rates to his own brother and others. Under his banner he organized formidable mercenary forces which in return for considerable sums he hired out to the Emperor and other princes. Little wonder therefore that at the end of his reign John left a sizeable surplus in his treasury while Joachim II left considerable debts.

From the outset, in spite of opposition from his father, John had been a supporter of the cause of the Reformation, but his brother Joachim was somewhat more reserved. He converted to Lutheranism in stages by adopting certain parts of it. In that way he avoided actual conflict with either Catholics or Protestants, while the net effect was the Lutheranization of the Kurmark. In the sphere of imperial politics he was entrusted with the command of the imperial army against the Turks in

1542, but his lack of any military experience, the rag-bag composition of his troops and other factors ensured the failure of his mission to relieve Buda from the Turks. Neither Joachim nor John considered it wise to participate in the Schmalkaldic wars (the war of Germany's Protestant princes and cities against Charles V between 1546 and 1547), one factor that brought the two brothers closer together again but also caused a split and then war with Charles V. This fear of imperial attack resulted in a considerable rapprochement between Brandenburg and Albrecht I of Prussia, but neither Joachim, John, nor Albrecht was prepared to go as far as their ally, Elector Moritz of Saxony intended and attack the Emperor in alliance with France.

The Peace of Augsburg brought a temporary solution to the religious question and its wars. The focus of discussion now was the succession in Magdeburg and in Prussia. Magdeburg provided a problem which kept Brandenburg and the imperial court busy for several decades, because the Emperor wished to avoid the secularization of this ecclesiastical territory – ultimately without success though. Brandenburg endeavoured to obtain a voice in any decision concerning the enfeoffment of the duchy. After lengthy negotiations this was obtained from Poland, but at considerable expense, the cost to be borne by the estates of Brandenburg. Secularization of church lands had increased the electoral domain but in order to pay the debts much had to be handed over to the members of the estates.

Joachim I's division of Brandenburg between his two sons had led to trade rivalries among the cities along the river Oder. Frankfurt-an-der-Oder was by far the most important trading centre of Brandenburg, but Landsberg as well as Krossen, which belonged to John's Neumark, tried to wrest the new monopoly position from Frankfurt. The two brothers came to an agreement which maintained Frankfurt's position but very much at the expense of Stettin in Pomerania, while John also tried to develop trade routes to Poland overland, again to the disadvantage of Stettin.

In 1571 both Joachim and John died within 10 days of one another. John did not leave any sons, only daughters. Hence the successor was Joachim's son John George, who once again united the Kurmark and the Neumark.

John George was not the ready spender that his father had been and immediately upon his accession to office he prosecuted the favourites of his father, as well as those merchants who had been ready to lend money. These included a number of Jews who were expelled from Brandenburg, as indeed were most Jews until they were readmitted again during the reign of the Great Elector. His internal policy aimed at reconsolidating Brandenburg economically; within the Reich he was mainly concerned with opposing the militant forces of the Counter-Reformation, without great loss to Brandenburg's treasury, while at the same time pressing a claim for succession to the territories of Jülich-Cleves. This was a claim which had derived from the marriage, in 1594, of George's son John Sigismund to a daughter of Albrecht of Prussia's feeble-minded son. Duchess Mary Eleanor of Prussia became his mother-in-law and she was the sister of the Duchess of Cleves. Spain, the driving force of the Counter-Reformation, until joined by Ferdinand of Styria, opposed the Protestant Brandenburg's claims, while Brandenburg gave open support to the Calvinist ruling house of Jülich-Cleves. John George died in 1598 to be succeeded by Joachim Frederick who at that time was already 52 years of age. He possessed extensive administrative experience and one of his first aims was to restore if not a cordial then at least a working relationship with the House of Hapsburg. Also John George had left debts which had to be paid. What had happened in Prussia was now also happening in Brandenburg. The *Landtag*, the diet, convened to grant taxation which at least paid two-thirds of the debts, but did so only after obtaining socio-economic prerogatives which secured in essence the economic power of the nobility. But they wanted no part in any venture which could involve them in further expense, be that a war against Spain, against the ecclesiastical princes or against the Emperor. Especially over the question of Jülich-Cleves they counselled moderation and patience. The ambitions of Joachim Frederick were therefore set definite limits.

Joachim Frederick's reign is distinguished by distinctive innovations in the administration of Brandenburg. Of course these had their precursors in other German principalities, but for the House of Hohenzollern in Brandenburg they represent the formal beginnings of a central administration. In December 1604 the Secret Council was founded, a collegiate body of nine councillors. Its task was the administration of external as well as internal affairs under the supervision of the Elector. The old system of councillors who individually advised the Elector disappeared as the primary administrative body and was transformed into the electoral *Kammergericht*, the Elector's Chamber Court. Next to the Secret Council and the Chamber Court came the *Amtskammer*, an office of general administration primarily concerned with the administration of the electoral domains. To reduce the influence of the estates Joachim Frederick brought in officials from outside who were capable of running a government of increasing complexity – a complexity with which the old system had no longer been able to cope.

Joachim Frederick's son, the electoral prince John Sigismund, forced a greater activism behind Brandenburg's support of the Protestant cause. However, in retrospect the most important event of John Sigismund's reign was his formal enfeoffment with Prussia in 1611. When Albrecht II died in 1618, the right of succession went to the House of Hohenzollern. John Sigismund's marriage with Albrecht's eldest daughter ultimately established his claims to Jülich-Cleves.

The Elector of Prussia was now a vassal of the Emperor as well as the King of Poland. Not that either mattered very much. What mattered was the increase in size of Hohenzollern territory, which now had almost doubled. Brandenburg comprised 697 square miles, East Prussia 672. The city of Königsberg had been a commercial centre since the days of the Teutonic Knights, unrivalled by any city in Brandenburg. But in Prussia as in Brandenburg it was the landed nobility which endeavoured to play the major political role and very often succeeded in doing so.

The increase in the Hohenzollern territories and the improvement of the central administration were soon overshadowed by signs of neglect during the reign of John Sigismund. The active role he played as electoral prince had promised much, but that promise remained unfulfilled. True, when he succeeded his father he was no longer a healthy man, and illness seemed to have eroded away his previous energies. This was hardly helped by his excessive eating and drinking habits. Nor was his relationship with his wife Princess Anne a particularly happy one, a relationship not helped by the stern Lutheranism of the Princess and the Calvinist leanings of John Sigismund. Perhaps their marriage was even rather conventional: in their disputes, prince and princess tossed plates and crystal glasses at one another.

In March 1609 Duke John William of Jülich died. Electress Anne was next in line of succession and Brandenburg formally took possession of Jülich-Cleves. The Emperor objected and the *Reichshofrat* was convened. The president of this imperial office, Count John George of Hohenzollern-Sigmaringen, deputized for the Emperor at the meeting. The Brandenburg claim was contested by the Neuburg family and in order to appease both claimants and offend neither the *Reichshofrat* decreed the joint rule of Jülich-Cleves by Brandenburg and Neuburg. The local estates agreed with the solution, as long as religious toleration for Protestants, Calvinists and Catholics was guaranteed within the principality.

But the question of Jülich-Cleves was more complicated than that. It involved the Spanish war in the Netherlands in which the German Protestants were allied with France and England in support of the Dutch. In the spring of 1610 the French endeavoured to take Jülich from the Emperor while an armistice between Spain and the Dutch was still in force. Nor was the German Catholic League ready to intervene in the Jülich affair as long as Catholic interests were not violated. French plans came to an abrupt end through the murder of their King Henry IV. Brandenburg now took full possession of Jülich because it did not trust the *Reichshofrat*, composed as it was exclusively of Catholics. Naturally the Neuburgs did not accept the Brandenburg claims and it came to open conflict in which the Brandenburg contingent did not show up particularly well. As a result of the mediation carried out by England and France, Brandenburg was deprived of part of the legacy. The income of the principality was halved between the claimants, as was the government, Brandenburg governing the predominantly Protestant regions of Cleves, Mark, Ravensberg and Ravenstein, while Neuburg took over the Catholic regions of Jülich and Berg. This solution was bound to be of a temporary nature, for which John Sigismund's half-heartedness in the pursuit of Branden-burg's interests was partly responsible, as was the attitude of the estates of Brandenburg which wanted to avoid any complications causing additional expenditure. For them the dynastic politics of the Hohenzollerns spreading into the north-western corner of Germany bore no relationship with their own interests, quite in contrast to the acquisition of Prussia, for example. In 1613 John Sigismund was converted to Calvinism. The Reformed church, a new and specifically German form of Puritanism, was to be of lasting influence upon the early Hohenzollern dynasty.

John Sigismund's health rapidly deteriorated, so much so that in November 1619 he handed over government to his son George William. Two months later, in January 1620, he died. In spite of its weaknesses his reign left a legacy for Brandenburg which was to shape its fortunes for the next two and a half centuries. The Hohenzollerns were now involved in the geographical extremities of northern Germany, in the north-east as well as in the north-west. Brandenburg had ceased to be simply a central-German principality but had become a neighbour of Poland and Russia on the one hand and of the Netherlands on the other. This also influenced its immediate future. Brandenburg could no longer insist on religious uniformity. The very composition of its population made religious toleration a political postulate which ultimately had to become policy of state. Brandenburg had ceased to be – if in fact it had ever been – a confessional territorial state.

George William, who at the time of his succession was 25 years old, was not in the best of health either, nor was his character that of a man of determination, foresight and quick decision, hardly an asset at a time when the first waves of those ravages cumulatively called the Thirty Years War swept over Germany. Because of his own weakness it was not difficult for the Elector's chief counsellor Adam Count von Schwart-zenberg, a Catholic nobleman from the Rhineland, to achieve pre-eminence and determine Brandenburg's policy.

George William's priority was to obtain the formal investiture of the Elector with the Duchy of Prussia by the King of Poland. But there was still one problem: his mother. She pursued a policy of her own, namely the marriage of her daughter with King Gustavus Adolphus of Sweden. George William was against this connection, primarily because the Polish King, at war with Sweden, opposed it, but while he was in Königsberg the Elector's mother sent her daughter to the Swedish chancellor Oxenstierna to be married in Sweden. King Sigmund of Poland at first considered the affair part of a Hohenzollern conspiracy and George William was highly embarrassed because of the delay in the investiture; he was prepared to join neither Gustavus Adolphus nor Sigmund. He preferred undisturbed neutrality. Swedish advances in Livonia seriously threatened Polish interests and as a result of this threat the Polish court showed a greater readiness to make concessions to George William. On 23 September 1621 he obtained Prussia under the same conditions as his predecessor. More extensive demands originally envisaged by the Poles were dropped.

Brandenburg had managed to keep out of the conflict between Sweden and Poland; it pursued an identical policy with regard to the war in Bohemia, even though Elector Frederick V of the Palatinate, the 'Winter King', was the brother-in-law of George William. Several other Hohenzollern princes supported Frederick but not so George William. After the battle of the White Mountain – perhaps the most decisive battle in Germany's political development, for had it been won by the Bohemian rebels it is doubtful whether there would have been the occasion and need for a Bismarck and his policy – these princes were on the side of the loser and were deprived of their properties. But George William did not seem to be particularly concerned with the dissolution of the Protestant Union, the conquest of the Upper Palatinate and the handing over of it to Maximilian of Bavaria.

However, neutrality also brought isolation. While his neighbour John George of Saxony conducted special negotiations with the Catholic party, George William's possessions in north-western Germany were occupied by the imperial troops under Tilly. Meanwhile the enemies of the Hapsburgs, notably France, England and the Scandinavian states, planned a coalition. Brandenburg participated on the periphery by negotiating with Gustavus Adolphus who planned a large campaign in Silesia. This was too close for George William's comfort and he tried to dissuade him by raising his interest for a campaign in western Germany with the object of reconquering the Palatinate. Eventually hostility between Gustavus Adolphus and King Christian IV of Denmark caused these plans to be abandoned. George William also toyed with one of the Emperor's most serious enemies, Prince Bethlen Gabor of Transylvania, but when challenged by the imperial court in Vienna he broke off negotiations with him and refrained, for instance, from joining the alliance of the Hague of December 1625 between England and Denmark and France.

To protect his neutrality George William mustered some 3,000 men – too late to prevent Mansfeld and his men from crossing the Altmark and Priegnitz. Wallenstein's victory over Mansfeld in 1626 temporarily deprived Brandenburg of Magdeburg and Halberstadt.

While traversing the territory of Brandenburg imperial troops tended to bear in mind the country's neutrality, but the arrival of Gustavus Adolphus forced George William to take sides against the Empire and from then on, like most other parts of Germany, Brandenburg and Prussia became a battleground of the Thirty Years War. Changing sides did not help. Brandenburg was ravaged and in the eyes of contemporaries it was at the point of dissolution when on 1 December 1640, at the age of 46, Elector George William died.

Chapter 3

The Great Elector

Just at the time when George William had gone to Prussia to obtain his investiture from Poland as Duke of Prussia, his wife Charlotte of the Palatinate, the sister of the Winter King, gave birth to her first son Frederick William. The first Christian name was given in honour of the Winter King, the second in honour of the child's father. The Electress's mother in turn was a daughter of William of Orange.

When Frederick William succeeded to the throne he was only 20 years old, with hardly any experience in government and administration. Indeed his father had deliberately held him back from any participation in the affairs of state. Quite apart from that, his political interests had been inspired by a deep admiration for Gustavus Adolphus, whose body he accompanied as a 13-year-old when it was transferred to the boat that was to take the dead king to Sweden. His political interests were both more active and less cautious than those of his father. Because of the Thirty Years War he was sent from Berlin to Küstrin to receive his education there, and then in 1634 he travelled to the Netherlands where at Leyden he studied mathematics, Latin, history and war studies. Besides German he spoke French, Dutch and Polish.

The Dutch influence upon him was deep and lasting; it made him sympathize deeply with the struggle of the House of Orange against the Catholic, Spanish and Hapsburg Empire. Consequently, when in 1637 his father decided that Brandenburg should join the struggle against the Swedes, he found himself not only in opposition to him, but was compelled to leave the Netherlands for Berlin where the tensions between father and son continued for some time, the embers of suspicion being kept alive by Schwartzenberg, the man also responsible for Brandenburg changing sides in favour of the Hapsburgs. Naturally Schwartzenberg ostensibly favoured a reconciliation between father and son, though Frederick William's mistrust of Schwartzenberg was so strong that he did not put it beyond the minister to poison him. When Frederick William did fall ill it seemed to confirm his suspicions, but in the end it turned out to be only measles.

The remaining time until his father's death Frederick William spent in Königsberg, depressed because of his enforced inactivity. By the time of his accession Brandenburg's fortunes were at a low ebb. The soldiers which Brandenburg had raised to aid the Empire were the plague of the land; they could hardly have been worse than the Swedes. In fact when, in 1639, the Swedes occupied Landsberg, Driesen and Frankfurt, the population there considered them less of a burden than their own *Soldateska*. At the time of George William's death those parts of Pomerania owned by Prussia were in the hands of his opponents, as was Jülich in the west; East Prussia too was threatened. One would hardly have thought that in terms of territorial expansion the Hohenzollerns were second only to the House of Hapsburg in Germany. Yet territory itself was not enough. What the Hohenzollern's lacked was the effective strength to maintain it – which really meant that their territorial possessions existed at the mercy of their neighbours. This in turn had allowed the estates to assert their own power and pursue their own special interests without considering the Hohenzollern possessions as a whole.

The Thirty Years War had ravaged, and was still ravaging, these territories badly. Brandenburg alone had lost over 50 per cent of its population, and its strategically most important areas were in the hands of the enemy. In Prussia the estates had exploited their position to the full, or played off the Hohenzollerns against the Poles. Yet from an economic point of view Prussia was more important to the Hohenzollerns than was Brandenburg. The Duke of Prussia possessed immense domains with considerable economic resources and a great number of subjects. This was a direct consequence of the settlement policy of the Teutonic Order which had concentrated in its hands the largest part of the territory, a large percentage of the population of which had, in the course of the preceding century and a half, been reduced to the state of serfdom. The economic importance of Prussia's population was that it could be taxed directly by the Hohenzollerns without first having to ask the estates. This made Prussia the Hohenzollern's most important single source of revenue, even more so because it had not suffered so much from the events of the war as had Brandenburg and their other territories.

Equally important from the point of view of revenue was the commercial significance of Königsberg. It exported the produce not only of Prussia but of Lithuania as well, major exports being wheat, wood, hemp and furs. The Teutonic Order had already attempted to acquire a share of the resulting revenue by introducing an export toll. As a consequence of the war the Swedes occupied Pillau at the exit of the *Frisches Haff* until 1635. After that date the toll revenues reverted to Prussia, but since the Duke of Prussia was still the vassal of the King of Poland at the time, the latter demanded his share as well. This the Duke had to concede, and Frederick William was compelled to accept the situation upon his accession.

The part of Jülich-Cleves held by the Hohenzollerns had been exposed to serious risk by George William's support of the Hapsburgs, which in economic terms meant that revenue obtained along the Rhine, from the forests and from other sources was taken by the Netherlands.

The political position of the Hohenzollerns in Brandenburg was, relatively speaking, still stable. After all they represented the resident ruling house. But economically their position was weak. Brandenburg relied on extensive sheep farming and wool production which had seriously declined because of the war. Another major source of revenue was the river tolls exacted on the Elbe and the Oder. As, however, the mouths of both these rivers were in the possession of other states, control of the trade lay outside the power of the Hohenzollerns. Stettin, for example, always managed to maintain its supremacy over Frankfurt-an-der-Oder. When Brandenburg itself became a battleground, trade came almost to a stand-still.

Thus the legacy left to Frederick William was not a very enviable one. In contrast to his father who had relied on Schwartzenberg, Frederick William preferred to rely on his mother. Upon her initiative several memoranda were drawn up to analyse Brandenburg's problems, but they failed to supply practical solutions. They emphasized the impossibility of conducting and continuing the war against the Swedes, but at the same time stressed the need for loyalty towards the Hapsburgs and the Empire. How the two policies were to be reconciled with one another remained an unanswered problem. But one point was made to which, in the final analysis, Frederick William paid great attention: the need for an effective army; for without an efficient army the House of Hohenzollern would not be in a position to pursue active politics at all but would simply remain the political objective of others. A policy of general appeasement towards the estates was recommended.

Instead of dismissing Schwartzenberg, Frederick William, step by step, curtailed his powers to the point of insignificance, either assuming them himself or handing them over to Sigismund von Götzen whom he appointed chancellor on the advice of his mother. At first Frederick William tried to follow the advice about establishing cordial relations with the estates. It was his express wish to involve them in discussion and ask their advice about the relationship of Brandenburg with the Emperor, the problem of Pomerania and the question of disarmament. From his experience in the Netherlands, his observations of the politics of the Estates General, he expected constructive assistance. But his expectations were not fulfilled. The estates showed little interest in questions of grand politics; all that mattered to them was the preservation and extension of their own material privileges. This was a lesson Frederick William remembered when formulating his future policy. In the process of joint consultation all that was agreed upon in the end was to investigate the complaints against the troops of Brandenburg and to reduce the army.

This seems in direct contradiction to the advice given to Frederick William about the need to build up a strong army. But it was a contradiction on the surface only. The combat value of the existing army was highly doubtful. Most of the officers and men represented the dregs of society, the scum swept to the surface by the Thirty Years War.

The precondition of a new army was the dissolution of the old one. On the other hand it was imperative to come to an arrangement with the Swedes as soon as possible, and negotiations without the backing of an army would be futile. When Schwartzenburg died unexpectedly in March 1641, Frederick William was relieved of one of his burdens, but the dilemma arising out of the joint necessities of negotiating with the Swedes and dissolving the army was not resolved.

The *Reichstag* in Regensburg looked at Frederick William's attempts to obtain an armistice with the Swedes with scepticism, if not with hostility. He therefore instructed his delegates not to raise this topic at the *Reichstag* level any more, and then proceeded to negotiate with the Swedes on his own. Negotiations continued for several months, first indirectly then directly. Finally on 24 July 1641 a two-year armistice between Brandenburg and Sweden was concluded. While it relieved Brandenburg from the effort of making war, the armistice left the Swedes in those positions they held in Brandenburg. In other words the armistice highlighted the political and military impotence of Brandenburg. Sweden had sacrificed nothing at all, which may have been the reason why Frederick William never exchanged the document of ratification, managing time and again to raise another point in need of further clarification until the general settlement of the Peace of Westphalia in 1648.

As was the case for his father, Frederick William's relationship with Poland was of primary importance, since as a Polish duke he was also the vassal of the King of Poland. The armistice of Stuhmdorf with the Swedes had given the Poles cause for alarm, for they feared that they would now be exposed to military pressure from the Swedes. Frederick William assured the Poles that he would not put Prussia's harbours at the disposal of the Swedes. But, in general, he tried to keep King Vladislav IV of Poland in the dark about his arrangements with the Swedes, so as to use them as a lever with which to obtain a formal investiture or the *de facto* assumption of power in Prussia through his deputy. The latter was achieved, but Vladislav, contrary to Frederick William's plan, insisted that he appear personally for the investiture which finally took place on 7 October 1641. Little less than a month later, on 1 November 1641, Frederick William entered Königsberg and attended the Prussian diet. The diet granted him, among other things, the introduction of the excise tax which was to become one of the most important forms of taxation throughout Brandenburg-Prussia. It represented a form of indirect taxation, by taxing consumption. But as the administration of taxation in Prussia lay in the hands of the nobility, this made sure that the nobility did not suffer too much.

That nobility consisted of those who have generally become known as the 'Junkers'. Yet it is a misleading term because its present-day connotation does not go back further than the revolution of 1848, when among liberals it became a term of abuse directed against the Prussian nobility. In fact a Junker was originally the son of a noble house, in the

Middle Ages often doing his military apprenticeship as the squire to a knight, in more modern armies also being a 'Fahnenjunker', or ensign, the rank held prior to a full commission.

Moreover, the term as generally used tends to obscure the fact that in Prussia as elsewhere the nobility itself consisted of what, for the sake of convenience, one might describe as a higher and lower nobility. In East Prussia there were the *Grafenfamilien*, the families of the counts or earls represented by famous names such as the Dohnas and the Döhnhoffs; below them were the knights bound to them by feudal obligations, and in the sixteenth and seventeenth centuries that class from which the higher nobility drew administrators such as the *Landräte*. But the greater number of lower nobility during the same period ensured that they ultimately dominated the provincial diet and to all intents and purposes entered into a lasting alliance with the higher nobility. With the development and extension of demesne farming and the decline of the manorial system came also a substantial increase in the economic power of the Prussian nobility east of the river Elbe in general.

It acquired and usurped privileges which were finally confirmed by the Great Elector in 1653 and remained fundamentally unchanged until the Prussian Reform Movement of the early nineteenth century. The population of the countryside east of the Elbe was made up of people falling into essentially four categories. Firstly there were the peasants, possessing between 30 and 60 hectares of land and whose service obligation to the local lord consisted in supplying between two and four horses and one or two agricultural labourers. Secondly there were the cottagers, most of whom held no more than 30 hectares of land and who were compelled to render manual service. Thirdly there were the small cottagers, who had little more than a small garden and supplied casual labour as well as full-time labour during harvest time. Fourthly there were the servants and peasants who served the lord directly and lived on or close by his premises. Apart from those services mentioned, the peasants also had to pay dues in cash or agricultural produce to the lord of the demesne. This peasant population was subject to the lord or the administrator of the electoral, and later royal, domain. They were not allowed to leave the estate without permission of the lord and could marry only with his consent. Nor could they learn a particular trade without his agreement. They were all subject to patrimonial justice, all police and judiciary power over them being concentrated in the lord's hands. Actual serfdom existed in Pomerania and the Uckermark. The lord could do with his serfs as wished, buying and selling them like livestock, and they had no right of appeal to any court. Towns and cities which had lost their independence to the lord of the demesne were in a similar position, the burghers subject to feudal obligations. However, the situation that applied to the lands east of the Elbe, those territories traditionally associated with the 'Junkers', did not apply to the territories west of the Elbe – or if it did was in a much milder form. Clearly the early social and economic development of Prussia was strongly influenced by the customs prevailing among its nearest neighbours, Russia and Poland. And indeed in the late sixteenth and early seventeenth centuries East Prussia in particular resembled Polish conditions very closely. In the words of Otto Hintze it 'turned into a veritable nobles' republic' – until the Great Elector put an end to this misrule.

While he was in Königsberg Frederick William also moved towards settlement of the Jülich-Cleves problem. After the death of Schwartzenberg the Netherlands believed that Brandenburg's pro-Hapsburg policy would come to an end, or at least would be modified favourably. The Prussian envoy in the Hague, Joachim Frederick von Blumenthal, took the initiative in trying to turn the eligible bachelor Frederick William into a respectable married man. The Polish court had already had an eye on him. Now Blumenthal suggested to Frederick Henry of Orange, the marriage of his daughter Louise Henrietta with Frederick William. At that stage the project was still somewhat premature and several years were to elapse before the first marriage of Frederick William was concluded, but against the background of the marriage project the arrival of the deputies of Cleves at Königsberg provided at least a basis on which a solution satisfactory for Frederick William could ultimately be arrived at.

As far as religion was concerned Frederick William was a Calvinist, receiving his final imprint as such during his stay in the Netherlands. But the majority of his subjects were orthodox Lutherans. Publicly, Frederick William supported the cause of religious toleration, which of course did not prevent him from selecting his closest circle from men of his own religious persuasion. The Lutheran clergy in Prussia feared the spreading of Calvinist doctrine, and consequently opposed militantly any sign of it from the very beginning. This threat convinced Frederick William all the more that for the sake of stability he had to pursue a policy of religious toleration and to open offices and honours to all members of the Christian religions.

Most of Frederick William's governmental and administrative activity took place within the Secret Council which met two or three times a week, usually with six to eight councillors present. At such meetings virtually all types of problems came under review or up for decision, from foreign to domestic policy. Since upon his accession the councillors were rather aged, Frederick William appointed several new ones. On the whole his role within the council meetings was that of an arbitrator between differing views rather than that of a man with a decided view on all matters.

His view of the function of the judiciary is best illustrated by a painting which he had put in the Berlin Chamber Court. It depicted how the Persian King Cambyses had skinned a judge found guilty of an unjust judgement.

The build-up of the army dates from the spring of 1644, after Frederick William had achieved a degree of internal as well as external consolidation. The first recruitments represent the beginning of the army of Brandenburg-Prussia. The strength of the army varied according to need and circumstance, and only after 1660 was it possible to transform it into a regular standing army. Nevertheless, Frederick William and his councillors were clear in their minds about the need for a small efficient army in Brandenburg to supply the necessary muscle behind the territory's political demands. Chancellor Götzen raised only two objections: the money an army would cost, and the suspicions it would arouse among the Swedes.

But against those objections stood the considerations in favour of an army and, more important, a memorandum submitted in 1644 by Curt Bertram von Phul, a member of the Brandenburg nobility who had served in the Swedish army. Phul argued in favour of an army because its existence would increase the diplomatic prestige of Brandenburg-Prussia, and he also made the important point that a disciplined standing army would be of considerable economic benefit, as it had proved to be in the Dutch Netherlands and in Sweden. Though basically sound, the expectations inherent in these ideas were not realized until the eighteenth century.

Frederick William proceeded cautiously with his recruitment programme, entrusting it first to a close confidant, Johann von Norprath. It was to be conducted in the region of the lower Rhine, in other words away from the close proximity of the Swedes who might become suspicious. The garrison fortresses in Brandenburg and in Prussia were also slowly increased. But the core of the standing army was built up in Cleves where, because of the war between Spain and the Dutch, the Estates General decided to pull out their forces, thus leaving it to Frederick William. By 1646 approximately 3,000 men were garrisoned on the lower Rhine, recruited mainly from Dutchmen and Prussians.

One major problem remained, however, namely how to pay the army and where to take the funds from to hire the soldiers in the first place. The main contribution came from the Duchy of Prussia, though the payments were highly secretive because of the Swedes and the estates were circumvented. Councillors, and individual members of the diet, as well as representatives of town and countryside were approached individually and persuaded to give their support. But there was still a substantial gap between Prussia's contribution and the amount needed. Loans were raised in cities, but we still do not know all the sources from which the army was financed in the early years.

Major difficulties were encountered in Cleves where the estates were rather vehement in their opposition to the army recruitment and the consequential levying of contributions. The need for an army, its purpose and function in the general context of the policy of Brandenburg-Prussia were explained to them. It was of no avail. They were willing to grant supplies only if Frederick William would pull out of Cleves the troops he had recruited. Although Frederick William was willing to concede the point and transfer the troops to the county of Mark, he could only do so once the respective garrisons there had been evacuated by the imperial troops. Therefore because of the unreasonableness of the estates of Cleves, Frederick William had little choice other than to raise taxation without consent. This was possible in the countryside but met with strong opposition in the cities, where because of their refusal to co-operate no administration existed to assess and collect the taxes. Frederick William also encountered the opposition of Austria and the Dutch who opposed this kind of taxation on grounds of political principle. For the time being Frederick William and the estates could reach no common ground; both got themselves involved in an extensive pamphleteering war about the rights and wrongs of taxation without consultation – arguments which, across the North Sea, John Pym and John Hampden, among others, had put forward in defence of the same principle a short time before.

Meanwhile Sweden was turning its attention away from Germany towards Denmark. Rumours circulated of a marriage project between Frederick William and Queen Christina. This project had once been actively promoted by the Swedes but it seemed that neither Christina nor Frederick William showed any enthusiasm for the scheme. Brandenburg, hoping of course for due compensation, tried to mediate between Denmark and Sweden, but the attempt was ignored. However, the military needs of the Swedes compelled them to give up their occupation of the fortresses of Frankfurt-an-der Oder and of Krossen, which they could have defended only with great difficulty against any attacks by imperial troops. Brandenburg-Prussia had to promise that it would not allow these fortresses to be occupied by the Austrians. Obviously this was an embarrassing demand because it was by no means certain that Brandenburg-Prussia had the necessary strength to prevent them, nor whether such forces as existed were strong enough even to prevent the transit of imperial troops. Apart from that, Brandenburg-Prussia was still, at least formally, the ally of the Hapsburgs. After lengthy and protracted negotiations in which by force of necessity the representatives of Brandenburg-Prussia were not always the most honest of men, a treaty was agreed upon and the fortresses evacuated by the Swedes in July 1644. The first members of the new army of Brandenburg-Prussia entered virtually upon the heels of the Swedes.

The Swedes also seemed ready to discuss the question of Pomerania, but because of its connections with the Empire Brandenburg-Prussia could not over-indulge in negotiations with the Swedes. But the impotence of the state when faced by a major power was demonstrated during the course of the same year, when in order to support the Danes imperial troops traversed Brandenburg-Prussia with impunity, leaving Frederick William in a position to do very little about it.

It was that impotence which caused Frederick William to look for support from any major power ready to give it. In 1643 when the first rumours spread about an impending major peace settlement, he had been quick to establish connections with France, since the Swedes could no longer be relied upon for support over the long term. On the other hand, the aim of France throughout the seventeenth century had been to weaken the House of Hapsburg in Spain and in the Hapsburg crownlands in Austria and Hungary, in order to prevent the re-emergence of the kind of power bloc which Charles V had once created. Richelieu and Mazarin (and later Louis XIV) with unswerving purposefulness had built up France to the status of Europe's leading great power. However, in the process they underestimated seriously the political, social and economic strength of sea-powers such as Great Britain and the Netherlands while overestimating that of Sweden, which after the Thirty Years War was showing serious signs of the erosion of its strength and resources.

For the time being the Danish–Swedish war caused the hopes of a general peace to recede. Sweden's ascendancy over Denmark was responsible for the adoption of a more haughty attitude towards Brandenburg-Prussia which expressed itself particularly in the key question affecting the relations between the two countries – the question of Pomerania. Frederick William had his allies though, for the Dutch Netherlands, vitally interested in trading in the Baltic, did not favour a solution that would further consolidate Sweden's position there. They also took a serious view when Sweden refused to evacuate further fortresses which it occupied in Brandenburg.

The hardening of respective positions became clear very quickly at Münster and Osnabrück, where the delegates of the various powers assembled to discuss a possible peace treaty to end the Thirty Years War. The Brandenburg delegation took its seats in both places in the spring of 1646. By August of that year the Swedes made it plain that they insisted upon Pomerania. Brandenburg refused arguing that Pomerania was so to speak, its own front garden, a territory essential for maintaining the connection between Brandenburg and Prussia and that its loss would ruin the Elector. The Netherlands, in spite of their fundamental opposition to the Swedish demands, held back their arguments for the time being, while the Poles complicated the position even more by demanding parts of Pomerania for themselves. Since Pomerania was only one item of a long list of Swedish demands, her ally France felt rather alienated and, envisaging a Franco-Swedish conflict, enquired whether Frederick William would support France. France's objective was to achieve a general peace which would prevent Vienna from aiding its Spanish relations. The danger was that Sweden could perhaps, by way of a separate peace with Austria achieve all of its aims, and as far as Brandenburg was concerned such a separate peace was likely to be concluded only at her expense.

Hence flexibility in the conduct of its negotiations became imperative for Brandenburg, which from the outright rejection of the Swedish demands moved to a position where on its own initiative it offered to

Sweden some Pomeranian territories without, however, sacrificing its basic objective which was to regain control of the mouth of the river Oder at Stettin. From there it hoped to build up extensive overseas trade and to obtain colonies, in other words to turn Brandenburg-Prussia into something of a carbon copy of the Netherlands whose stability and wealth Frederick William so much admired.

But Sweden was not to be tempted. Vienna, interested in the speedy conclusion of a peace with Sweden, now submitted its own proposals. These would have granted the Swedes the majority of their demands in northern Germany, the whole of Pomerania, and the cities of Wismar, Bremen and Verden. All that Brandenburg was to receive was Halberstadt and financial compensation. Brandenburg replied with equally strong counter-demands which almost produced a total confrontation with Sweden and Austria on one side and Brandenburg on the other. The French intervened in this situation, with a compromise solution according to which Pomerania was to be divided. The eastern part of Pomerania, Vorpommern, the mouth of the Oder, including the city of Stettin, was to go to Sweden; western Pomerania, Hinterpommern to Brandenburg.[1]

Lacking the support of powers which would have been prepared to continue the war solely to see Brandenburg-Prussia's demands fulfilled, Frederick William was compelled to agree. His ambition to create a state modelled commercially on that of the Netherlands had been frustrated. He had been cut off from the Baltic at its most important point. However, benefit of considerable magnitude was achieved by the mere fact that Brandenburg-Prussia was now no longer involved in the war which had reduced the population of many of its towns by half, some even by two-thirds and more. One-third of all the farms had been devastated, the destruction by its very nature affecting the peasant more than the nobleman.

The Peace of Westphalia signified the end of the ascendancy of the House of Hapsburg on the one hand, and the rise of France on the other. Spanish power along the Rhine was at the point of collapsing, though it was to take another 11 years before this finally occurred.

Paradoxically, the rise of Brandenburg-Prussia during the seventeenth and eighteenth centuries was favoured also by the Peace of Westphalia which brought to it important territorial acquisitions. Although for the time being Sweden exercised control over the mouths of the rivers Elbe and Oder, Brandenburg-Prussia's position along these rivers ensured it an important rôle since these rivers carried by far the greater part of German exports. In addition her territorial holdings along the river Weser and the lower Rhine placed her in a key position between Germany's north and south, between the northwest, particularly Hamburg, and the territories southeast of Brandenburg, those of the upper Oder and their neighbouring territories. A policy of opening up and expanding the existing network of communications, particularly roads and canals, which was pursued for over a century cemented that position. It allowed the export of east Prussian grain into the densely populated regions of northwestern Europe and this trade contributed to Brandenburg-Prussia recovering relatively quickly from the destruction of the Thirty Years War. The territories of Cleves, Mark, and Ravensberg provided additional economic resources. While Ravensberg produced cotton, Mark possessed a sizeable iron and steel industry and Cleves cloth and silk manufacture.

Brandenburg-Prussia, still relatively insignificant and considered not particularly trustworthy because of the vacillating role it had played during the Thirty Years War, was in danger of becoming a pawn in the diplomatic game of the Great Powers. That it survived the way it did was mainly due to Austria's exhaustion and the diversionary influence exercised by the Turks who unexpectedly favoured the rise of Brandenburg-Prussia. But because it did not represent a single compact territorial unit and instead was spread east to west across northern Germany, it was highly vulnerable, a vulnerability duly exploited by its neighbours. The Swedes, for instance, did not feel themselves bound by the provisions of the Treaty of Westphalia and kept the whole of Pomerania under occupation. Brandenburg-Prussia's possessions in western Germany, such as Cleves and Berg, were also insecure, though mainly because of differences over the religious settlement there. Frederick William tried to settle the question by military intervention but succeeded only in ranging Vienna against himself. However Emperor Ferdinand III, wishing to secure the voice of the Elector in favour of the royal title for his son, was prepared to assist him in another more vital matter, that of compelling the Swedes to evacuate Hinterpommern as agreed. This was finally achieved by the spring of 1653. But with the election secured, the Emperor again reverted to his original opposition to Frederick William. The issues contested were mainly complaints by Frederick William of the suppression of Protestants in areas such as Silesia, while the imperial court lent its support to the estates of Brandenburg-Prussia against the Elector. On the whole the relationship between Brandenburg-Prussia and the Empire was one of tension rather than co-operation.

In July 1655 war broke out between Sweden and Poland, which posed a serious problem for Frederick William for he was the vassal of King John Casimir of Poland and as such obliged to rally to his support. By that time, however, Poland was already showing serious internal weaknesses of the kind that little more than a century later were to lead to its destruction. The Swedes advanced victoriously, casting an eager eye upon Prussia which they much desired, and which was also important as an operational base against Poland. Frederick William endeavoured to mediate but met outright rejection by the Swedes. Confronted by the choice of supporting Poland or eventually being destroyed himself, he abandoned his liege lord. The victorious Swedes chased John Casimir out of his country, from where he sought refuge in Upper Silesia, and Frederick William now was forced to accept Swedish overlordship. On 17 January 1656 he concluded the Treaty of Königsberg in which he accepted Prussia from the hands of Charles Gustavus (Charles X). He also opened his Prussian harbours of Memel and Pillau to the Swedes and divided with them the revenue from the harbour dues. Apart from that he had to promise to support the Swedes with 1,500 of his own men.

Hardly had the treaty been concluded when the fortunes of war turned decisively against the Swedes. With the support of a great popular movement and the church John Casimir returned to Poland, attacked the Swedes and expelled Charles Gustavus. This of course further increased the value of Brandenburg-Prussia as Sweden's ally and on 25 June 1656, by the Treaty of Marienburg, the former was promised part of the Polish spoils should Poland be defeated.

The alliance culminated in the three-day battle of Warsaw in which the army of Brandenburg-Prussia received its baptism of fire. It proved also highly superior to its opponents. To be sure it was hardly in Frederick William's interest to ensure complete Swedish victory, and thus perpetuate Swedish dominance. Moreover Vienna and the new power of the East, Russia, under Czar Alexei, began to rally to the support of Poland, putting the Swedes once more on the defensive. The moment seemed opportune for Frederick William: he was now in a strong enough position to demand that Charles Gustavus agree to the revocation of the bonds of vassalage and recognize Frederick William as Duke and sovereign of Prussia in his own right. And precisely this was agreed upon at the Treaty of Labiau on 20 November 1656. Negotiating in all directions, Frederick William would have been quite prepared to change sides to support John Casimir, only the King of Poland overestimated the strength of his position and rejected demands identical to those accepted by Charles Gustavus. However, the court of Vienna indicated to Frederick William that he would receive its fullest support if he refrained from supporting the Swedes. The Swedes, now being attacked also by the Danes, were in a dangerous position and demanded that Frederick William take on the Poles by himself while they turned against the Danes.

Again an election proved decisive. Emperor Ferdinand III had died on 2 April 1657, and it was therefore important to win over the Elector of Brandenburg-Prussia to the Hapsburg side. The Elector's main condition was the recognition by Poland of the sovereignty of Prussia, a condition to which the King of Poland only agreed under the severest of pressure from the court of Vienna. By the Treaty of Wehlau of 19 September 1657, Prussia once again became sovereign. The territory which had once been that of the Teutonic Order once again became a German state.

The Swedes quite rightly felt betrayed, but Frederick William could not in view of the general vulnerability of his territories, afford to pursue any policy other than one that actively furthered the interests of his house. Adherence to rigid loyalties would have been credited by none of the surrounding powers; his situation demanded a degree of flexibility, involving changes in alliance according to the changing needs of Brandenburg-Prussia.

Renewed Swedish hostility caused him to conclude a defensive alliance with Austria which also included Poland and without further ado he gave his full support to the election of Leopold as Emperor of the Holy Roman Empire of the German Nation, who on 18 July 1658 at the age of 18 was duly elected.

A month later Charles Gustavus renewed the war, but instead of turning against Prussia as expected he sailed with his fleet first against Copenhagen, where the Danish King Frederick III put up such a spirited defence that Charles Gustavus was in dire straits. Precisely at this moment Frederick William decided to attack the Swedes. At the head of a 30,000-strong army composed of Brandenburg, imperial and Polish contingents, he expelled the Swedes from Schleswig and Holstein while the Dutch appeared with a fleet breaking the Swedish blockade of Copenhagen.

Sweden's only major ally, France, had its hands tied by its war with Spain. Only after the Peace of the Pyrenees had been concluded was Mazarin in a position to give support to the Swedes. He objected to the occupation of Vorpommern by Brandenburg and assembled an army of 40,000, a threat strong enough to persuade the Poles and the Empire to give up supporting Frederick William. Poland had liberated its territory from the Swedes. The Emperor was not interested in continuing the war since Spain had made its peace with France. Brandenburg-Prussia was on its own.

France now acted as mediator, but only the death of Charles Gustavus helped a peace settlement to be arrived at. At the Peace of Oliva near Danzig on 3 May 1660, Frederick William was in an isolated position and had once again to cede Vorpommern to the Swedes. The only major concession he obtained was the confirmation of Prussian sovereignty. He was a disappointed man whose ambitions seemed to have come to nought.

For almost 20 years now he had governed by listening to his closest advisers. Oliva represents a watershed in his style of government, because from then on he accepted no counsel other than his own and became one of the main representatives of princely absolutism in Europe. His position was emphasized by a sense of mission to establish Brandenburg-Prussia as a major power within the Holy Roman Empire, a sense of mission strengthened by his stern Calvinism. As the Elector, elected by divinity, he took it upon himself to turn his state into a formidable power, come what may, if necessary against the will of the representative organs such as the estates. Already in 1653 the Brandenburg *Landtag* had met for the last time.

The scattered nature of the Elector's possessions meant they were lacking in natural unity. Consequently it was easier for him to ignore the estates of the various regions and pursue and impose his own policy. By the same token the pursuit of this policy met the greatest resistance in the largest and most consolidated of his territories, Prussia itself. There the estates demanded that the Elector's sovereignty over Prussia required also the prior consent of the estates. They went as far as to conspire with the Poles against their ruler. So far the Polish crown had always been a force which the estates could deploy as a countervailing power against the absolutist aspirations of the Elector. Deprived of that backing they now challenged the legality of the declaration of sovereignty.

Open conflict between the Elector and the estates of Prussia broke out in the first Prussian *Landtag* or diet, to be held after the conclusion of the Peace of Oliva. This was held at Königsberg in 1661. By means of a constitutional document, Frederick William informed the assembled estates that he now possessed the *jus supremi et absoluti domini*. While the privileges of the *Landtag* were to remain the same, it should be convened only with his permission. The estates refused to accept this change and therefore refused to pay homage to the Elector. Attempts to persuade the members of the estates to change their minds failed. The heart of the opposition was to be found in Königsberg in the person of the chairman of the City Court, Hieronymus Roth. He was widely popular and enjoyed the full confidence and support of the guilds. Roth also made contact with the Poles, and at one time even found it necessary to escape to Poland. But when he returned to Königsberg the city council protected him and refused his extradition. There seemed nothing that could be done about the situation, until in 1662 the Elector decided to come to Prussia himself and enforce his demands. In October of that year, coming from Danzig, he landed with 2,000 men and entered Königsberg. While the city council and the population in general maintained passive resistance, they nevertheless avoided open hostility. But one of the Elector's patrols managed to capture Roth which meant that one of Frederick William's main aims had been achieved.

The guilds, facing the choice of war against a superior military force or acquiescence, chose the latter and sacrificed Roth. The Elector in turn confirmed the privileges of the estates within the confines of his own absolutist claims and the estates duly paid homage. One of the modifications introduced was that the rule by which only orthodox Lutherans could serve in public offices was abolished. Frederick William's Calvinist confidants could now be employed. All government councillors were now required to submit regular reports to Frederick William about activities in their districts.

Roth, however, was charged with treason. A special commission investigated his case and found him guilty, but in view of the complex legal situation recommended mercy. This Frederick William was ready to grant, provided that Roth submitted a plea for mercy. Roth, convinced that he was in the right and the Elector in the wrong, refused and stayed a prisoner in the fortress of Peitz until he died in 1678. But this was not the end of the Elector's troubles with Prussia. In 1669 he asked the estates for new money grants for military purposes. The estates refused and tensions grew. One of the main opponents was Colonel Christian Ludwig von Kalckstein, who had first been in the service of the Polish crown and then in that of the Elector. Dismissed for embezzlement, he was subsequently convicted of *lèse-majesté*, but escaped to Warsaw where he acted as self-appointed spokesman for the Prussian estates. His extradition was requested but the Polish court refused. Finally he was abducted by the Elector's men and taken to Prussia, where he was tried for treason, subjected to torture in order to find out if he had any fellow conspirators and finally found guilty and convicted. He was beheaded at Memel in 1672.

Whether the judgement and the execution can stand close scrutiny is open to argument. The action was primarily politically motivated, a demonstration that the Elector would tolerate no opposition and that any hopes which the Prussian nobility placed in Polish support were futile. The example served its purpose. In 1673 and 1674 the first taxes not specifically granted by the estates were demanded and paid; also the first troops stationed in Königsberg without the estates consent.

The struggle with the estates had less severe results in Brandenburg, where of course the reigning dynasty was not considered as an alien intruder as was the case in the Elector's other possessions. However, even there the maintenance of a standing army was a major topic of controversy but a controversy that never went beyond complaints. Neither did the estates refuse to grant money to Frederick William, primarily because of concessions made to the land-owning nobility such as the confirmation of their personal jurisdiction over the serfs on their estates and their freedom from taxation and excise. The victim was the peasant, who, if he was free, had to prove it first.

One point which Frederick William failed to push through in Brandenburg was the introduction of a uniform system of taxation, particularly the introduction of the excise. In this the nobility defied him successfully, because the excise by its very nature would of course have ended their own freedom from taxation. The result was that the excise could be introduced in the towns only. In other words a dual system of taxation developed, one system for the towns and another for the countryside. It also meant two different kinds of revenue administrations and, in order to maximize the returns from the excise, the prohibition of commercial transactions between the towns and countryside. At first the excise was administered by the towns themselves, but from 1682 onwards it was transformed into official state taxation with the corresponding administrative offices. This system put an end to whatever community of interest had existed between the towns and the landed nobility.

A rather more difficult situation was presented by the Rhenish possessions, for in Cleves the estates could find ready support from the Dutch, and in Jülich-Berg, the Catholic section could expect support from the Emperor. The Elector's attempts to curb the estates there came to nought; the estates preserved their right to convene at will. Also, only officials native to the area could be employed, which meant that no official from Brandenburg or Prussia could take up office in Cleves. The Elector had even to promise not to keep troops in his Rhenish possessions or build fortresses there. Only after the Peace of Oliva does the period of consolidation of the Elector's power in these provinces begin. His Rhenish lands were no longer allowed to conduct negotiations with foreign powers. Any complaints had to be directed to the Elector, not to the Emperor. Also the Elector obtained the right to station troops there without the consent of the estates. With the introduction of a standing army, as in Brandenburg, the Rhenish provinces acquired also a relatively uniform system of taxation.

The incorporation of Hinterpommern into the state of Brandenburg-Prussia was carried out without any serious complications. After all it was a region accustomed to the regular and severe contributions which had been exacted during the Thirty Years War. The Elector's taxation system was a major improvement by comparison. A more difficult case was the city of Magdeburg, which after the Peace of Westphalia was required to pay formal homage to the Elector. He also demanded the stationing of permanent Brandenburg garrisons there, but the city refused. Then, in 1666, he appeared with a sizeable contingent of troops before the city gates. It was not long before the councillors of Magdeburg gave in to the demands of the Elector.

Given the diverse characters of his territories, their different political traditions and historical development, there was no unified government nor the possibility of imposing one quickly. A centralized and efficiently functioning government needed time to develop and expand. The Elector's government in each territory consisted basically of a *Statthalter*, as his direct representative, aided and advised by a collegiate body of councillors. There was no division of that collegiate body into an administrative and judicial branch and it fulfilled both functions.

The nucleus of a central government developed out of the Secret Council of the Kurmark, which slowly became the central organ of the administration reaching beyond the confines of the Brandenburg territory. It began to be organized into departments, but for these to act effectively they had to be accepted in all the Elector's territories. This took time and the obstacles put in their way locally were considerable.

The most effective instrument making for centralization was the Elector's financial policy, consisting of the imposition of a uniform system of taxation administered and used mainly for the maintenance of a standing army. Hence taxation was collected and administered by the 'war commissaries' under the central institution of the General War Commissary, which in turn was headed by the most senior active general, who at the same time was also a member of the Secret Council.

Thus financial administration was closely connected with the administration of the army, since the function of the former was, in the main, to serve the needs of the latter. Otto Hintze quite rightly describes the army of the Great Elector as the product of 'the nationalization of the *Soldateska* of the Thirty Years' War'. From an instrument of a military entrepreneur it was transformed into an instrument of state. The army in Brandenburg-Prussia developed along similar lines to the French army. The policies of Louvois were closely emulated by the Elector.

An army that in peace time was kept in its garrisons with apparently little purpose other than drill, was something which most of the Elector's subjects were not to understand. At best it was a useless luxury which heavily increased taxation. For every cow, pig or sheep slaughtered, a fee had to be paid which went into the coffers of the army. After his previous abortive attempts to explain his reasons to the estates, the Elector saw neither need nor purpose to try again to elucidate his views as to why an army was required. One innovation finding general approval was the introduction of severe discipline in the army. The parsons and chaplains in their pulpits and the officers before their men, had to announce that any act of plundering would be punished by hanging. Any officer who physically attacked a civilian would be stripped of his rank for a year and have to carry the musket as a common soldier. Every unit had its own Bible and a religious service was to be held every morning and evening.

Some of the new measures did not survive Frederick William's reign. For instance, he proscribed beating of soldiers by their officers and prohibited running the gauntlet. Even deserters did not any longer automatically go to the gallows. Every court martial sentence had to be confirmed by the Elector personally. All recruitment was to be carried out in the Elector's name, not in that of *condottieri*. Artisans and peasants were exempt from recruitment. In other words he tried to professionalize the army and give it a degree of the respectability which other trades and professions enjoyed.

Frederick William created the regiments and appointed its colonels, though throughout his reign the general practice continued that the regimental officers were still appointed by their colonels and not by the Elector. He recognized that there was need for reform and recognized equally that an officer corps of some homogeneity could not be created overnight but would be the product of decades of growth. As a result he was quick to see the advantage in an innovation of Louis XIV, who had created his own cadet corps for the training of officers. Such officers were thus essentially products of a common mould shaped by the French absolutist monarchy. The Elector adapted this idea and founded a cadet institution for the training of officers for the next generation. The officers of Brandenburg-Prussia were no longer to be soldiers of fortune that came and went as they pleased, but a group of military leaders whose fate was closely associated with the country which they served.

This, over the long term, made the army an ideal instrument for integrating the nobility into the Hohenzollern state, but in the short term it was precisely the nobility who provided some of the main opposition to the standing army. Reasonably enough the Elector did not trust his officers from the nobility to the same extent as did his successors. In the composition of his officer corps the attempt is clearly discernible to balance against officers of native Brandenburg-Prussian origin those, though certainly of repute, of social origins which to say the least can be described as doubtful. His most redoubtable General, Field Marshall von Derfflinger was an Austrian, the son of peasants according to one source, of a tailor according to another. He had made his fortune as a *condottiero* in the Thirty Years War before he joined the service of Brandenburg-Prussia. The Great Elector made a point of keeping counsel with his senior officers. These meetings were the origin of the Prussian general staff.

It took time to infuse the officers with a sense of personal loyalty towards the dynasty; equally it took time to organize them into large military units capable of operating within a centralized framework of command. Problems of insubordination were endemic. The bulk of the army came from recruitment on the 'open market' and the size of the army depended on whether there was war or peace. The Elector did once entertain ideas of introducing, at least in Prussia, something like a regular national service, but quickly abandoned this idea because as yet he did not trust his subjects enough, least of all those of the duchy of Prussia. In peace time the army averaged approximately 7,000 men, in time of war about 15,000 up to a maximum of 30,000.

In spite of his introduction of a uniform system of taxation and its efficient collection, the revenue thus obtained was not enough to keep a force of that strength under arms. Consequently he depended on subsidies paid by the Great Powers – the Dutch Netherlands, Austria, Spain and France – subsidies which necessitated a considerable degree of dependence on the foreign policy of other powers and a flexibility of policy which amounted to frequently changing sides, always according to the advantages offered by one side or the other.

When, in 1667, Louis XIV, made the attempt to bring the Spanish Netherlands under his control, Frederick William's attitude to the situation was determined by another problem. In Poland John Casimir had abdicated and the French advocated the Prince de Condé as his successor, which was hardly promising for the security of Prussia. But Louis XIV was prepared to drop the candidacy of Condé providing Prussia maintained neutrality in the war over the Spanish Netherlands. Frederick William agreed. Michael Wisnowiecki, a native Polish nobleman, was crowned King of Poland and proved the weak monarch the Elector had hoped for. Meanwhile Brandenburg-Prussia refused to join the alliance between the Netherlands, England and Sweden. But Frederick William went even a step further. In return for an annual subsidy of 40,000 thalers, he promised Louis his and his army's active support after the death of the King of Spain. It would have amounted to a secret alliance against the Netherlands, against which, in spite of admiring them in principle, he had serious practical grievances. Because of debts he owed to them they still occupied parts of his Rhenish territories; they maintained constant contact, so he believed, with the unruly estates there. Yet there was another side to this question as well. Which would be preferable, an uncomfortable and occasionally uncouth Netherlands as neighbour of his possessions, or a strong France whose ambition to acquire the left bank of the Rhine was clear to everyone?

The issue was debated by the Elector's family, by his councillors and by his generals. It divided all, but gradually a majority in favour of an alliance with the Netherlands emerged. Finally on 6 May 1672, an alliance with the Netherlands was concluded, the Netherlands assuming half the cost for the recruitment of an army of 20,000 and their pay. But Frederick William ended up in the position of the cheated cheat. England and France opened hostilities against the Netherlands, but the Netherlands remained isolated, save for their alliance with Brandenberg-Prussia. And the Netherlands did not pay the subsidies they had promised.

The Empire refrained from interfering and although Frederick William had as yet not declared war upon France, this did not stop the armies of Louis XIV from occupying his Rhenish possessions. The quick collapse of the Netherlands enabled Frederick William to extricate himself from the entire affair with as little damage as possible. He undertook to give no further aid to the Dutch while the French returned to him most territories which they had occupied; all were to be returned after conclusion of peace with the Dutch.[2] Louis XIV also undertook that in the course of a negotiated settlement with the Dutch he would press them to pay the arrears of subsidies due to BrandenburgPrussia. At the same time he granted a subsidy of his own. In the wake of this settlement France embarked upon a series of annexations, for example the Reich cities in Alsace, which mobilized public opinion in Germany against France.[3] In the pamphlet literature of the period, popular Francophobia caused by fear of French predominance was closely allied with ridicule of Brandenburg-Prussia in general and the Elector in particular because of his inconsistency and untrustworthiness. Vienna now aimed at a grand coalition against Louis XIV. Austria allied with Spain, Denmark and the Netherlands, an alliance ultimately also joined by Frederick William. Spain and the Netherlands paid his subsidies. But the campaign brought no laurels for his troops. They suffered several reverses and outright defeat at the hands of Turenne. Imperial generals and those of Brandenburg-Prussia blamed each other for the adverse outcome. While the mutual recriminations reverberated through Central Europe and the Elector's forces were moving into their winter quarters in Franconia, alarming news arrived: on Christmas Day 1674 the Swedes had invaded

Brandenburg and were ravaging the territory. Sweden had already joined the French and in 1674 a treaty promising French subsidies was renewed on condition that Sweden give all its assistance to the King of France. And that was precisely what it was doing. Frederick William was now again standing on his own. No imperial troops rallied to his support and the problem that faced him was to cross the whole of central Germany as rapidly as possible to meet the Swedes. A seventeenth-century army in this situation was not an army on the march but a migration, because apart from supply and baggage trains there were the dependants of the soldiers as well. For every 7,000 soldiers there were approximately 2,000 to 3,000 dependants.

The achievement of getting the army to Brandenburg in time was mainly that of Derfflinger, who in order to give it greater mobility, divided it into small contingents spread over a distance of 130 kilometres, maintaining continuous contact between the contingents by the use of cavalry units. Within two weeks the army was back in Brandenburg. Derfflinger, at that time already 70 years old, surprised the Swedes at Rathenow and they pulled their armies out of the fortress there. The Swedes were superior in numbers, but simply did not know it. At Fehrbellin Defflinger's dragoons caught up with them. He had only 13 artillery pieces but was able to place them on a commanding height, while of 38 Swedish guns only 7 managed to fire. The battle cost the Swedes 2,000 men; the casualties of Derfflinger's troops totalled 500 wounded and killed. Fehrbellin taken by itself was a minor battle, but it established the fame of the Prussian army. To ensure that the Swedes would be chased out of the country entirely, Derfflinger took a force of selected soldiers, covered 500 kilometres in 10 days on horseback – one has to bear in mind that cavalry horses of that period had all the graces and characteristics of cart horses! – and inflicted another defeat upon the Swedes at Tilsit. Frederick William realized immediately that if he could maintain his success against the Swedes it would cost them Pomerania. He allied himself with Denmark, and the Danes as well as the Dutch fleet exerted pressure upon the Swedes. The campaign now became a drawn-out one, slow, systematic and thorough, lasting throughout 1675, 1676 and into 1677. Frederick William's main objective was the capture of Stettin in order to control the Oder. From July 1677 until December of that year Stettin was besieged, bombarded from sea and land. Finally towards the end of December the walls of the city were breached and the final assault was about to be launched when it capitulated. The garrison was offered, accepted and received honourable conditions, the city's privileges were fully confirmed by the Elector and on 6 January 1678 he entered it and was paid homage.

If Frederick William believed that the other powers would agree with his conquest he was seriously mistaken. The Netherlands and Spain had already made their separate peace with France and in Vienna it was said that it would not be in the interests of the Emperor to allow the emergence of a new *Vandalking* on the shores of the Baltic. In the meantime the French had encouraged their Swedish allies to undertake a new diversion against Brandenburg-Prussia culminating in a winter campaign of 1678–9 which was far more demanding than the battle of Fehrbellin. It was a campaign of attrition in which the Swedes sustained heavy losses of both men and equipment. On the other hand the gains Frederick William expected were not forthcoming. At the Peace of Nymwegen on 5 February 1679 the Emperor made peace with France and Sweden. The Elector had only one ally left; Denmark. He did not possess the strength to maintain his position in the north and north-east as well as in the west. Peace with France and Sweden became imperative. In the Peace of St Germain of 29 June 1679 the Elector had to return Pomerania to Sweden. All he gained were minor frontier corrections.

Frederick William believed himself betrayed by Emperor and Reich, conveniently forgetting the vacillations of his own alliance politics. His policy was also influenced by the Silesian question, or rather by the Emperor's attitude towards it. In 1675 the last of the Silesian Piasts, Duke George William of Liegnitz, died. By a treaty dating back to 1537, parts of Silesia were in that case to become Hohenzollern possessions. But Vienna would not hear of it and simply annexed it as part of the crown lands of Bohemia. Even the demand for compensation in lieu of Silesia was rejected. As a result of the Emperor's treatment of him Frederick William once again turned towards France. Having been deprived of Pomerania by the power of France he now accepted the inevitability of its rise and, by joining it, hoped to regain what he lost.

Complex secret negotiations ensued. At the same time Louis XIV was engaged in a policy of annexation towards German territory which he chose to call 'reunions'. The Empire and opposition raised the value of an alliance with Brandenburg-Prussia correspondingly. But Louis and Frederick William wanted an alliance with one another for different purposes: Louis in order to back his policy of reunions, Frederick William, who also wanted to draw Denmark into the alliance, in order to direct it against the Swedes. The alliance was concluded, but without Denmark, and ultimately benefited France but not Brandenburg-Prussia. Louis XIV's 'Rape of Strassburg' in 1681 tarred Frederick William with the same brush, probably even worse, for his support of France was taken as a betrayal of the Reich. Frederick William continued to entertain hopes that France would support him against the Swedes. Only in 1683, when Sweden instead of renewing its treaties with France accepted subsidies from the Emperor and the Netherlands, was France interested in keeping Sweden in check with the aid of Brandenburg and Denmark. On 30 April 1683 two alliance treaties were concluded, one between France and Brandenburg the other between France, Brandenburg and Denmark. Sweden was to be expelled completely from Germany. In point of fact the agreements were not fully-fledged alliances at all but preliminary provisional agreements. Frederick William made the mistake of not realizing this. The treaties were never ratified. Furthermore, additional aid arrived on the political scene of Europe for France, which was less expensive and still threatened the Empire: the Turks. Realizing how low his value had sunk *vis à vis* France, Frederick William now offered his aid to Vienna in return for subsidies and territorial compensation. Thoroughly disillusioned and distrustful of Frederick William by now, the Emperor rejected the offer, insisting that as a prince of the Empire it was the Elector's duty to come to the assistance of the Empire threatened by the armed might of the heathens. The relief of Vienna from the Turkish siege took place with the help of the King of Poland – John Sobieski – and Elector Max Emanuel of Bavaria. Troops of Brandenburg-Prussia had no part in it. In the meantime the Emperor was once again deeply involved in negotiations aiming at a settlement with France, or at least an armistice. Louis was prepared to conclude it providing he could hold the gains he had made by his policy of reunions. In this he was successful. His alliance with Brandenburg-Prussia had served its purpose: a French one, but not a Brandenburg, let alone German one.

Frederick William, known since Fehrbellin as the Great Elector, had succeeded in transforming his state into a formidable power, but not, as he had hoped, into a major one. All his foreign policy objectives had been frustrated. Even belatedly turning his back on France did not change anything. Nor was he able to transform Brandenburg-Prussia into a commercial power of any significance. Ventures into sea power, the creation of an African colony Gross-Friedrichsburg, illustrate the direction of his ambitions, but their ephemeral character also illustrates that these ambitions lacked the solid base of power, political and economic, with which to sustain and expand them. Hence it is not because of his vision that he is an impressive monarch of the Baroque to be remembered, but because he laid foundations upon which later, able successors could build and transform at least part of his ambitions into concrete reality. What he left behind were beginnings of the Prussian state, its army, its bureaucracy and perhaps among its subjects a nascent awareness of Prussian statehood.

Notes

1. In addition she was to obtain the bishoprics of Halberstadt, Minden and Cammin, as well as the claim to Magdeburg which was realised in 1680.
2. This undertaking was given at the Peace of Vossem in 1673.
3. This was the French 'reunion' policy which began with the seizure of Lorraine and extended to the Reich cities after 1679.

Chapter 4

From duchy to kingdom

When the Great Elector died he left an army 30,000 strong. Taxation and subsidies from other powers alone were no longer sufficient to maintain the army. The need to finance the army was one major factor responsible for his expanding trade and commerce in Brandenburg-Prussia. One of the major aspects of his domestic policy had been to attract immigrants to Prussia and in this context, during the last years of his life, the revocation of the Edict of Nantes in 1685 had played into his hands because it brought some 20,000 French and Walloon Huguenot emigrants to Brandenburg-Prussia. Possessing more highly developed commercial and industrial skills than the majority of the native population, and having also a rather better education, the Huguenot immigrants represented an asset the value of which to the commercial, industrial and intellectual development of Brandenburg-Prussia can never be overestimated.

In terms of institutions it was the General War Commissary and the Secret Court Chamber, as well as the Secret Council, that represented the nucleus of the bureaucratic machinery which was to develop over the next century and impose a centralized administration over geographically, socially and economically highly diverse territories. Naturally even this nucleus changed in the course of time. The Secret Council declined into insignificance while the Secret Court Chamber, assuming the administration and control of all the electoral domains, gained immensely in importance until in 1713 it was transformed into the General Finance Directory.

Of the three aims of the Great Elector's foreign policy, namely the achievement of sovereignty in Prussia, the acquisition of Vorpommern and a general rounding off of his territories to give his state greater coherence, only the first had been achieved. Of this he was very much aware, so much so that after the Peace of St Germain, he had a memorial medal struck bearing a line of Virgil: *Exoriare aliquis nostris ex ossibus ultor* – may from my bones an avenger arise. He did.

The political subordination of the estates established the absolutist regime, a regime which in spite of the concessions that had been made to the nobility could, in the light of the political and economic circumstances, hardly afford to degenerate into a dictatorship of the nobility, let alone the dictatorship of one prince in the interest of one group. The very fragility of Brandenburg-Prussia demanded the integration of more than just one interest group into the state.

Brandenburg-Prussia was in the process of emerging as a European power, but its fundamental problem remained – its inherent vulnerability resulting from its geographical position, scattered dynastic possessions and poverty in natural resources. Within the confines of the Germanic body politic this emergence of the new state was of revolutionary long-term significance. But it was revolutionary also at its very sources. In terms of colonial territory of the Holy Roman Empire of the German Nation, Prussia represented the north-eastern marches. As Great Britain's American colonies were later to demonstrate, colonial existence tends to weaken the ties of tradition and encourage creative independence.

Like England, the Prussian state rested upon a single radical act of the secularization of land, carried out in Brandenburg-Prussia by its adoption of Protestantism. With one single stroke Duke Albrecht had cut the ties with the past and his excommunication inevitably elevated Protestantism into a constituent principle of state. The subsequent influence of Calvinist modes of thought simply underlined this fact.

A further revolutionary feature of Prussia the origin of which can be attributed exclusively to the Great Elector, was its character as a military state, a military state which extended its territory and maintained its existence on the battlefields of Europe for almost two centuries.

Prussia as a state was a work of art, a Renaissance state in the true sense of Jakob Burckhardt's term. 'With immense effort, Brandenburg-Prussia raised herself from the debris of Germany' (Burckhardt). It would hardly have survived had it served the interests of only one group exclusively or predominantly. During the reign of the Great Elector a major constituent principle of this new state became visible, namely a kind of *étatisme* an ideology of the state community which subjected dynasty, aristocracy and subjects alike, and which represented a revolutionary break away from the still-prevalent feudal dynastic conception as represented by the Hapsburgs.

Given that condition of natural weakness compensated only by highly artifical devices, it had to be the object of the dynasty, of the state, to regulate society in a manner which on the one hand would prevent periodic discontent from becoming a source of internal unrest and potential revolution, while on the other making it unnecessary for the state, whose external foundations rested upon bayonets anyway, to maintain law and order with their aid as well. It had to be a major point of policy to prevent dissatisfaction from arising in the first place, and, to use the phrase first coined by Thorstein Veblen and applied by Ralf Dahrendorf, to a much later period, to absorb political, social and economic conflicts by the institutional framework. Again the first signs of this policy are discernible during the reign of the Great Elector, as are the beginnings of an institutional framework capable of initiating and carrying out reform from above and thus preventing revolution from below. Prussia's governmental apparatus was to be the very embodiment of the ideology of the state community.

By the time of the Great Elector's death the general European situation was changed in a way that favoured the rise of the Hohenzollern state rather more than had been the case during his lifetime. Sweden, whose external ambitions were in inverse proportion to its actual resources, lost its predominance in the Baltic, while Russia emerged as a great power. This did not immediately lead to Brandenburg-Prussia acquiring the position she desired in the Baltic region, but Sweden's decline nevertheless removed a major threat. Poland, in the throes of dissolution under its future Saxon rulers, moved towards greater dependency on Russia, a situation which, for the time being, removed another threat from the frontiers of the Hohenzollern state.

Most important was the Anglo-French conflict, global in character but crystallizing itself in Europe over the question of the Spanish succession, in which Great Britain supported the House of Hapsburg and thus effectively contained the French attempt at achieving hegemony in Europe. The Peace of Utrecht re-established a balance of power in Europe between Great Britain, France and Austria, without endowing Austria with the additional power that could make it a serious threat to Brandenburg-Prussia.

Elector Frederick III introduced his reign by establishing primogeniture in Brandenburg-Prussia in 1692, in part invalidating the will of the Great Elector. But with this action a precedent was established and the inviolability of the territorial unity of the state of Brandenburg-Prussia secured. Frederick III showed none of the political ambition of his father, nor the desire to run the affairs of state himself. Preferring the appearance and the outward trappings of absolutist monarchy to its actual substance, he entrusted the conduct of affairs of state to the hands of prime ministers, first Eberhard von Danckelmann (1688–1697) and then Kolbe von Wartenberg (1702–1711). The first period was marked by Prussia's membership of the Grand Alliance against France under Louis XIV, an alliance which ended with the Peace of Ryswick in 1697.

Danckelmann had been instrumental in once again ranging Prussia firmly on the side of the Netherlands, moving strong troop contingents to the lower Rhine to cover William III of Orange in his venture across the sea to carry out the 'Glorious Revolution' in England. One Brandenburg general, Marshal Schomberg, participated directly in the operation and landed with William in England.

In the War of the Grand Alliance, Brandenburg-Prussia received subsidies from Great Britain, the Netherlands, Austria and Spain: Brandenburg-Prussia was as yet not in a position to conduct wars independently. Her inability to press her demands expressed itself time and again. Subsidies which were due to her were not paid in full, and at the conclusion of the Peace of Ryswick compensations previously promised to Frederick III were withheld or ignored. As usual a scapegoat for such failure had to be found and so Danckelmann was dismissed, mainly as a result of an intrigue initiated by Frederick's wife, a Hanoverian princess, the Electoress Sophia Charlotte. Danckelmann's fall led to a serious neglect of the administration of the state; its bureaucratic institutions, still in their infancy, were allowed to deteriorate. The immediate result was a decline in financial revenue.

This seems to have mattered little to Elector Frederick because his entire efforts were concentrated on achieving his major ambition: the royal title and crown. Frederick the Great used to say that his grandfather aimed for and obtained the royal crown before he actually possessed the requisite power. This is quite true and Frederick III realized that he could not achieve his ambition by a stroke of power, but by remaining a faithful vassal of the Emperor and ignoring the slights and humiliations he suffered in the course of this relationship. But as king he did not wish to be the vassal of the Emperor, and so he based his royal claims upon the duchy of Prussia over which he was sovereign. This meant that he needed only the agreement of the Emperor rather than the conferment of the crown to him. Negotiations in this direction first took place in 1690, two years after he succeeded his father. Certain minor territorial issues complicated them and in Vienna the old phrase about a new Vandal King on the shores of the Baltic could be heard again. The religious issue also played a role. Conceding to the wishes of the Elector of Brandenburg-Prussia would mean establishing another Protestant royal house. Objections on religious grounds were only dismissed after the confessor of Emperor Leopold, Father Wolf S.J., endeavoured to bring about a marriage between the Prussian Electoral Prince Frederick William and one of the daughters of the Emperor.

In the end it was the imminent resumption of war with France which was the decisive issue, for Austria was badly in need of Prussian forces, as well as Frederick's promise to support the House of Hapsburg in a future imperial election. On 16 November 1700 the Emperor promised the immediate recognition of Frederick's royal title, based on his duchy of Prussia, whenever he chose to assume it. Hardly had agreement been reached when the news was received of the death of King Charles II of Spain. The War of the Spanish Succession was imminent. The Elector, in a hurry to clinch the deal while the situation was in his favour, crowned himself King *in* Prussia in the city of Königsberg on 18 January 1701. Considering that electorates such as Hanover or Saxony existed in connection with non-German territories – Great Britain in the one case, Poland in the other – the Hohenzollern crown ruled over exclusively German territory.

The new King was annointed by two Protestant bishops, but he gave no notification whatever to the Catholic church, which therefore until 1787 – after the death of Frederick the Great – listed the Kings of Prussia in its papal calender merely as the Margraves of Brandenburg. The coronation ceremony was a fairly costly affair. The estates of

Brandenburg made a grant of 100,000 thalers in advance and a special coronation tax was levied.

At his coronation ceremony Frederick wore scarlet clothes and when seated upon the throne placed the crown on his head himself, then took the sceptre in one hand and the orb in the other. Next he went to the rooms of the Queen in order to place the crown upon her head. After that a church service was held, followed by the coronation meal. After his coronation Frederick I stayed for two months in Prussia and finally returned to Berlin on 6 May 1701. As he entered his capital all the church bells rang, the artillery pieces fired their salute and the entire city was illuminated. Someone had turned the name Berolinum into *lumen orbi* – light of the world – a somewhat extravagant claim for a still relatively undistinguished middle-sized town.

Frederick I was determined to enjoy his crown and not dilute this enjoyment with any complications. Hence his policy was essentially peaceful. In his testament for his successor he had already by 1698 written that he should take care not to start an ill-considered war and should maintain peace as long as this was possible, in order that the common man should prosper rather than be ruined. What is fed by peace, is consumed by war.

Still, he was aware that the position of his House rested very much on an effective army, which therefore needed always to be well trained and disciplined in order that the neighbouring states would fear it. His caution derived from the realization that because the territories of his kingdom could easily be isolated they were therefore very vulnerable. A kingdom such as his, spread in several pieces across northern Germany from East Prussia to the Rhine, made defence a permanent problem. In other words any military action directed against the Reich was bound to take place in the immediate vicinity of the Prussian borders and was likely to involve the risk of territorial losses.

Nevertheless, in spite of this apparent realism, Frederick's reign was full of contradictions, the major one being the power of the absolute monarch projected in Baroque dimensions and the empty coffers of his treasury. After Wartenburg became the King's prime minister Prussia was heading towards financial ruin. Wartenburg, aided by the Court Marshal, Count von Sayn-Wittgenstein, and the General War Commissioner, Count von Wartensleben, mobilized every penny he could lay his hands on in order that the King might live according to his newly gained status. Because of their oppressive and destructive financial policy towards the Berliners, who have never been short of wit nor short of readiness to give it quick expression, they were referred to as 'the treble pain'.

Under the influence of his wife, Sophia Charlotte, Frederick became a great supporter of the arts in Brandenburg-Prussia. Early in his reign he engaged the famous international jurist Samuel von Pufendorf to write a work entitled 'The Life and Deeds of Frederick William'. Historiography of the period was mainly interested in the history of antiquity, so Pufendorf's work represents a major and important attempt at the writing of 'contemporary history', and is also free from the hagiographic distortions which one would normally expect in a work of this type. Together with Christian Thomasius he laid the foundations for the secular theory of enlightened absolute monarchy according to which the prince has only one duty: governing for the welfare of his subjects.

Frederick also encouraged Philipp Jakob Spener to come to his court. Spener had previously been court preacher at the electoral court of Saxony in Dresden, but had been expelled because of his apparently unorthodox religious views. In Berlin Frederick immediately made him *Probst* of St Nicolai as a public gesture in support of his policy of religious toleration – similar to his father's Edict of Potsdam of 1685 when the Great Elector had publicly responded to the revocation of the Edict of Nantes by inviting the Huguenots to his state.

Frederick is also the founder of the University of Halle, which opened its gates in 1694 to a total of 449 students. Its main purpose was to train future administrators, so in its early years the emphasis was on the law faculty, which had five professors, while other faculties, such as philosophy, were granted only a maximum of two chairs. Frederick had a good eye for talent, and by attracting Christian Thomasius to the university gave immediate distinction to the new institution. Thomasious himself the son of a university professor and a pupil of Pufendorf, challenged the purely biblical concept of 'natural law', basing his own interpretations of law upon the power of purposefully directed reason. He also challenged the power of superstition, still expressed in various parts of Europe in the form of witch-hunts and torture. Furthermore he brought innovation into German university life by giving his lectures in German rather than Latin.

The person who perhaps more than any other was to influence the thought as well as the politics of Prussia in the long term and whose life was closely connected with the University of Halle, was August Hermann Francke. He joined the university, the *Fredericiana*, as an expert in old and new philology and oriental languages; after 1695 he turned to theology. His importance is not to be found in his academic contributions but in his social and religious activities. He was a preacher, a founder of schools and a missionary whose educational foundations enjoyed the support of Frederick I to the extent that he even ordered his diplomats to raise money for them outside Prussia. Francke was one of the main representatives of the Pietist movement in northern Germany. In his schools, whether the royal *Paedagogium*, his Latin School and his *Seminarium Praeceptorum* or his *Seminarium Orientale*, he founded communities of teachers and students, students selected by ability not by social background and destined to become a natural elite. Throughout his work he was continuously aware that it was not enough for man to work and suffer in the present in order that he might enjoy the blessings of the hereafter, but that man's first service to God lay in his duty to his neighbour. Through changes in the social conditions and institutions of man, human society could be substantially improved, and in that way the divine will fulfilled.

After the University of Halle, Frederick I founded the Prussian Academy of the Arts, patterned on Italian and French examples. It defined itself as a community of painters and sculptors in which some taught and others learnt. Its first director was a Swiss, Joseph Werner, who had been a pupil of Merian and had received most of his artistic training in Italy. As an artist he showed little originality; his gifts were more those of a pedagogue. He had aspired to become a court painter for Louis XIV at Versailles but failed to make an impression there. The Prussian Academy was no doubt an ambitious project at a time when the splendours of the Counter-Reformation as exemplified in the art of the Baroque were already, if not fading, then at least undergoing a slow process of stylistic transformation. The great talents had already found their sponsors and there seemed little attraction in the barbaric north. But the Prussian Academy did produce one major talent whose work has, at least in part, survived in Berlin to this day and stamped its imprint upon the architecture of that city. It was a sculptor and architect from Danzig by the name of Andreas Schlüter. His first work was carried out in Poland where he designed and built the Krasinki Palace, a gem in Warsaw's architecture until it was reduced to rubble during the Warsaw rising of 1944. A famous work of his is the statue of the Great Elector which now stands outside the Charlottenburg, the *Schloss* which Frederick I had built for his wife. The original building was in the style of the late renaissance. It was virtually rebuilt by Schlüter in a style frequently described as the Prussian baroque, a style which while maintaining the essence of baroque splendour contains an element of severity characteristic of the barren landscape of northern Germany, much in the same way as the severity of the baroque style of the music of Bach distinguishes it from the occasionally excessive stylistic exuberance of his south German and Italian contemporaries.

Finally, another important foundation associated with Frederick I is the institute which was later to be named the Royal Prussian Academy of Sciences. It was originally the brainchild of Leibniz, who had conceived the idea during the reign of the Great Elector but was unable to put it into practice at the time. The claim that it served as an example for similar foundations in Leipzig, Göttingen and Munich, and outside Germany in Turin and Stockholm, cannot unfortunately be substantiated. Leibniz's aim was threefold: to support and encourage the further development of the natural sciences (which had just made their first major strides); to preserve scientific results attained by individual effort which might otherwise be forgotten or disappear into oblivion; and to train scientists with wide intellectual horizons (he abhorred the narrow specialist).

In contrast to such academies as already existed in Paris, Florence and London he was not interested in scientific, or for that matter human, curiosities, but – and in this respect he reflected a very modern trend which dominates the natural sciences to this day – he endeavoured to combine theory and practice towards very practical ends. He himself had applied his considerable ingenuity to problems of the mining industry, the development of a fire pump and the rearing of silk-worms for farming. He also wanted to establish close connections between Europe and China, probably partly because of his deep admiration for Confucius, but also because Leibniz saw in China an alternative model of civilization to that in Europe and believed that contact between them would yield fruitful results for both of them. Berlin to him seemed to be the ideal location for the preparation of an undertaking of this kind because it possessed substantial library holdings about Far Eastern studies. Furthermore Prussia's good relations with Muscovy meant that the land route to China would be open to her.

Frederick gave his support to the cultural currents that had been coming to the surface in Germany since the end of the Thirty Years War, especially the reaction against the predominance of France in this sphere. He insisted that the new academy should promote and develop the German language and also instituted a department of national philology. And his wife, whose diverse interests included astronomy, insisted that an observatory be built and attached to the academy. (It was in fact Sophia Charlotte who was responsible for Leibniz being called to Berlin in the first place.)

After his coronation Frederick was officially called King *in* rather than *of* Prussia. This was because of objections from the Poles who still held some parts of the former territory of the Teutonic Order.[1] Nevertheless he immediately began to refer to his entire possessions as the Prussian Kingdom, while the Prussian army and all his administrative organs began to carry the prefix 'royal'.

In a purely German context the further expansion of the centrifugal forces within the German body politic is exemplified by the increasing jurisdiction obtained by Frederick I at the expense of the Empire. Whereas previously the Reich courts represented the ultimate legal arbiter, in December 1702 Frederick I received the imperial privilege, the *privilegium de non appellando*, of supreme jurisdiction in law suits up to the value of 2,500 gulden. An unlimited privilege had already existed in Brandenburg since 1356. Because a vast range of cases was now excluded from the right of appeal to any of the Reich courts, Prussia (the term being used in its widest sense) was in need of creating its own Supreme Appeal Court. By December 1703 this had been done. This does not mean that legal uniformity had now been established throughout the kingdom – far from it – but the first steps in this direction had been taken. The Supreme Appeal Court was as yet not the supreme court of the country. It was not the superior of but an equal institution to the Chamber Court. The province of East Prussia had its own superior tribunal, and even some of the new King's Reich territories were exempt for some time from the jurisdiction of this new court. Only under Frederick the Great was the whole legal system in Prussia ultimately unified.

After the fall of the prime minister Danckelman, Frederick chose to look after his own affairs for several years. But during that period a new favourite slowly emerged in the shape of John Casimir Kolbe von Wartenberg, who had entered the service of Brandenburg after serving in the Palatinate. He soon became an excellent diplomat, and his good connections with the imperial court in Vienna had made him the almost ideal person to negotiate the Emperor's agreement to Frederick's royal title. Wartenberg soon became the King's closest advisor. When, on the eve of his coronation, Frederick founded the Order of the Black Eagle, Wartenburg was the second person he invested with it (Crown Prince Frederick William being the first). He made himself virtually indispensable by his unique ability of knowing how to handle the King while at the same time looking after his own interests and securing a substantial, perhaps even exorbitant, income for himself. The fact that he was the King's prime minister does not mean that he was ever formally installed as such; he was not even a member of the Secret Council. He was the chief courtier in whom the King confided fully, whose advice he took almost without any reservation, and who formulated and executed the King's policies, yet he did not in fact possess any institutional backing or sanction other than the King's full support. Needless to say that under such circumstances intrigues and counter-intrigues were rife at the court of Brandenburg-Prussia, and the measure of Wartenberg's skill is demonstrated by the fact that he won or survived them all.

The King's desire for the visible spectacular trappings of absolutist monarchy had their effects upon the finances of the kingdom. Expenditure trebled without new sources of revenue being opened up. Financial administration, the further development of the institutions which the Great Elector had founded to this end, were sadly neglected. The idea of a fixed budget matched by revenue received was completely abandoned. The Secret Chamber, originally the supreme central organ of the administration, was relegated to second place by the Supreme Directory of the Domains headed by Wartenberg. The Directory made policy, and the Secret Council executed it and was held responsible for it. Aided by Sayn-Wittgenstein and Wartensleben they milked the Prussian state for all it was worth to raise the funds which their Lord and Master required in order to live with pomp and circumstance.

One of the first issues to come to the fore after Frederick became King was a reform project put forward by the chamber councillor Christian Frederick Luben (who when raised to the nobility was called von Wulffen). Luben's plan had as its immediate aim the opening up of new financial resources. He suggested dividing up parts of the royal domain and renting them out. To make the scheme more attractive, the lease should be an inheritable commodity. The parts of the royal domain to be leased in this way were, in the original plan, to be mainly mills, inns and smaller estates. If carried out, the consequences for the entire social structure of the kingdom of Brandenburg-Prussia would have been immense. In addition to the landed nobility there would have been a number of smaller estates held by members of what one may even for that period call the middle class. Simultaneously peasant serfdom – at least within the royal domain – would have been abolished. Although the state would have had to part with some of its domains a substantial new source of revenue would have been created. Luben argued very much on the basis of the incentive principle. An estate farmed by someone who could expect both personal profit as well as security of tenure for himself and his family would work the domain far more intensively than someone who did so because he was forced to do so and who had little or no personal stake in what he was doing. In our age of mechanical farming the idea of breaking up large agricultural units into small and medium-sized holdings may sound anachronistic, but in the context of the time and bearing in mind the farming methods used in Prussia during the eighteenth century, the project made economic as well as social sense. The social benefit was that it would help to elevate the state of the peasantry, which Luben had described as being 'extraordinarily sad'.

Wartenberg and Wittgenstein saw the financial potential in the plan and immediately tried to adapt to it for their purposes. Luben realized this and put up considerable resistance against what he took, and rightly so, to be the perversion of his project. The struggle over the project dragged on for the rest of Frederick I's reign. But on the whole, in spite of its original and socially progressive character, it was a failure. The regional domain chambers opposed and sabotaged it. They wanted to hold on to the old order, and were able to do so reasonably successfully because the King's civil servants were recruited from the same families which held the land. The landed nobility opposed the scheme because, not without justification, they considered it to be the explosive core of a movement likely to dissolve the existing feudal relationships. Naturally wherever the existing social order was most vulnerable to criticism, such as in Pomerania, the resistance to Luben's reform project was the most vociferous. And finally Wittgenstein's financial mismanagement was blamed upon Luben himself. While Wittgenstein got away with a money fine Luben had to leave the country, simply because Wittgenstein had pursued a policy aimed solely at filling the royal coffers.

Besides the administration of the royal domain, another example of mismanagement was provided by the town of Krossen. The town, which had been virtually destroyed by fire in 1708, had received a considerable royal grant for its reconstruction. But when it came to the task of rebuilding there was hardly any money, the funds having been misappropriated by Wittgenstein – to what purpose it was never discovered. On the principle that the King can do no wrong, it has been said that this fact had remained hidden from the King for two years, but considering that the King's primary objective was the satisfaction of his own personal needs it is not unreasonable to assume that Frederick I really did not want to know until he had no other alternative than to face the deplorable facts.

Towards the last years of Frederick's reign the Black Death, coming from the east during the terribly cold winter of 1709, reached East Prussia, causing immense suffering, depopulating vast areas and extending into neighbouring regions. Bad harvests and starvation added to the problems and suffering. Again the administration, and with it Wittgenstein, failed abysmally to cope with the situation. A memorandum of 1 November 1710 from the Secret Court Chamber, also signed – somewhat reluctantly – by Wittgenstein, admitted the total inefficiency of the administration and its partial responsibility for the deterioration of the province. But in the wake of this disaster a whole series of embezzlements came to light. It was the end of Wartenberg and his camarilla. On 31 December 1710 he had to leave office, the King parting from him with tears and giving him an annual pension of 24,000 thalers.

Waiting in the wings was Crown Prince Frederick William and an administrator who enjoyed his confidence, the Secret Councillor von Kameke. When they began to move into the centre of affairs they immediately abandoned Luben's very promising reform project, but tarred as it was with Wittgenstein's and Wartensleben's brush, it was too discredited to be pursued any further, especially in the face of opposition from the East Prussian nobility who justifiably pointed to the previous corruption. They also abolished the Superior Domain Directory and restored the Secret Court Chamber as the highest administrative body for the royal domains. It was a restoration of the old order, but one that was reasonably clear, precise and efficient. Kameke became President of the Secret Court Chamber in 1711 and immediately began to assume responsibility for other sources of revenue, turning the Chamber ultimately into the permanent administrative organ which it became under Frederick William I.

In the realm of foreign policy the major event after the accession of Frederick to the royal title was the War of the Spanish Succession. By agreement Frederick was obliged to support the Emperor with 8,000 men, but that was out of a total of 30,000. The question of how and where to deploy the rest of his forces was to a large extent determined by the powers which paid his subsidies, for without them the Prussian army could not have been kept in being. At the same time as the War of the Spanish Succession the threat from the north re-emerged. But subsidies could not be expected from Russia, Poland or Sweden, whereas the Netherlands and Austria were prepared to pay. Consequently necessity required the concentration of Prussia's military effort in the west. The Spanish succession was only one major consideration. The other was the Orange Legacy. William III of Orange had died in 1702 leaving no issue, and Frederick I was his nearest relation.

Theoretically the possibility of Frederick's succession to the throne of England could not be excluded, but it was never seriously considered. From a practical point of view the territorial possessions of the House of Orange, spread across the Netherlands, Germany and Burgundy, were rather more attractive. In Germany there was the duchy of Mörse, bordering directly on to Cleves and the county of Lingen. On Swiss territory there was the duchy of Neufchatel with the county of Valengin. Apart from these there were several other territories and towns belonging to the House of Orange upon which Frederick I could now lay claim. However William of Orange had left a will in which he appointed a remote relation as universal heir. Therefore as far as the House of Hohenzollern of Brandenburg-Prussia was concerned there was, besides the question of the Spanish succession, also the question of the succession to the legacy of the House of Orange – a question not finally resolved until 1732. But it also represented a major influence on Frederick I's decision to assemble his troops on the Lower Rhine rather than in the north-east of his territory.

Brandenburg-Prussia joined the Grand Alliance against France on 30 December 1701 and, in contrast to the policy of the Great Elector, adhered to it with remarkable consistency. The military significance of Prussia's contribution in the War of the Spanish Succession is difficult to assess because Prussian troops were deployed here and there but never in very large formations. The *Alte Dessauer*, Prince Leopold of Anhalt-Dessau, earned the highest praise from the Duke of Marlborough and Prince Eugène at Blenheim. At Turin, Cassano and at Ramillies, Prussian troops showed extraordinary bravery. And they participated in the conquest of Naples as well as in the occupation of the papal territories. Prussian troops also formed part of the occupying forces in Bavaria. (Elector Max Emanuel of Bavaria, unlike Frederick, had failed to obtain royal status from the Emperor and had allied with the Empire's arch-enemy Louis XIV, but was defeated and exiled in Belgium.) The reports to Vienna about conditions in Bavaria stress time and again the exemplary discipline of the Prussian troops, discipline which stood in strong contrast to that of the other Reich troops. The Austrian forces were especially bad and their behaviour precipitated a major peasant rising which for a time seemed to jeopardize the whole position of the imperial troops in Bavaria.

But the Prussian contribution to the war was judged by the major powers, especially the Emperor, to be essentially an auxiliary one, so Frederick, and his demands, were treated accordingly. His claim to the succession in the Netherlands was dismissed and he was fobbed off with territorial morsels like Lingen, Mörs, Geldern and Neufchatel.

Had Frederick I possessed not only the inclination but also sufficient financial resources to keep his army in being, the Great Northern War of 1700–21 contained much more solid and promising possibilities for the territorial aggrandizement of Brandenburg-Prussia than did the

War of the Spanish Succession. Considering the situation in 1705, when the decision as to whether to support Sweden or Poland–Saxony had not yet been taken, there were several promising opportunities. For example Poland, anxious for Prussian support, offered in return for a successful conclusion to the hostilities Pomerelia, Ermland and Elbing. But, in the first place, Frederick I would have had to be personally more inclined to ally with Sweden's Charles XII; secondly, sharing Marlborough's judgement he considered this Lion of the North as unbeatable; and thirdly he resented Augustus the Strong of Saxony because of his conversion to Roman Catholicism, which he considered as an act of betrayal. Even the reversal of the fortunes of war as a result of Poltava in 1709 did nothing to change his attitude.

Towards the end of his life Frederick's baroque splendour began to wear thin under the hammering of fate. The two eldest sons of the Crown Prince and Sophia Dorothea, the daughter of the future George I of England, died very early. A third marriage which Frederick had entered into in the autumn of 1708 with Sophia Louise of Mecklenburg ended in disaster when, not long after the wedding, his wife became mentally ill. And his own friends began to die. The only happy event left for him was the birth on 24 January 1712 of another grandson, Frederick. A little more than a year later, on 25 February 1713, Frederick I died. The influence of Versailles disappeared; that of Sparta was to come.

Notes

1. Objections were also raised by the Emperor who would not allow him to be a king in the Reich.

Chapter 5

Frederick William I

The body of Frederick I lay in state in full baroque splendour, with the trappings of an age he had loved, admired and done so much to emulate in his barren kingdom. At his feet, deep in thought, stood the new King, Frederick William I. Rather abruptly he straightened himself, turned on his heels and walked out of the room leaving behind him not only the body of his father, the guard of honour and the dim light of the candles, but also another age. The threshold which he crossed was one into an era he meant to be vastly different from that of his father.

Macaulay has described him as being a man whose 'character was disfigured by odious vices, and whose eccentricities were such as had never been seen before out of a madhouse. . . . the mind of Frederick William was so ill regulated, that all his inclinations became passions, and all his passions partook of the character of moral and intellectual disease'. A nicely turned phrase alone does not make good history, though Macaulay is not the only one to have fallen victim to this superficial impression. After all it was one shared by many of Frederick William's contemporaries. With utter incomprehension they observed the unfolding of a spectacle that seemed to contradict the very essence of the spirit of the time, the beginnings of the European Enlightenment. The generous and careless rule of the first Hohenzollern king was to be followed by the rule of a man who carefully appreciated the resources of his territories, or their lack of them, a man who reversed the principle of the Baroque age that revenue had to be adequate to meet expenditure by stating that expenditure should on no account exceed available revenue.

His succession to the crown was tantamount to being a revolution against the hitherto prevailing form of princely absolutism. While the art of the Baroque as the propagandist expression of the Counter-Reformation appealed to the senses and dominated not only the Hapsburg Empire, Spain and France but also the Protestant courts, Frederick William's Calvinist heritage quickly asserted itself by drastically reducing pomp and splendour, making way in his kingdom for a functionalism in the style and appearance of government hitherto unheard of. No wonder contemporaries viewed him as the 'Barbarian from the North'.

Within hours of the death of his father, he assembled his first council around him and ordered that all valuables such as precious stones, silver and rare furniture in the various royal residences be listed and then the latter sealed. The following day the army swore their loyalty to the new King. For the next eight days his father's ministers were forbidden to approach him about government matters. After that period had elapsed he confirmed everyone in his office and emphasized to them that while his father had found his pleasure in architectural ostentation and great amounts of jewels, he himself would find the same satisfaction in a great quantity of good troops. Only Rüdiger von Ilgen, who had hitherto looked after Brandenburg-Prussia's external affairs, had two new officials attached to him. Together they formed the Cabinet Council whose members were later to be known by the title Cabinet Ministers.

Five weeks later came drastic economy measures. They began with horse fodder. Ministers and other notables who had until then received fodder for 20 or even 30 horses were reduced to fodder sufficient for 6. Lesser mortals, such as the court chaplains, received none at all. The royal stables were reduced from 600 to 120 horses. 'My father gave everyone horse fodder so that they would follow him across the country, but I cut it down so that everyone stays in Berlin', said Frederick William. This measure was followed by a military reorganization which he had had in mind and even planned in great detail when still Crown Prince. The costly and splendid-looking force of guards, who gave great pleasure to the eye but were of little fighting value, were transformed into regiments of the line. The Swiss guards were dissolved completely. All that remained of the guards was one batallion, the King's very own tall grenadiers, which he had commanded as a Crown Prince and which he paid and equipped from his own personal revenue. The cavalry was reorganized into 55 squadrons, each numbering 150 horses, while the infantry was ordered into 50 battalions, or 25 regiments; the artillery for the time being was to number 2 battalions. These economy measures enabled Frederick William to save enough money actually to increase the total number of his army from 39,000 men to 45,000. His father's death, from that point of view, had come at a very convenient moment. On the eve of the Peace of Utrecht the Prussian forces, until then tied down in the west, became free, and Frederick William was able to maintain them with his own resources rather than being dependent on foreign subsidies.

After the army it was the turn of his own court to feel the royal economies. Its members, that is to say its officials had their salaries cut, in many cases down to 25 per cent of what they had received under Frederick I and in one particular case even down to 10 per cent. These were the lucky ones, for the majority of personnel at court was made redundant, and from there transferred either into the administration or the army 'according to their inclinations to the sword or the pen'. The office of master of ceremonies was one that was abolished, making a short-lived reappearance only in the form of a practical joke by Frederick William when he appointed his court jester, Gundling, a disreputable historian addicted to drink, to the post. Even Andreas

Schlüter, the sculptor and architect to whom Berlin owed the *Schloss* and the masks of dying warriors at the Zeughaus (the royal arsenal now the Museum for German History in East Berlin), could no longer expect any royal commissions and therefore went to St Petersburg, where he died shortly after.

However, to explain the King's economy measures exclusively in terms of economic motives would show only one side of the coin. Calvin's teachings of divine predestination had played an important part in the King's education. His teacher Philippe Rebeur, himself a French Huguenot refugee, posed the question to his pupil as to whether he belonged to the Lord's chosen few, to the elect, and whether he could thus be sure that the House of Hohenzollern would be blessed with fortune, the sign of the Lord's divine benevolence. This question was to preoccupy Frederick William throughout his life, causing hours of brooding and searching torment, so much so that in the education of his own children he explicitly prohibited the teaching of Calvinist predestination. Upon Frederick William himself it had left its indelible mark. Indeed, one of the vital motivating forces behind Frederick William I was religion, his own brand of reformed Lutheranism. One of the reasons why his personal rule never degenerated into absolute tyranny was his deeply rooted conviction that one day he would have to account for his deeds to his maker. Of considerable importance in this context is the Pietist movement and its influence upon Prussia, both in the short and long term.

Though the importance of the personal connection between Frederick William I and August Hermann Francke, the Pietist reformer at Halle, can be overstressed, the Pietist influence as an integrating force of Prussian society in the eighteenth and the nineteenth centuries seems to have been frequently underestimated, if not altogether ignored. By Pietism, very crudely summarized, one understands primarily the German brand of Puritan reaction to the Thirty Years War with its upheaval of the Lutheran faith. The Pietists confronted the Lutheran acceptance of the world as it is and the submission of the individual to it, with reform proposals. They did not oppose Luther's hope for the day of judgement, but they critized man's social environment penetratingly. To Luther's call for a reform merely of the church, they added the call for a reform of the world and its social institutions. Pietism as a religious and social force was highly complex and world-wide in its aspirations.

As far as Prussia was concerned the Pietists aimed at producing responsible subjects, and a society whose members, irrespective of the station they occupied in life, would have their social conscience turned towards the common weal. Their schools were by far the most advanced in the kingdom and hence, through what at first was a personal connection between Frederick William I and Francke, the avenue was opened for products of the Pietist schools and academies to enter the Prussian civil service, the army and its officer corps. Pietism produced a social and religious ethos which characterizes the Prussia of the eighteenth and early nineteenth century. It was a religion ideal for civil servants, as much as Puritanism was a religion ideal for entrepreneurs, a religion sober and hard, drawing into its circle all the estates of the kingdom. In conjuction with the transformation of the feudal estates of the Junkers into private holdings in return for financing and officering the army, Pietism played a major role in the de-feudalization of the Prussian aristocracy. In the army Pietists obtained chaplaincies and thus the army and the administration became the major channels through which Pietist influence and thought percolated to the lower levels of Prussian society.

Theoretically at least, 1717 saw the beginning of compulsory elementary education in Prussia, and among the new schools that were founded those of the Pietists were the most numerous. The ideal product of their education was not the aristocratic cavalier of the Age of the Baroque, but the businesslike, matter-of-fact state functionary. This, perhaps, supplies one explanation as to why Germans outside Prussia rarely considered the highly placed Prussian civil servants or the Prussian officers worth emulating, but looked rather to the French *grand seigneur* and the English gentleman.

Class lists from 1700 onwards supply ample evidence of the great number of Prussian officers and higher civil servants who were graduates of Pietist schools, schools which selected talent from all social classes. Even Prussia's commercial policy was influenced by the Pietist movement, which believed that commerce must be for the benefit of the state and through the state for the benefit of all rather than for the exclusive enrichment of the individual. There is certainly a case for arguing that whereas in Britain the rise of Puritanism may have coincided with the emergence of a modern capitalist economy, the Pietist strain of the Puritan movement in Prussia lay at the foundations of an emerging state socialism – a feature of particular long-term significance when we look at the emergence of liberal institutions in Britain and their absence in Germany a century later.

Actively supported by the dynasty, Pietism permeated all levels of society with an ethos in which all efforts were directed towards maintaining and securing the whole, even if this operated at times at the expense of the individual. The demand of unconditional, unflinching fulfilment of their duties by all – nobility, burghers and peasants alike – led to situations of which it can well be said that Frederick William I and his son Frederick the Great treated their subjects worse than dogs; but it must be said that they treated themselves no better. Duty and the common weal were principles enforced at a time when their harshness was giving way elsewhere in favour of comfortable, humane and liberal ideas, in an age inclined more towards Epicurus rather than Seneca, when insistence upon the fulfilment of human duties receded and was replaced by the demand for human rights. While other powers were satiated, Prussia still meant to catch up, thus causing considerable discomfort all round. The moral implications of Seneca's maxim *vivere est militare* had validity by the end of the eighteenth century only in Prussia.

Frederick William I continued the policy initiated by his father of supporting the Pietists and their institutions, a policy which he realized was yielding immense dividends for the Prussian state. Yet he never became a Pietist himself and in spite of his reformed Lutheranism the stern Calvinist streak in him never disappeared. He saw himself and his every action as accountable to God. The prosperity of the state was a sign of divine approval; given Prussia's fragility, positioned in the midst of great powers, the task of the monarch was that his every action be an example to his subjects lest divine approval be withdrawn. It is against this background that one ought to examine the conflict with his son; it makes the excesses of the King more explicable than transposing nineteenth-century liberal value judgement on to eighteenth century Prussia.

Against this background and in this spirit Frederick William acted from the day he succeeded to the throne. It determined his attitude towards his own family as much as it did towards the nobility and his other subjects. And his reign marked also the final phase of the struggle between the Hohenzollerns and their Brandenburg and East Prussian nobility against the former's policy of centralization. However, in Frederick William's reign this struggle no longer took the form of personal confrontation but rather obstruction of the administrative reforms of the King, reforms which whittled away what powers the nobility still possessed in relation to the monarchy. As he put it himself: 'I shall ruin the authority of the Junkers; I shall achieve my purpose and stabilize the sovereignty like a rock of bronze.' The provincial diets, the strongholds of the Junkers, were allowed no other function than implementing the King's ordinances. But to ensure that even at that level no obstacles would be placed in his way, he deprived the diets of their administrative effectiveness by appointing his own officials at all administrative and executive levels of his kingdom. In that step really lay the origin of the Prussian civil service.

Even in a predominantly agrarian society such as eighteenth-century Prussia the successful functioning of the bureaucracy required specialized knowledge, an increasing measure of expertise and thus a division of labour. Even an absolute monarchy cannot concentrate all knowledge and all expertise in one man or small group of men. Hence intrinsic in the growth of any bureaucracy is the tendency towards its independence, towards emancipation from an absolutist monarchy. Frederick William I was well aware of this danger, as was also his son, and what he therefore built up was a very dependent, purely technically functioning apparatus which was meant to do very little else other than carry out the will of its princely managing director.

But even this was not enough: if among other things the bureaucracy was to check the nobility, the danger of the bureaucracy becoming too independent could, according to Frederick William, only be met by recruiting the bureaucracy from the aristrocracy as well as from the educated middle class. This would foster rivalry between the two social classes, now side by side within one institution, and prevent an alliance between the two against the monarchy. Besides, the religious ethos which permeated Prussian society of the eighteenth century in general, and the army and bureaucracy in particular, was itself a major check against conflicts of interest ever taking on such proportions as to endanger the fabric of the state.

In fact the effective replacement of the remnants of medieval institutions by a centralized monarchic state run efficiently by a civil service constitutes the major achievement of Frederick William I. Army and civil service became the main pillars of the kingdom of Prussia, a kingdom made up of highly diverse components artificially held together by the two institutions which represented most prominently the state community.

A major step towards the consolidation of the Prussian state was taken by Frederick William's ordinance of 13th August 1713 which declared all royal domains and property as indivisible and inalienable. Already his father had abolished the ancient rule according to which each nobleman could do as he liked on new lands or territories he had acquired. Frederick William's measure constituted a further move towards the transformation of the territories into a unified state. Since for more than a century and a half the nobility of Brandenburg-Prussia had encroached upon the royal domain as well as upon the property of free peasants, substantial land transfers had taken place without ever having been officially registered. In East Prussia, for instance, this process was not really noticed until Frederick William I replaced the multitude of dues and taxes by one general land tax, a tax determined by the size of the holding and the quality of the soil. This in turn required a survey of the lands of the province. In the course of the survey it was revealed that one-third of the land holdings of the Prussian nobility in East Prussia had been illegally acquired from either the royal domain or the peasants.

Upon Frederick William's accession to the throne, the Prussian administration consisted essentially of two main bodies: the General Finance Directory responsible for the administration of the royal domains, and the General War Commissary responsible for the administration of the army and the revenue. Both bodies possessed far-reaching judicial powers in administrative affairs, while each had its branches in every province of the kingdom. However, until the reign of Frederick William these provincial branches had been subject to a considerable degree of control by and interference from the local notables. With the beginning of his reign the influence of the estates in the provincial branches of the central administration was eliminated. In other words, what to all intents and purposes had been provincial tax offices became commissaries, which were staffed and controlled from the centre. And in order to facilitate their smooth functioning the chief administrators in each province, the *Landräte*, posts hitherto filled by nominees of the estates, now became the King's civil servants which the King without the consultation of any other body filled with his own men. Of course changes of this sort were not brought about without encountering resistance, resistance from the nobility but very often also from the office-holders themselves. The latter had previously been recruited from the province in which they took up their office; Frederick William insisted that his civil servants should not work in the area of their origin. Two officials who because of this ruling were to be transferred from Königsberg to Tilsit and who opposed the move were told by the King: 'One has to serve one's Lord with one's life and possessions, with honour and good conscience, with everything except one's salvation. This is for our Lord, but everything else must be mine. They shall dance to my tune or the devil will fetch me.' Again the emphasis upon *himself* rather than that the devil should fetch *them* is noteworthy!

In a wider European sense the seventeenth and eighteenth centuries saw the transformation of a state and society based on the power and economic resources of the estates, their origins rooted in medieval Europe, into an absolutist state. In Brandenburg-Prussia this period covered the time between the Great Elector and Frederick the Great. Yet not one absolutist monarchy ever had truly absolute power because of the historical accretion of interdependent relationships which no ruler could sever entirely and which in themselves represented checks to the freedom of action of any monarch.

In economic terms this change was paralleled by the rise of the mercantilist system which found its first classic expression in the France of Louis XIV. Economic power was subordinated to the purposes of the state. The beginnings of this process in Brandenburg-Prussia can be seen in the construction of an administration serviceable to the whole state. But these were only tentative beginnings which under Prussia's first King, with neither inclination and ability for administration nor the vision to realize the importance of an efficient administration for the stability of the state, were not further developed. Hence the accession of Frederick William I meant a resumption of the policies of his grandfather.

One would misunderstand not only the essence of his work but also the character of the man if his domestic policy were considered as an imitation of the French example. On the contrary: France, that is to say the French monarchy, had worked herself into a serious national debt; Frederick William I ended his reign with a surplus. In France the maxim was that revenue had to be created to meet the demands of the monarchy. In Prussia the financial expenditure of the state, including the monarchy, was adjusted to the available revenue. The Age of the Baroque whether in France, Austria or Spain was built on credit, credit obtained through banks and through increasing burdens of taxation for its subjects. The splendours of the Baroque, whether at Versailles, in Salzburg or at the residence of the Bishop of Würzburg, were built on the backs of the people and in the main that meant the peasants. With their toil and sweat 'culture' was created.

Frederick William's determination to reverse this trend, to create a stable state and society by living according to the available means, obviously meant that there was no longer any place in Berlin for a talent like Schlüter. According to Frederick William the state could not afford his grandiose architecture. For the first time in Prussian history an annual budget was established, based on the revenue that could be expected, and from that determined the expenditure for the individual departments or areas.

The pronouncement of the eternal indivisibility of all royal domains and other landed possessions amounted to a proclamation of the indivisibility of the entire territory of the state, thus removing the ruler's privilege, as practised hitherto, of doing with his territories and subjects as he liked. But it also meant a rejection of the plans of the discredited Luben, plans which from Frederick William's point of view would have amounted to a disposal of the royal domain. It was the first step towards transforming Prussia from a royal state into a state community.

In his encouragement of trade and manufacture he gave considerable support to two young merchants, David Splitgerber and Gottfried Adolph Daum, who in 1712 had set up a small store in Berlin. Since they were not citizens of Berlin but originated from Pomerania and Saxony respectively the Berlin guild prohibited them from trading in actual goods, so they concentrated their activities in buying and selling wholesale and on commission. In so doing they developed their connections to Leipzig, Hamburg and Danzig and even as far as London, Amsterdam, Bordeaux, Venice and Lisbon. The King took due notice of this and soon became their customer. They supplied him with ammunition and rare metals, and soon other members of the royal court and Berlin's society were among their clientele. They expanded Prussian trade into Russia by founding the highly successful Russian Trading Company. From there they went on to buy arms factories (and to found new ones in Potsdam), ironworks and sugar refineries.

Frederick William's policy towards the textile industry was determined by the requirements of the army. Upon his accession to the throne he had his close confident Johann Andreas Kraut, later to be a minister, found a warehouse and factory in Berlin. It produced the cloth for all the uniforms of the Prussian army. In 1723 it was turned into a state enterprise subject to the General Directory. On the eve of his reign almost 18 per cent of the Prussian labour force employed in manufacturing trades was concentrated in the textile industry, supplying the home market and carrying on an extensive export trade to Prussia's eastern neighbours. The industry was centred in Berlin, Prussia's western provinces, Brandenburg, and, after the Seven Years War, Silesia.

Neither the Great Elector nor Frederick I had been in a position to conduct wars or for that matter even to keep an army of the size they possessed without subsidies from abroad. At the death of Frederick I the Prussian army had reached a total of 39,000 men. During the reign of Frederick William I that figure was doubled, paid for out of Prussia's own resources. To turn the army into the kind of instrument which displayed its versatility for the first time under his son at Mollwitz, or its resilience after Kunersdorf, required first of all thoroughgoing reforms. First to be affected was the officer corps, which under his predecessors still consisted in parts of noble, or allegedly noble, adventurers from all over Europe. Frederick William I dismissed all doubtful elements from his officer corps and on principle refused to recruit new members from countries other than German ones. Then, to ensure a supply of officers as well as to tie closer the bonds between the Prussian nobility and the monarchy, he virtually compelled the native nobility to serve as officers in the Prussian army. The nobility was discouraged to serve in armies abroad and although after the allodification of the estates of the nobility (that is to say the granting of proprietary rights to the land holdings of the nobility) there was no longer the feudal tie based on land between monarchy and nobility, Frederick William nevertheless insisted on vassalage expressed in terms of service to the crown and state. In that way the Prussian army proved to be a major institution through which in due course the aristocracy was integrated into and absorbed by the state.

Nevertheless, at first Frederick William's allodification of the estates did cause some protest, because with this measure the higher nobility was also deprived of such services as the lower nobility had been obliged to render them. Frederick William wished these services to be commuted into money payments. It caused legal wrangles before the Imperial Court Council which were never resolved. In the meantime Frederick William proceeded on the basis of the decrees he had issued.

It was not a policy carried out without meeting resistance, for in its core it was revolutionary and changed existing social relationships, yet within a very conservative context. This coexistence of revolutionary policy and conservatism was very largely facilitated by Brandenburg-Prussia's social structure. Until well into the nineteenth century Prussia's economic power base was its agrarian economy. The ratio of rural to urban population towards the end of the eighteenth century has been calculated as 7 : 2 and the increase in royal revenue between 1713 and 1786 was not due to increased taxation, specifically land tax or the excise affecting the towns, but was the result of additional land being put under cultivation and agricultural output being maximized. The Prussian provinces supplied by far the larger part of the revenue and the significance of the role of the towns, cities and their manufacturing industries at this time has, as the result of a remark once made by Frederick the Great, frequently been overestimated. Equally of course, it was neither city nor town which formed the recruiting ground for the army, but the land, and it was precisely the relationship between Prussia's military system and its agrarian economy that determined the kingdom's social structure.

The standing army of the Great Elector, a remnant of the private armies of the Thirty Years War, was, during his reign and establishment of princely absolutism, 'nationalized' by being turned from a private into a state instrument. The initial heterogeneity of its officer corps was of considerable advantage when the landed nobility was still powerful enough to obstruct the ruler's policies when the Prussian Junker aristocracy, despite fiscal and land concessions, was slow in being integrated into the new state. Yet after the reforms of Frederick William I the army became the major institution through which the nobility could be absorbed into the state.

Until 1730 the army was recruited at random, and frequently by force, from among the German and East European population and very substantially from the peasantry of Brandenburg-Prussia. As a result Prussia's western provinces suffered a great depletion of their population as the peasants simply fled into neighbouring German territory – a trend almost as pronounced in Prussia's eastern provinces. Over the long term, therefore, a decline in agricultural output was inevitable and with it a decline in state revenue. That prospect was sufficient to compel Frederick William I to seek a compromise between the demands of his military policy and the requirements of Prussia's agrarian economy.

First he hoped to meet the situation by prohibiting the forcible recruitment of peasants in Prussia and the escape of his subjects to territories outside Prussia. Neither of these measures proved satisfactory. On the contrary, as the regiments had now to extend their recruitment to areas outside Prussia, expenditure was increased and so, by implication, was the drain of gold away from Prussia. The problem was finally resolved when Frederick William I combined two expedients that had been in use throughout his kingdom. First of all he realized that with its increasing influx into the officer corps the function of the Prussian nobility was now military as well as economic. That is to say regimental and company commanders alike were also agricultural entrepreneurs, and in order to reduce their recruitment expenditure they tended to look for recruits among the peasants of their own estates. This in turn was bound to affect agricultural production adversely unless the serving peasants were given leave in order to look after the estates of their Junker landlords/officers during certain periods.of the year. This expedient ensured not only agricultural output but also meant that the officer/land-owner saved the pay which his peasant received, pay which now could be used for recruitment outside Prussia. The other expedient, which had been in use for some time, was that individual regiments enrolled all the young males living in the district in which the regiment was garrisoned, to ensure that when called upon they could serve in that particular regiment. The main purpose of this was to curb competitive recruitment by other regiments in one's own regimental area.

Frederick William's policy was a combination of these two expedients. He divided the country into clearly defined recruitment districts, regimental cantons, and made the enrolment of the youth of each canton compulsory, stipulating at the same time that after the initial basic training every soldier would be subject to three months' military service per year. For the rest of the year the soldier would be 'on leave'. Thus a balance was established, one that had previously been lacking, between the needs of Prussia's agrarian economy and the requirements of its army. In addition to the regular soldiers there were now the serving peasants, soldiers who 9 months out of 12 would also be the serving peasants on their masters' estates.

The result of this *Cantonal Reglement* of 1730 was a rapid acceleration in the growth of the Prussian army, between 1731 and 1733; not only that, it caused a transformation in Prussian social structure. The peasant now played an important threefold role which Frederick the Great clearly recognized when he said that the peasants formed that class 'which deserves the greatest respect of all, because their fiscal burdens are the heaviest, they supply the entire state with essential foodstuffs and at the same time the largest number of recruits for the army and also a steady addition to the number of burghers'. A state whose economic strength depended on the maximization of existing agricultural resources and on increasing the amount of land under cultivation could not afford depopulation and had to 'maintain that species of peasants which is most admirable'. The estate of the peasantry was consequently of fundamental importance to Prussia, for 'it represents its foundation and carries its burden, it has the work, the others the fame'.

More than any other action of Frederick William I this piece of legislation integrated aristocracy and peasantry into the state, by integrating the needs of the Prussian army with the agrarian social structure. The burghers in the towns, as yet too insignificant to matter very much, were exempt from military service, but they too had to play their part by quartering the troops, and, more importantly, by supplying the members of the lower echelons of the growing bureaucracy.

The bureaucracy as an institution was the necessary executive arm of Prussian absolutism. However, that royal absolutism and as well-functioning bureaucracy are in the long run mutually exclusive was a fact of which Frederick William I quickly became aware after his accession to the throne. His father had allowed this institution to grow into a serious contender for supreme power in the dynastic state. Frederick William quickly counter-acted this situation by a highly personal policy 'which restricted and widened the appointment to the upper grades of the executive hierarchy'. While in general the number of law experts and of non-military nobility declined, three groups in

particular were in ascent. Firstly there were the businessmen who had
been successful in their careers, men who knew how to produce and how
to be efficient. Secondly there were the officials who had been raised
from the status of petty-officials by royal grace, men familiar with the
'red tape' of day-to-day administration and capable of cutting it at
points where it was thought unnecessary. Retired soldiers, usually
former non-commissioned officers, also belonged to this group and
they filled numerous posts in the bureaucracy and the teaching
profession in lieu of a pension. These, together with the third group of
military bureaucrats, in the last analysis introduced the military tone as
well as the high professional ethos into the Prussian civil service. They
set a model of obedience, chaired royal committees and boards, and
exercised an important influence on urban administration in particular.
That this produced an uneasy balance 'between commoners and heirs of
superior social rank' (Hans Rosenberg) is a contention devoid of proof.
There is nothing to show that the representatives of these classes were
aware of the existence of any such uneasiness.

There existed as yet hardly any garrisons for the army. Soldiers were
quartered in burghers' houses in the towns and had to buy and cook
their own food. Many of them were married and in their spare time
pursued a trade. In order to look after the orphaned children of soldiers
or those who were neglected by their parents Frederick William I
founded the Potsdamer *Militärwaisenhaus*, the Potsdam Military
orphanage.

Of the soldier's equipment only uniform and weapons were supplied
by the army; a whole host of smaller articles of clothing had to be
bought by the soldier himself and paid for by means of deductions from
his wages. This really ensured that the army as such was also an
economic driving force within the urban economy. Given the fact that
the excise tax was levied on the towns only and that the presence of
troops in the towns inevitably increased consumption, then it is
understandable that Frederick William I once remarked: 'When the
army is on the march then the excise loses one-third.' This primarily
economic motivation explains Frederick William's reluctance actually
to deploy his forces in any warlike action; it also goes some distance
towards explaining his foreign policy.

Frederick William was not simply the commander of his army, he was
also its royal drill sergeant, inspired and influenced by his friend Prince
Leopold of Anhalt-Dessau. The latter's introduction of the iron ramrod
increased the fire power of the Prussian infantry to a degree unmatched
by any other army. But since an attack was based on linear tactics, that
is to say bringing three lines of infantry against the enemy, the bayonet
attack was considered especially important and for that tall grenadiers
were the most suitable. It has been said, correctly, that it was from this
that Frederick William I when still Crown Prince acquired his passion
for the tall grenadiers which he later formed into his own personal
bodyguard. This was the one passion he possessed for which he was

prepared to spend considerable sums quite recklessly. However, the source of income which financed this hobby did not come from the normal state revenue but from two other sources: the King's own private income derived from his estates and a specially established recruitment fund to which voluntary contributions could be made. This fund was the one and only avenue by which venality in office-holding entered the Prussian bureaucracy. It was possible, by making a suitable contribution to the recruitment fund, to obtain a desired office – which however, did not mean that the holder would continue in that office if found to be incompetent. Moreover, considering the venality of office-holding in other European countries, that in Prussia was almost insignificant.

To maintain and supply the army was the major task of the financial administration, as had in effect been the case since the days of the Great Elector. To further consolidate and centralize the administration Frederick William immediately elevated the General Finance Directory to a dominant position in place of the old Secret Court Chamber. It was also superior to another institution founded at the same time, the *Generalfinanzkasse*, the General Finance Administration. Theirs was the task to administer all royal domains and other possessions. Parts of the royal domain were leased in six-yearly periods, with the lessees being personally responsible for the annual income being paid into the *Generalfinanzkasse*. He could sub-let, but the responsibility was his alone. Nor was the lease inheritable. To avoid any overlap of interests between the royal domains and the landed nobility, only commoners could become lessees.

Parallel with the General Finance Directory existed the General War Commissary which headed the administration of the army and taxation. Formerly it had been the command centre of the army, but gradually it mutated into the administrative centre for taxation and police affairs. It should not be forgotten that at the time the term *Polizei* implied rather more of a welfare role than this term does today, the functions of the Police in Prussia being public welfare and public health problems.

The installation of the General Finance Directory and the General War Commissary at the apex of the central administration was followed by a transformation of all commissary offices in the provinces into provincial departments, as already existed in East Prussia and Cleves. The participation of the estates in the provinces in questions of taxation was completely abolished.

The provincial commissaries, now organs of the central adminis- stration, extended their influence considerably. Originally part of the military and financial administration they acquired policing powers over their districts; powers of economic administration, particularly in the towns and cities; of supervision of the guilds; and of promotion of the manufacturing industries and their protection against foreign competition.

Yet in spite of this centralized administration competition between the two major instruments of government and their respective subordinate organs was keen. The General Finance Directory, because it administered the royal domain, was primarily influenced by agrarian considerations and thus had a ready ear for agrarian interests. It also represented essentially the principle of Free Trade. The General War Commissary on the other hand was rather more urban-orientated, understandable in view of the facts that the towns were the garrisons of the army and that the towns brought in the excise. In essence it represented mercantilist interests and pursued policies accordingly. Friction between these two interest groups was frequent and the King's intervention was often necessary. Ultimately he could find no other solution to end the feud than to unify the two offices, giving them the name General Superior Finance War and Domains Directory. The name was too complex and was ultimately reduced to General Directory. In instructions devised by the King and written in his own hand, he laid down the powers of this new office. It was now responsible for the entire financial and internal administration, including the military finance and army supplies. It was composed of four provincial departments, each department headed by a minister under whom were three or four councillors. The first department encompassed East Prussia, Pomerania and Neumark, the second the Kurmark, Magdeburg and Halberstadt, the third the Rhenish Provinces and the fourth the Westphalian provinces of the kingdom. To ensure that the horizon of each department was not limited to the geographical area under its control, the King delegated to each department specific tasks which affected the whole of the kingdom. Thus the first department was responsible for questions affecting the frontiers of the kingdom and for turning forests into arable lands; the second for the maintenance of the main roads, the marching routes of the army, and for military finance; the third for postal affairs and the mint; and the fourth looked after the general accounts.

This fusion also took place at provincial level, the new offices, called War and Domain Chambers, being responsible for the towns as well as for the countryside, for general taxation as well as for the revenue derived from the royal domains. As in the central authority, the decision-making process was a collegiate one, every councillor being head of a particular department or area consisting of towns, country and domains, and decisions being taken after joint discussion. In contrast to the practice of his father and grandfather, Frederick William insisted that none of the councillors in the chambers was a native of the province in which he worked, a move to prevent local interests entrenching themselves in the local administration.

As to the background of his administrative personnel, Frederick William was still very flexible, his choice often being determined by whether a candidate for office was dynamic and mentally alert, with eyes opened to the practical aspects of life and having the ability to deal with them. Therefore one very often finds councillors with a military background – regimental auditors, quartermasters and the like – though during the latter part of his reign the increasing complexity of affairs required specialization and expertise and so there was an increase in personnel with better academic qualifications.

Before the fusing of the two main branches of government Frederick William had deliberately kept in being two separate treasury offices, one responsible for the income from the royal domains the other for receipts from taxation destined mainly for the upkeep of the army. The latter was called the War Treasury, the former the General Domain Treasury. There were correspondingly two separate budgets, the military and the civilian budget. In 1714 Frederick William created the post of *General-Rechenkammer*, General Auditor, to control both budgets. When the General Directory was created the General Auditor was subordinated to it, and his task became the exercise of financial control over the War and Domain Chamber, control over the Auditor's Office being exercised by the General Directory.

Under the War and Domain Chamber functioned the *Landräte*. If the administrative apparatus was completely reformed so was the administration of the cities. For centuries they had operated under their own constitutions, ruled usually by a patrician oligarchy anxious to preserve and extend its existing privileges. At the accession of Frederick William there was hardly a city or town in his kingdom that was not seriously in debt, which provided the lever by which he could introduce major reforms. With the more rigorous enforcement of the excise tax and the quartering of garrisons, the organs of the central administration in the towns reached a greater degree of efficiency, pushing aside the old traditional ruling powers. Committees of investigation examined the finances of each town and regulated the settlement of existing debts. In practice this led to the elimination of most forms of communal self-administration. City councillors were now no longer burghers of the town they lived in, elected or appointed by a small group of fellow citizens, but royal civil servants coming from other parts of the country. As at state level the financial administration of each city or town was based on a firm annual budget. Specifically communal taxation was abolished and urban taxation made uniform throughout the kingdom. Treasury officials supervised financial administration, as well as most public affairs, jointly with the garrison commander. These treasury officials were formed into a *Steuerrat*, a revenue council, each revenue council supervising six to 12 towns.

At the very apex of the administration was the King himself. While the central administration was located in Berlin, the king resided mainly in Potsdam or in one of his hunting chateaux, his favourite being Wusterhausen in the Mark Brandenburg. His ministers had to submit their reports to the King, and the King in turn would formulate his answers and decisions in his own cabinet with the aid of several personal secretaries. The Cabinet Order was the ultimate piece of legislation in the state of Brandenburg-Prussia. This method of government, highly personal and concentrated upon one person as it was, naturally required immense diligence and detailed knowledge from the King. He possessed both to an extraordinary degree, making him, together with his son, unique in the age of absolutism.

He had not long to wait before success began to show. Royal debts accumulated by his father were rapidly paid off, royal domains pawned to obtain money were taken under control of the crown again. This was the case especially in East Prussia, the former Swedish Baltic provinces and Poland. Opposition raised by the nobility he quelled firmly, and throughout his reign he expanded the royal domain by buying up estates from members of indebted nobility to the extent that by the end of his reign one-third of all arable land was crown land. The income derived from the royal domains by that time amounted to approximately half of the total state revenue received.

The system of taxation too was reformed, particularly the land tax. It was not so much a question of levying new taxes as of distributing the existing taxes more equitably, from the poorer to the richer. Although as a result of the financial policies of the Teutonic Knights the nobility in East Prussia had never been formally exempted from taxation, after the decay of the order they more or less exempted themselves. And as the administration of revenue affairs lay in the hands of the nobility anyway, this had not been very difficult to achieve. Frederick William instead of continuing with a system of taxation which was as confused as it was evaded, replaced it with a general tax based on an assessment of the income of each estate.

But what proved possible in East Prussia was much more difficult to implement in other areas of the kingdom, where the nobility countered with greater opposition and where on occasion taxes had to be collected by the use of military force. In order that not only the cities should carry the financial burden of a military garrison, Frederick William levied a contribution upon the peasants. Remnants of feudal services by the peasants were commuted into money payments, again for the benefit of the army. The towns, of course, paid their excise, as a means of obtaining revenue on the one hand and a tool of the mercantilist policy of Frederick William on the other, a protective tariff for the benefit of local trade and goods. As the kingdom was territorially fragmented it was not possible to raise customs duties at the frontiers. Consequently, excise tax was to be paid at the point of destination of imported goods. Whereas the money derived from contributions remained fairly constant throughout the eighteenth century, the income derived from the excise tax rose continuously.

Frederick William I also introduced the firm distinction between the state budget and the ruler's personal budget. From 1713 to the end of the eighteenth century Prussia's finances showed a surplus; in other words there was no need for a national debt as was the case in Great Britain, the Netherlands, France and Austria. Emergencies were to be met with by funds put aside for that purpose, the state treasury.

Even after the reforms the burden of taxation was heavy and could only be carried if the economic development of the kingdom continued. Since agriculture was the prime industry, the King directed most of his attention there. Though inclined towards liberating the peasants, in the light of his other policies this was one point on which he had to appease his nobility. But he seriously endeavoured to ameliorate the lot of the peasants and reduce their burdens. Beating of peasants was prohibited and peasants' services reduced to three or four days a week or replaced by money payments. But these reforms were restricted in the main to the royal domains; they made only very slow headway, if any at all, on the estates of the nobility. Agriculture was protected against the import of foreign grain, and to encourage domestic cloth manufacture, Frederick William prohibited the export of sheep wool to ensure the availability of cheap raw materials.

Of all the provinces of the kingdom that of East Prussia was most affected by the reform work of the King, domestic and foreign policy being inextricably intertwined here. The Great Northern War brought for Prussia the desired access to the sea at the mouth of the Oder. Poland, as an aristocratic republic, was moving towards internal dissolution, but Russia under Peter the Great had emerged as a great power. During the Great Northern War its troops had entered Pomerania, to the rear of East Prussia. Peter the Great seemed to display an interest in the harbours of Memel and Pillau. Avoiding direct confrontation, it was one of the cardinal points of Frederick William's policy to develop and maintain cordial relations with Russia. The domestic pendant to this policy was the '*Retablissement*' of East Prussia, for one-third of its population had perished by the Black Death and hunger. It benefited most by his administrative and fiscal reforms.

The worst-hit areas of East Prussia were in the north-east and the south-east, a total of 27,000 farms in those areas being without tenants. It was there that in the wake of the institutional reforms a vast scheme of colonization was embarked upon. Of 30,000 Protestants expelled because of their faith from their native Salzburg region of Austria, and who had taken up Frederick William's invitation to Prussia, 15,000 found their homes in East Prussia, all on the royal domain. Wherever necessary the state built houses for them, supplied agricultural implements, seed and livestock. Throughout his life the successful recolonization of East Prussia was Frederick William's great pride, the link between the colonizing activity of Teutonic Order and the consolidation of the Prussian kingdom. At the time of Frederick William's death in 1740 the population of East Prussia was back to the level it had been before the great famine.

Casually related to the *Retablissement* of East Prussia are the beginnings of the judicial reforms in the entire kingdom. The root cause of the need for reform was the different judicial traditions existing in the various territories of the kingdom. Leibniz had already tried his hand at it and in 1701 he devised a uniform legal code; others did so after him, without much success. Samuel von Cocceji, a discerning legal brain of middle-class origins, had been previously entrusted by Frederick William with bringing order into the legal system of East Prussia and he proved resoundingly successful. It was in his hands, therefore, that the King placed the entire problem of judicial reform. Whereas the judiciary had been a collegiate body Cocceji now became its first head, but given the complexity of the task he could only make beginnings and even then suffered setbacks. The only improvements achieved in Frederick William's lifetime were in the realm of the penal code, and the problem of judicial reform accompanied the entire reign of his successor, not finding its final solution until the reign of Frederick William II.

Of equal long-term importance as his practical reforms is the spirit with which Frederick William I infused his administration and which until its end characterized the Prussian bureaucracy. Army and bureaucracy alike were instilled with the same spirit of service for the state, one major reason why the monarch succeeded in preparing the base from which his son could lift Prussia from the ranks of an auxiliary power to that of a major European power.

The Prussian state rested upon the triple foundations of an agrarian economy, strong military power and an efficient civil service, all three closely integrated and subordinated to one aim, the maintenance and prosperity of the state. This had little or nothing to do with the perpetuation and increase of power for the sake of one individual: it was the expression of the growing ideology of the state community pure and simple, a secularized version of that ideology which in their heyday had made the Teutonic Knights outstanding colonizers, administrators and politicians. It was a subjugation of all sectors and aspects of public life to the purposes of state.

In his policy towards the churches Frederick William aimed at unifying the orthodox Lutherans with the Reformed Church. He himself remained an adherent of the Reformed church, like his ancestors open-minded enough to listen to other Christian denominations. Hence his inclination towards Pietism. But to prevent religion from becoming a divisive force in his state he, like the Great Elector, prohibited the exposition of theological controversy from the pulpit. Because of their alleged excesses in Poland he was extremely hostile towards the Jesuit Order, whose members were not allowed to cross the borders into his kingdom. But his toleration of Roman Catholicism was rather greater than that of his grandfather, not least because of military reasons. His numerous Catholic soldiers pleaded for Catholic chaplains and they got them.

Frederick William's objective in his foreign policy was to consolidate and maintain what had so far been achieved by his ancestors and by himself. In his testament of 1722 he implores his successor:

I beg you not to begin an unjust war, because God has forbidden unjust wars. You must give account for every man killed in an unjust war. Look at history and you will see that nothing good has come from unjust wars. This, my dear successor, demonstates the hand of God. . . . Therefore, my dear successor, I beg you not to commence an unjust war in order that God's blessing may lie always upon you and your army, and give you courage. You are of course a great lord upon this earth, but you have to account to God for all the blood spilt in an unjust cause. That is a hard fact. Therefore I beg you to keep your conscience clear before God and you will enjoy a happy reign.

Repetitious though this passage is, it makes clear the intensity of the religious conviction in Frederick William's character. His preoccupation with the state's economy also finds expression when he writes that 'The welfare of the regent is based upon the fact that the land is well populated; population is the real treasure of your land. When your army is on the march outside Prussia, the gate taxes will not be one-third of their usual level when the army is in the country. . . . the administration of the domain will be unable to pay rents and that is tantamount to total ruin'. Prussia's army did not only consume two-thirds of her revenue, it also provided a large market for Prussia's young domestic industries and was a part of the domestic market that Frederick William industriously fostered.

The role that Frederick William envisaged for Prussia in international affairs was one that would enable her to gain modest advantages out of the wars of the great European powers, 'because he who can hold the balance in the world, will always profit for his land and command the respect of your friends and the fear of your enemies'. This policy was securely founded on domestic stability and was also in accord with his religious principles. 'The state had as yet not become the content of religion and the sole subject of reason.'

Upon his accession, after the conclusion of the Peace of Utrecht on 11 April 1713, Prussia once again regained her freedom of action. But cautious by nature Frederick William I was loath immediately to involve himself in the confused pattern of the Great Northern War. When Peter the Great visited Berlin in 1713 he tried to draw Prussia into an alliance with Russia. But for the Prussian King the domestic situation in the kingdom had priority; he said it would take at least a year to get the country's finances in order. After that he would make his decision. Nevertheless, not only did he immediately commence financial reforms, he also simultaneously increased the army by seven regiments, just in case.

His major objective was, like that of his father and grandfather, to obtain Stettin and thus have direct access to a major harbour of the Baltic and control of the river Oder. Since Charles XII of Sweden was most likely to die without leaving any heir, the question of the succession to the Swedish throne was uppermost in the minds of the

European cabinets. One very likely contestant for the succession was the Duke of Holstein-Gottrop, a brother-in-law of Charles XII. Frederick William I promised to support the Duke's claims in return for which he received the promise that he would cede to Prussia Vorpommern up to the river Peene. Nothing came of it; in fact Stettin was conquered by a combined force of Russians, Poles and Danes. This incident was enough for Frederick William to decide which side's support he really needed in order to further his aims. He needed Russia. On 6 October 1713 he concluded at Schwedt a treaty with Prince Menshikov according to which Prussia was to receive in trust Stettin and Vorpommern up to the river Peene until the conclusion of the hostilities. For the duration of the war Prussia was to undertake the occupation of the region. To give this temporary arrangement greater permanency, he supplemented this treaty with a secret treaty with the Russians on 12 June 1714 which was to guarantee Prussia obtaining the region occupied, while Russia would acquire other Swedish Baltic provinces including Estonia and Carelia. Shortly after, in November 1714, George, the Elector of Hanover, who had just succeeded to the British throne, joined this alliance and so did Denmark.

The sudden return of Charles XII from exile in Turkey introduced further alarm and confusion. Frederick William believed in adopting an attitude of reserve hoping that by way of negotiations Sweden would grant the same concessions. But these bore no results and on 1 May 1715 Prussia declared war on Sweden. The latter, in a militarily very unfavourable situation, under-strength and no longer enjoying the kind of support which France had given before, had to yield to its opponents.

It has rightly been said that in the context of international relations the most important result of the Great Northern War was the growing conflict of interest between Great Britain and Russia, the latter in search of a warm-water port and control over their routes of access, the former, like the Dutch the century before, seeing in the Baltic not only an important trading area but also an important supplier of the timber and naval stores which were so important for the maintenance of a large navy very well on the way to becoming the mistress of the seas.

For Prussia in particular the outcome of the Great Northern War meant the partial fulfilment of those ambitions which the Great Elector had cherished. All of those ambitions were no longer practicable, nor were they in the mind of Frederick William. Prussia had obtained Stettin and parts of Vorpommern; overshadowed by the great powers, by necessity veering towards Russia rather than Britain. In addition to a division within his own family over the issue, relations between Prussia and Britain took on a sharper tone. On the other hand, the greater independence with which Frederick William acted also alienated to some extent the Emperor Charles VI, who felt that Vienna could no longer depend on the immediate support from Prussia that they had enjoyed in the reign of Frederick I. This brought about closer relations between Vienna, Hanover and London while the Elector of Saxony also felt his interests threatened by the Russian menace and therefore joined the other powers. This alliance actually prevented the complete destruction of Sweden and under pressure from these powers Prussia forsook its Russian ally and made a separate peace with Sweden on 1 February 1720. Russia fought on alone for another year until it signed a peace with Sweden at Nystad in 1721. But to symbolize where his sympathies lay, Frederick William did not accept the homage of the city of Stettin until the final conclusion of the hostilities of the Great Northern War in 1721.

Four years later the existing European alliances were dramatically reversed. Spain, resenting Britain's presence in Gibraltar and the frequent clashes with her in the West Indies, concluded an alliance with the Emperor in Vienna, an alliance also joined by the German Roman Catholic principalities. The former enemies France and Great Britain also concluded an alliance which was joined by Hanover and on 3 September 1725 also by Prussia. The Prussian move does not seem to have been motivated by any *raison d'état*, but rather by Frederick William's annoyance and anger over the treatment he was receiving from Vienna. On his part it was an emotional outburst, the dangerous character of which he quickly recognized when the widow of Peter the Great, Catherine I, joined Austria. Prussia was now likely to be the most vulnerable defender of French and British interests and to prevent this he concluded a treaty with the Emperor in 1726 which two years later was expanded into a fully-fledged alliance, the Treaty of Berlin of 23 December 1728. Prussia now became a firm supporter of the Reich and in 1726 ratified the Pragmatic Sanction of 1713 which confirmed the indivisibility of the Hapsburg crown lands and admitted a female successor to the Hapsburg throne.

Family rivalry exercised considerable influence in the formation of Frederick William's foreign policy, especially that between the Hohenzollerns and the Guelphs, in other words Berlin and Hanover. This was in spite of the close relations between the two families – after all Frederick William was the brother-in-law of George II for his first wife Sophia Dorothea was the sister of the British King. This rivalry also divided the court in Berlin into a pro-British and a pro-Emperor party and against this background the tensions existing between Frederick William and his son Crown Prince Frederick reached crisis-point.

The relationship between father and son had already been deteriorating for some time. From Frederick William's point of view his son had no other task than to continue his father's work; to do so his son was to display the same qualities as distinguished his father and there was every sign that he did not. Frederick was drawn by every fibre of his intellect towards the European Enlightenment and French culture. His first instructor was a Frenchman, Duhan de Jardun, who had a profound influence upon Frederick, much more so than any subsequent German military instructor. His interests in literature, philosophy and science were in the King's view, hardly a help in equipping the Crown Prince adequately for his future task as king. Given Frederick William's firm religious conviction that the prosperity of the state was a sign of divine approval, and his belief that the duty of the monarch was that his every action be an example to his subjects lest divine approval be withdrawn, his son's interest and his way of life were the very opposite of all that he believed in. Frederick William demanded, prohibited and cursed; his son obstructed, evaded and made sarcastic jokes which soon got back to the ears of the father. Frederick loved music and had secretly taken tuition in playing the flute, an instrument on which he excelled; on the other hand he loathed the army and called his uniform 'the death shirt'. In a court such as Frederick William's which was run on a very tight budget, his son's comparatively lavish way of life cost money, money which he borrowed from outside. Tension between father and son was ever-present, violent outbreaks of the royal temper very frequent.

Moreover the situation was further complicated by the ambitious marriage projects of Sophia Dorothea. Her main desire was to see her eldest daughter Wilhelmina, the close confidant of Frederick, upon the British throne. George II on the other hand wanted the Princess Royal Amelia to marry the Prussian Crown Prince. Frederick William had his doubts as to how a British princess would be able to adjust to the Spartan way of life of the Prussian court, but he raised no fundamental objections. But when Frederick William once more allied with the Emperor, the marriage project was considered by the British as well as French as a lever with which to force Prussia back onto their side. Intrigue and counter-intrigue were spun in Berlin, the victims being Frederick and Wilhelmina. Although Frederick had never set eyes on her, he adored his British cousin and together with his mother loathed the pro-Austrian party.

On Sophia Dorothea's initiative a British envoy extraordinary, Sir Charles Hotham was despatched to Berlin from London, to promote the marriage project. Frederick William now began to develop doubts about the political consequences of the marriage for he wished to adhere to the alliance with the Emperor. Therefore, though he was ready to agree to a marriage between his eldest daughter and the Prince of Wales, at the same time he let it be known that it was much too soon to consider any marriage for the Crown Prince. However, when the time was ripe a British princess would have preference over any other. Sir Charles Hotham, acting on detailed instructions, replied that the Court of St James desired to see the realization of both marriage projects together or none at all. Mission and projects had come to an end. When before his departure Hotham made his final visit to the King, he handed him a set of documents showing that one of the King's closest confidants and advisors, who was also the leader of the pro-Austrian faction, was in fact in Austrian pay. The King was disgusted with Hotham's behaviour; Hotham felt that the diplomatic niceties had been violated. They parted in anger.

Shortly afterwards the King undertook a journey to southern Germany on which the Crown Prince accompanied him. Frederick had long planned to escape and saw this as his opportunity to make his way to England. But the servant who had already obtained the necessary horses had second thoughts and betrayed the plan to the King. Frederick William was furious, treated his son as a deserter from the army and had him court-martialled. The court, made up of generals, virtually rejected the charge as well as the suitability of holding the trial. But Frederick's close confidant, Lieutenant von Katte, who had known of the plan was sentenced to death for *lese majesté* and beheaded in the fortress of Küstrin before the eyes of the Crown Prince who was forced to watch the execution from the window of his cell.

For some time the King continued to entertain plans of excluding Frederick from the succession, and it was another six months before the formal reconciliation between father and son took place. The event was a watershed in Frederick's life: he ceased to play and began to work, first in the War and Domain Chamber of Küstrin where he learnt the rudiments of administration.

The Anglo-Prussian marriage project had come to nought. Frederick's sister Wilhelmina was compelled to marry the Margrave of Bayreuth, and Frederick, in 1733, Princess Elizabeth Christine of Brunswick-Bevern. From 1736 until Frederick William's death, the Crown Prince was given *Schloss* Rheinsberg, where among the circle of his close friends, he was allowed to pursue his interests, and spend what in Frederick's later opinion were the four happiest years of his life.

In the subsequent major questions of European foreign policy, such as the Polish succession, Prussia played only a small part on the periphery of the main events. Frederick William's attempts to enlarge his territorial holdings on the lower Rhine and obtain an imperial guarantee for Berg and Ravenstein were thwarted by the Emperor, something the King did not forgive him for to the end of his days. He rested his claims on the basis of various assurances, none of them free from ambiguity, given to him by the Emperor, but they failed in face of the opposition raised by the great powers of Austria, France and Great Britain as well as the Netherlands. On the eve of his death he turned towards France, thus paving the way which his son was to take upon his accession.

Similar to the state of the Teutonic Order in its own time, the Prussian kingdom under Frederick William I had succeeded in an epoch-making achievement, significant not only in the history of Germany but also in that of Europe. With a total population of two and a half million it maintained from its own resources an army of 60,000 whose annual budget amounted to about five million thalers out of a total state budget of about seven. By 1740 Frederick William had accumulated reserves of about eight million thalers. In terms of its population Prussia occupied the twelfth position among the European powers, in terms of the peacetime condition of its army the fourth, and in terms of the military effectiveness of its army the first.

By the end of his reign Frederick William could look back on the solid achievement of the consolidation of a state based upon an institutional framework within which the endeavours of all elements it contained were directed towards maintaining this artificial structure. The militarization of an agrarian society, the Pietist ethos, all were very well on the way towards combining into a specifically 'Prussian' way of life which was bound to retard liberalization of Prussia's political, social and economic order. The accent lay on stability and conservation rather than allowing room for the free flow of social forces. By 1740 the God which Hegel was to adulate was already in existence: the God by the name of *der Staat*.

Chapter 6

Frederick the Great

It was rather remarkable that the state of Frederick William I found its completion in his successor – because considering not merely the conflict between father and son but, at least on the surface, the entirely different personalities and inclinations of both, this gave good reason to expect a radical change of policy internally as well as externally, and not a continuation and completion of Frederick William's.

Already in 1731, when he was Crown Prince, and eight years before he wrote his *Anti-Machiavel*, Frederick realized the geo-political factors underlying his conception of the lines along which Prussia's foreign policy should be conducted. In his view a territorially fragmented kingdom stretching across the northern part of Central Europe had only two alternatives. The first was to live in harmony with all its neighbours, which would be equivalent to a permanent state of fearful impotence and mean a hopeless defensive position in case of conflict. The second alternative was to acquire, without too much regard for existing dynasties, such territories as would consolidate and round off the territory of the kingdom. Heavenly retribution need hardly be feared as long as within the state the fear of God and a sense of justice reigned supreme over atheism, party faction, greed and selfishness. Territorial consolidation of the state outwardly, accord and harmony within, were the determining principles of Frederick's policy. From that position of strength the state could develop into a 'refuge of the persecuted, the widows and orphans, the supporter of the poor and the terror of the unjust'.

Yet at first it did seem that his accession to the throne was bringing about radical departures from policies hitherto pursued. Hardly upon the throne, he set about doing two things. Firstly, unlike his father, he completely ceased all further attempts to recover royal lands, thus formally acknowledging the right of private property of the nobility, and secondly, he abandoned the caution and timidity which had characterized the foreign policy of both his father and grandfather and instead pursued, recklessly at first, power politics. He made his 'Rendezvouz with fame', a policy which was to take the state to the brink of absolute disaster on several occasions, but from where it managed to emerge victoriously. And on the battlefields of Silesia was finally forged the alliance between crown and aristocracy which henceforth was to characterize the Prussian state until 1918. However, it was an alliance in which the moment the crown was represented by a man of lesser stature than Frederick, the nobility was bound to gain weight, though without ever eroding that common denominator of Prussian society as a whole, the ideology of the state community. This ideology on which the Prussian state rested ensured that the social preponderance of one social class did not turn into abuse, a feature which strongly influenced contemporary observers and inclined them towards generalizations which, though true of Prussia, were hardly applicable to all parts of Germany.

The importance of the welfare of the community was not based upon altruistic motives but upon *raison d'état*. In Frederick's secret testaments, destined solely for his successor, he repeatedly urges that the monarch must be mild because he would be ruling over a diligent and well-tempered people from whom unprovoked domestic resistance was not to be expected. He implores his successor to encourage by rewards rather than urge through punishments, 'to ease as much as possible fiscal burdens and to be aware at all time that . . .' [the ruler] '. . . is only the first servant of the state. His guiding star should be exclusively the interest of the state to which his entire life should be dedicated. The welfare of the people must be his primary concern; it is inseparably connected with his own.'

In his domestic policy, viewed as a whole, he continued along the path laid down by his father: the encouragement of agriculture but with a greater emphasis on trade and manufacturing interests. The pillars of the state, economic and military, were still the aristocracy and the peasants, while the growing middle class could find access to the higher ranks of society via the bureaucracy where expertise had always been a prerequisite, even more so with the increasing complexity of government. It 'could not dispense with people of this kind because the work for which high-born councillors were unqualified simply had to be done', especially during the years when Frederick's reign was drawing to a close.

Where one notices a significant difference between father and son is in their attitudes to religion. Frederick William I still accepted that he would ultimately be accountable to God while his son saw his task as acting exclusively in the interests of the state as he interpreted them, a state whose first servant he considered himself to be and to which he owed his duty. Religious sceptic that he was, 'duty' to him became an *ersatz* religion. In contrast to the Hapsburgs domestic and foreign policy ceased to be subject purely to dynastic considerations, and became instead subject solely to *raison d'état* as Frederick understood it, even if that meant a total disregard for his own person. In 1741 he wrote to Count Podewils: 'In the event of the misfortune that I should be captured alive, I order you at the risk of your head, to disregard any order I may issue from captivity, that you support my brother with your advice, and that the state undertakes nothing for my liberation which would be below its dignity. On the contrary! . . . I am king only when I am free.' Or again in 1757: 'If I should fall into the hands of the enemy I forbid you to take the slightest regard for my person and disregard whatever I may write from captivity. In the case of such a misfortune occurring I shall sacrifice myself for the state ... no province, no ransom must be offered and the war must be continued by the exploitation of all advantages as though I had never lived.'

This makes very clear Frederick's idea that state and prince, irrespective of the person involved, are one and indivisible; the state was no longer a mere apparatus used by the prince for his individual ends, but a body to which the prince subordinated himself. It ceased to be an instrument of power wielded by the ruler and instead acquired a supra-individual personality. The unity of the state is emphasized, as opposed to the agglomeration of territories held together by the dynasty.

Many who had believed that with the accession of Frederick a reign of Epicurus would begin, found themselves very quickly and drastically disappointed. True, torture was, with certain exceptions, abolished and the whole legal process of punishment made more humane. The Academy of the Sciences which under Frederick William I had been in a state of decay was given a new injection of life by the appointment of the famous mathematician Maupertius as its president. Frederick's relations with Voltaire could now be deepened and expanded. The initiative for the building of the Berlin Opera, built between 1741 and 1743 by Knobelsdorff, came during the first months of Frederick's reign.

However, the primary focus of his attention was Prussia's position as a power and his ambition to turn it into a great power. Although immediately after coming to the throne he dissolved his father's Guard of Giants, he increased the army by seven infantry regiments which meant that by 1741 Prussia possessed an army of more than 100,000 men. Frederick was fully aware of the disproportion that existed between Prussia's military might and the political role it played in Germany and Europe. He was not prepared to accept the humiliations which his father and grandfather had found necessary to accept. From the first moment of his accession he was determined to convey the impression of being a strong man. He personally conducted the correspondence with his envoys from his cabinet, which from the point of view of structure and purpose remained the same as it had been under Frederick William I. Absolute secrecy in his foreign policy was of the essence, therefore no ministers were informed; only his cabinet secretary, the Secret War Councillor Eichel who conducted the King's correspondence, was informed of all the secrets of Frederick's policy.

At the time of Frederick's accession tension mounted between France and Great Britain as a result of a war that had broken out between Great Britain and Spain in 1739. The Bourbon courts of Spain and France adopted a united front. This situation tempted Frederick to renew the old Prussian claims on the duchy of Jülich and Berg. By negotiating with France or Great Britain, both of which were anxious to secure

Prussia's military support, he hoped to gain decisive support. Another minor affair, but nevertheless characteristic of the new broom that was to sweep across Germany, concerned territory which had come to Prussia from the Orange legacy. But it was a claim strongly contested by the bishop of Liège. Frederick simply despatched a few battalions from his Wesel garrison to occupy the territory and then compelled the bishop to buy the territory from him for the round sum of 200,000 thalers.

While the negotiations over Berg were still in process, Emperor Charles VI died quite unexpectedly on 20 October 1740. This changed Frederick's horizon of ambitions. In Russia the Czarina had died, and her death and the ensuing confusion ensured for the time being Russia's inactivity. Hapsburg territory, in particular the economically prosperous Silesia, would also provide Prussia with an advantageous springboard *vis à vis* Poland (if, as seemed likely it disintegrated in the near future) and at the same time threaten Saxony. Two days later he called a meeting with Minister Podewils and Field-Marshal Schwerin and informed them of his decision to obtain the richest province of the House of Hapsburg: Silesia. He wanted to hear their view as to how he could achieve this, not as to whether or not he should attempt it.

Of course there were claims dating back to the sixteenth century to the time of the Elector Joachim II, and the treaty of 1537 according to which three Silesian duchies (Liegnitz, Brieg and Wohlau) were to come to Brandenburg after the death of the last of the line of the Piast princes. That line had in fact become extinct in 1675 but nothing had been done to press these claims seriously. For Frederick they now became pretexts with the aid of which he would break the jewel of Silesia out of the Hapsburg crown.

Podewils suggested settling the matter by negotiation. Frederick decided to confront Europe with a *fait accompli*: march before the winter, negotiate during the winter was his motto.

Frederick's generalship was to develop to unexpected heights during the next 23 years, but that does not mean that on the eve of the First Silesian War he was a relative novice in the craft of war. For one thing he possessed the military training of every Prussian officer; for another, besides reading as Crown Prince the French philosophers and men of *belle lettres*, he was also an avid student of the publications of the military writers of the period.

The Prussian army which Frederick commanded may well have been the first in Europe, but as an army it was still inexperienced. The true importance of light cavalry had not yet been recognized, the infantry had yet to withstand the test of fire. On the whole there existed general agreement among the tacticians of the period that with linear tactics of attack and defence concentrated fire was preferable to general fire or, as Scharnhorst was to put it later, individual firing was to be avoided, only entire salvos would yield any results. Ten men killed or wounded simultaneously would more likely result in the enemy battalion's withdrawal than 50 killed by a salvo over the entire front of a battalion. Individual fire would lead to wastage of ammunition and the quick wearing out of arms. Finally, the officers would lose control over their men. How effective concentrated fire could be was demonstrated at Fontenoy when British–Hanoverian guards met French ones. The respective officers even complimented each other on the first shot, and when the French guards suffered such heavy losses after the first salvo fired by the British, the rest of the French took to their heels.

The ideal way of firing was thought to be to divide each battalion, which in battle would be lined up three deep, into eight platoons which fired rapidly one after another, thus maintaining continuous fire and preventing the enemy's cavalry from breaking into the infantry formations. This manoeuvre could be carried out on the parade ground but in actual battle it was another matter. Frederick too considered these the ideal firing tactics but was aware that in practice they might not be carried out successfully. What tended to happen was that the first salvo was discharged according to the rules, perhaps even three or four platoons might fire correctly, but then despite strict discipline it would degenerate into general firing and the officers could do little other than wait until they could advance or withdraw.

It was generally accepted that the attack was to be carried out by the entire line of infantry, which would be advancing while firing; the enemy was finally to be felled by a bayonet attack. But the actual use of the bayonet was relatively rare and it was more of a psychological threat than a real one. Moreover, ramming a bayonet into an enemy is one thing, extracting it is another, which quite often can be achieved only with considerable effort, wasting far too much time in the heat of battle. In practice once the attacking line met the defence face to face, the latter tended to give way. These tactics corresponded very closely with the composition of the armies at the time. The soldier had no other function than to obey orders, advance in equal step, an officer at the flank of each formation and one behind. Salvos were fired according to command until one had broken into the enemy's lines, where no real combat was expected. These tactics place a premium on obedience and stifled individual initiative, but were ideal for armies large parts of whose soldiers fought for the pay they received, with little personal allegiance to the state or dynasty to which the army belonged. The speed with which the salvos were fired was a maximum of four per minute, the average being two or three rounds per minute.

The most difficult problem was that of firing whilst in motion. Theoretically an advancing platoon should halt and then fire. Again it was an exercise that could be nicely demonstrated on the parade ground but was hardly equalled in actual battle. The development that took place during the wars of Frederick's reign was to let the infantry storm forward without firing, using fire only in pursuit or defence. Preparatory fire was to be carried out by artillery. Yet it was a development not uniformly followed in the Prussian army and throughout the three Silesian Wars it varied from battle to battle. More often than not the Prussian army attacked accompanied by rapid rifle fire. This resulted in heavy enemy losses which, however, were matched by the losses inflicted by the defenders. In the end all that was gained by these tactics was the maintenance of what Delbrück calls the 'stability of the tactical body'.

One of the problems of linear tactics was that a line of infantry three deep could tear or could be broken through all too easily. The tacticians of antiquity had already realized this weakness and tried to meet it by introducing a second line whose function was to strengthen the weak points of the first and to ward off attacks from the flanks and the rear. Particularly because of the vulnerability of the flanks, battalions were positioned facing and fighting outwards against any attack from the sides. The aim of most generals was to place their troops on as wide a front as possible, so that as a result of the length of one's own line it was possible to carry out a flanking movement, enveloping one of the enemy's wings and cause him to falter from the side rather than defeating him by means of frontal attack. The disadvantage in this was that the longer the line the thinner it was, and therefore the forces attempting the manoeuvre lacked that superiority of numbers necessary to bring it to a successful conclusion. Topographical factors introduced immense difficulties, particularly when the battlefield was not flat but hilly or undulating. In effect this manoeuvre was hardly ever successfully deployed, but the problem which gave birth to it occupied Frederick seriously and resulted in the 'oblique' order of battle. That is not to say that Frederick was its inventor. The significance of the flanks had been recognized for centuries; Frundsberg, the 'father' of the *Landsknechte*, for instance, always barricaded his flanks; during the Thirty Years War at the Battle of the White Mountain similar precautions were taken both by the imperial and the Protestant forces. Already in the Wars of the Spanish Succession attacks were no longer carried out with equal intensity over the entire front but tended to be weaker on one wing in order to strengthen that one which was to envelop one of the enemy's wings. Blenheim, Ramillies and Turin are appropriate examples. The origin of the oblique order of battle is found in antiquity, in the writings of Vegetius, while the first most modern military theoretician to take up the problem was Montecuccoli (the prominent imperial general against the Turks and French in the seventeenth century) with whose writings Frederick was intimately familiar. He advised that the best troops should be positioned on the flanks. The initiative in the battle should then originate from that wing which qualitatively and quantitatively was the stronger.

The French writer Folard, from whose works Frederick ordered extensive extracts to be made, paid considerable attention to the importance of and his preference for the oblique order of battle, while from the writings of another French military theoretician, Feuquières, whose views were identical with those of Folard, Frederick adopted entire passages to include in his instructions. In short, the concept of the oblique order of battle had existed among military theoreticians and generals for some time. Frederick was deeply familiar with it; his contribution to it is really that after several attempts, which involved at least one near defeat and a complete one, he applied it successfully.

Actually to strengthen one wing more than another is fairly simple, but as soon as the enemy recognizes this he does the same thing, strengthening his wing that is opposite the weaker one. In theory the result could well have been a battle in which one wing chased the other, the whole thing revolving like a cartwheel. For the oblique order of battle to become fully effective one would have to envelop the enemy flank with one's own attacking flank. But since no enemy is fool enough to expose his flanks deliberately and therefore positions himself at right-angles to the direction of the expected attack, the attacking force is faced with the major task of wheeling around. This was a movement of considerable complexity because the traditional linear tactics had made little allowance for that degree of mobility. To facilitate a greater degree of mobility Marshal Puységur, another formative French influence on Frederick's military thinking, suggested breaking up the linear formation into battalions. However, this carried the intrinsic risk of multiplying the number of flanks, each battalion now having its own flanks instead of being part of a continuous line. Consequently it was of the utmost importance to keep the intervals between the battalions as small as possible, yet large enough to allow for greater mobility. In addition to protection of the flanks it was one of the tasks of the cavalry to protect these spaces.

Furthermore the oblique order of battle is only then of advantage when the attacking wing is the stronger, while the rest of the forces tie down the maximum number of the enemy's forces; speed is of the essence, to prevent the enemy from taking counter-measures. In other words the attack must come as a surprise, and success will be achieved the moment the enemy's front has been enveloped on one of his wings.

The oblique order of battle is therefore what Delbrück quite rightly calls 'a tactical work of art', which Frederick developed not at one stroke but over the years, putting into practice at least eight different variations of it. Just because it won Frederick some highly spectacular victories does not mean that by itself it was a guarantee of success; it could very well happen, as it did at Kunersdorf, that an enemy not thrown at the first attempt would hold his position which would ultimately lead to both lines meeting head on and thus to a battle with all the available forces deployed with none in reserve. That such an order of battle could be defeated by other tactics was amply demonstrated when it was carried out by the Prussian army against the forces of Napoleon in 1806. The best definition of the oblique order of battle is that supplied by Delbrück who describes it as that

'form of wing battle in which the entire line of battle represents a little-

interrupted or uninterrupted front. It is a characteristic of the wing battle that one wing is advanced while the other is withheld, and that the attacking wing is strengthened to catch the enemy in the flank or even in the rear. . . . The oblique battle order is a sub-form of the wing battle which was adapted to the elementary tactics of the epoch. The reinforcement of the attacking wing can consist of infantry in the form of preliminary attacks preceding the main attack or adding reserves during the battle as well as of cavalry or artillery.'

This represents approximately the body of ideas on military tactics which Frederick II possessed on the eve of the outbreak of the First Silesian War.

Without knowing or foreseeing the ultimate consequences of his action Frederick was determined to annex Silesia. The issue of the Pragmatic Sanction, that is to say the succession after the death of Charles VI of his daughter Maria Theresa to the Hapsburg throne, did not play any role at all, except as a tactical manoeuvre. In principle the question of the succession was completely without interest at all; it was an irrelevancy. Therefore his venture had nothing to do with those of the two princes who refused to sign the Pragmatic Sanction, the Electors of Saxony (who finally signed in 1733) and Bavaria. After all, Prussia began the war not Bavaria. Initially Frederick attempted to cover his action with a veneer of respectability. George II of Great Britian, his uncle, received assurances from his nephew that the latter's troops were really on the march to safeguard the interests of the House of Hapsburg. He emphasized that since the death of Charles VI Austria had been at the point of disintegration, vulnerable to all its enemies. His action was a preventive one, designed to ward off the evil plans of others: 'My sole purpose is the maintenance and the true interests of the House of Austria.' With such hypocritical nonsense Frederick tried to justify what, contrary to his expectations, became the greatest bloodletting which Central Europe experienced between the Thirty Years War and Wars of Napoleon. Privately he did not even attempt to justify his action: 'Who would have thought that destiny has chosen a poet to topple the political system of Europe and to turn upside down the political combinations of its rulers!' he wrote to his friend Jordan. 'My youthfulness, the burning embers of my passion, my thirst for fame, yes, even curiosity admittedly, a secret instinct, have torn me from the joys of tranquillity. The satisfaction of seeing my name in the gazettes and later in history has seduced me', he admitted on another occasion. And this from the same man who only a few months before, while still Crown Prince, had described Europe's conquering monarchs as crowned robbers and criminals decorated with royal insignia. One should not take that too seriously any more than his Anti-Machiavel. Even during his period of imprisonment in the Küstrin fortress he described himself in a letter to a confidant as a prince who 'strides from country to country, from conquest to conquest and, like Alexander, chooses new worlds for subjugation'. Even Poland was on his list of potential conquests. On moral grounds Frederick's action deserves utter condemnation, but that view is softened, or even made irrelevant, by the actions of his contemporaries, his predecessors and successors.

The First Silesian War was undoubtedly a *Blitzkrieg*; the army was in a state of complete preparedness, utter secrecy was maintained and all stratagems of diplomacy were exploited. When his regiments were already on the march he told the Austrian envoy to assure the Empress Maria Theresa that he would do nothing directed against the House of Hapsburg. On the evening before his departure to join his troops about to cross the frontier into Silesia he attended a ball given by the Queen, the wife who had been forced upon him and from whom he had lived in informal separation since three weeks after the marriage. When he had reached his army he still continued negotiations with Vienna, promising in return for Silesia the maintenance of the Pragmatic Sanction and Brandenburg's vote for the election of Maria Theresa's husband, Francis of Tuscany, as Emperor. Indeed the statesmen in Vienna were at first not disinclined to accept Frederick's proposals, but the energetic 23-year-old Maria Theresa was every ounce a match for the 28-year-old Prussian King. Taking perhaps his own mother as well as his wife as his yardstick for judging women, Frederick had seriously miscalculated. Maria Thersea intervened and rejected Frederick's offer outright. Frederick entered Silesia's capital, Breslau, when news of the rejection of his proposals reached him.

Aware that a long war would be ruinous for Prussia, he decided in favour of swift decisive victories, rounded off by an advantageous peace settlement. He also included in his calculations not only the possibility but the probability that one of the two major powers, France or Great Britain, would, in their own interest, join his side. But Cardinal Fleury was no longer ready to risk the laurels which in the course of a long life he had obtained for France, while Great Britain's Hanoverian interests inclined towards Austria rather than Prussia. Hanover and Saxony had an interest in several of Prussia's territories; and in Britain's wake sailed also the Netherlands. Russia, too, seemed to range herself with what appeared to become a Grand Coalition against Prussia. But Frederick's skilful diplomacy managed to break out the very linchpin of that coalition – Hanover. With it came Great Britain and that meant the end of the Grand Coalition.

Just at that point Frederick gained an impressive and temporarily decisive victory, at Mollwitz on 10 April 1741. In order to occupy Silesia, Prussia's troops had been scattered widely over the province. Meanwhile Austria's forces, some 14,000 strong under Field-Marshal Count Neipperg, managed to cross the Sudeten passes from Bohemia into Silesia almost unnoticed and were about to cut the Prussian army into two, forcing Frederick to accept battle. At Mollwitz the Prussian army under Field-Marshal Schwerin gained its first major victory. It was not Frederick's victory, though he had drawn up the plan of battle, which envisaged a tentative application of the oblique order of battle. Although superior to the Austrians in infantry and artillery, the Prussian cavalry was inferior qualitatively as well as quantitatively and the Austrian cavalry virtually swept the Prussian cavalry from the battlefield. Defeat stared the Prussians in the face. The King left the battlefield for his own safety – whether in panic or whether acting on the advice of Field-Marshal Schwerin matters very little. Then Schwerin, grabbing hold of the colours of the First Battalion of Guards, rallied the Prussian infantry and artillery again and in one massive effort, attacking as though he was on the Potsdam parade ground, threw the Austrians. The Austrian attempt to separate the Prussian forces had miscarried. However, parts of Silesia remained in Austrian hands, with only the small area of Brieg going to Prussia.

More important was the battle's political effect in bringing about the alliance between France and Prussia. Cardinal Fleury's hesitance gave way and an alliance was concluded in Breslau on 5 June 1741. Together Prussia and France became the main supporters of Bavaria, whose Elector Charles became their candidate for the imperial throne instead of Maria Theresa's husband. In 1742 he was duly elected in Frankfurt as Charles VII. But to prevent the French from gaining too much influence in Germany Frederick, with British aid, concluded a secret convention with Austria at Klein-Schnellendorf. From this he received assurances of Austria's neutrality, the territory of Lower Silesia, Breslau and Neisse, and winter quarters in Silesia. The war was now conducted by the Saxons, Bavarians and the French who succeeded in taking Prague. In the light of the success of his allies Frederick broke the convention and resumed the war against Austria. The creed of the isolated *raison d'état* once again gained the upper hand.

In the meantime he had learnt some of the lessons of Mollwitz and reorganized his cavalry. Cuirassiers, who had been the dominant part of the cavalry on heavy horses, were retrained on lighter horses that were quicker and less clumsy to manoeuvre; the hussars under General von Zieten were expanded, as were the dragoons. The Prussian cavalry earned its first laurels at the battle of Chotusitz on 17 May 1742 in which the Austrian army was again defeated, a defeat of sufficient impact to persuade Maria Theresa to make peace with Prussia at Breslau on 28 July 1742. Silesia in its entirety now remained in Prussian hands.

Frederick's allies were again left in the lurch. The frequency with which he broke treaties, conventions and other agreements during the First Silesian War left its mark on the judgement of contemporaries to the end of his days. Whatever fame he had achieved and was to achieve in future years, a reputation for trustworthiness was something he was never to attain.

The Peace of Breslau was not of a very long duration. Austrian forces expelled the French beyond the Rhine. It seemed as though the French would also have to yield Alsace which they had appropriated in the previous century. Maria Theresa's military successes became a cause for concern for Frederick who, after Saxony had also joined the Austrian coalition, considered his own spoils threatened, especially as Russia under the Czarina Elizabeth gave signs of giving up her neutral attitude which had secured his back so far. From France he could expect little support; he would have to carry the weight of any combined attack of the allies alone. In the light of this prospect Frederick decided to take the initiative and in August 1744 broke the Peace of Breslau; the Second Silesian War began.

Frederick's armies conquered Prague compelling the Austrians to leave Alsace. They returned from the Rhine by forced marches and threatened to cut Frederick's lines of communication. This forced him to withdraw from Bohemia into Silesia. As expected French help did not materialize, while the Saxons, supported by British subsidies, joined Austria and thus added another 20,000 men to Frederick's enemies. At no stage was he able to force the enemy to give battle; time and again he was simply outmanoeuvred. Doubts about his capacity as a military leader began to be voiced within the Prussian officer corps; the example of Mollwitz was invoked. Even more drastic consequences could be seen among the rank and file of his army of which 17,000 deserted either to the enemy or simply just out of the army. Maria Theresa, seeing herself on the threshold of the liberation of Silesia, proclaimed that the citizens of the province no longer owed any allegiance to the King of Prussia.

And now a quality began to show in Frederick which represents the basis of the claim to greatness that his contemporaries and posterity made on his behalf. This claim does not rest on the brilliance of his victories, for they are matched by the severity of the defeats he suffered. It rests in part on his capacity when threatened, when near to the point of defeat, to generate unexpected resources and, despite great odds, once again force fortune in his direction.

Bavaria made its separate peace with Austria after the counter-Emperor Charles VII had died in January 1745. Elector Maximilian pledged his voice for Maria Theresa's husband and Bavaria, largely occupied by the Austrians, was returned to him. Britain refused any attempt at mediation. Frederick's war treasure was slowly beginning to show signs of exhaustion. Since the middle of March 1745 the King had been with his army, relentlessly drilling and training his troops.

Instead of guarding and defending the mountain passes that led from Bohemia into Silesia, Frederick decided to meet the Austrians on Silesian ground. All avenues into Silesia were kept under close observation during the spring of 1745, every move of the Austrian forces reported to Frederick in his headquarters in Schweidnitz. On the evening of 3 June 1745 reports were conclusive. Seventy thousand Austrians and Saxons formed into eight army columns moved from the Sudeten passes into Silesia between Hohenfriedberg and Pilgramshain. The commander of the Austrian army, Prince Charles of Lorraine, finding the mountain passes unoccupied, had no doubts about the outcome of any battle: 'There would be no God in heaven, if we should not win this battle.' Apparently there was not.

Contrary to the Austrian expectation Frederick attacked their left wing. First the Saxons then the Austrians were thrown. For the first time the Prussian cavalry proved superior to that of the Austrians. The dragoons of Ansbach-Bayreuth rode into attack, sweeping everything before them, their 10 squadrons destroying six battle-hardened Austrian infantry regiments, conquering 66 flags. The enemy lost 10,000 men killed and wounded. In military terms it was a splendid victory for Prussia's soldiers, the air of triumph still captured in the ringing tunes of the Hohenfriedberger March, the composition of which has been attributed to Frederick himself and probably rightly so. This victory once again established confidence in his leadership; it was his first personal military victory. Mollwitz had been that of Schwerin, Chotusitz was argued by the Austrians not to have been a victory at all, but there was no doubt as to who had been the victor at Hohenfriedberg. Frederick had triumphed with a concept that ran contrary to established thinking. Instead of taking the initiative himself he had left it to the enemy, thus tempting him into Silesia. Once there he had attacked him and inflicted a resounding defeat upon Austria's army. Frederick pursued the enemy for another three days. Then the fronts came to a halt again, for the Austrian army in Bohemia still represented a formidable force and in the light of the experience of the previous winter Frederick did not dare to venture beyond Königsgrätz.

If Frederick could have had his way now he would have made peace, provided that he could have retained Silesia. But his great opponent Maria Theresa was not so quickly discouraged. London was now ready to accept the task of mediation but George II, behind the back of his ministers, advised Austria against making peace and concluded an agreement with Saxony according to which Hanover and Saxony were to acquire sizeable Prussian territories. Moreover the French who had moved into Germany with an army of 40,000 men were expelled again by the Austrians. On 13 September 1745 Maria Theresa's husband was crowned as Emperor Francis I, with the Electors of Brandenburg and the Palatinate dissenting.

In the early autumn of 1745 Frederick was preparing to withdraw from Bohemia and take up winter quarters in Silesia. Mistakes had led to numerous mishaps. Frederick's cabinet secretary Eichel had been captured by the Austrians, so had his baggage. The threat of the Saxons diverted a substantial part of the army, the main part of which was now only 22,000 strong. Under such circumstances Prince Charles of Lorraine decided to do a Hohenfriedberg in reverse on Frederick. Frederick's army was encamped at Soor, which Charles intended to attack by surprise with a numerically much superior force of 39,000 men. On 30 September 1745 at five in the morning Frederick received the first news while already with his generals. Frederick was trapped, withdrawal or evasion being made impossible by the geographical factors. He decided that the only salvation lay in attack. This unconditional readiness to accept battle and to attack with a fervour as though all the odds were in favour of the Prussians decided the battle. Again the Prussian cavalry made the ultimately decisive contribution. Frederick's military reputation soared once more, but still no sign was discernible that peace could be obtained. Hence he turned against the weakest link, the Saxons.

To prevent the Austrian and Saxon armies from uniting, the Prussian armies attacked the Saxon forces at Kesselsdorf near Dresden on 15 December 1745. The Prussian army was commanded by the very man who had given it decisive shape, the close friend of Frederick's father, Prince Leopold of Anhalt-Dessau, *der alte Dessauer*. While his battalions were lined up in battle formation Dessauer, on horseback in front of his troops, took off his hat, drew his sword, raised it to the sky and loudly prayed: 'Oh Lord if today you should not bless us with victory, please make sure that the scoundrels on the other side will not get it either.' The battle was won, the Saxons were beaten, the joining up of the armies prevented. The immediate consequence of this victory was Frederick's entry into Saxony's capital, and this was the point at which, for the time being, Maria Theresa decided to terminate a venture which had brought her armies serious reverses while raising Prussia's military glory to hitherto unknown heights.

On Christmas Day 1745 Austria and Prussia concluded peace in Dresden. Prussia retained Silesia. Frederick returned to Berlin and for the first time the title 'the Great' made its appearance in the popular vocabulary. Believing, if only for a short time, that his career as a general had reached its point of culmination and at the same time its end, he decided to devote himself to more peaceful pursuits. But the consequences of his actions at the beginning of his reign had not yet run their full course.

The Peace of Aachen of 18 October 1748, which endeavoured to bring about a general European settlement, guaranteed the Treaty of Dresden but did not bring about a general acceptance of the power relationships in Europe. Whether France or Great Britain should be the first sea and colonial power was still an open question, while in Germany both Prussia and Austria were vying for supremacy, with Russia (which had been on the verge of entering the war against Prussia when the Treaty of Dresden was signed) time and again trying to infuse Austria with new offensive spirit. Also, because one of Frederick's sisters was the wife of the Swedish Crown Prince, who exercised considerable political influence, the Russians were endeavouring to bring about a change in the succession to the Swedish throne, by force if necessary. By early 1749 another war seemed imminent, but Prussia's firm attitude and skilful diplomacy made the Russian plans come to nought. Frederick, mistakenly as the evidence later showed, firmly believed that the machinations were really inspired by the Hofburg in Vienna.

In the meantime Frederick proceeded with opening up Silesia's resources for the benefit of the entire Prussian state. The province's agricultural resources were more than sufficient to feed a population of greater than a million. Extensive sheep farming provided wool for export to Austria, Bohemia and Saxony as well as to Holland and Great Britain. It also possessed its own finishing, dying, spinning and weaving industries. But on the eve of its conquest by Frederick the province's main mineral resource, coal had hardly been touched. However such metals as iron, zinc, lead and silver were already being mined. Geographically Silesia lay in a favourable position because through it led the major trade routes between the Baltic and a large part of Central and Eastern Central Europe.

At first Frederick failed to follow a consistent policy concerning the economic development of this new Prussian province. The question for him was whether to treat it as a backward agrarian region whose raw materials could be utilized by the Prussian economy or whether it was a relatively advanced region in the early stages of industrialization with well-developed craft industries. His first priority was to restore the economic life of the region as quickly as possible. Trade in woollen clothes reached record heights within three years after the conclusion of the Treaty of Dresden. But set-backs were soon experienced as the result of Austria's imposition of high tariffs on goods coming from Silesia, a measure designed to deprive Frederick of the economic benefits of his conquest. Saxony followed suit with similar measures. Prussia retaliated, but the real victim of this tariff war was Silesia herself, and only after the Seven Years War is a consistent economic recovery of the province evident. Frederick also realized the importance of the mining industries, and on the eve of the Seven Years War he decreed that the crown should receive one-tenth of the output of the Silesian mines. Attempts to establish ironworks and to increase the output of iron, as well as to explore systematically Silesia's coal deposits, go back to 1753. Since it was difficult to recruit labour to these iron works soldiers were drafted in, but in the long run skilled workers were attracted by special privileges such as reduced taxation, welfare benefits and exemption from military service. The benefit of the additional output of the new ironworks was substantially felt by Prussia's army during the Seven Years War.

But if the opening up and exploitation of the newly annexed province was a major task which occupied Frederick during the 10-year period between 1746 and 1756 this must not be seen in isolation but rather as part of the continuation of the policy of his father Frederick William I to strengthen the kingdom economically and extend as well as further evolve the administrative apparatus to run it efficiently. Actually Frederick created the instrument of his policy of industrialization in 1740, almost immediately after his accession to the throne, namely the fifth department of the General Directory responsible for commerce and manufacture. A sixth department was added after the end of the

Second Silesian War which was responsible for military administration and supplies. It was very much the product of Frederick's disastrous experiences during the Bohemian campaign of 1744 in which supplies had been seriously mismanaged. Within the General Directory these new departments were not simply a novelty, but because they were responsible for specific functions concerning the whole of the kingdom they differed in character from the other four departments which were organized basically according to provinces with only some tasks relevant to the kingdom as a whole. The new departments by contrast were a sign of the growing unity of the kingdom.

By comparison with his father Frederick showed little inclination for collegiate gatherings and decisions. At the lower levels of the administration he distinctly preferred individual responsibility, which in practice meant both the delegation of greater authority to and its acceptance by the chamber president. The office of the *Landrat* was now, with the exception of the two regions of Geldern and Eastern Frisia, introduced in all areas of the kingdom. Silesia was reorganized administratively immediately after, its conquest, the Hapsburg structure being replaced by that of Prussia. Unlike his father Frederick favoured rather more communal self-administration which in 1756 led to the reintroduction of the right, abolished by Frederick William I, to elect the *Landrat*. The same applies to his policy towards the towns, where the magistrates regained the right to submit suggestions as to who should be a member of that collegiate body and also the right to make their own appointments to communal offices. On the other hand, in his appointments to the higher ranks of the civil service, for example to the post of chamber president, he closed the avenues which Frederick William had opened to the talent of the middle class and appointed only members of the nobility. But like his father he kept a constant eye upon his civil servants; chamber presidents had to prepare a conduct sheet on each of their civil servants in which their degree of efficiency was judged by a very high standard.

In 1748 he issued new instructions for the General Directory, that is to say he revised those issued by his father. Whereas the latter's aim had been to economize in order to yield a financial surplus each year, Frederick's revision is evidence that he kept his eye on the general development of the kingdom's economy. In order to provide greater incentives for the peasants to increase their productivity he expressly reduced their dues and burdens.

The most impressive document illustrating his policies and attitudes is his Political Testament of 1752. On the nobility he writes:

An object of policy of the sovereign of this state is to preserve his noble class; for whatever change may come about, he might perhaps have one which was richer, but never one more valorous and more noble. To enable them to maintain themselves in their possessions, it is necessary to prevent non-nobles from acquiring noble estates and to compel them to put their money into commerce . . . It is also necessary to prevent noblemen from taking service abroad, to inspire them with an esprit de corps and a national spirit. This is [why] I did everything possible to spread the name 'Prussian', in order to teach the officers that, whatever province they came from, they were all counted as Prussians, and that for that reason all the provinces, however separated from one another, form a united body.

Of the towns and burghers he said:

I have left the towns in the old provinces the privilege of electing their own magistrates, and have not interferred with these elections unless they were misused and some families or burghers monopolized all the authority to the prejudice of the rest. In Silesia I have deprived them of the franchise for fear of their filling the councils with men who are devoted to Austria. With time, and when the present generation has passed away, it will be possible to restore the electoral system in Silesia without danger.

On the peasants he commented:

I have relaxed [on the royal domain] the services which the peasants used to perform; instead of six days service a week, they now have to work only three. This has provoked the nobles' peasants, and in several places they have resisted their lords. The sovereign should hold the balance evenly between the peasant and the gentleman, so they do not ruin one another. In Silesia the peasants, outside Upper Silesia, are very well placed; in Upper Silesia they are serfs. One will have to try to free them in due course. I have set the example on my crown lands, where I have begun putting them on the same footing as the Lower Silesians. One should further prevent peasants from buying nobles' lands, or nobles peasants', because peasants cannot serve as officers in the army, and if the nobles convert peasant holdings into demesne farms, they diminish the number of inhabitants and cultivators.

From the same year dates a letter by Frederick which aptly illustrates his attitude towards industrialization:

Since I have seen from your report . . . that you are of the opinion that except for the few factories listed by you, which in themselves are very good and necessary, we need no more factories in this country, but have more than enough, I cannot refrain from informing you that I must conclude that you can have made only a very superficial survey and examination of the extracts and balance sheets of imports and exports sent in by the Chamber; certainly, if you had looked attentively at the rubrics in them of imports from foreign countries, you would have easily seen from the details specified in them how very many objects there are which at present we have to get from abroad, and that we could spare ourselves that necessity by setting up our own factories here or sometimes by extending beginnings already made . . . Besides these examples, you would have found a hundred more similar things for which we have at present no factories and will gradually have to establish them . . .'

What stands out in the first document is that in spite of Frederick's obvious preference for the nobility he clearly realizes that it is in the interests of the state that nobility, burghers and peasants are integrated. The second document shows that he realizes industrialization was not stumbled upon by accident but forced itself upon the monarch out of the logic of dire economic necessity.

One major problem which preoccupied Frederick between 1746 and 1756 was the relationship between Prussia and the Roman Catholic church. Prussia for almost a century now had pursued a policy of religious toleration, but with the acquisition of Silesia a solidly Roman Catholic province had become part of Prussia. Papal jurisdiction over its Roman Catholics in Silesia had previously been exercised via the papal nuncio in Vienna. Several alternative solutions were suggested, one of them being to transfer papal jurisdiction to a papal vicar general whom Frederick wanted to appoint himself. The Curia resisted successfully and finally a compromise was reached by which these powers were to be exercised by the nuncio in Warsaw instead of the one in Vienna.

Frederick also at first tried to influence the Breslau chapter in order to have his nominee appointed as bishop of Breslau. When the chapter turned a deaf ear to his suggestion, Frederick claimed the privilege which existed in the Hapsburg lands and in France and simply appointed him. Pope Benedict XIV acquiesced.

Frederick also resumed a piece of work begun by his father, namely the reform of the judiciary and judicial proceedings. This time Samuel von Cocceji, the son of Frederick William I's legal expert, was entrusted with the task. First Frederick discussed with him the principles on which this reform was to be based. In Cocceji's view the reform required a thorough change in personnel and in the method of proceedings, and the introduction of a uniform legal code applicable throughout the country in conformity with the principle of centralization of the kingdom. One of the major concerns of the King was the hitherto lengthy and therefore very costly method of legal proceedings. To test Cocceji's ideas Frederick suggested that he try out his reforms on one of the Pomeranian courts renowned for its slowness and backlog of cases. Cocceji agreed and in 1747 managed to get through some 3,000 cases, although occasionally by the use of methods which suggest recourse to rough and ready justice for the sake of speed. Nevertheless his performance was judged a success and Frederick now entrusted him with the reform of the Chamber Court. Immediate conflict ensued between Cocceji and Frederick's minister of justice von Arnim, who considered the reform unnecessary and, if carried out according to the pattern established in Pomerania, disastrous to the judicial process in

Prussia. Around Arnim rallied the forces of the opposition, in part consisting of judges who in the days of Frederick William I had obtained office by contributing generously to his recruitment fund and who now had to fear losing their positions. Indeed 11 of them, all members of the Chamber Court, were dismissed. In spite of the sizeable opposition to Cocceji, Frederick backed him throughout, even though this meant Arnim's resignation. Cocceji moved from province to province replacing old, very often highly diverse, structures by a unified court system and the principles of the judicial process were clearly laid out in the *Codex Fridericianus Marchicus* of 1748.

Reform of the apparatus was accompanied by reform of personnel and venality in the holding of judicial office was completely abolished. Frederick William I in order to curb state spending had allowed judges to take case fees from both plaintiff and defendant. Cocceji's argument was that to ensure reasonable, sound and fair judgement the judge would have to be free from financial considerations, and consequently ought to be paid by the state. Frederick accepted this but nevertheless argued that the cost of judicial reforms must be kept as low as possible. Cocceji managed to persuade the estates in the various provinces to make regular extra contributions which would fund salaries for the judges and secure their relative independence.

Lawyers were equally closely scrutinized and undesirable elements removed. In the course of his reform Cocceji had subjected those judges who were to be re-employed to a severe examination, a practice hitherto unknown in Prussia. With that he set a precedent which under Cocceji's successor Jariges was transformed into a regular examination that had to be passed before anyone could be appointed as a judge and, more importantly, an entire set of examinations that had to be passed before any step upward on the ladder of a judicial career could be made.

Within the realm of civil law Cocceji insisted upon the principle of non-interference by the supreme judge of the kingdom, the monarch, which Frederick accepted. Cocceji would have liked to have seen the complete independence of the judiciary, but the King insisted on maintaining his prerogatives in criminal law, mainly, he argued, since this would allow him to remove corrupt judges. However, the beginning of a separation between executive and judiciary became discernible, as did the creation of a uniform legal code for the entire kingdom. But the latter remained the major problem, interrupted by the Seven Years War and making progress slowly over the two following decades to be completed only after Frederick's death. The judicial reforms that were achieved, though, commanded the attention of most of Europe.

The principles of Frederick's economic policy remained unchanged from those of his father; they were of a mercantilist nature designed to protect and further Prussian produce by exacting heavy dues on imported goods. In his agricultural policy he gave his support, in accordance with the principles set out in his Political Testament of 1752, to the nobility which provided him with his officers, but at the same time tried to ensure that the peasants would not be exploited by their masters. His reforms which actually benefited peasants remained restricted to his royal domains, within which he allowed, for instance, the development of peasant estates. He considered an economically healthy peasantry essential for the welfare of the state and the success of his policy is demonstrated by the high number of peasant immigrants he managed to attract and settle in Prussia. Between 1746 and 1756 90 new peasant villages were founded in Pomerania alone, 50 in the Oderbruch region, 96 in the Kurmark and 40 in the Neumark.

Overseas trade was another aspect towards which he directed his attention. He would have liked to export Silesian linen to the colonies of France and Spain and a special company was founded at Emden with this object in mind. Four shiploads sailed to China and did successful business, but when in 1755 naval warfare was resumed Prussia, which possessed no navy of her own, could do nothing to protect her infant overseas interests. The French Admiral Labourdonnais, disappointed by the lack of gratitude for his services to his own country, in 1751 submitted a detailed plan to Frederick for a Prussian navy. But Frederick wisely rejected this far-reaching scheme pointing to Prussia's limited reserves which allowed the maintenance of a Prussian land army only. The major threat for Prussia existed on land. True, the Russians could land troops in Danzig; perhaps once Danzig was in Prussian hands one could think over again the idea of a Prussian navy.

Frederick had retired from the Second Silesian War with hopes that all 'which now remains for us is to philosophize according to our heart's content, to cultivate the sciences in the shadow of the olive tree and to work at the ennoblement of our souls'. He wanted 'at long last to enjoy my life'.

From that perspective the 10-year period between the Second Silesian War and the Seven Years War was probably the happiest for the ruler. These were the years of the 'Round Table of Sanssouci', of the flute concerts, in which the King as an accomplished flute player not only played the solo passages but also performed his own compositions. These were by no means merely the works of a talented amateur, but displayed a genuine musical versatility combined with emotional range and depth unparalleled by any of his contemporaries on the royal thrones of Europe. His music, like his writings, displays a man who has little in common with the hard stern picture of Frederick the Great. His music exudes harmony, the adagio dominates over the fortissimo, even the most exhillarating flute solo is of a tenderness behind which one would not expect to find the victor of Hohenfriedberg, let alone the grim bundle of sheer willpower that confronts the observer during the Seven Years War. As are all men, Frederick was a living contradiction, a contradition brought into sharp relief by his position, by the brilliance of his gifts and inclinations and by the stern dedication to what he considered he owed his position, his dynasty, his state. His dedication to what he took to be his duty came first at all times, even though this meant neglecting that which he preferred, the arts.

Frederick had begun building his own miniature palace, Sanssouci, in 1745 during the Second Silesian War. The architect was Hans Georg Wenzeslaus von Knobelsdorf, a worthy successor of Schlüter whose style manifests the transition from Rococco to Classicism. His style also influenced the architecture of the rising middle class. In 1747 Frederick was able to occupy his new palace and three years later that man became his guest for whom he had had the greatest admiration since his days as Crown Prince: Voltaire. The King of the Enlightenment met the enlightened King. But in the course of almost three years what, at a distance, had previously been mutual admiration gave way to a mutually more critical view of one another. Neither admiration nor resplendent prose could dim the critically observant eyes of either Frederick or Voltaire. They all too quickly recognized one another's flaws and finally produced that blend of admiration and contempt that characterized their relationship until death.

Voltaire quickly grasped the antithesis within Frederick's character, 'the enthusiasm of thought and of action'. Philosophic reflection and political action confronted one another continuously, a confrontation between the demands of a very exacting concept of duty and Frederick's natural talents. He had characterized himself as a 'philosopher by inclination, a politician by force of circumstance'. Yet it was not force of circumstance that compelled him to unleash the First Silesian War, but vanity and personal folly. It was the consequences of that folly that he had to live with and master.

Therefore the army was not neglected during this 10-year period either, all the manoeuvres of the Prussian army at the time being aimed at perfecting the oblique order of battle. Unlike most of his contemporaries, Frederick believed in reaching a rapid decision on the battlefield, and not in mere manoeuvre. His offensive spirit set him apart from his contemporary commanders in the field. Only in the final phase of the Seven Year War, when his army had been decimated, when he lacked both manpower and supplies, was he forced to resort to traditional strategy and tactics. His instructions to the army just before the Seven Years War exemplify his offensive spirit. The infantry after a few strong salvos was to attack in quick step and with a bayonet charge push the enemy out of his positions. Never was the cavalry to wait to be attacked, but was always to attack first. Cavalry was to attack in large formation at the greatest possible speed, sword in hand. Firing of pistols during the attack was forbidden. Frederick's aim was to raise the strength of his army to 180,000 men and his war chest to at least 20 million thalers. When war did break out in 1756 he was still short of his aim; the army was 150,000 men strong and his war chest had barely reached 13 million thalers.

Since 1746 there had existed an Austro-Russian defensive alliance, potentially directed against Prussia. Great Britain, increasingly engaged in war with France over colonial predominance in North America, in September 1755 concluded a treaty with Russia according to which the latter would protect Hanover with more than 50,000 men. The spectre of encirclement stared Frederick in the face, so in January 1756 he concluded with George II the Convention of Westminster, guaranteeing the neutrality of Germany in the imminent Anglo-French colonial conflict. Prior to the conclusion of the convention Frederick had tried to enlist the services of France to break the ring that circled him, seeking to goad it into an attack on Hanover. But France was already busily negotiating with Austria. It was not interested in Frederick's suggestions. After the conclusion of the Convention of Westminster Frederick also hoped that the existing treaty between Britain and Russia had given the British a large enough lever to keep the Russians neutral. Because within that ring forming around Prussia it was Russia which he feared most and he was highly alarmed by news of extensive Russian military preparations. The suspicion that he was being encircled was further hardened when in May 1756 Maria Theresa's chancellor, Count Kaunitz, brought about the 'diplomatic revolution' by inducing the French to reverse their alliances. In April 1756 the Franco-Prussian alliance expired. But irritated by the previous erratic behaviour of her ally, and even more so by the Convention of Westminster, France felt herself once again betrayed and entered into a defensive alliance with Austria, the preliminary stage of an offensive alliance.

Yet Frederick was wrong with his theory of encirclement, the force behind which he believed to be Vienna and a vengeful Empress-Queen set upon reconquering the lost province. He assumed there would be co-ordinated concerted action masterminded by Maria Theresa's Chancellor Kaunitz. Action did in fact take place, but it was neither co-ordinated nor concerted because the Russians had decided upon their own course of action against Prussia irrespective of what Austria would or would not do. A plan 'to wipe Prussia off the map' did exist and it existed in Russia. British alarm at Russian military preparations was countered by the Russians with assurances that these were being made in order to keep to the terms of her treaty with Britain. Frederick, on the other hand, assumed that it was precisely the British who would be able to keep the Russians under control. What he did not realize was that Russia was rather more anxious to make war on Prussia than was Austria, her motives being territorial aggrandizement and commercial expansion, and Russia's aggressive policy towards Prussia had been very much in evidence since shortly before the end of the Second Silesian War. Bestuzhev, the Russian chancellor, aimed at war against Prussia in collaboration with Austria. The alliance with Britain gave him the necessary pretext to assemble his troops in Livonia. Even when the conclusion of the Convention of Westminster became known – a convention which after all went behind the back of the Russians – Bestuzhev chose to ignore it publicly, because had he reacted against it with hostility he would have deprived himself of the pretext and cloak behind which he made his preparations against Prussia. Towards the end of March 1756 a Secret War Council was set up in St Petersburg.

From the start it set out to produce a systematic plan for the reduction of the power of Prussia, and it continued in existence almost to the end of the Seven Years War, dealing with all aspects of that conflict, diplomatic, military, financial and administrative. It was a Council especially intended for the direction of what we call the Seven Years War – only it began that work in March 1756, five months before Frederick the Great attacked Saxony. (Sir Herbert Butterfield)

Russia was the driving force, hoping that by her immediate war preparations she would provide an incentive for Austria, making Maria Theresa realize that now would be the right moment to reconquer Silesia. When the Austrians speculated about the size of the Russian contribution to the war effort, estimating it at about 60,000 men, Russia offered 20,000 more. Russian preparations went ahead, militarily and politically, with Austria if possible, without it if need be. Evidence exists suggesting that part of the political preparation by Russia and Austria was 'to goad Prussia into making the attack'.

Of all that Frederick was only partially aware, if at all. Though viewing Russia as the chief danger militarily, he was convinced that the centre of the anti-Prussian conspiracy was in Vienna – that there were two centres he never knew. Austria planned originally for a war in the summer of 1756 but the protracted negotiations with France in which Austria demanded French agreement to the *destruction totale de la Prusse* made a delay necessary and the timing was put back to the spring of 1757. Austria asked Russia to delay action until then. Russia however, continued, in her preparations. From the middle of June onwards news reached Berlin of Russian troop movements along the Russian frontier. While he had received the news of the 'diplomatic revolution' with calm, the Russian preparations immediately put Frederick on his guard and he decided to arm himself quickly with a good deal of noise to show his neighbours that he was not to be caught unawares, in other words using the same tactic with which he had successfully dampened war-like Russian spirits in 1749. But then came news that Russian preparations had been halted, though only temporarily and merely as a gesture to the Austrian request to postpone the attack until the spring of 1757.

The piece of news which finally decided Frederick to take action was that Austrian troops were marching into Bohemia and Moravia via Hungary. Though the news ultimately proved to be false, possibly planted deliberately, for Frederick it was decisive. On 18 July 1756 Austria was asked by Prussia whether the increase in its armed forces was being carried out with the intention of attacking Prussia. The Hofburg's answer was very polite and very evasive. In the meantime Frederick had also found out the reason behind the temporary halt in

Russian movements and decided on preventive action. But he wished to gain time, to start the attack as late as possible in order to prevent French and Russian intervention for the rest of 1756. Another enquiry was despatched to Vienna similar in content to the previous one. It received a similar reply. This Frederick followed up with a proposal amounting to a Prussian annexation of Saxony, fully aware what the Saxon response would be. On 28 August 1756, after having sent a third enquiry to Vienna, he put himself at the head of his army and occupied Saxony.

Frederick's view had always been that any war in which Prussia was involved and which did not add to its territory would be a waste of men and resources. In 1756 he expected that the eventual outcome of this conflict would be the incorporation of Saxony into Prussia and the conquest of West Prussia, thus establishing territorial unity between the territories of Brandenburg, Pomerania and East Prussia. But these were not the motives for which he entered into the conflict, rather they were the prospects he entertained once he felt that for the sake of the survival of his own state he had to act, even if that action included ignoring diplomatic niceties such as a declaration of war.

The Saxon army was quickly encircled at Pirna, while an Austrian army under Field-Marshal Browne, intended to bring relief to the Saxons, was defeated by the Prussian army on 1 October 1756 at Lobositz in Bohemia. The Saxon army capitulated, and with the exception of its officers Frederick incorporated its 20,000 men into the Prussian army. In doing so he committed a serious mistake in not dispersing the Saxons over the entire Prussian army. The assumption that to the common soldier it does not matter under whose colours he fights as long as he gets his pay proved wrong. Later the Saxons deserted in entire formations.

By occupying Saxony Frederick gained an operational base as well as military and financial resources which he intended to exploit fully for the benefit of Prussia. With speed and efficiency he imposed the Prussian system of administration upon Saxony with the aim of extracting annually five million thalers from the country; Berlin not Dresden became the capital of Saxony.

After Lobositz Frederick was quick in withdrawing his forces from Bohemia, which he did not believe he would be able to hold during the winter. He was interested in making peace, and assured the French that he would not hold on to any piece of Saxon territory if peace could be made, but France in the face of serious losses at the hands of the British in North America was set upon compensating for these losses by eventually acquiring the Austrian Netherlands and perhaps even putting a hand on Hanover. It transformed its defensive alliance with Austria into an offensive one, which had been preceded on 2 February 1757 by the conclusion of an offensive alliance between Russia and Austria. The war aims of the allies were clearly spelt out: Prussia was to be defeated and divided up among its neighbours, with Silesia and some other smaller territory going to Austria, Magdeburg and Halle to Saxony, while Poland was to receive East Prussia and Russia Courland. Sweden too joined the anti-Prussian coalition; the brother in Berlin and the sister in Stockholm had been estranged for some time. The Holy Roman Empire of the German Nation declared war upon Prussia, that is to say its princes, because where the population at large stood was made abundantly clear on several occasions during that war.

It was a mighty coalition that had assembled against Frederick but it contained a number of intrinsic weaknesses. In the first instance, this coalition included too many mutually exclusive interests and was too heterogeneous in character to be able to maintain stability in the long term, though of course there was no guarantee that Frederick would not be defeated in the short term. In the second instance, and this was of immediate importance, with the appointment of William Pitt the Elder as George II's first minister, a statesman headed Great Britain's administration who put British interests before those of Hanover. In order to pursue relentlessly the war against the French overseas he was prepared to entrust the fortunes of Hanover to Frederick, thus strengthening Frederick's hand militarily, morally and financially (financially by Parliament granting him large-scale subsidies).

Originally Frederick's campaign strategy for 1757 had been to expect the enemy in Saxony and beat him there. But, mainly on Schwerin's advice, he moved two Prussian armies, one commanded by himself the other by Schwerin, into Bohemia towards Prague, the supply base of the Austrian army which confronted him. On 6 May 1757 the battle of Prague was fought in which Frederick applied his oblique order of battle but lacked the strength to envelop the enemy's flanks. Schwerin's army was in trouble because a General von Manstein had attacked prematurely and was thrown back by the Austrians. Signs of a rout were evident when Schwerin, as he had at Mollwitz, took hold of the regimental colours and at the head of his regiment stormed the Austrian positions. Under the murderous Austrian defensive fire the aged field-marshal was killed, his body entwined with the regimental colours. The Prussian army failed to carry out the oblique order of battle successfully, but the Austrians were thrown in the centre. The infantry attack was decisively supported by a spirited attack of the Prussian cavalry under General von Zieten. It was the bloodiest battle in the war so far and in the history of warfare. The Austrians alone lost over 15,000 men. However, these losses had not annihilated the Austrian army and its bulk withdrew into the fortress of Prague which Frederick now held under siege, expecting in vain that it would fall shortly. To starve the army out of Prague would take too long; for Frederick the battle had brought new fame but no political conclusion. To discourage the hopes of the besieged he decided for the moment upon attacking the Austrian army under Field-Marshal von Daun that was coming to the relief of Prague.

However, unlike at Hohenfriedberg Frederick did not possess the element of surprise. Daun expected him at Kolin and was well prepared with his army of 54,000 against Frederick's 33,000. In well-fortified positions Daun's men waited for the Prussians to attack; Frederick once again decided in favour of the oblique order of battle but again the over-hasty action of General von Manstein, who prematurely decided to initiate a cavalry attack, turned it into a battle over the entire front. Time and again the lines of the Prussian battalions advanced against the volleys of the Austrian army, time and again they were thrown back. When the Saxon cavalry regiments from Poland rode a devastating attack against the weakest link in the Prussian line of battle, the Prussian troops would no longer go forward. Frederick in person had gathered 40 men of the regiment of Anhalt-Bayreuth to attack when an Englishman, Major Grant, called to him, 'But Sire, do you intend to conquer the batteries on your own?'

The battle was lost for the Prussians; to turn it into a disastrous defeat would have been possible had Daun pursued the Prussian army. But cautious as he was the idea of pursuit did not appeal to him. The defeat at Kolin on 18 June 1757 gave Frederick's plan of campaign an entirely different face. He now had to give up Bohemia altogether; the siege of Prague was raised. Within his family doubts about Frederick's generalship were voiced. His brother, Prince Henry, on the evening of the battle wrote a letter to his sister Amalie: 'Phaeton has fallen, we do not know what will become of us.'

Moreover problems emerged elsewhere. The French had beaten the Hanoverian forces of the Duke of Cumberland, which put the Duke in a position where the wisest course was the conclusion of a convention according to which the British forces would be dissolved. Frederick dealt with that problem at once by returning to the tactic of the strategic defensive but combining it with the tactical offensive. A French army under Prince Soubise supported by troops of the Empire moved towards the river Saale intending to attack Frederick in Saxony. Frederick anticipated this attack with 20,000 of his own men against his opponent's 50,000. On 5 November 1757 at Rossbach the Prussian army attacked the enemy while it was still on the march. The attack demonstrated the high degree of mobility achieved by the Prussian army, which while itself on the march parallel to the French columns formed itself into attacking echelons without the slightest difficulty. The Prussian attack threw the French into confusion, confusion that was turned into a rout by the Prussian cavalry under General von Seydlitz which scattered the enemy in all directions. Henceforth the armies of France ceased to play a significant part in the Seven Years War in Central Europe.

'That battle,' said Napoleon, 'was a masterpiece. Of itself it is sufficient to entitle Frederick to a place in the first rank among generals.' The French guns, their colours, their baggage and their mistresses had fallen into the hands of the Prussian army. The victory of Rossbach had an immense psychological impact on Germany.

Never since the dissolution of the empire of Charlemagne, had the teutonic race won such a field against the French. The tidings called forth a general burst of delight and pride from the whole of the great family which spoke the various dialects of the ancient language of Arminius. The fame of Frederick began to supply, in some degree, the place of a common government and a common capital. It became a rallying point for all true Germans, a subject of mutual congratulation to the Bavarian and the Westphalian, to the citizen of Nuremberg. Then first was it manifest that the Germans were truly a nation . . .
(Macaulay)

Rossbach also symbolized the beginning of Germany's literary and cultural emancipation from the French – in spite of a Prussian King who culturally was rather more a French product than a German one. Rossbach was the Agincourt of the German people.

But not only in Germany was the effect widespread. In Macaulay's words:

Yet even the enthusiasm of Germany in favour of Frederick hardly equalled the enthusiasm of England. The birthday of our ally was celebrated with as much enthusiasm as that of our own sovereign; and at night the streets of London were in a blaze of illuminations. Portraits of the hero of Rossbach, with his cocked hat and long pigtail, were in every house. An attentive observer will, at this day [April 1842], find in the parlours of old-fashioned inns, and in the portfolios of printsellers, twenty portraits of Frederick for one of George II. The sign-painters were everywhere employed in touching up Admiral Vernon into the King of Prussia. This enthusiasm was strong among religious people, and especially among the Methodists, who knew that the French and Austrians were Papists, and supposed Frederick to be Joshua or Gideon of the Reformed Faith.

But Frederick had no time to enjoy his victory. While he was busy in Saxony the Russians were devastating East Prussia and Prince Charles of Lorraine had entered Silesia. Schweidnitz, Bevern and then Breslau fell into his hands. Forced-marching his army of 35,000 men towards Breslau, soldiers whose morale had been elated by a great victory, he arrived at the village of Leuthen west of the city on 4 December. On the evening of that day, after supper, he ordered all generals and commanding officers to come to his quarters, and addressed them:

Gentlemen! I have had you brought here, firstly, in order to thank you for your loyal services that you have rendered to the fatherland, and to me. I recognize them with feelings of deep emotion. There is hardly one among you who has not distinguished himself by great and most honourable feats. Relying on your courage and experience, I have prepared a plan for the battle that I shall, and must, wage tomorrow. I shall, against all the rules of the art, attack an enemy which is nearly twice as strong as ourselves and entrenched on high ground. I must do it, for if I do not all is lost. We must defeat the enemy, or let their batteries dig our graves. This is what I think and how I propose to act. But if there is anyone among you who thinks otherwise, let him ask leave here to depart. I will grant it him, without the slightest reproach . . . I thought that none of you would leave me; so now I count entirely on your loyal help, and on certain victory. Should I fall, and be unable to reward you for what you will do tomorrow, our fatherland will do it. Now go to the camp and tell your regiments what I have said to you here, and assure them that I shall watch each of them most closely. The cavalry regiment that does not charge the enemy at once, on the word of command, I shall have unhorsed immediately after battle and turned into a garrison regiment. The infantry regiment which begins to falter for a moment, for whatever reasons, will lose its colours and its swords, and will have the braid cut off its uniform. Now gentlemen farewell: by this hour tomorrow we shall have defeated the enemy, or we shall not see one another again.

The Austrians were spread out over a front of two kilometres in a defensive position, while Frederick's forces occupied a considerably shorter front. The Prussians succeeded in concentrating their main effort against the left wing of the Austrians who, instead of attacking the Prussians while they were still in the process of forming up, were content to wait and let them come. They also failed to recognize until it was too late where Frederick would attack. At first it seemed to the Austrians that the main force of the Prussian attack would be directed at their centre; then, before they realized what was happening, the Prussian troops re-formed and attacked the Austrian left flank. The oblique order of battle proved a complete success and Leuthen a resounding defeat for the Austrians. In a state of disorganization and chaos they left Silesia and withdrew into Bohemia. Frederick had once again secured his prize. On the evening of that day on that snow-covered blood-stained ground of Leuthen dimly lit by camp fires, among the groaning of the dying and wounded a voice began to sing and within seconds the entire Prussian army took up the hymn: 'Now thank thee all our Lord' – *der Choral von Leuthen*. Even Frederick, the religious sceptic, was deeply moved.

Elsewhere, too, Frederick was lucky; the Russian army which had invaded East Prussia withdrew behind Russia's borders after rumours – which proved to be false – of the death of Czarina Elizabeth. Prince Ferdinand of Brunswick took over command of the Hanoverian army which, contrary to the previous Convention of Klosterzeven, had not dissolved itself. He immediately took the initiative against what had remained of the French after Rossbach and by March 1758 the French were well beyond the left bank of the Rhine. A month later a new agreement was signed between Britain and Prussia in which both powers promised not to enter into a separate peace and Prussia was given an annual subsidy of £670,000.

Frederick believed that things were looking up again, that he could return to his original plan of attack against Austrian territory. But for 1758 he chose Moravia rather than Bohemia as his area of operations. He hoped to force Maria Theresa to make peace, by conquering the fortress of Olmütz, but Olmütz was not to be conquered and this compelled him once again to abandon the strategic offensive. The Russians had returned to Prussia, conquered Königsberg and compelled the city to pay homage to the Czarina. There was little that Frederick could do about East Prussia, but when the Russians approached the Neumark, bombarding Küstrin with their artillery, their objective became clear, namely to link up with the Austrian forces. This he had to prevent at all costs. On 25 August 1758 at Zorndorf Prussians and Russians encountered one another for the first time in a major battle. It lasted all day. The Russian infantry fought with the steadfastness and bravery, with a defiance of death that made even Frederick shudder. The Prussian battalions showed signs of exhaustion and at one point Frederick personally led his regiments into the attack. The Prussian Cavalry under General von Seydlitz, riding attack after attack once again stabilized the situation in favour of the Prussian army. The battle ended not because the Prussians had defeated the Russians but because night intervened. Short of ammunition, the Prussian army looked forward rather apprehensively to the renewal of the struggle on the following day, but next morning they registered with relief that the Russians had withdrawn, leaving behind 20,000 casualties, half of their original strength. The Prussians had lost 11,000 out of 36,000 men. Frederick had secured his objective of preventing the Russians from linking up with the Austrians.

Using the advantage of interior lines of communication, Frederick now turned towards the River Lausitz where Daun seriously threatened the Prussian army commanded by the King's brother, Prince Henry. The Austrian surprise attack upon Frederick's unfortified camp at Hochkirch during the night of 13 October, cured him of underestimating Daun. The Austrians captured more than 100 pieces of Prussian artillery. But Daun repeated his mistake of Kolin and failed to exploit his success. This allowed Frederick to grasp the initiative again and in the end keep control of Silesia as well as Saxony.

By the beginning of 1759 Frederick came to accept that because of limited resources of men and materials he could only fight a defensive war; to maintain his territory including Saxony. Manpower shortage slowly made itself felt in the Prussian army, and a number of the best generals had been killed. In his personal sphere he suffered tragedy; his favourite sister had died of gout, the family disease of the Hohenzollern family with which he himself had been afflicted since his thirty-fifth year. It was taking its toll of his own physical stamina. In the spring of 1759 the Russians renewed their attack, beating the Prussian forces under General Wedel in the Neumark and approaching Frankfurt-an-der-Oder. Frederick decided to attack them at Kunersdorf near

Frankfurt. On 12 August 1759 he had 53,000 men under his command; the combined force of Russians and Austrians numbered 70,000. The Prussian army concentrated its attack upon the Russians, who were waiting in well-entrenched positions with their artillery positioned upon the commanding heights of the north-east. Frederick again took recourse to the oblique order of battle, but the Russian commander, General Shaltikov, resourceful as he was, thought of an answer. By fortifying his centre heavily he made it virtually invulnerable to attack, enabling him to use the forces of the centre as reinfocements for either the left or right wings. Frederick attacked the Russian left wing across extremely difficult ground and the attack soon got bogged down in the Russian defensive fire. Attack succeeded attack, each suffering the same fate, the intervention of the Prussian cavalry being cut short when Seydlitz was wounded. Two horses were killed under the King. Then the Austrian cavalry commanded by Marshal Laudon, an officer whom Frederick had once rejected for service in the Prussian army, attacked and routed the Prussian forces. As at Zorndorf Frederick took up the colours of Prince Henry's regiment and shouting to his soldiers 'Lads, do you want to live eternally?' tried to lead a battalion into attack. When that failed he tried to form a defensive line, but the Prussian army was in disarray, fleeing back towards the river Oder in the west. The King himself was nearly captured by Cossacks.

The Prussian Army was beaten, and soundly at that. For the next 24 hours Frederick thought that his end, and the end of his state, had come. But while the King was in a state of utter defeatism, Prussian discipline reasserted itself. His adjudants collected what remained of the army again. It had lost 25,000 men, the Russians 19,000. Instead of Austrians and Russians venturing upon a common pursuit of the Prussian army they followed their different aims. Shaltikov over estimated the Prussian resources and after the losses he had sustained he was not prepared to sacrifice much more for Austria's benefit, while Daun was more interested in reconquering Silesia than in marching into Berlin. Russians and Austrians moved off in different directions. Frederick had also lost Dresden; Saxony now became the theatre of operations again. Only Prince Ferdinand of Brunswick in the west could show successes against the French. But Prussia's prospects remained gloomy. By the end of the year its situation seemed desperate and it seemed that it would no longer be able to carry on the war.

But the King carried on war as no European power has ever carried on war . . . He governed his kingdom as he would have governed a besieged town, not caring to what extent property was destroyed, or the pursuits of civil life suspended, so that he did but make head against the enemy. As long as there was a man left in Prussia, that man might carry a musket; as long as there was a horse left, that horse might draw artillery. The coin was debased, the civil functionaries were left unpaid; in some provinces civil government altogether ceased to exist. But there was still rye-bread and potatoes; there was still lead and gun powder; and, while the means of sustaining and destroying life remained Frederick was determined to fight it out to the very last. (Macaulay)

Shortages of every kind increased his wish for peace. Jointly with England he proposed peace negotiations in November 1759, but Austria, encouraged by her successes, rejected the proposal. On the contrary, to ensure the continued assistance of the Russians, she agreed that East Prussia should go to Russia, providing of course that Silesia became Hapsburg territory again.

Frederick failed to achieve his campaign objective for 1760, namely to recapture Dresden. Consequently he had to give up Saxony and withdrew into Silesia, while Prince Henry kept the Russians in check in the north-east. The Austrian armies under Daun and Laudon followed Frederick into Silesia and there, a year almost to the day since Kunersdorf, Daun and Laudon with their 90,000 men against Frederick's 30,000 planned a battle of annihilation by a concerted attack from three sides. Frederick, quick in recognizing the intention, evaded the manoeuvre and attacked Laudon's corps at Liegnitz, completely defeating it. Daun's innate caution reasserted itself and he abandoned his plan. Confidence resurged among the Prussians. Frederick thought that now he could force fate and attempt one more bid for Saxony. On 3 November 1760 he fought and won the battle of Torgau. But the weakness of his forces did not permit him to follow up this victory and achieve his actual objective, the capture of Dresden.

Since the death of George II in 1760, Pitt, Prussia's most faithful ally, had been hard pressed in the Lords and Commons by that faction which, after Britain had achieved supremacy in Canada, wished for peace. That wish was shared by France, Russia and Austria, who now agreed to Frederick's earlier suggestion of convening a peace congress at Augsburg. But because Frederick made Prussia's participation conditional on the acceptance of its demand that it should not lose any of its territory, the congress was never convened. Britain's ally now became the most serious obstacle to a much-desired settlement.

Frederick's lack of manpower resources was approaching dangerous proportions. Volunteer regiments were set up, while in the regular regiments two-thirds of the men were foreigners and cadets from the age of 14 were called into active service. With such devices Frederick managed to bring his army to a strength of about 100,000, but its offensive capacity was doubtful. Encamped at Bunzelwitz in Lower Silesia he awaited the attack of the enemy, an attack which could well have been the *coup de grâce* for his forces had not Daun overestimated the Prussian strength and refrained from attacking. But Laudon stormed Schweidnitz, the Russians took Kolberg, and set up their winter quarters in Pomerania. Both Prussians and Austrians set up theirs in Silesia, the Austrians for the first time since the First Silesian War. On 5 October 1761 Pitt resigned. Faced by the lack of alternatives other than his own and Prussia's destruction, Frederick began to evolve plans that moved into the realm of fantasy. One of them involved a simultaneous attack against the Hapsburg Empire and the Russians by the Turks.

Then, on 5 January 1762, a miracle happened that Frederick had not expected: the Czarina Elizabeth died and her nephew, the Duke of Holstein-Gottorp, became her successor, Peter III. Russia reversed its policy. Peter, an ardent admirer of Frederick, declared little more than a month later Russia's disinterest in all conquests and recommended to his allies a speedy conclusion of peace. Peace between Russia and Prussia was signed on 22 May 1762 on the basis of the *status quo ante bellum*. Precisely at this moment the alliance between Prussia and England was broken. Britain wanted peace and expected of Frederick that he cede Silesia. Frederick rejected the suggestion out of hand. His optimism had returned and with it plans to grasp the initiative. Together with the Russians he hoped to march against the Austrians. These hopes, however, were brought to nought by the deposal and murder of Peter III. The Russian forces received orders to return home. Hence most of the campaign of 1762, with the exception of the battle of Freiberg on 29 October in which the Austrians were defeated, followed the traditional eighteenth-century pattern of warfare, the strategy of attrition through manoeuvre and counter-manoeuvre.

Maria Theresa, too, felt that the war was exacting sacrifices hardly justified by the reconquest of one province. In fact, Austria faced financial ruin. Dire economic necessity compelled Austria and Prussia to agree on an armistice for the winter of 1762/3. Britain concluded its separate peace with France at Fontainebleau on 3 November 1762. This settlement had repercussions upon Prussia and Austria in the sense that for the first time peace negotiations were taken up, in the first instance between Prussia and Saxony. Frederick gave assurances that he would hand back what he still held of Saxony but without any indemnities. Ultimately these negotiations led to direct peace negotiations between Prussia and Austria and thus to the conclusion of the Peace of Hubertusburg. By that Frederick retained what first he had gained in 1740.

When in that year he had embarked upon this venture he was a minor king. He had become a great one by the spirit of sacrifice with which he defended that which he had robbed. However, the king that returned to war-weary but nevertheless cheering Berlin was devoid of any sense of greatness. He too was weary, so much so that he could not face his subjects. Avoiding the main avenues he entered the city through side streets, finding peace only in seclusion.

He had maintained his possessions; to reconstruct them and to restore the army were the immediate post-war tasks. With hardly a rest after the war he took it upon himself to travel through his provinces and personally discuss the regional problems, their amelioration and cure with the respective Chamber Presidents and *Landräte*. Six hundred thousand bushels of wheat, 408,000 bushels of oats and 35,000 horses were made available free of charge to the war-ravaged provinces. Within the first 12 months after the conclusion of peace Frederick spent six million thalers for purposes of reconstruction.

In 1764 Frederick began to build the first garrison in Berlin for soldiers hitherto quartered with the burghers. To utilize their services in the interests of the Prussian economy soldiers in garrisons were ordered to spin cotton yarn, and to maximize the number of troops petty criminals and vagabonds were pressed into their ranks. By 1776 the Prussian army numbered 187,000 men again, 90,000 of whom were Prussian subjects stationed in the heartlands of the Hohenzollern kingdom, while the rest, mainly in Prussia's western provinces, were other German or foreigners recruited voluntarily or pressed.

To put the economy back on a sound footing, the debasement of the coinage which had been necessary to carry on the war was stopped and public confidence restored by the withdrawal of all debased coins. Already by 1764 only sound coinage was in circulation. However, the restoration of Prussia's economy was seriously affected by a general crisis in trade and commerce which affected Amsterdam and Hamburg and had its repercussions in Berlin also. Yet precisely this crisis produced in Frederick the initiative for a plan which envisaged the concentration of all capital and money traffic in the hands of a central authority, as well as state planning and state control of trade and manufacture. The centre of the scheme was to be a central bank modelled on the Bank of England whose function would be to regulate and control all money traffic. Several large monopoly-holding companies were to be created to be associated with the bank, the centre of economic control. From that centre production was to be planned and regulated according to the general requirements. It was a vision of a modern form of state capitalism, but for the time being it remained no more than a vision. Although the bank was created – the *Giro-Diskonto-und Leihbank* – as well as several trading companies, the bank did not possess the teeth necessary to enforce its own rules. The new companies remained separate units rather than integrated parts of the structure envisaged. Vested interests against it were too strong and the merchants who were to raise the necessary capital were financially still too weak to do so. The General Directory was also opposed to the scheme. In a report of 1 October 1766 it alleged that these new institutions of the King were responsible for the general economic depression, a charge which Frederick promptly dismissed. Mercantilist that Frederick was, he aimed at the extension of internal trade, but even more at the expansion of the manufacturing industries, in order to reach the maximum possible economic self-sufficiency. Frederick's aim was one thing, that of the bankers, merchants and manufacturers another. Apart from being short of funds anyway, they were reluctant to invest large sums in a venture and a policy the outcome of which seemed rather uncertain. As Frederick put it, they were content to remain commissioners for foreign merchants and manufacturers, content in return for a moderate commission to conduct the business of the Dutch, the Hamburgers, Saxons and French, and supply the Prussian market with their goods. Frederick's plan had been to counteract this diffusion of capital by replacing the numerous small companies by a few which were strong enough to meet the competitive challenge; but their monopoly status he considered to be of a temporary nature only, for as long as it took to establish and consolidate themselves.

In some other economic ventures Frederick was more successful. The Berlin wool manufacturer Wilhelm Caspar Wegely had succeeded in buying from someone the secret of the manufacture of porcelain. In 1751 he founded his own factory in Berlin but had to give it up during the Seven Years War. While the Prussian troops were occupying Saxony they also acquired the secrets behind the Meissen porcelain and in 1760 the Berlin merchant Ernst Gotzkowsky founded a new porcelain factory which two years later already employed over 150 workers. When the problem of 'cash flow' began to affect him he was forced to sell; the purchaser was Frederick and the firm became the *Königliche Porzellanmanufaktur*, a prosperous enterprise which has remained so to this day.

In the field of agriculture he forced the expansion of potato planting, a vegetable which throughout Europe prevented a serious crisis in the supply of staple foods. Large-scale dairy farming was also promoted by Frederick especially in East Prussia where the royal domains represented one of the most progressive agricultural areas in Germany. While in the rest of Germany the number of cattle rose relatively slowly between 1756 and the turn of the century, in Brandenburg-Prussia it more than doubled. Sheep farming had to give way to cattle farming, the sheep farmers moving to the easternmost provinces of Prussia while cattle farmers took their place.

As a result of the dislocations of the Seven Years War the excise administration had suffered badly. Cases of embezzlement were not uncommon. To return it to its previous efficiency required a thorough overhaul of institution and personnel. Frederick separated the excise and tariff administration from the general administration of which they had been part. Within the General Directory he created the fourth department for excise and toll administration. For the Rhenish territories the third department fulfilled that function. Effective though the reform was, Frederick's employment of approximately 200 Frenchmen in leading positions in the excise administrations of the provinces met wide resentment. But Frederick believed that Prussia could substantially gain by the introduction of the rather more refined administrative practices used in France. The reform of the administration of the excise was accompanied by reform of the excise and tariff duties. While the excise on brandy, beer and meat was increased, that on flour was abolished. During the period 1766 to 1786 the result of these reforms in this particular field was a net increase of 23½ million thalers.

The excise was what it had always been – unpopular; that it was administered very largely by Frenchmen made it even more so, but there was nothing that could be done about it. Other measures were equally as unpopular but less successful in terms of the financial returns, such as the introduction of a state monopoly on coffee and tobacco.

The increased yield in the state revenue made it possible for Frederick to spend more than 40 million thalers for welfare purposes alone between 1763 and 1786, as well as stocking up the state treasure to 55 million thalers at the time of his death. During the 23 years of his reign that followed the Seven Years War he acquired the reputation of being everywhere, of controlling everything. He visited his provinces annually, first to inspect his troops, secondly to inspect his administration, thirdly to inspect his subjects, particularly those whom he had attracted to settle in Prussian territory. During the time of his reign Frederick settled 57,475 new families on the land, in terms of total population over 300,000 people. At the time of Frederick's death every fifth Prussian was a colonist. The population increases average $1\frac{1}{4}$ per cent per annum. No doubt the wars made serious inroads into the population, but whereas in 1756 Prussia had 4.1 million subjects, by 1775 this figure had risen to 4.5 million, excluding the territories annexed as a result of the Polish partition.

In the realm of foreign policy Frederick endeavoured to escape the danger of renewed isolation by concluding a new alliance with Russia on 11 April 1764. The King of Poland, Augustus III, had died the year before and so once again the Polish question moved into the international arena and became the bridge of a Prussian–Russian understanding. Obviously Russian predominance in Poland posed a mortal danger to Prussia. Austria, which after the conclusion of the Peace of Hubertusburg had established closer ties with France again, was equally averse to Russia's aims in Poland, as was France. The result was a rapprochement between Prussia and Austria, with Prussia representing the link between Russia and Austria. Frederick and Catherine were agreed that the new Polish King should not be a candidate of the French, Austrians or Saxons. Catherine's own candidate was one of her former favourites, Stanislav Poniatovski, who under Russian pressure was elected King of Poland in 1764. On the other hand, on the pretext of protecting the subjects of the Russian Orthodox church in Poland, the Czarina ensured the continued weakness of Poland by supporting the state of political anarchy in the country. When war broke out between Russia and the Ottoman Empire, Prussia had to honour its treaty obligations, which included paying subsidies to Russia. This in turn alarmed Austria and a Russo-Austrian war seemed imminent. As this would have involved Prussia actively on the side of Russia, it was therefore in Frederick's interest to avoid this by trying to mediate between St Petersburg and Constantinople. As a pre-condition of any peace the Turks insisted upon Russia returning the provinces of Moldavia and Walachia. To make this retrocession possible Frederick suggested as compensation the division of Poland between the three powers of Prussia, Russia and Austria. His own objective was West Prussia, the piece of territory that would round off the Prussian state in central Germany and make it into a territorial entity by linking Prussia with Brandenburg. A tricky and shameful piece of diplomacy culminated in the first Polish division of 1772 in which Prussia received West Prussia, but still without the cities of Danzig and Thorun. Former colonial territory was once again in German hands, while the first step had been taken in a process which was to wipe the Polish state off the map of Europe for over a century and a half. But that state and nation are not necessarily conterminous the people of Poland have demonstrated impressively: the state was dead, but the nation, by means of immense sacrifices, survived, forever an example to all those nations whose organic unity has been broken asunder with brute force by the politics of an epoch.

In West Prussia the existing Polish administrative and legal system was replaced by that of Prussia, German immigrants were encouraged, and serfdom, which under Polish and Russian conditions had amounted to abject slavery, was made to conform to Prussian standards. Education, especially in the countryside, was improved. Between 1772 and 1775, 750 schools were built; by 1778 there were 177 Protestant and 58 Catholic teachers employed in the Bromberg region (the present-day Bydgoszcz), with strong preference being given to those who could speak Polish in addition to their native German. Frederick's instruction to his successor to acquire a knowledge of Polish also dates from this period. This instruction was followed for almost a century. Every Prussian Crown Prince was required to know Polish, until the liberal Crown Prince Frederick in the case of his eldest son, the future Kaiser Wilhelm II, stopped it in the interest and pursuit of the Germanizing mission which was particularly pronounced among German liberals.

The other foreign policy problem that affected the later years of Frederick's reign originated over the question of the succession in Bavaria. With the death of the Elector Max Joseph the Bavarian line of the House of Wittelsbach became extinct. As so often before Austrian troops moved rapidly into Bavaria and occupied it – a belated compensation for Silesia. The Austrian Emperor Joseph II, trusting in his alliance with France on the one side and in Russia's preoccupation with the Turks on the other, believed that Frederick would not be prepared to make war on his own. But Frederick was prepared to accept the risk and in 1778 the old foes confronted one another again in Bohemia.[1] However, no serious battles were fought. The great powers of France, England and Russia were too busy elsewhere to have any wish to be drawn into a conflict in Central Europe. Hence as a result of Russo-French mediation Joseph II was persuaded to give in and after the conclusion of the Treaty of Teschen in 1779 Austria removed its troops from Bavarian soil – except for a small slip of territory along the right bank of the river Inn – while Frederick managed to gain acknowledgement for the claims of the House of Hohenzollern to the succession in the Franconian duchies of Ansbach and Bayreuth.

In 1780 Frederick's great antagonist Maria Theresa died. Her son, Joseph II, ambitious as he was, set the course for drastic domestic reforms, designed among other things to ameliorate the lot of the peasants, but also to centralize the institutions of the Hapsburg monarchy after the Prussian example and to ensure German predominance in the multinational Empire. Unwittingly his policies became the trigger of the national *risorgimento* of eastern Central Europe, especially among the Hungarians and the Czechs. The reaction was such that he had to abandon many of his original intentions. In his foreign policy he aimed at breaking up the alliance between Prussia and Russia, in which, however, he did not succeed.

Joseph II made one further bid for Bavaria, in return for the Austrian Netherlands. The new Elector of Bavaria, Charles Theodore of the Zweibrücken line of the House of Wittelsbach, had already been won over when Frederick objected to the violation of the Treaty of Teschen. Then in 1785 the League of the German Princes (the successor of the Schmalkaldic League and the precursor of the North-German Federation) came into being under Frederick's leadership, and this effectively blocked any further ambitious projects of Joseph's. In the face of increasing internal problems Joseph II's urge for internal reform and external expansion and consolidation was curbed.

A year later on 16 August 1786 Frederick died at 74 years of age. No other Prussian monarch has exercised such profound influence, far beyond the political sphere. The history of his reign is not merely the history of the emerging dualism between the two major powers in the Reich. Already during his lifetime his personality became for many the focal point of a reawakening of the German national consciousness. Through him the name of Prussia exercised the magnetism that attracted so many non-Prussians, among them almost all the members of the Prussian Reform Movement of 1807, to serve the Prussian state. Goethe, born in the Reich city of Frankfurt-am-Main, remarked that in his youth he had been 'Fritzisch' minded. 'What mattered Prussia to us? It was the personality of the Great King which affected the emotions of us all.' When after the Seven Years War preparations were made in Frankfurt for the election of Joseph II as Emperor of the Holy Roman Empire of the German Nation, Goethe, together with the rest of the Frankfurt population, stood at the roadside to cheer the arrival of the Prussian representative. 'All eyes were directed upon him. So high stood the King . . . in favour of the masses among which, in addition to Frankfurters, Germans from all regions were to be found.'

Goethe describes Frederick's effect upon German literature:

Germany, so long submerged by foreign peoples, permeated by other nations, in learned and diplomatic negotiations dependent on foreign languages, was unable to form its own . . . If one looks closely, what German poetry was lacking was content, national content; we were not lacking in talent. The first true and higher content entered into German poetry through Frederick the Great and the deeds of the Seven Years War . . . Every national poetry must be shallow, must become shallow, if it is not based upon the humanly unique, upon the events of the peoples and their shepherds . . . Kings have to be described in war and danger, in situations where they appear to be the first, because they decide the fate of the ultimate and therefore become much more interesting than the Gods themselves. In that sense every nation that has pride in itself must have an Epopöe, for which the form of the epic poem is not really necessary . . . The Prussians, and with them Protestant Germany, gained for their literature a treasure which lacked opposition and which even later efforts could not replace. They approached the great concept which the Prussian writers had of their King, and the more diligently they did so the less he under whose inspiration they worked wanted to know of them . . . Also, Frederick's dislike of German as a literary form proved fortunate. One did everything to be noticed by him, not in order to be respected by him but in order to capture his attention; one did it in the German fashion out of inner conviction. One did what one considered to be right, and wished and wanted that the King would recognize and esteem this German right. This did not happen and could not happen. Because how could one expect a King who wanted to enjoy life intellectually to waste his time in recognizing and enjoying as cultured and pleasurable that which he holds to be barbaric? . . . One work, however, the true product of the Seven Years War, of complete northern German National content, must be mentioned here as occupying a place of honour: Minna von Barnhelm . . . One recognizes easily how this piece of work has been created between peace and war, hate and deep attachment. It was this production which opened the eye to a higher more significant world . . .[The play Minna von Barnhelm by Gotthold Ephraim Lessing is set in the immediate post-war period and has as its major theme the conflict between the concept of honour of a Prussian officer and the apparent ingratitude of Frederick the Great.]

When Goethe stayed in Strassburg for the purpose of widening his horizons, he wrote:

Well we had not much to say in favour of the constitution of the Reich; we admitted that it consisted entirely of lawful misuses, but it rose therefore the higher over the present French constitution which is operating in a maze of lawless misuses, whose government displays its energies in the wrong places and therefore has to face the challenge that a thorough change in the state of affairs is widely prophesied. In contrast when we looked towards the north, from there shone Frederick, the Pole Star, around whom Germany, Europe, even the world seemed to turn . . .

Goethe was not the only contemporary who spoke and wrote of Frederick the Great in such terms. Without being aware of it, for the Germans he was culturally the great emancipator. Words of Frederick's rejection of German literature and culture are frequently quoted, yet with particular reference to literature he said on the eve of his death: 'I am like Moses, I can see the promised land, but I am too old to reach it.' Frederick was not absorbed by Prussia. As a private person and thinker he maintained his detachment, but without him Prussia would not have existed as a concept.

He represents the root cause of a process of abstraction consisting of norms of behaviour, attitudes and characteristics which acquired a life of their own, together with other postulates which had nothing to do with the King. They became an independent quantity, over which Frederick's name was imposed. It was a unique process, a thoroughly individualistic even narcissistic human being became the representative of a supra-individual attitude, an attitude depersonalized, motivated only by the state and the community and the individual's duty towards them.

Frederick William I had run through Berlin, swinging and wielding his cane upon the backs of the burghers shouting: 'You should not fear me, you should love me!' His son Frederick was not loved either; he was respected, admired and honoured. There must have been only a few who loved him. He reigned as the 'greatest curiosity of the century'. Life to him was the concrete, the empirically verifiable, for the concrete represented the challenge to change it according to his desire, his insight and his aims. This applied to his character as much as to his state or his attitude towards other states. As regards his personal conduct Frederick was honest enough to admit that he was what he was and what he wanted to be without trying to be an example to others, without caring what his contemporaries or later generations thought about him.

Whenever the predicate 'Great' is applied, it is a natural reaction to look immediately for the victims upon which that claim is based. If one is prepared to admit the attribute of greatness to Frederick, then let it be not because of his generalship or the battles he won, but for the stamina and dignity he showed in adversity. He was the last of Seneca's disciples upon a Hohenzollern throne, even though Epicurus supplied some lighter touches to that otherwise ascetic appearance clad in shoddy uniform, a figure bent in pain over his cane, a face clear and severe, dominated by the penetrating gaze of his eyes.

Notes
1. Frederick was determined to prevent any further Hapsburg aggrandisement in Germany.

Chapter 7

Prussian absolutism in crisis

With the death of Frederick the Great ended a phase of the political development of the Prussian state which had begun with the reign of the Great Elector. Within a century and a half a state had been formed, but not only that, it had developed its own specific character, unique within the context of the Age of Enlightened Absolutism. Frederick as King, like his father, had demonstrated the professional aspect of monarchy in a manner which could hardly be continued or surpassed. His figure stands at the end of a thousand years of European history, at the beginning of which period there was interdependence between crown and church while at the end royal dignity had become entirely secularized. Frederick William I had still considered himself a servant of God; not so his son, whose concept of royalty was entirely secular yet ennobled through the monarch's own absolute subjugation to his duty to the state.

The role of the monarch had changed profoundly in the Age of Enlightened Absolutism. No longer was his role determined by the consciousness of the divine origin of his office but by his ability to rule his subjects. One of the inherent consequences of this change was one of potentially revolutionary character. No dynasty could expect to produce a trinity of such high ability as was shown by the Great Elector, Frederick William I and Frederick the Great, and lack of ability was bound to lead at least to the demand to transform the absolute monarchy into a constitutional one, a move which while removing the monarch from public criticism set quite clearly defined limits on his power. Furthermore, a state built upon the principles of the Enlightenment removes the influence of the estates and with it the traditional boundaries to its power. In other words, there is no longer any area left free from state intervention or, so to speak, from reform from above. The resulting inevitable infringement of ancient liberties by the state was bound to collide with the principles of liberty as advocated by the Enlightenment. Indeed the Enlightenment saw in the enlightened despot the executor of its principles; it used enlightened absolutism as much as the latter used the Enlightenment. As the example of Frederick the Great eloquently demonstrates, the monarch himself determined which reforms he desired and which could in practice be accomplished.

Again as Prussia shows, enlightened absolutism seen from an economic perspective was an attempt to catch up economically with countries such as Great Britain. Prussia's rigid mercantilist policies pursued this objective, yet towards the end of the reign of Frederick the Great and even more so under his successors a younger generation of administrators such as Stein argued that this objective could be achieved only by greater economic liberty, by the introduction of the principles of free trade, leaning heavily on Adam Smith.

There is no doubt that the implementation of the policies of en-lightened absolutism was a revolutionary process, during the course of which structural social changes took place, such as the rise of middle class in Prussia and the improved status of the peasantry (although throughout the nineteenth century the nobility managed to preserve a privileged position). Since the ideal of enlightened absolutism was the welfare of the community it was bound to clash with the principle of the liberty of the individual, the ideal of the Enlightenment. These con-tradictions are inherent in the alliance between the Enlightenment and enlightened absolutism, and dominated Prussian politics during the reign of Frederick William II and the decades thereafter until the forces of restoration temporarily reasserted themselves.

Any successor of Frederick was bound to be measured by the yardstick he had established and to fall short. Inevitably he would stand in the shadow of the Great King. Even more so when the successor was a man of the character of Frederick William II. 'The much beloved', as Berliners used to call him because of his paramours, or 'fat William', because of the width of his girth as well as his truly Herculean proportions, was the son of a younger brother of Frederick, Prince Augustus William and his wife Princess Louise Amalie of Brunswick-Bevern, the sister of Frederick's wife. After the death of Augustus William his son Frederick William, born in 1744, was next in line of succession. Like all Prussian princes he was compelled to participate actively in the profession of arms and in his early years at least seems to have made a good impression upon his uncle, an impression which Frederick was to revise a year before his death when he said to his minister Hoym: 'I will tell you what will happen after my death: there will be much merry-making at court, my nephew will squander the treasure and let the army degenerate. Women will rule and the state will come to ruin. Then you will have to say to the King: "This is impossible! The treasure is the country's, not yours!" And if my nephew reacts with anger, then you tell him "It is *I* who have ordered it!" Perhaps this will help because he has not a bad heart . . .'

When Frederick William came to the throne in 1786 at the age of 42, he was already too set in his ways for them to be changed by the assumption of the duties of high office. The strict regime of Frederick gave way to greater flexibility which in the course of a few years blended into carelessness and neglect. By removing the state monopoly on coffee and tobacco he temporarily made himself widely popular among the population. But after a while the very same population could not fail to note that, as Mirabeau described it, 'the King remained faithful to his preference for the theatre, the concert, to his old and new mistress. One was astonished also that for hours he could examine paintings, furniture, shops or play the violincello or listen to the intrigues of the ladies at court while having obviously so very little time to listen to his ministers who under his eyes guided the interests of the state.' It was also Mirabeau who noted about the monarch that instead of trying to raise the populace to a higher level 'he stepped down to it'. His reign was the classic case demonstrating that absolute monarchy is as strong and as absolute as the monarch himself – or as weak.

The combination of Prussia's social structure (reflecting in turn its economic base and military necessities) and its foreign policy had, under the sometimes forceful guiding hand of two monarchs, produced a degree of stability and integration that could hardly have been foreseen a hundred years earlier. Yet, although aristocracy and peasants were still the main components of society, the growth of the towns brought forth a middle class which as yet had to find its place in an essentially agrarian-orientated state.

The last third of the eighteenth century saw a rise in land values which specifically in Prussia gave an uplift to a speculative agrarian capitalism with the inherent tendency of giving greater economic independence to the Prussian landed nobility. At the same time, the slow but steady growth of industrialization favourably affected the middle class. As both aristocracy and, to a lesser extent, the middle class were represented in the Prussian bureaucracy, unmistakable signs of the latter's growing self-confidence became frequent, signs which Frederick the Great had duly noticed and endeavoured to counteract. Succeeded by an incomparably weaker monarch, the power of the crown declined; the death of Frederick the Great was also the end of royal absolutism in Prussia. Into its place stepped bureaucratic authoritarianism, rule by a bureaucracy whose implicit task it was to administer the state in such a manner as to prevent the eruption of civil unrest.

Under Frederick William, Prussia experienced its *belle époque* during which Berlin became a flourishing centre of culture and education. And as education was not the privilege of the aristocracy but became increasingly dominated by the intellects of the middle class, their opinions found greater articulation, culminating in an enthusiastic adulation of the principles of the French Revolution – an adulation, however, which when these principles were extended beyond the boundaries of France in the interest of Napoleonic expansionism, was to turn into the very opposite sentiment. At the turn of the eighteenth century the general tendency in Prussia's bureaucracy seemed to be towards a decline in the position and status of the aristocracy of birth in favour of a middle class – and without the revolution such as France had experienced. Already under Frederick the Great, but much more so under Frederick William II, the influx of middle class blood into the bureaucracy tended on the one hand to dilute the existing blue blood, if this had few other qualifications to recommend it, on the other hand to raise members of the middle class to the same level as their social superiors by means of a shared higher education. Their common aim was to prevent erratic royal interference and to ensure the continuity of administration as well as personal security by obtaining security of tenure and pensions by right, rather than as a demonstration of royal favour. Security of tenure was achieved by the Code of 1794, though its final draft had been prepared and available since 1784, two years before the death of Frederick the Great. The granting of pensions by right had to wait until 1820. In general, the period between 1786 and 1806 is one in which a socially heterogeneous bureaucracy established its ascendancy, placing the King under the law and transforming the executive arm of royal absolutism into an autonomous bureaucratic body. However, during this period this transfer of power had little effect on the over-centralized structure of the Prussian bureaucracy. Without the personal drive of the monarch it stagnated and consequently the defeat of the remains of the Frederician state in 1806 meant that the task of reconstruction involved a fundamental reappraisal as well as a reconstruction of Prussia's social structure and its political institutions. In contrast to the situation in 1730 Prussia's middle class could now be seen to be clearly emerging – as demonstrated by the role it played in the bureaucracy.

The most significant piece of legislation enacted during the reign of Frederick William II was the Code of 1794, the *Allgemeine Preussische Landrecht*. Yet in the words of that most incisive analyst of his time, Alexis de Tocqueville,

Of all the works of Frederick the Great, the least known, even in his own country, is the code drawn up by his orders, and promulgated by his successor. Yet I doubt whether any of his other works throws as much light on the mind of the man or on the times in which he lived, or shows so plainly the influence which they exercised one upon the other.

This code was a real constitution in the ordinary sense of the word. It regulated not only the mutual relations of citizens, but also their relations to the state. It was a civil code, a criminal code and a charter all in one.

It rests, or appears to rest, on a certain number of general principles, expressed in a highly philosophical and abstract form and which bear a strong resemblance in many respects to those which are embodied in the Declaration of the Rights of Man in the Constitution of 1791.

The Code of 1794 indeed represents the final phase of the judiciary reform initiated by the predecessors of Frederick the Great. He had resumed this task after the Seven Years War when Cocceji's reforms were extended throughout the kingdom. Cocceji had planned a general codification of the laws of Prussia but it had been a task for which he had not lived long enough. Frederick therefore entrusted the Silesian minister of justice von Carmer with it, and Carmer together with another Silesian councillor, Suarez, continued it until in the hands of

Suarez and Klein it was concluded and finally promulgated. The Code does not by any means represent new law but merely the codification of existing laws which because of their diverse origins, in themselves a reflection of the diverse territorial acquisitions of the Hohenzollerns, had caused many contradictions and sometimes even injustice. The intention was to create a law book free from contradiction and unclearness, understandable to all, capable of supplying the answers to all practical legal problems. Therefore the Code did not consist of an enunciation of general principles, but of laws intended to cover all conceivable situations. Precisely this approach, the concentration on every detail, had been a major cause of the long delay in the Code and when Frederick the Great received the first draft he understandably commented 'But this is very thick; laws must be short and not copious.'

Even de Tocqueville described it as something of a monster. But it is also a major document demonstrating the transition of Prussia from the Age of Absolutism towards an age in which subjects became citizens. The Code represents a posthumous constitutional gift by Frederick to an age in which the political and social conditions that had given birth to the code in the first place were waning. 'The paradox in this law work consists in the fact that as a theoretical design it was far ahead of the social reality that gradually became more permeable, while in its execution this reality was codified through a vast number of laws which hindered the development of that which was envisaged, or even contradicted it.' (R. Kosselek)

Theoretically the Code, or what de Tocqueville sees as a constitution, was based on a social contract in which individuals part with their natural rights only in so far as this is necessary for the state to ensure the free development of their personality, their prosperity, their education and their private happiness. From that derive a number of basic rights: protection of person and property, equality before the law, independence of the judiciary, equality of the sexes, liberty of religion and of conscience, the right to education and the pursuit of one's own happiness, 'general rights of mankind' which determine and limit the task and the duties of the state. In the final draft Suarez, influenced by the First Constitution of the French Revolution, argued that it was impossible to deny man the right to develop his abilities and to deploy all the qualities he had been given by nature in the pursuit of his own happiness. These natural and inalienable rights would remain with man after his transition into a bourgeois society and there could be no legislative power which possessed the right to deprive him of these. This also meant pruning royal sovereignty, especially in its interference in the judiciary process. In the promulgated version of the Code Frederick William II had this clause eliminated; nevertheless the tendency is clearly visible to create a *Rechtsstat*, a state based upon law, in which liberal basic laws are made binding upon the monarch as well as the judiciary and the administration.

Even the final version of the code

makes no allusion to any hereditary rights of the sovereign, nor to his family, nor even to any particular right as distinguished from that of the state. The royal power was already designated by no other name than that of the state.

On the other hand, it alludes to the rights of man, which are founded on the natural right of everyone to pursue his own happiness without treading on the rights of others. All acts not forbidden by natural law, or a positive state law, are allowable. Every citizen is entitled to claim the protection of the state for himself and his property, and may defend himself by using force if the state does not come to his defence. (de Tocqueville)

But the actual application of the Code differed rather from its underlying liberal philosophy. Prussian society according to the Code is still essentially envisaged as an organic growth, a corporate structure of estates of times past, rather than a growing bourgeois society. It remains the old three-tier system of peasants, burghers and nobility. Each tier has its own substructure. But whereas in the Middle Ages, for instance, this type of society gave to each of its estates and their subgroups their own privileges, and to some extent even legal autonomy, the Code deprived them of these and subordinated them to the purposes of the state, a state which as a conceptual abstraction was conterminous with the general welfare of all its components. Hence the Code carried in itself the contradiction between a traditional society and a bourgeois-liberal constitution. All estates were directed towards the state as the focal centre for their activity. Hence a paradox again that for the purpose of achieving ultimately liberal ends, traditional norms of social, political and economic behaviour were transformed into legal decrees which regulated all these aspects down to the smallest detail. Once again we see a typical example of the traditional policy inaugurated by Frederick William I, that of the institutional absorption of social, economic and political conflict in order to maintain and strengthen the state.

Again de Tocqueville's discerning eye saw the forces of the future at work in the Code: the tendency towards a centrally directed democracy, even towards a state socialism.

By the side of this work, which was more than half borrowed from the Middle Ages, are provisions whose spirit borders on socialism. Thus it is declared that it devolves on the state to provide food, work and wages for all who cannot support themselves, and have no claim for support on the lord or the community; they must be provided with work suited to their strength and capacity. The state is bound to provide establishments for relieving the poor. It is authorized to abolish establishments which tend to encourage idleness, and to distribute personally to the poor the money by which these establishments were supported. (de Tocqueville)

The *Allgemeine Preussische Landrecht* was a paradox – but which written or unwritten constitution is free from them? The American Constitution at a most critical point in time had no clear answer as to where sovereignty resided – in the nation, as the preamble in the phrase of 'We the people' would suggest, or in the several states, as would the method of its ratification suggest. The United States found an answer, though not a constitutional one: force.

But in spite or even because of the paradoxes and ambivalences which the Code contained, it also contained the potential for, on the one side increasing liberalization through gradual reduction and ultimate elimination of the privileges and rights of the estates, and on the other a social welfare state which absorbed in its service the liberated energies. As has been correctly observed, neither of these alternatives actually came about. What did happen was the further continuation of a state directed by a more or less authoritarian bureaucracy which according to issue, interests and situation was backed or opposed by the traditional estates, and at the economic level endeavoured to develop a liberal society.

When the Code was promulgated it was noticed only by a few. 'Lawyers were the only persons who studied it; and even in our own time there are many enlightened men who have never read it' (de Tocqueville).

Much more noted was the King's private life. Almost 20 years before he came to the throne he had formed a deep liaison with Wilhelmine Enke, the daughter of a horn-player in the royal orchestra. What she lacked was education; what she did not lack was a high degree of intelligence. The formal instruction Frederick William gave her personally as well through teachers, transformed an urchin into a lady of considerable refinement and distinction whose common sense was not without influence in the affairs of state. Like his uncle, Frederick William had been forced into marriage. By his marriage to Princess Elizabeth of Brunswick he had one daughter, and his second marriage to Princess Frederica of Hesse produced seven children. But at the same time he continued his relationship with Wilhelmine who bore him five children. He ended the liaison six years before coming to the throne as a result of the influence of the Order of the Rosicrucians, a secret order which considered itself as an opposing force to the Freemasons – of which, incidentally, Frederick the Great had been a Grand Master – and to the ideas of the Enlightenment. But while the physical relationship was terminated, the friendship between the two continued to the end of his life and she never seems to have misused her influence. In 1794 he had her made Countess of Lichtenau and he provided well for her and her children.

Yet though he relieved his conscience by discounting his sexual relationship with Wilhelmine he was quick in burdening it again with a number of other affairs, two of them morganatic marriages to the Queen's ladies-in-waiting Julie von Voss and Countess Sophie

Dönhoff. As in the case of the marriage of Margrave Philip of Hesse, who knew his scripture well and appealed to Luther and Melanchthon to have his polygamy confirmed, so in the case of Frederick William and Countess Sophie a consistory was convened and on the basis of the opinion submitted by Melanchthon more than two .centuries before agreed to a ceremony of marriage sanctioned by the church.

Frederick the Great, like his father, had been his own minister of finance. Frederick William II showed no such inclination, nor any interest in being his own minister of war. In spite of the ultimately serious consequences, the waning of the tough discipline which had characterized Prussia under Frederick William's two predecessors was not entirely without benefit. A fresher, freer air blew through the streets of Berlin. The literary salons flourished in the capital of Prussia and the arts in general experienced an upward trend. There would not be a Brandenburg Gate in Berlin (completed in the same year in which the Bastile was stormed) had it not been for Wilhelmine Enke who discovered Johann Gotthard Langhans who designed and built it – as indeed she discovered many another artistic talents. The sculptor Schadow reached his peak of creativity during this period. The Academy of the Sciences received a substantial injection of new blood, this time German blood, in contrast to the reign of Frederick the Great when the majority of its members had been Frenchmen.

To be sure Prussia's *belle époque* has its origins during the reign of Frederick the Great when the literary salons of Rachel Levin and Henriette Herz, both Prussians of the Jewish faith, gathered Berlin's intellectual talents while Friedrich Nicolai, the editor of the widely read *Allgemeine Deutsche Bibliothek*, Moses Mendelsohn, an influential popularizer of the ideas of the Enlightenment, and Lessing left their mark upon the Enlightenment in Prussia. In the realm of philosophy Immanuel Kant, Johann Georg Hammann and Johann Gottfried von Herder were making their contributions, pushing forward to new dimensions. What under Frederick the Great had been a beginning reached its full blossoming, influencing Schleiermarcher, Kleist, the brothers Humbolt and many others whose subsequent work was to shape the culture and the political fortunes of Prussia. Literary and scientific clubs and circles began to proliferate, like the 'Monday Club' of which Lessing and Mendelsohn were members, and the 'Society for the Friends of the Natural Sciences', which met weekly. Both had already existed during the reign of Frederick the Great. On the initiative of Suarez a 'Wednesday Society' was founded in 1793, having among its members famous doctors like Marcus Herz, the sculptor Schadow and the actor Iffland. Lessings plays *Emilia Galotti* and *Nathan the Wise* (the latter was a plea for tolerance and reconciliation between Jews and Christians) were first performed before these societies. Another society, the 'Society for the Friends of Humanitarianism', had as its expressed aim the reform of the Prussian school system.

But these activities were not limited to the capital. One finds them throughout the provinces of the Prussian kingdom, acquiring and building up extensive libraries, and even introducing mobile lending libraries to reach the countryside. Officers of the Herzog von Braunschweig regiment in Halberstadt were members of a society professing pacifist aims, who did not hold back their disapproval once Prussia involved herself in the French revolutionary wars. All this was accompanied by the spread of newspapers, which began to transform themselves from purveyors of official court news to purveyors of political, cultural and economic news added to which was much critical comment.

When Wilhelm Iffland became director of the Royal Playhouse in Berlin Schiller's plays gained immense popularity, while the operas of Gluck and Mozart conquered the operatic stage. Gottfried Schadow, Karl von Gontard and Friedrich Gilly further developed and refined Knobelsdorff's architectural style, thus preparing the foundations upon which Karl Friedrich Schinkel was to complete his classicist style during the early decades of the nineteenth century.

The domestic policy of Frederick William II and his ministers added little that was new; on the whole it amounted to a process of diluting Frederician principles not because they set out deliberately to do so, but because letting things slide was so much more comfortable for all concerned. But there was one area where this was not the case, and that was religion. The Lutheran church in Prussia, as the result of benevolent neglect by Frederick the Great, was showing signs of decay and much needed to be reformed. Frederick William entrusted that reform to his close confidant Wöllner, another Rosicrucian. Wöllner got to work, insisting upon complete Lutheran orthodoxy among the clergy, free from all influences of the Enlightenment. Insistence upon orthodoxy also prevailed in the teaching profession, and by the end of Frederick William's reign had invaded even the press which so far had been free from censorship. But at the same time Prussia opened doors for the advancement of Jews, doors that had hitherto been closed to them (the fact that Frederick the Great's army had even one Jewish general was the exception to the rule). In Frederick's reign the Jews had served him a useful purpose but he was never free from an instinctive dislike of them and had burdened them with considerable financial and economic duties. In Berlin, every Jewish couple prior to their wedding was compelled to buy a specific amount of porcelain ware from the Royal Porcelain Manufacturer (KPM), a company which in private hands had been at the point of ruin when it was bought up by Frederick. Unwittingly this onerous duty led to many Jewish families in Berlin having some of the best porcelain collections in Germany. Under Frederick William II the decrees upon which this and similar duties were based were not revoked but simply ignored. Berlin's Jews enjoyed a better and freer atmosphere and in general a change in attitude developed which culminated in the laws for Jewish emancipation during the Reform Movement.

Prussia's foreign policy at first remained very much within the pattern established by Frederick the Great. Count Hertzberg, who guided the course of this policy under Frederick William II, continued to base it on the assumption that Prussia's eternal enemy was and would remain Austria and therefore the League of the German Princes was to be an instrument for the maintenance of the constitution of the Reich. In practice this meant the maintenance of the political and territorial *status quo* within the Holy Roman Empire. By contrast one of Prussia's allied princes, Duke Charles Augustus of Saxe-Weimar, the prince whose friend and counsellor was Goethe, endeavoured to turn the league into an instrument for the reform of the constitution. A precondition to the necessary reforms was the transformation of the league into a closer association under Prussia's leadership, very similar to what the North German Confederation was to be. But Hertzberg rejected this idea and instead envisaged a Northern League to balance the Austro-French alliance, the core of this league being an alliance with Great Britain. A development favourable to this plan occurred in 1787 with the revolution in Holland against the House of Orange. Behind the republicans opposing Prince William V, whose wife was a sister of Frederick William II, stood France; behind the House of Orange and its supporters, Great Britain. By making use of Prussia's military resources, comprising an army of 20,000 men under the command of the Duke of Brunswick, William V was returned to The Hague. France's influence in Holland suffered a severe setback, that of Great Britain dominated. For Prussia the only gain was an alliance with Holland in April 1788 which was supplemented by one with England in August of the same year.

Hertzberg seemed to have achieved his aim at a time when the situation appeared to be very favourable towards Prussia. Both Austria and Russia were engaged in a war against the Ottoman Empire which diverted their attention from Central Europe while in the Hapsburg Empire the centralizing tendencies of Emperor Joseph II created serious unrest in Bohemia and Hungary. The Austrian Netherlands, too, were in a state of unrest and violence, caused by the striving towards separate statehood. This was actively supported by Prussia. Hertzberg sought to exploit the problems confronting Austria to Prussia's benefit, specifically to obtain possession of Thorun and Danzig together with part of the province of Posen from Poland. War between Prussia and Austria seemed imminent when on 20 February 1790 Emperor Joseph II died. His successor Leopold II approached Frederick William II with the aim of starting negotations. Their result was the Convention of Reichenbach of 1790 by the terms of which Prussia was to cease supporting separatist movements in the Austrian Netherlands and in Hungary, while Austria, pressed by Great Britain and Prussia, agreed to an armistice in its war against Turkey with the prospect of a peace without territorial annexations. For Prussia it was an empty diplomatic victory. It yielded no practical returns and

Hertzberg's policy had only caused expense. On the other hand it put an end to the League of the German Princes, or any attempt to transform it into an instrument for the reform of the Reich.

However, there was one power that had not participated in the Convention of Reichenbach and which was insistent on further pursuing its own aims: Russia. Catherine successfully continued the war against Turkey on her own and was not prepared to make peace without achieving territorial gains. Frederick William II made preparations for an offensive into Livonia while the Royal Navy was to attack in the Baltic as well as in the Straits of the Dardanelles. But the ascendancy of Fox over Pitt, due to the growing unpopularity of the latter, caused a change in British policy. Prussia was compelled to stop its preparations against Russia, while Catherine the Great forced the Turks to make peace at Jassy in 1792 involving considerable losses of Ottoman territory. Diplomatically at least, Prussia had been defeated.

The true significance of the Convention of Reichenbach, however, lies in the way in which it caused a fundamental reversal in Prusso-Austrian relations. Since 1740, for over half a century, antagonism had been their characteristic feature. Reichenbach inaugurated a policy of alliance and co-operation between the two major German powers which continued 50 years. One of the external factors making for this development was the outbreak of revolution in France in 1789, which made particularly those monarchic powers whose territories bordered directly onto France realize the common interest they had to defend against the forces of revolution. In Prussia Hertzberg's influence was at an end, while that of Bischoffswerder, another Rosicrucian associate of Wöllner, increased. It was his aim to establish a common front against revolutionary France, the main pillar of which was to be an alliance between Prussia and Austria. A preliminary alliance was concluded on 25 July 1791 which dealt with two aspects. Firstly, Poland's integrity was to be respected in principle; it was to be reformed and transformed from an elective monarchy, into one of a hereditary character under the Saxon dynasty. Secondly, Prussia expressly gave its backing to Leopold's II Padua Circular, which had been addressed to all the courts of Europe and called for consolidated action in support of France's royal family. Frederick William II, believing that the French revolutionary army could be dispersed by disciplined Prussian troops much in the same way as the Dutch revolutionaries had been a few years before, actively supported a policy of war against revolutionary France. On 7 February 1792 Prussia and Austria concluded a formal alliance in which Prussia promised 20,000 men in support of the war against France. Although Leopold II died on 1 March 1792, his successor Francis II received the French declaration of war on 20 April 1792.

Catherine the Great thought this moment opportune to obtain easy gains in Poland, especially since she was aware that Frederick William for his part had similar ideas for the further aggrandizement of Prussia. Austria would have preferred to see a restoration of Poland as envisaged in its preliminary alliance with Prussia, for this would have contained Russia as well as Prussia. But Russia was already moving troops into Poland in 1792. Prussia came to an understanding with Russia about a further partition of Poland without prior consultation with Austria, and Russia's invasion of Poland was followed by a Prussian invasion in 1793, each power occupying the territories it wished to annex. Austria was seriously offended, but there was little it could do to reverse the *de facto* annexation of Danzig, Thorun and the regions of Posen, Gnesen and Kalish, 2,716 square kilometres containing 1,130,000 inhabitants. In the face of the rape of their country patriotic Poles made one last stand under Thaddeus Kosciuszko. They gathered their remaining strength and dissipated it in one mighty uprising which ended with the defeat of the Polish cause by November 1795. The rising was treated as an attempt at revolution, with the consequences usually attendant upon such occurrences when they fail. Vast confiscation of land took place in Prussian-occupied Poland, characterized by greed and corruption among the higher echelons of the Prussian civil service. In the meantime Francis II had recognized the second division of Poland of 1793 securing for himself the Galician region, a division formally recognized by a treaty concluded between Austria, Russia and Prussia on 24 October 1795. The internal instability which had characterized Poland for more than a century and a half had given cause for many to ask the question as to how long Poland would last as a sovereign state. This question was of course aggravated by the rise of Russia in the east and Prussia in the west. With that development Poland's days as a great European power were numbered. And as our own century has shown, the existence of a buffer state with the ambitions of a great power contains too many contradictions to ensure its independence.

No similar ambitions could be realised in the west. In 1792 Frederick William had felt himself the major representative of the German cause against that of the Gaul, and in moments of enthusiasm he spoke of reversing the rape of Alsace and Lorraine. The campaign began well enough. The allied armies under the command of the Duke of Brunswick captured Longwy and Verdun, marching in the direction of Paris. But contrary to expectations based upon reports from French emigrants, the people of the territories captured did not consider the allies as their liberators, a truth driven home dramatically by the cannonade of Valmy. In effect the Duke of Brunswick lost his campaign, the French royal couple their heads. French revolutionary forces penetrated to the left bank of the Rhine.

In the spring of 1793 the war of Prussia and Austria against France was formally transformed into a war of the Empire against France. The Duke of Brunswick once again captured parts of the left bank of the Rhine, but through lack of co-ordination in the planning of their operations every one of the allied armies acted as it thought fit without much consultation with the others. By the end of the year French forces were again on the offensive. In protest against the Austrians' lack of co-operation with the Prussian forces the Duke of Brunswick had resigned his command, and in 1794 the continuation of the war in the west was in doubt. The Duke was replaced by Field-Marshal von Möllendorf, one of the veterans of Frederick the Great's army. Now the financial effects of Prussia's *belle époque* made themselves felt: the state treasure of 50 million thalers which Frederick the Great had left behind was spent. Prussia was in need of foreign subsidies if it meant to continue the war. Negotiations with Great Britain over this problem were initiated, but yielded no conclusive results. The Prussian army was ordered to return home except for the 20,000 men stipulated in the Austro-Prussian alliance. When a British monthly subsidy of £50,000 was finally forthcoming Prussia agreed to leave 62,400 men in the west. But the subsidy was accompanied by the express stipulation that they should operate in the interest and according to the wishes of the sea powers of Great Britain and Holland. That touched the very core of Prussia's self-esteem, which had risen considerably in the previous decades. Continuous quarrels between Prussian and British leaders resulted, and these reached such a pitch that the British discontinued their subsidies. Moreover, in spite of Prussian victories such as that at Kaiserslautern in May 1794, in the overall conduct of the campaign the French armies demonstrated a clear superiority over their eastern opponents, and in response to the Polish rising of the same year the Prussian army left the west. The Peace of Basle ended Prussia's participation in the war for the time being.

The campaign had also left its mark on Frederick William II. His health deteriorated rapidly and a long illness ensued during which he was cared for with unsurpassable dedication by his first love, Wilhelmine Enke, the Countess of Lichtenau, until he died aged 53 on 16 November 1797.

No one will understand how Frederick William III became what he did become. He did not witness the happiness radiated by a happy marriage and yet was the best of husbands, he did not enjoy the fortune of paternal love and yet was the most loving of fathers. He received his education at a time when free thinking and derision of piety were the order of the day and yet he was a pious prince; his feelings awakened at a time when shameless libertinage spread over all the estates, but he remained free from infection. In face of all temptations he remained a virtuous man. (Johann Carl Kretzschmer)

This judgement by one of his contemporaries immediately after his death throws some light upon the salient features of the King's personal life. Born on 3 August 1770, in his early formative years he still experienced the Frederician state. Frederick the Great himself, in view of the low expectation he had of his nephew, held the opinion that his grand nephew would one day have the task of beginning anew his own work. Therefore, deliberately excluding the influence of the Crown

Prince – who showed little sign of being offended by this – Frederick personally attended to the education and training of the future Crown Prince, the future King. It was he who selected his teachers and instructors and issued them with detailed instructions.

Some defects could not be remedied. One was his speech. Except in his closest personal circle, among wife and family, he found it difficult to speak without halting or without a stammer. He spoke in short, sometimes abrupt sentences which on the first encounter tended to make his partners in conversation somewhat shy, a shyness which soon passed when it emerged that as Frederick William warmed up he demonstrated a remarkable lack of preconceptions and an openness of mind one did not expect from his severe-looking appearance. He did not possess a wide range of gifts such as were his grand-uncle's; what he did possess was a solid character. Mirabeau, who met him at the age of 15, remarked: 'He is not particularly attractive, rather without adroitness, but of expressive physiognomy, devoid of varnish, but true. Above all he wants to know why; only reasonable answers will satisfy him. Strict and determined to the degree of inflexibility and yet not closed to warm and refined feelings he knows what to estimate highly and what to despise. His admiration for the great Frederick borders on to adoration and he expresses it loudly. Perhaps this young man ripens for great tasks.'

Religious sceptic that Frederick the Great was as far as his own person was concerned, he nevertheless recognized the importance a solid religious foundation played in the lives of other men and society as a whole. Therefore he demanded that the instruction of the prince be entrusted only to those who were not religiously indifferent. He should develop unhindered and free but should not grow up without religion. And religious he remained throughout his life, but at the same time free from intolerance: 'I know how much misfortune has been caused in the world because one wanted to insist upon decreeing what people had to believe, and I recognize the force of conscience for a cause which may be contrary to justice and good sense as well as contrary to the teachings and behaviour of Christ . . .' but 'the only means of putting them on the right path can be to enlighten them by instruction and by convincing them'. Suarez was one of his instructors, who also emphasized to him the importance of religious toleration. As his reign demonstrated, he endeavoured to represent a synthensis between a brand of conservatism which saw as its task the preservation of all that he thought worth preserving and a progressivism which sought slowly to change what he and his advisors considered necessary to change.

He was fortunate enough in 1793 to meet the 17-year-old Princess Louise of Mecklenburg-Strelitz and the couple were married on Christmas Eve of 1793. It was one of the few love matches within the Hohenzollern dynasty. She complemented him almost to perfection. Her liveliness compensated for his reserve and he knew how to value it. In 1795 the heir to the throne, the future Frederick William IV, was born;

in 1797 the second son, the future William I. Seven further children arrived, among them the future Czarina Alexandra of Russia. At the age of 27 Frederick William and Princess Louise ascended to the throne.

Directly after Prussia's departure from the struggle against revolutionary France, Napoleon's ascendancy began and, associated with it, the territorial expansion of the war which enmeshed the whole of Europe and spilled over into the Baltic, the North Sea and the Mediterranean. It was an upheaval of an unprecedented scale at the root of which is at least one major cause – a revolution in the conduct of war. France's entire resources, economic and human, were deployed to conduct war. The principle of *levée en masse* was only another expression of that process of the French Revolution which demolished the last institutional barriers between the individual and the state. Where once estates, guilds and the church had been intermediaries between subjects and monarch, now the individual, the *citoyen*, confronted the state face to face. No longer was it the profession of arms which carried the glory of victory or the burden of defeat, it was the nation as a whole, and therefore those among the nation capable of carrying arms had to assume the duty of doing so. The first step towards total war had been taken.

The conduct of war in the outgoing Age of Absolutism had been typified by a relatively small professional army divided strictly into officers and other ranks; it was characterized by its tactics, a set game of chess consisting of carefully thought-out moves with the aim of achieving a maximum at the least possible cost to one's army. Soldiers were expensive. They became less so when with the advance of mass democracy soldiering was no longer a choice but became a citizen's duty. Even Frederick the Great had to operate within the limitations this system imposed upon him. But by comparison the French revolutionary armies numbered hundreds of thousands of men who lived off the land, exacted contributions without any consideration, made requisitions in a manner akin to that Gustavus Adolphus or Wallenstein. Napoleon accelerated this development to hitherto undreamt of dimensions; the speed and flexibility with which he moved his mass armies had no precedent. And underlying this revolutionary change was the proud consciousness of being one nation, one and indivisible, and the conviction that the principles on behalf of which this revolutionary army marched were universal and victory therefore inevitable.

The one major European power which ventured to raise doubts about any such change was Great Britain. With short interruptions she fought France from 1793 until 1815 to maintain her predominance at sea and re-establish a balance of power in Europe. The only other power which showed similar though not equal determination was Austria, the House of Hapsburg. But both powers not only derived their strength from the current of historical continuity, that very current had sharpened their eyes and minds. They thought on a continental or even global scale and had the vision to discern what mattered over decades or longer, what development was likely to endanger their interests, as well as the pattern of culture and society they represented, over the long term. Thus arose the determination not to suffer a Napoleon any more than, in the case of Great Britain more than a century later, a Hitler.

After Prussia had left the coalition in 1795 Austria had battled on for another two years and ended the First Revolutionary War with the Peace of Campo Formio, suffering heavy losses in territory among them the entire left bank of the Rhine. Two years later the second round was fought in league with Great Britain and Russia, Naples, Portugal and Turkey. They were no match for Napoleon, who had speedily returned from Egypt. In 1801 Emperor Francis at the Treaty of Lunéville had openly to acknowledge the cession of the left bank of the Rhine. And then, in 1805, again in league with England and Russia, Austria fought Napoleon to maintain the established political order in Europe. Napoleon's victory at Austerlitz put an end to that attempt as well and the Peace of Pressburg of December 1805 gave Napoleon a free hand in Europe while Austria suffered further territorial losses.

Napoleon's impact upon Germany was profound. In the territories on the right bank of the Rhine rapid transformation took place. The chequered political and territorial pattern made way for one that was simpler and more rational. Irrespective of the claims of the church and the nobility ancient structures were demolished and replaced by those thought to be suitable to the time; changes and replacements carried out under the auspices of the principles of the French Revolution and Napoleon's urge to expand his power. Napoleon, since 1804 Emperor of the French, became the initiator and protector of the Confederation of the Rhine, that league of German princes who sought their fortunes under the sign of the tricolor, some of the princes, like the Elector of Bavaria, lowering themselves to the level of receiving royal dignity at the hands of the usurper.

Prussia, too, had benefited from some of the changes introduced by Napoleon. Its territorial holdings in western Germany had increased; and hopes were entertained that perhaps Hanover could also be obtained without too great a sacrifice. Prussia had not participated in the second and third wars against revolutionary France but had maintained a strict neutrality which was of benefit to Napoleon. Irrespective of this neutrality, however, as a result of the division of Poland close contacts existed between Prussia and Russia which on the eve of the Third Coalition War were extended into an alliance according to which Napoleon was to agree to the convening of a European Congress to settle all existing differences. If this should fail Prussia would be prepared to assist the allies with its forces. But Austerlitz came too quickly for the Prussian troops to take to the roads.

All that was still in the future though when Frederick William and his wife Louise were crowned and moved into the *Kronprinzenpalais*. (The

Berlin Palace was considered to be too extravagant by Frederick William III.) One of his first actions was to carry out a thorough purge at court, removing former mistresses and other morally undesirable subjects. Wilhelmine Enke, the Countess of Lichtenau, was thoroughly investigated. Nothing really objectionable could be found out about her, but she lost some of her property and was banished to one of her estates. At first the new King maintained the principle of personal rule, but lacking the capacity and range of Frederick the Great government *by* the cabinet developed rather than government *from* the cabinet as had formerly been the case. Under Frederick the Great the cabinet officials – although they carried the title councillor – had had very little to counsel, but simply wrote down the King's instructions. Under Frederick William II cabinet officials had begun to develop a greater degree of independence and during the early part of Frederick William III's reign that independence developed enough for cabinet councillors to exercise an influence greater than that of the ministers. However, the councillors were not burdened with actual responsibilities as were the ministers of the various departments, who were held at considerable distance from the King. Stein, who was in the employ of the General Directory, and Hardenberg, who together with Haugwitz looked after foreign affairs, felt serious annoyance at having to carry out measures which had not originated in their departments, which had never been discussed, but had their source in the King's cabinet. Perhaps all this would not have been too serious a matter had the councillors been men of ability and distinction, but they were persons more inclined to acquiesce to the King's every wish, to anticipate what they thought were his desires and to avoid conflict at any cost. Frederick William's strongest desire at first was to keep Prussia at peace come what may. The events leading up to the Treaty of Basle had shown the extent to which the Prussian army had deteriorated in less than a decade after the death of Frederick the Great. A commission of investigation had been appointed which was given new impetus by Frederick William III. Various reforms were proposed but the pressure which would have led to their implementation was lacking.

Frederick William II had left 55 million thalers of debts. Frederick William III succeeded in having 22 million paid off by 1806 as well as accumulating a reserve of 17 million thalers. But this still left a considerable debt yet to be paid. In spite of the need for greater financial revenue to meet increased expenditure, and the need for the renewal of military equipment, no increase in taxation took place even though it was a period of general economic prosperity. Fortresses were neglected, the officer corps was over-aged, and while the French had demonstrated that campaigns could also be fought during the winter, the Prussian army had no winter coats. The issue of increasing the level of taxation, particularly by increasing the land tax, was raised on various occasions, but the Prussian nobility always objected. Many of the reform proposals which were implemented after 1807, such as the setting up of a ministry of state in which various ministers could meet to discuss and decide their specific policies and co-ordinate them with a general policy of state, were first aired during that early period.

The need for social reforms was recognized too and the traditional policy of institutional absorption of conflict is reflected by the remark one Prussian minister made to the French envoy in 1799: 'The beneficial revolution which you have made from below to the top, will take place in Prussia slowly from above to below. In his own way the King is a democrat: he is working ceaselessly on the limitations of the privileges of the nobility and in that respect pursues the plan of Joseph II, only by slower means. In a few years there will be no longer a privileged class in Prussia.' Like Frederick the Great and Frederick William I, the King saw as one of his main aims the final liberation of the peasantry from bondage. In the period between 1799 and 1806 alone 50,000 peasants were freed from all services to their lords and became free peasants, but mainly on lands where the crown could exercise direct influence. It was a more difficult process to carry out on the private estates, one that did not see its conclusion until 1850. Frederick William III lacked the firmness of will to confront his nobility with unpopular measures. Thus, in summary, the first nine years of the reign of Frederick William III were years in which the need for reform in many sectors of public and social life, and in the economy became apparent, when men began to think in practical terms of what these reforms should consist of, but when at the same time the crystallizing point that would have transformed the recognition of the need for reforms into a co-ordinated reform movement was still lacking.

The Peace of Amiens which Great Britain has concluded with France in 1802 was of no great duration. In 1803 war broke out again between France and Great Britain. Napoleon immediately moved troops into Germany to occupy Hanover. The Prussian court had been given prior notice, and although it was recognized that French troops in the proximity would pose a danger, the King and his councillors were too faint-hearted to object. The guiding principle was always to maintain neutrality, at the same time maintaining the existing connections with France and Russia while avoiding involvement in any warlike action against Great Britain. But when Napoleon broke with Russia, Prussia's policy inclined towards Russia. On 24 May 1804 an agreement was signed between these two countries to the effect that if Napoleon should endeavour to expand even further from his Hanover base then Russia and Prussia would jointly oppose him. During the War of the Third Coalition the neutrality of Prussian territory was in fact violated by the French. Bernadotte marched from Hanover through Ansbach and Prussia mobilized in reply without, however, taking any military action. When at that time Czar Alexander visited the Prussian royal couple they visited the tombs of Frederick the Great and Frederick William I in the garrison church of Potsdam. Before the tombs in an emotion-laden moment the two monarchs and the Prussian Queen concluded a friendship pact which found its concrete expression in the Treaty of Potsdam of 3 November 1805. According to its terms Prussia should first try armed mediation between Napoleon on the one hand and the Emperors of Austria and Russia on the other on the basis of the Treaty of Lunéville If this should fail then Prussia would join the coalition by the middle of December 1805 at the latest. Prussia was then to occupy Hanover with the possibility of retaining it later. Napoleon's military blows were delivered with greater speed than the time taken for the Prussian diplomatic machine to get into gear and move. By the time the attempt at mediation was undertaken, it had been overtaken by Austerlitz. The timid Prussian foreign secretary Haugwitz arrived at the Palace of Schönbrunn near Vienna where Napoleon had taken up residence and instead of trying to mediate signed a formal alliance with France. Prussia agreed to cede Ansbach, which was to become the property of Napoleon's ally Bavaria, while Napoleon himself took Cleves, Wesel and Neufchatel. In return Prussia received Hanover which it was to hold against the British. Furthermore Prussia had to agree to the territorial changes which Napoleon planned to carry out or had carried out already as a result of the defeat of the Austrians, such as the annexation of the Tyrol by Bavaria. On seeing the treaty Frederick William showed signs of consternation; he was willing to sign it only if several changes were made. Napoleon would not accept any of these and since in the meantime the Treaty of Pressburg had been signed between Austria and France a new treaty was drawn up, the Treaty of Paris of 15 February 1806. Prussia now had to close its harbours to British shipping, thus entering Napoleon's system of continental blockade. The terms of Prussian military aid and its contingencies were more clearly specified, to the extent that should Napoleon demand it Prussia would have to assist him against Russia. Prussia ratified this humiliating document and closed its harbours to the British, which led to war with Great Britain on 11 June 1806. What Prussian shipping there was on the high seas was swept away by the Royal Navy, and a period of economic prosperity in Prussia ended, to be followed by one of economic stagnation and decline.

But all will to resist the Corsican had not evaporated within Prussia's leadership. Prussia's political attitude was feeble, it was humiliating, but if its lack of resoluteness in adhering to its former allies is clear, equally clear is the lack of decisively siding with Napoleon. This not only illustrates the lack of decision at the centre of Prussia's leadership, but also the fear that once on the side of Napoleon, Prussia's position would be reduced to that of a satellite power. While having concluded the treaty with Napoleon, Prussia still maintained its connections with Russia. Napoleon suggested that as a pendant to the Confederation of the Rhine, Prussia should call into being a North German Federation which together with Austria should be one of the three powers in Germany. While making this proposal Napoleon was preparing for a campaign against Prussia. French armies were approaching the

Prussian frontiers from southern and western Germany. Rumours circulated that Napoleon intended to deprive Prussia of Hanover again in order to use it as a bargaining object in negotiations with Great Britain.

At long last on 6 August 1806 Frederick William III mobilized the Prussian army and sent an ultimatum to Napoleon demanding the withdrawal of French troops from the frontiers of Prussia and the return of several Prussian territories on the lower Rhine which were held by the French. Napoleon did not bother to reply to the demands; he simply demanded that Prussia withdraw its mobilization orders.

Frederick William III was now under pressure, especially from public opinion within Prussia. The people still believed Prussia to be the state it was under Frederick the Great and in every respect as effective, so the humiliating foreign policy pursued by the King and his councillors gave cause for public expression of disgust. Young officers sharpened their swords on the steps of the French Embassy in Berlin and when in a performance of Schiller's play *Wallenstein's Lager* the song came up

> Auf, auf Kameraden aufs Pferd, aufs Pferd,
> in das Feld, in die Freiheit gezogen,
> nur im Felde da ist ja der Mann noch was wert
> ja da wird sein Herze gewogen . . .

> *Up, up, comrades to horse, to horse*
> *towards the battlefield and liberty*
> *only on the battlefield can a man show his worth*
> *then his heart will be put on the scales . . .*

the entire audience joined in. Under that pressure and finally recognizing that no step short of subjugation would satisfy Napoleon, Frederick William III refused to withdraw his mobilization orders and war with France ensued. He could not have chosen a worse moment. Prussia's policy of neutrality in the preceding years had alienated many of those who were Prussia's potential allies. Austria had been beaten and was not in a position to assist, a state of war existed with Great Britain, Russian forces were too far removed to intervene in the decisive early stage of the war. In effect Prussia was alone. If her policy shows one redeeming feature it is that she had refused to humble herself in the manner of the princes of the Confederation of the Rhine, for even if the difference is one of degree, yet there is still a difference.

The Prussian army expected to meet Napoleon west of the Thuringian forest. Totally underestimating the rapidity with which Napoleon could move his forces the Prussian army approached that region. But already on 10 October 1806 the Prussian vanguard was defeated by the French at Saalfeld, an engagement in which Prince Louis Ferdinand was killed.[1] In their rapid advance the French forces bypassed the Prussians on their flank, penetrating to their rear. On 14 October 1806 the battles of Jena and Auerstädt were fought, which for Prussia were absolutely disastrous. At Jena a Prussian army under the command of Prince Hohenlohe-Ingelfingen confronted a force three times its own size; a few miles to the north of it stood the bulk of the Prussian army near the village of Auerstädt, where it had the numerical superiority over the French. The army's commander, the Duke of Brunswick was wounded early in the battle. This put the King, who nominally held supreme command, directly in charge of operations, but whilst not lacking in personal bravery he lacked the gift of generalship, the capacity and vision necessary for quick, momentous decisions. At Auerstädt the Prussian army was beaten as soundly as at Jena. The linear tactics of the eighteenth century proved of little use against Napoleon's *tirailleurs*, for whom the solid Prussian lines proved an easy target. The fact that the Prussian forces had been bypassed and were taken from the rear meant that the French fought with their backs to Berlin and the river Oder, while the Prussians faced east. Their communications cut, they lacked any base to withdraw to, and thus after having been defeated they were also routed, the army being in complete disarray. Unit after unit capitulated, fortress after fortress surrendered.

Frederick William III immediately attempted to enter into negotiations with Napoleon but these were rejected outright; Rossbach was to be avenged to the full. On 27 October 1806 the Corsican entered Berlin. One of his first visits was to the tomb of Frederick the Great at Potsdam. Deep in thought before the coffin containing the last remains he turned to his attending generals and said; 'Gentlemen, if this man were still alive I would not be here.'

Frederick William III and his family, together with the government, fled beyond the river Oder. Freiherr von Stein just managed to save the state treasure from the French. Now Napoleon put forward his demands: the cession by Prussia of all its territory to the west of the river Elbe. Frederick William III tried to get milder terms without success. A preliminary peace was signed at the Charlottenburg on 30 October 1806 but the ink had hardly dried when Napoleon changed his mind, saying he was willing to conclude an armistice only if Prussia was prepared to serve as an operational base for a French attack against Russia. The majority of the King's councillors advised him to accept the condition, but in one of his rare moments of quick decision Frederick William III decided in favour of the minority opinion, to reject the armistice offer and continue the war. That the war could only be continued if Russia's support was forthcoming, of that he was certain. The King's decision separated the wheat from the chaff among his advisors. Cautious and fearful men like Haugwitz now resigned. One of them had to be taken under the personal protection of the Queen to save him from the wrath of the population of Stettin. Men like Stein and Hardenberg now came to the fore to direct Prussia's fortunes. By that time Frederick William and his court had moved to Königsberg, the French army close on their heels.

Napoleon, convinced that he would only be able to beat his main enemy Great Britain after having first beaten the Russians, now tried to rally support. He backed a national rising by the Poles in Prussia's Polish provinces, promising the reconstitution of the kingdom of Poland. To Austria he offered Silesia in return for the cession of Galicia, but Austria refused and insisted upon its neutrality. Saxony, which had been in league with Prussia, yielded to Napoleon's tempting offer, and the Elector of Saxony, like that of Bavaria, became King by Napoleon's hand.

In 1807 the main theatre of war was East Prussia where Napoleon had a force of approximately 600,000 men, which lived off a land the population of which was already hard-pressed. Upon encountering the first Russian forces he forced them back to the Lithuanian border districts. On 7 and 8 February 1807 he met them at Preussisch-Eylau in the first major battle in East Prussia, the Russians under the command of General Bennigsen, supported by the Prussian Corps L'Estocq whose chief of staff was Gerhard von Scharnhorst. It was the first battle Napoleon did not win and in response he sent an envoy to Frederick William III, now at Memel, to make peace on the basis of the original condition of Prussia's cession of its territories west of the Elbe. Frederick William III, now counselled by Hardenberg, refused in the hope that Russia's strength would soon make itself felt and change the situation in Prussia's favour.

But because the Russians failed to exploit the situation after Preussisch-Eylau, the French went on to make further gains such as Silesia and Pomerania. In the former province of Silesia only Glatz and Kosel held out against the French; in Pomerania only the city of Kolberg under the heroic inspiration of its mayor Nettelbeck and the military leadership of a hitherto relatively unknown officer, Neidthardt von Gneisenau, resisted.

Prior to Preussisch-Eylau, on 28 January 1807, Prussia had concluded peace with Great Britain, but the expected British support was not yet forthcoming. An alliance with Sweden was concluded, and more importantly an alliance with Russia, negotiated by Hardenberg and concluded on 26 April 1807. According to its terms the war was to be continued and no separate peace to be concluded until Napoleon had been defeated and thrown back beyond the Rhine. Prussia was to be restored within the territorial limits of 1805 and in place of the Holy Roman Empire of the German Nation, which had ceased to exist, a German Confederation was to be created within which Austria and Prussia were to exist as equal partners. However, the new alliance was not blessed with any military victories. When on 14 June 1807 Napoleon beat Bennigsen at the battle of Friedland, Czar Alexander asked Napoleon for an armistice. Eleven days later, on 25 June, the two Emperors met on a raft on the river Memel and concluded an agreement at the expense of Prussia. While Russia was not to sustain any losses, Prussia was to pay the bill, its existence suffered by Napoleon only as a favour to Alexander. Queen Louise by personal intervention with

Napoleon hoped to get easier terms for her country. In vain; on 9 July 1807 at the Treaty of Tilsit Prussia lost all its territories west of the Elbe including the city of Magdeburg and her Polish provinces to the Duchy of Warsaw under the King of Saxony. Prussia was reduced to 7311 square kilometres with a population of 4.5 million. From the western provinces Prussia lost, the kingdom of Westphalia was formed, on the throne of which Napoleon put his youngest brother Jerome. The Treaty of Tilsit was supplemented by the Convention of Königsberg of 12 July 1807 in which Napoleon stipulated that he would withdraw his occupying forces from Prussia only when the reparation payments demanded had been paid. As yet no figure had been determined.

Notes
1. The Prince was the nephew of Frederick the Great.

Chapter 8

The Prussian Reform Movement

Prussia had suffered defeat and humiliation at the hands of Napoleon, a defeat not expected by the seemingly invincible. Yet that defeat came at a moment in time when Prussia's leaders were convinced that the state was badly in need of reform. They had already cautiously made their own preparations for reform and found themselves surprised by the disaster, but soon afterwards recognized that this disaster provided the opportunity to implement their plans.

It is one of the salient features of the Prussian Reform Movement that an obsolete cabinet government was replaced by a small articulate group of critically thinking civil servants and officers whose main objective was not the revolutionary transformation of the state, but reform from within and, more important, the reconstruction of the administrative and military pyramid. The decisive and determining point was that reconstruction should proceed from within the existing Prussian institutions and not outside them. Harmony in place of discord, absorption in place of conflict were the guiding stars of the Prussian Reform Movement – but also one of the major reasons for its failure and the reassertion of the powers of reaction after 1815.

It is only natural that reformers like Stein, Hardenberg, Scharnhorst, Gneisenau, Boyen, Schrötter, Schön, Frey and Wilhelm von Humboldt should be attracted by Kant's concept of liberty, liberty defined as the privilege and ability to dedicate one's self to the fulfilment of duty – or the practical application of Kant's categorical imperative. The royal subject was to become the citizen, a process which required the abolition of the limitations which had so far prevented him from accepting full ethical and political responsibility. Fichte simply carried Kant's idealism one stage further in arguing that the state represented the focal point of the community, towards which the attention of each individual component should be directed.

Of the group of reformers four in particular gave that reform impetus, power and a sense of direction: Stein, Hardenberg, Scharnhorst and Humboldt. Reichsfreiherr H. F. Karl von und zum Stein had begun his civil service career under Frederick the Great, had become president of Westphalia and from 1804 until 1806 had been minister of trade. He was born in Nassau in 1757, the year of Rossbach, the ninth of 10 children. The von Stein family were members of the *Reichsritterschaft*, the Knights of the Reich, a corporate body which during the second half of the seventeenth century and throughout the eighteenth fought a continuous battle against the centralizing and rationalizing forces of princely absolutism, against princes who sought aggrandizement at the expense of both Emperor and knightly nobility. At a time when Germany had disintegrated into something like 60 major princely courts the Knights of the Reich still maintained their corporate identity, their sense of unity and the consciousness of the essential unity of the Holy Roman Empire of the German Nation. Precisely that gave Stein the strength and independence of mind which characterized his relationship with Frederick William III. The Knights of the Reich enjoyed legislative, fiscal and judicial privileges; they were subject only to the Emperor but were without representation in the *Reichstag*. But they were a declining caste; their economic base shrank, the feuds with the local princes were no longer fought with sword or lance but with costly legal action before the Reichs Chamber Court. To escape the downward spiral of decline many Knights of the Reich sought service and career at a powerful court, as did Stein, and it is significant that he and many others chose Prussia rather than any other German court.

In the course of his service in Prussia Stein recognized the weakness of the Prussian administration during the last years of Frederick the Great and the reign of Frederick William II. He complained about the lack of co-ordination between the various departments of the General Directory, the degradation of ministers to the level of office boys who carried on the day-to-day running of routine office affairs, and their lack of participation in major decisions. At the heart of the administration Stein envisaged a greater centralization and the establishment of a council of ministers.

Moreover, he was able to read the signs of the times. In spite of a tradition-orientated mind which thought in terms of the restoration and the unity of the Reich, rather than in terms of the particularist territorial state, he felt certain that the future could only be mastered on the basis of new relations between government and the people. Therefore in his famous Nassau Memorandum of 1807 he demanded the regeneration of the public spirit by permeating it again with a national feeling and, above all, by ensuring that the public participate in public affairs. Prior to 1807 he had already laid down that this participation could best be carried out in representative assemblies consisting of elected members of the estates. He believed that the estates should be based on the nobility because by the nature of their social and economic position, they possessed influence and were bound by indissoluble ties to the interest of the country. But the nobility were not the only land-owners, and the bourgeois landowners, including peasants who owned land of a size for which they paid land tax of 500 thalers upwards, should also be represented in the diet.

One of his first actions while still a member of the General Directory was the abolition, on 26 December 1805, of internal tolls in Prussia, and he generally endeavoured to turn Prussia's economy away from the mercantilist policies that had predominated in the eighteenth century towards a policy based on the principles of Adam Smith, whose faithful disciple Stein confessed himself to be on more than one occasion. He wanted to curb the power of the guilds, to make them accessible to all trades, crafts and professions, to break down the barriers which so far had existed in Prussia between town and countryside. Trade should prosper throughout the kingdom, and there was little point and even less justice in levying on the countryside a relatively low land tax and on the towns a very high excise. He suggested a general income tax along the lines decreed for the first time in history by the French Convention in 1793, and carried out in England under Pitt the Younger in 1799 and again, after the reopening of hostilities between Great Britain and France, in 1803. There was basically very little that was new in the reforms suggested by Stein. They were reforms which had first been demanded from the *ancien régime* by the French physiocrats, had then been adopted by parts of the French nobility and the bourgeoisie, and in the execution of which Turgot had failed to overcome the entrenched forces of the opposition.

Stein was to experience a similar opposition, particularly from the nobility. Although himself a member of the General Directory, between King and minister there still stood the royal cabinet, the removal of which Stein deemed essential if the reforms he had conceived were to be carried through before the tide of revolution and war overcame the whole of the kingdom. The entire administrative structure of the Prussian state was in need of reform. His thoughts on this subject he expressed in his 'Description of the faulty Organization of the Cabinet and the Formation of a Ministerial Conference'. In this memorandum he blandly observed that the Prussian state did not possess a written constitution, that supreme power was not divided between supreme head and 'the deputies of the nation', that the Prussian state was nothing other than a new aggregate of its provinces. These provinces were governed by the King and his cabinet in whose hands lay the only decision-making power. Ministers could only appeal to the cabinet or submit petitions. They had to carry out decisions, nothing else. They did not even form a council in order to communicate with one another. The ministers possessed the expertise, but the cabinet, lacking expertise and carrying no responsibility, had all the power. This was bound to affect the morale not only of the ministers but of the entire bureaucracy. He demanded the establishment of direct contact between King and the highest members of the civil service, so that the persons 'which have to submit business of state to the King's final decision' should be 'by law and publicly called upon to do so' and their 'assemblies be purposefully organized and carry responsibility'. This ministerial organization, divided up into departments, was no product of Stein's mind; it was developing already in Western Europe, even in the states of the Confederation of the Rhine. Stein concluded his memorandum with the words that if the King could not agree with the changes demanded then 'it is to be expected that the Prussian state will dissolve altogether or lose its independence and that respect and love for it will disappear among its subjects'. Stein's memorandum was not acted upon, and the consequences were such as he had prophesied. After the defeat, Frederick William III while at Danzig tried to entrust Stein with the conduct of foreign affairs, but the latter refused because the influence of the cabinet still continued to exist and 'the change of a system from which so much misfortune has originated is the first condition for our salvation'. It was an unprecedented action in Prussia's history for a civil servant to decline an office because the reforms he demanded had not been carried out and, on top of that, to suggest another official, Hardenberg, whom he considered more suitable for the post. This in Frederick William III's eyes lent even more support to the rumours emanating from his cabinet officials that Stein was after nothing other than supreme power for himself; Stein was alleged to be trying to prevent the King from seeking advice from whatever quarters he desired. Still, Frederick William tried to find a compromise and suggested a ministerial council, responsible to the cabinet, of which Stein would be a member. But again Stein refused because the ministerial council would either be useless or misused by the cabinet. He told the King that he did not intend to leave his service, but that he would have to cease to cherish the deception that a truly functioning ministerial council existed. The King now assumed that Stein was at least prepared to collaborate and sent him some business matters for the department of the interior which Stein promptly returned with the remark that he did not consider the ministerial council as being constituted. Frederick William III was incensed by such behaviour and threatened to dispense with Stein's services. Stein submitted his resignation and it was accepted. The absolute monarch had confronted the man of the new age and for a short time he had won.

Stein returned to his native Nassau and there contemplated the causes of the disaster that had befallen Prussia as well as Germany as a whole. One of the root causes for Prussia's misfortunes he believed to be the total apathy of the people, apathy that was a product of a bureaucratic state whose subjects did not share in the formulation of the policies that ultimately affected them all. The French Revolution had seemingly succeeded in making the citizens actively participate in the fortunes of the state. Stein argued that in Prussia state and society must be elevated to the same level. For Prussia 1806 was the year of the final defeat of the *ancien régime*. This *régime* had undoubtedly produced great achievements but the connection between people and government, which according to Stein had existed in the Middle Ages, had been lost. To bring together people, society and state once more had been a challenge which the French Revolution had accepted and risen to. But Stein sought no imitation of the French example. In many respects he reflected Prussian opinion in general, which on the whole approved of the French Revolution without thinking for one moment that it could be a model for Prussia or Germany as a whole. While the French had tried to translate natural law directly into practice, Stein's essentially conservative mould preferred the connection with Germany's historical tradition. He did not seek to raise forces from the depth of the people which, as the French example had demonstrated, escaped the control of their originators, but demanded that in Prussia 'absolutism overcome itself' by legal means, through laws, decrees drafted and signed by the King and his ministers. Reform itself should be the means of liberation from the Napoleonic yoke, a liberation carried out by its citizens infused with a new patriotic spirit, citizens who now could identify with the state because they participated actively in its affairs. Prussia should become a model for Germany as a whole and he hoped that Austria too would follow its example. German unitarian that he was, the Hapsburg monarchy was too valuable to be sacrificed, and he believed that its contribution, like that of Prussia, would be a valuable and essential component of his aim – the restoration of German unity. 'I know only one fatherland and that is Germany.'

In his Nassau Memorandum of June 1807 he goes into considerable detail about the reforms he considers necessary for the rejuvenation of respect for the fatherland, independence and national honour. As before he demanded the replacement of the cabinet by a Permanent Ministerial Conference; also ministries for specific purposes rather than divided regionally, for only that would complete a unified state. He demanded the separation of the judiciary and the executive, which implied the abolition of the judiciary privilege of patrimonial justice as still practised by the estate owner. He demanded a special ministry for public education, as well as ministries for Protestant and for Catholic affairs. This implied the separation of education from religion, and the limitation of clerical influence to the religious sector – which Stein considered its only field of competence.

Ironically enough Stein had no one other than Napoleon himself to thank for being recalled to office. When Frederick William III remarked to Napoleon that it was really only Hardenberg to whom he could entrust high office, Napoleon replied '*Prenez le baron de Stein, c'est un homme d'ésprit.*' There had been talk that Stein and Hardenberg had had difficulties in getting on with one another. Napoleon may have thought that after Stein's recall any Prussian attempt at recovery would be blocked by the mutual rivalry between the two men.

On the day of the Treaty of Tilsit, 10 June 1807, the King, through Hardenberg, sent Stein the call to return to office, to forget old grievances. That Stein could be moved to return was mainly due to Hardenberg's ability to persuade him. On 4 October 1807 he resumed office for exactly one year, a year of momentous decisions that were to influence Prussia's and Germany's history for a century. Within five days of Stein's return the first great reform measure was published, the 'Edict concerning easier Possession and free Use of Landed Property as well as the Personal Relations of the Population on the Land'.

Hardenberg had already prepared the ground for Stein. One of two commissions which he had appointed was to examine and replace the old order of the estates by a more modernly structured organization of society and to articulate anew the legal rights of the rural population. In spite of the reforms begun by Frederick William I and continued by his first two successors much needed to be done, and that need was recognized. Since Napoleon's creation of the grand duchy of Warsaw all forms of serfdom there had been abolished. This in turn exerted pressure upon Prussia to do likewise. The leading man in the commission appointed by Hardenberg was minister von Schrötter, who as minister for East Prussia had been actively engaged in the cause of liberating the peasants over several years. He now was to advise Stein on this particular aspect. Schrötter was supported in the commission by Theodor von Schön, an East Prussian infused with the ideas of Kant and Adam Smith who had travelled widely, including an extensive stay in England. In the negotiations to obtain the co-operation of the nobility, its representatives were surprisingly open to the suggestions made concerning the emancipation of the peasants. All they demanded was that in return the Prussian government would do away with those measures which had been enacted under three previous monarchs which protected specific rights of the peasants.

It is important when talking of serfdom in the eighteenth century to be aware that this condition varied from country to country. In Russia and in Poland it was a condition of abject subjugation, little short of actual slavery. In Austria, until the reforms of Joseph II, it was somewhat milder. In Prussia, however, the peasant serf was a man with certain specific duties to carry out for his lord, with the right of every citizen to go to court, and a watchful bureaucracy to ensure that the land-owner did not abuse his rights.

But there was one major underlying reason why the nobility seemed so readily agreeable to the reforms suggested. Since the turn of the century agrarian prices had suffered a serious economic depression, so the financial returns of the land-owner had decreased while his obligations towards his rural population remained the same. Thus if the protective measures that secured the economic basis of the peasant serf and the land he held were revoked, the land-owner could without much ado evict any number of peasants he thought necessary, consolidate his own estate and employ seasonal farm labour as and when he needed it. This provided the basis of the economic upsurge which Prussian land-owners experienced after 1810.

Stein's first action was to extend the reform which had until then been thought to apply to East Prussia only, to the whole of the kingdom. He realized the danger which this could bring to the peasants in connection with the revocation of the protective measures which they had enjoyed so far. Therefore upon his initiative the decree contained additional provisions which should have made it easier for all to buy, own and cultivate land. Everyone should have been able to follow his own inclinations and in this instance pursue his agricultural calling, so to speak, if he so wished. But the easing of the restrictions on the purchase of land, the right of the peasant 'freely to use his resources', was only a palliative, because by entering into competition with the established landlord he had an unequal chance: 'the revolutionary destruction of the private economic basis of the nobility was out of the question' (Kehr). Only the great land-owner possessed capital enough to react to changing economic fortunes, to learn the newest agricultural techniques by sending his sons to schools or agricultural institutes. Stein's intention of giving every peasant a stake in his country was not fulfilled. Perhaps Eckhart Kehr's formulation may be considered as somewhat extreme, but nevertheless it touches the core of the matter when he says that 'bureaucracy divided its rule over the state, with the landed nobility sitting on the back of a non-participating third, the "liberated peasantry" . . . '.

This may apply to the bureaucracy as an institution but not to Stein himself, who soon enough recognized the tendencies at work, endeavoured to counteract them, and thus found himself attacked by the peasants or their self-appointed spokesmen and by the Prussian nobility. The nobility's most vociferous spokesman was F. A. L. von der Marwitz, who complained about the evil influence the 'foreign' nobleman Stein exercised: 'Stein began the revolutionizing of the fatherland, the war of the have-nots against property, of industry against agriculture, of the flexible against the stable.' General Yorck, soon to become famous as one of the generals of the War of Liberation, commented about Stein shortly after the publication of the decree:

Much to our misfortune this man has been in England and there has obtained his stately wisdom; and now the institutions of a seapower grown over the centuries, those based upon trade and manufacturing in rich Great Britain should be made tasty for us poor, agricultural Prussians . . . Is the spice pedlar or the tailor who buys himself an estate, or the speculator who only thinks in terms of profit and already is thinking about re-selling what he has acquired, likely in times of misfortune to serve the monarch with his property and blood?

No doubt these words too contain elements that cannot be dismissed out of hand. But the opposition to Stein was not aware of his nationalistic motivation, nor of the connection of that motivation with German history, which represented one of the driving forces behind Stein's actions and thoughts. In effect Stein's reform, followed up by the measures of Hardenberg dissolved the traditional lord–peasant relationship; serfdom was completely abolished, the entire social structure of Prussia was altered. Land-ownership was no longer the privilege of the nobility. However, some aspects of the reform still had to wait to be implemented; patrimonial justice was only abolished in the wake of the revolution in 1849 and the policing power of the estate owner in 1872.

Subsequent reform measures only helped to consolidate the opposition. For Stein the liberation of the peasants was the very foundation on which all other reforms and their success had to rest. From serfs he could not expect an interest in the state, let alone the possibility of participating in self-government, the other important aspect of his reform endeavours. Stein wanted citizens, but not every citizen could work at the centre of the state and hence the necessity of having participation at all levels, from local government to the top. The citizen should participate in his village or town, in the communal diets or assemblies, in the diet of the province and finally, so Stein hoped, in a Prussian diet and a German national assembly. Of course he was aware that it was not possible to institute overnight the type of self-government he envisaged. It would require years not only of hard work but of getting the people accustomed to this practice. The City Ordinance published on 19 November 1808 represents a return to the principle of the liberty of the cities that was characteristic of the Middle Ages, but in its practical aspects was based upon the requirements of a modern society. The concept of an autonomous independent community was part of the law of medieval Germany. As elsewhere in Europe this concept was gradually pushed back by the forces of royal absolutism. Under Frederick William I the autonomous body of the city magistrates fulfilled only a perfunctory function: the cities were really run by his military and fiscal authorities. Even Frederick the Great had attempted to restore a small part of the privileges which the towns had once enjoyed. It was Stein's intention to push back this bureaucratic over-centralization. However, he realized that this could not be done by returning to medieval corporations such as the guilds, but instead took as his example the French revolutionary practice of determining the social structure not by birth but according to income. The City Ordinance contains various passages which are copied from the French Constitution of 1791.

Obviously, introducing self-government in the cities did not really amount to starting at the lowest level of society. But the cities represented a good starting point because in them the remnants of a corporate structure, though hollow and impotent, were still present – all they needed was to be filled with a new content and purpose. Reform in the rural areas was all the more difficult because of the political predominance of the landed nobility; moreover in Prussia east of the Elbe local self-administration was not known in the countryside. Here the lord ruled, as he had done since the days of the Teutonic Order. Hitherto the Prussian crown had refrained from touching the privileges of the nobility. Stein had drafted legislation for the introduction of self-government in rural areas but the difficulties and the opposition by the nobility were so great that it was not enacted. But as a problem it remained a major issue for almost another century of Prussian history.

The City Ordinance intended, as Stein put it, 'not only to liberate [the burgher] from the shackles of useless, clumsy habits but also to develop the consciousness of the burgher and a sense of community which had been destroyed by abolishing participation in the administration of municipal affairs and which should now be awakened again by new life'. The function of the state was cut back to a supervisory capacity. The inhabitants of the cities and towns were divided into burghers and those under the protection of the city or town. Burghership by definition included all political rights within the community, but also the exclusive right to own city property and to carry on a trade or craft in the city. Burghership could not be denied to anyone who settled in the city and was of good repute. This meant the removal of the inheritable caste system of the German medieval cities, while the political function of the guilds was now carried out by property-owners. Only the Jews were excluded from burghership by birth (most likely in accordance with Stein's personal convictions), only soldiers by profession. They were to enjoy the protection a city or town could provide so also had to carry fiscal burdens, but were excluded from administration and could not own property or carry on a business. Burghership brought not only privileges but also duties. It was punishable not to accept unpaid municipal office or not to take part in elections. Each city had only a few fully paid members of the magistracy; the rest of its members were unpaid honorary, but nevertheless fully responsible, members. For the Prussian state this carried the advantage that the cost of administration was drastically reduced, while the expenses of the city were in theory covered by municipal taxation. Stein's model had at least in part been clearly derived from his experiences in Great Britain.

While cutting back the role of the bureaucracy in the administration of Prussia in order to allow firm roots of self-government to develop, Stein was nevertheless also convinced of the need to curb or eliminate such forms of particularism as might endanger the unity of the state. Although Frederick the Great had fostered the tendency to refer to 'Prussia', meaning all the King's possessions, up to 1807 the country was still referred to as 'all his Royal Majesty's provinces and domains'. In 1807 it was decreed 'that the entire country will be called Prussia from now on'. It was the Prussian Reform Movement which in fact completed the unification of Prussia. Of course this was necessary for the Prussian diet that was envisaged, but it also required an efficient streamlined civil service. Stein was very well aware that a modern state was in need of an efficient central administration. The old administration with its collegiate procedure was costly, clumsy, and year by year proved to become more and more inefficient. Stein began by energetically pruning the civil service almost to the point of ruthlessness. Nearly 50 per cent of its members lost their jobs and were given a pension – at that time still a sign of royal favour rather than a right – but pensions were also drastically lowered and the amount to be paid made dependent on the individual's needs. Salaries were cut, the royal opera and the royal ballet dissolved.

On the same day on which Stein left office, 24 November 1808,

Frederick William III put his signature under the 'Ordinance concerning the changed Constitution of the supreme administrative Organs of the Prussian Monarchy'. In it modern ministries were founded, departments created which were no longer limited by territorial responsibility but were responsible for specific functions. Furthermore a month later, on 26 December 1808, a corresponding decree was issued concerning the provincial administration. In place of the old District and Domain Chambers came provincial government, but devoid of judiciary function. At a provincial level it combined all the internal administration of a province, including education and church affairs. Prussia was given a new administrative division, the provincial government district. But the president of the provincial government was a mere administrator, his powers limited by the central authorities above him and by the self-administration of the towns and cities below him. Then of course there were also the provinces, four of them in 1808 – East Prussia, Pomerania, Brandenburg and Silesia – which, since the office of the minister for the territory had been abolished, had at their head an *Oberpräsident*.

Before Stein left office, forced out on Napoleon's demand, he suggested to the King that he put Prussia's envoy at the Holy See, Wilhelm von Humboldt, at the head of the administration of culture and education. In a way it was a surprising choice and it is not known what prompted Stein to put him forward as a suitable candidate. Humboldt had not been in touch with the reformers, he was very much an aesthete, and had become envoy in Rome only because his own means were no longer sufficient to continue his stay in the Eternal City. Unlike his brother Alexander von Humboldt he had not excelled at anything so far, except at gaining a reputation as an elegant essay writer and correspondent. When the royal call came he was just visiting Prussia, and confronted by the abject misery defeat had caused he accepted the appointment, though not without showing some reluctance. In contrast to the philosopher Johann Gottlieb Fichte, Humboldt's principle was that the state should not regulate educational affairs in detail; he considered it his function to assist the state towards spiritual and moral maturity until it could look after the educational sector itself. State and nation were to be a community held together not only by legal ties but also by a common culture. To strengthen and to create an awareness of these deep cultural bonds he considered his primary task. But he was well aware that these cultural bonds were not specifically Prussian but German, and in that respect he fitted well into the group of the Prussian Reform Movement, whose ultimate frame of reference was Germany, within which and for which Prussia was to become a model to be emulated.

But in the cultural and educational sector Humboldt did not operate in a vacuum. Herder's idea of the *Volk* as the natural organic community of the nation, had in the hands of Fichte been turned into a weapon of national defence against French domination, political, military, but above all cultural. The fear that Germany's cultural emancipation from France, not yet 50 years of age, could be once again buried underneath alien influences turned him into a radical who used the concept of the *Volk* as the antithesis of the social contract theory. Therefore, education was a vital weapon with which to fight the French intruder, and even more the influence of the Romano-Gallic world in Germany. While Humboldt envisaged the state's function as educating its future citizens irrespective of power factors and other interests, Fichte, though agreeing that they should be educated, believed that, at least for the time being, education should be deployed as a weapon against intrusion in any form by an alien world. He seems to have been the first to lift patriotism and the concept of the *Volk* from a religiously and humanistically influenced context into a mainly secular and political one. Above all he stressed time and again the need to preserve the individuality of the German language because only through it did the German *Volk* exist. The German language as opposed to the Romance languages was, so he argued, largely unadulterated by foreign influences, and that gave it immeasurable depth and a virile force of expression, whereas other northern European languages, heavily Latinized, were capable of expressing the surface of life only. They were dead languages. Hence, he went on, to compare these languages with German was futile – one cannot compare life with death. Germany, as the unique possessor of a living language, represented the original *Volk*, the *Urvolk*, the only one with a living language. It did not matter in this view that the German nation was politically disunited, as long as it maintained the integrity of its language. For sooner or later this common language would resurrect the nation, the German *Volk*, as one political unit.

Humboldt had to carry this trend of thought in mind and hoped to make allowances for it in his concept of 'national education', by which he meant education to produce men who were whole and free and capable of fully developing their entire range of faculties for the benefit of the nation. Humboldt thus engaged in an experiment, the consequences and range of influence of which, at both the national and international levels, he could hardly have foreseen. To the Prussian state, and ultimately to Germany as a whole, it opened a new area of activity.

A national spirit was to develop in a society consisting of citizens who were politically aware and responsible. A major source of and impetus to this development were the ideas and the example of the Swiss educational reformer Johann Heinrich Pestalozzi. Like Rousseau he objected to the philosophic abstractions which as a result of the Enlightenment had also entered into education. In his view it was not the task of education to convey to the pupil words and concepts that he must then absorb mechanically; the pupil must be left to himself to find things out so that he can then observe his own intellectual growth, enjoy it, and derive from it the courage for further expansion of his mind. A child must first listen, see and act before it can judge. The teacher's function in its every essence is one of guidance rather than mechanical instruction. Man and the circumstances under which he lives have to be brought into their proper relationship. True, man is the product of circumstances, but circumstances are again, at least partly, the product of man himself. Hence, as Pestalozzi put it, man is the product of himself. Education is essentially a threefold approach: education of the mind, of the heart and of the hand.

One cannot say that Pestalozzi ever developed his ideas in a systematic form, consequently only parts of them were accepted here and there while other parts were ignored as unsuitable. The first evidence of the reception of Pestalozzi's ideas in Germany is contained in Fichte's 'Addresses to the German Nation' which he delivered to German students in French-occupied Berlin during the winter of 1807 to 1808. In them he argued that the German fatherland had really been brought to ruin by the selfishness of its own sons, and that to restore it would require generating new strength which would transcend personal considerations, material advantage or disadvantage. But the process of this regeneration would have to begin at the very heart of the people through the process of education. Education must not consist of memory work, it must raise love and desire for truth and goodness; it must completely shape the human being, not only parts of him. Education should not limit itself to the conveyance of facts, it should strengthen the will and activate the intellect. Fichte transformed Pestalozzi's teachings, which were directed mainly towards the lower orders of society, in accordance with Prussian – and from Fichte's point of view – with German needs. Fichte wanted to break down the barriers between the intellectuals and the people and by applying new principles in education create one nation and one state. He rejected schools for the privileged. He saw in national education a system of first-class schools for all in which all talents would have room for further development. Pestalozzie's ideas were to Fichte practical means towards political ends; unlike Pestalozzi he did not consider man exclusively but also the nation and the state. Nation and state were in need of a system of unified education, and it was the task of the state to create it. In true Prussian tradition Fichte was the apostle of state socialism in the cultural sector. In many aspects he preached ideas practised to some extent in National Socialist Germany and in Soviet Russia, ideas which to the present day have their place in the list of demands put forward by reformers Fichte demanded the separation of the child from the family and its education in a school community run by the state; he demanded co-education because the 'whole man' was to be achieved irrespective of the sex. This demand for the separation of child from family was based on Fichte's assumption that the society of the time was corrupt and that in order to create a new society a child had to be removed from its influence. The child should see the value of labour and that it is evil to derive one's income other than by one's own labour. Within the school community it should develop a responsibility towards the community of which it is part so that once adult it can act responsibly towards nation and state. The national community stood in Fichte's view above everything else, and towards it were to be directed all loyalties. Fichte asked, in different words, the same rhetorical question that Luther had asked before him: If the state could force its citizens into war and into military service, why should not the state also have the right to compel its citizens into a system of education? Fichte's ideas in the educational sector then, amounted to the postulate that the state should possess the monopoly in culture and education.

Fichte's ideas were never fully put into practice in his own time – they elicited too much opposition from a society moulded by tradition, however chequered – but they nevertheless exerted an influence strong enough to result in the acquisition, in the name of personal liberty, of powers by the state which through the process of education narrowed the spectrum of existing liberties. Above all, Fichte's idea of a unitary school system determined by national and secular considerations and over which the Prussian state would possess monopoly powers, influenced not only the Prussian but also the German system of education profoundly. The Prussian Reform Movement in general, and Wilhelm von Humboldt in particular, hoped that by fusing elements of Pestalozzi's ideas with his own and those of Fichte, it would be possible to maximize the power of the state by increasing the intellectual and physical capabilities of its citizens. Humboldt did not want the demonstration of knowledge, but the full development of a pupil's faculties. An entire generation of Prussian youth was to go through this process before specializing in order to train for a vocation. His concept of general education rejected schools for noblemen or purely professional schools: 'All schools which are not part of any particular estate, but part of the entire nation or state, must have as their purpose the general development and education of man. What corresponds with the practical requirements of life or a particular trade must be separated and obtained after the completion of a general education. If one mixes both, then education will become impure and one will obtain neither the complete human being nor the complete classless citizen.' Unity and continuity of school education were based on the assumption that education was part of an organic whole, a reflection of the organic theory in all spheres of life as developed by Herder. The confusion and proliferation of existing educational systems had to make way for a three-tier structure of education: the basic schools, whose function was primarily social in that they were to develop the beginnings of a responsible citizen; the higher schools, for the exercise of ability and its further development as well as the acquisition of the deeper knowledge without which scientific insight is impossible; and the universities, which were to be institutes for the creation of knowledge even if this only meant the development of insights already obtained. Since knowledge represents a unity and a totality, social considerations were to play no part in the transition from one educational stage to another, the only criterion for advancement being an intellectual one.

Humboldt threw down the gauntlet to private schools. He was partially successful in eliminating them – though he did not succeed in doing away with the cadet institutes or the War Academy – but his influence was strong enough to make all of them include in their curricula strong elements of a classic humanist education. The basic school, the *Volksschule*, gave Humboldt great scope for implementing his ideas. But to run the *Volksschule* successfully trained teachers were badly needed, for teachers jobs until then had often been filled by retired non-commissioned officers of the Prussian army. Humboldt quickly founded numerous teachers' seminaries which in time supplied new teachers. The higher schools too experienced thorough reforms: they became ultimately the *Gymnasium*. Humboldt ensured that only qualified teachers could teach in a *Gymnasium*, which eliminated patronage and the arbitrary powers of urban education offices. The influence of the clergy was also reduced. A *Gymnasium* was to be an institution from which the pupil left after having taken the matriculation examination (an examination which had existed in Prussia since 1788). There was to be a 10-year course, divided into six classes, with the main subjects being Latin, Greek, German and mathematics. All other subjects were subsidiary, but they too were part of Humboldt's idea of a general education and were therefore examinable. This reform introduced by Humboldt and carried on by his successor Suevern was to determine the entire pattern of secondary education in Germany throughout the nineteenth century.

Universities in Germany had been in a state of decay for several centuries. But Germany was not unique in this for Adam Smith, himself a former university don, had described England's universities as refuges of laziness. In Germany they degenerated into institutes training future civil servants. Already in 1802 the philosopher Schelling had made a serious public stand in the cause of a thorough reform of the universities. He conceived of knowledge as one body, one and indivisible, and challenged the atomization of knowledge while insisting on the autonomy of human thought. Humboldt and numerous others shared his conviction. Humboldt described his idea of the purpose of the university as follows: 'It is not important that this or that is being learnt, rather that learning exercises the memory, sharpens the intellect, justifies judgement, and refines ethical feeling. Only in this way will we ensure that people have the ability, the liberty and the strength necessary to be able to choose a profession at will, not simply to earn a living, but for its own sake.' He demanded that students and teachers alike consider 'knowledge not as something found complete but rather as something that can never be fully found, and therefore continuously to be searched for.'

Lehre – teaching rather than instruction – and research together represented an entity; one could not be separated from the other. The emphasis upon this essential unity was the cornerstone of the development of Prussia's and Germany's universities for most of the nineteenth century, until the age of technology led away once again from the universal concept of education and towards a degree of atomization more dangerous than that experienced in the three centuries prior to 1810. As to the role of the state in university education, Humboldt wanted it to supply the necessary finance but to refrain from any intervention in the areas of teaching and research. He insisted upon complete liberty in these two areas. Nor should students be compelled to study at the university in their home region. All in all Humboldt's reforms and those carried out by his successors widened the spectrum of people who were receiving education, while at the same time reorganizing the educational system from the bottom to the top and ensuring efficiency and continuity. The hope that Humboldt's high ethical ideals could be maintained was, in accordance with the nature of all things, not realized. But this thinking left an impression on German idealism through the concept of education as a universal idea, embracing man in his entirety. Under Humboldt's inspiration the Frederick William University of Berlin was founded; its first chancellor was Fichte, and Hegel was to be one of its most prominent teachers.

For personal reasons Humboldt found it increasingly difficult to work with Hardenberg and therefore in 1810 left his post to act as Prussian envoy in Vienna. Within a little more than a year of activity he had mobilized the intellectual strength in Prussia's society as it had never been mobilized before.

Karl August von Hardenberg, like Stein a non-Prussian, like Scharnhorst a Hanoverian, was already 60 years of age when in 1810 as chancellor of state – an office called into existence by cabinet order and which disappeared again after his death – was entrusted with the conduct of Prussia's affairs. Stein's departure from Government was followed by the Dohna/Altenstein Ministry which, heavily influenced by the nobility and giving in excessively to French pressure, was dismissed in 1810 when it supported the French demand that Prussia should yield the province of Silesia to France in lieu of indemnities.

Hardenberg, like Stein, had been in Prussian service for some considerable time; unlike Stein he was flexible, ready to compromise as long as he won the essentials, as he saw them, of any particular issue. He belonged to that circle of liberal nobles who supported reforms in the interest of the bourgeoisie but who looked with some suspicion at the political rumblings among the fifth estate – the 'mob'. In 1807 Hardenberg had had to yield his post under French pressure and he withdrew to Riga; like Stein at about the same time he expressed his reflections in a memorandum, the Riga Memorandum of 12 September 1807. In it he argued the case for a reform of social and political life on the basis of individual liberty, but within the framework of a strongly centralized state bureaucracy which did not envisage self-administration to the extent to which Stein was to carry it. But he shared with Stein the realization of the need for a national representative body.

When called to office again he set about putting his ideas into practice. Whereas Stein in his short tenure had left his subordinates free to work on their own initiative, Hardenberg, not devoid of intellectual arrogance, soon collided with ministers and counsellors who begged to differ with him. For this reason Schön and Niebuhr had to resign, in addition to Humboldt. In bold broad strokes the chancellor sketched his reforms on a large canvas and then left the completion of the detail to his office staff under the young Friedrich von Raumer (who was later to be the historian of the Hohenstaufen dynasty). Without any inhibitions Hardenberg borrowed and adopted from the French what he thought was useful. A particular model he copied was the newly created kingdom of Westphalia. One of his first edicts was the complete secularization of all church lands, Protestant and Catholic alike. Most of the land which the Prussian state obtained by this measure was, due to the deflationary spiral, sold at extremely low prices to speculators. But Prussia badly needed money to meet the French demands for contributions and to avert the threat of territorial sanctions, particularly as Hardenberg's foreign policy was at first aimed at a reconciliation with France and thus the lightening of Prussia's burdens.

On 2 November 1810 Hardenberg introduced general taxation in the kingdom of Prussia. The taxation laws eliminated all tax exemptions, made general land or property taxation applicable throughout the kingdom, and introduced a general taxation on consumption as well as on luxury goods. With these measures came *Gewerbefreiheit*, which meant that anyone who paid a trade tax could now carry on any trade, with the exception of those trades where excessive competition or the absence of professional skills could be disadvantageous to the community as a whole (pharmacy for example). Stein, grumbling from the distance, did not agree with this measure: he had not wished to eliminate the guilds, only their powers of exclusion. But Hardenberg, another avid student of Adam Smith, believed competition to be the greatest incentive and regulator 'of our industry'. This reform did away completely with the old corporations and their privileges and established the basic legal equality of free property and liberty of contract. Hardenberg foresaw a protest from those with vested interests in the old system, and was aware of the need to institutionalize this protest and the debate it engendered. Hence on 27 October 1810 he promised diets for the provinces as well as one for the entire Prussian state. He then called together a provisional national representation, the members of which he appointed himself, consisting in the main – and this is a reflection of the continuing agrarian basis of Prussia's economy at the time – of the landed nobility. But instead of being appeased by this measure, the nobility – who were also of the erroneous opinion that they had played a decisive part in the removal of Stein – voiced their strong opposition to Hardenberg's policies, which they saw as the policies of a 'foreigner' who wanted to turn honest-to-God Prussia into a modern *Judenstaat*. These rumblings of anti-industrial sentiments were to acquire unforeseeable proportions and produce sinister consequences. The leaders of the opposition, Count Fincken-stein and Ludwig von der Marwitz, were put into the Spandau Citadel because they were alleged to have led a conspiracy, while several regional civil servants who had supported them were relieved of their posts.

Stein's edict of 1807 in respect of the peasant liberation had abolished personal serfdom and its consequences but had not abolished such services as were due by right to the land-owners. Hardenberg now suggested that such services should be commuted into money payments, or that part of the land held by the peasant should be handed over to the landlord. By the peasant being relieved of these services Hardenberg hoped to achieve higher agricultural productivity than was possible under the old feudal system. His 'Edict concerning the Regulating of the Relations between Peasants and Manorial Estates' did just this. Like Stein's reform it was not wholly in the interest of the peasants. Many of them could no longer survive after they had handed over part of their land as compensation for services due and were reduced to the status of agricultural wage-labourers. Those that could survive became, in Hardenberg's view, the core of a healthy peasantry. It was the beginning of *laissez faire* in Prussia, based on the experience of the Agricultural Revolution in England.

On a broader level Hardenberg found support for his measures from the influential economist Albrecht Thaer who had made himself a name as an economist before he entered Prussian service in 1804. Thaer argued that landed nobility and peasants were no longer lords and servants but managers of a business designed to yield profit which in turn would maximize the state's income from the taxation derived. When the Berlin University was founded, Thaer became one of its teachers. But his views did not remain unopposed. The Prussian nobility found another middle class intellectual, Adam Müller, to oppose him. The struggle between Hardenberg on the one hand and the Prussian nobility on the other was now conducted by the pens of two middle class academics. Müller protested against the rationalization of agriculture as inhuman and disagreed with the theory of agriculture as an industry. While Müller argued about the close relationship existing between the soil and the men who cultivated it, Thaer denied the existence of such ties and compared the relationship of a landlord to his land with that of a factory manager to his factory. Müller was the representative of the organic world view, Thaer the progressive liberal-minded advocate of industrial attitudes in all sectors of human production. Müller saw agriculture as reflecting the divine order of things, strictly hierarchical, based on divine revelation and in Christian institutions. He succeeded in articulating the agrarian protest with arguments that were to be heard for the rest of the century. Practically, he attacked all aspects of the reform government and those who profited by it. He attacked the increasing bureaucratization of life, the economists influenced by the ideas of Adam Smith, arguing that 'nobles and peasants are perishing, and in the end there will be only merchants, artisans and Jews'.

This latent anti-Semitism among the forces of Conservatism was given support by the 'Edict concerning the Citizens' Rights of the Jews' of 11 March 1812. The edict, prepared by Friedrich von Raumer, proclaimed that the concept of Jewishness would cease forthwith; that Jews merely represented a religious community like any other. Hardenberg himself said that he would not opt for a law concerning the Jews that contained more than four words: 'same rights, same duties'. As a result of this edict approximately 70,000 Jews became Prussian citizens. In the War of Liberation more than 400 Jewish volunteers were registered, 72 of them earned the Iron Cross, and many of these now emancipated Jewish families – names like Friedberg, Liebermann, Friedlander, Rathenau, von Mossner and von Bendemann – were active supporters of the Prussian state and all it stood for.

By that time new military complications loomed on the horizon; Prussia's military forces, humiliated at Jena and Auerstädt, were once again considered a desirable ally. That this was the case was the achievement of another Hanoverian in Prussian service, General Gerhard von Scharnhorst, the son of a soldier who himself had started in the ranks and made his way up. Like Napoleon he had begun in the artillery. From early in his career he displayed a great talent for education. He was also probably the first German officer to realize fully the implications inherent in the colonial militia of the North American settlers and the important role they played in the defeat of Britain's mercenary forces. They enjoyed the advantage of knowing their country, of fully exploiting its geography. Once they were organized into a proper army, they were victorious. What had been demonstrated in North America was confirmed by the French Revolutionary Armies, particularly in Flanders where Scharnhorst participated with distinction in Hanoverian service. In other words, Scharnhorst had realized the significance of the *levée en masse* before it was put into practice in France.

Like Stein and others he recognized the need for thorough reforms in the Prussian army even before Jena and Auerstädt and dedicated himself to this purpose. Time and again he called for new strategies and tactics because those of the Frederician age were no longer adequate to meet the needs of a new age. As director of the War Academy, which was founded upon his initiative, he developed a new theory for the conduct of war; one of his most dedicated pupils was Carl von Clausewitz. But his calls for reforms were turned down time and again by the remnants of the Frederician school, till the defeats at the hand of Napoleon created a climate of opinion more favourable to the reception of his ideas.

Clausewitz summarized the ideas of Scharnhorst and his fellow reformers in four points:

1. *New structure, armaments and equipment for the army in accordance with the new methods of warfare.*
2. *Ennoblement of its [the army's] constituent parts and the raising of its morale. Therefore abolition of the recruitment of foreigners; an approach towards a system of general military service; abolition of corporal punishment; introduction of good military educational institutions.*
3. *Careful selection of those officers commanding the larger formations. The principle of seniority which had so far exercised so great a role in the Prussian army and had provided its leaders was to be subjected to serious limitations and replaced by the principle, of particular value at the time, that preferential treatment should be given to who had served in the war and had distinguished themselves in various ways . . .*
4. *Exercises adequate and corresponding with the present methods of warfare.*

What these aims implied was no more or less than a fundamental change in the relationship between army and state. So far the middle class, small as it was, had been exempted from military service. Scharnhorst argued for the opening up of the army to members of the middle class from which he himself had come. This proved to be a step of considerable long-term significance. Hitherto, the commissioned ranks had been almost exclusively the preserve of the nobility, while peasants constituted the rank and file. Scharnhorst's aim was to make members of the middle class eligible for commissions and to introduce higher education as the prerequisite for advancement into the upper echelons of the army.

The relations between army, state and society were to be reformed in such a way that the army would adopt the system of values and political consciousness of the middle class. Thus it became an institution which was to play a vital role in the process of political and social integration in the Prussian state. In July 1809, at a time when many of the reforms had been carried out, Scharnhorst answered the objections against entry of commoners into the Prussian officer corps in a memorandum, in which he wrote: 'If only children of noblemen possess the privilege to be employed as officers, and despite their gross ignorance and tender age men are made subordinate to them who have knowledge and courage, then this will help the noble families, but the army will rot and never obtain the respect of the nation – it will become the object of derision for the educated.'

Education was a vital factor in Scharnhorst's reform programme:

If the education of a nation is to prosper, then the entire school system of a nation must originate from one source which is at the very foundation of the nation. The same concept of the nation must predominate in all educational institutions; the same organic connections must embrace the entire education of youth and all be directed towards the same goal. There is only one humanity, and every nation represents one entity within it; therefore the national educational institutions should not educate individuals or classes, but the nation as a whole, and all schools must represent one school for the nation.

Two demands are reflected in this concept: a national aim and a democratic aim, interrelated with one another. The school should not be an institution for the state, nor for the education of a particular class, nor for the preparation for a particular profession, for this would only serve particularist interests and as such be in opposition to the whole idea of national education. Specialization, too, at school level would breed separate interests and would not lead to the unity of all citizens in one nation that was the ultimate aim. For this reason also, all citizens should serve in the army. 'Only by arming the whole of the people will the smaller establish a kind of equilibrium of might in a defensive war conducted against the larger who carries on a war of subjugation by aggression.'

The new army was to be based upon honour and bravery, with opportunities for anyone with ability. Wars of conquest, so Scharnhorst argued, are always dependent upon the great man who has the ability and charisma to lead and inspire his army but wars of defence depend to a much greater degree on the character of the soldier than on the talents of a great general. 'We have begun to estimate the art of war higher than the military virtues – this has been the downfall of peoples at all times. Bravery, sacrifice, steadfastness are the cornerstones of the independence of a nation; as soon as our hearts no longer beat for them we are lost, even in the midst of great victories.'

After Jena and Auerstädt Scharnhorst was called to head a military commission of which Gneisenau, because of his brilliant defence of Kolberg, was also a member. The commission was to enquire into the causes for the defeats and weed out those that had proved themselves incapable; also to submit and carry out the reforms considered necessary.

One must give the nation the feeling of independence; one must provide the opportunities for it to become familiar with itself, so that it looks after itself, for only then will it respect itself and know how to compel others to respect it. To work towards this aim is all that we can do. To destroy the old ways, remove prejudice, lead the rebirth, watch over it and not stop its free growth, more than that we cannot effect.

In many ways one can argue that the principle of general military service had existed since Frederick William I's *Cantonal-Reglement* of 1733. But any such view would not take account of the vast number of exemptions, which included all towns and cities, and which had meant that the recruitment of mercenaries was still a necessity. During the Seven Years War, especially its later stages, forcible recruitment had been carried out, but no one had conceived of the 'citizen soldier', of the duty of every citizen to carry arms for his country and to prepare for the day when he should need to use them. But then the citizen did not yet exist in Prussia, only the subject, and among the royal subjects of Frederick the Great the burghers were important only for trade and manufacture and were essentially unmilitary.

Stein fully supported Scharnhorst's demand for the introduction of general conscription. One of the first obstacles was of a financial nature, namely what would an army suddenly based upon universal conscription cost? The figures proved staggering, bearing in mind the financial obligations of Prussia towards France. Hence it was necessary to accept what existed already, namely the standing army, and merely add to it another component which was very cheap, this being the *Landwehr* or militia. Forcible recruitment as it had existed was adapted and turned into a general duty of all citizens to serve in the army. In that way the Prussian army experienced its most thoroughgoing transformation since the days of the Great Elector.

But first of all the standing army was badly in need of reform, especially its senior officers. Scharnhorst's commission purged it to the extent that of 143 generals who in 1806 were still on the active list, on the eve of the Wars of Liberation only two remained: Blücher and Tauentzien.

Scharnhorst wanted to turn the army into the school of the nation, but in practical terms he had to form an efficient but cheap military force for an impoverished state. The solution he envisaged was firstly to draft all who were able to carry arms into the army – though because the Treaty of Tilsit had limited the Prussian army to 42,000 men this could not be fully carried out until 1813. The national service men were to serve for a limited but uninterrupted period of time in the army, then be released but with the duty to remain in the reserves. Standing army and reserves were to constitute the regular army, ready to be mobilized the moment war threatened the country. But to ensure that everyone served in the army the *Landwehr*, the militia, was to be called into being to act as reinforcements or for the protection of the lines of communications. At first of course the *Landwehr* was bound to include many who as yet had never served in the army, but as the system of national service developed, ultimately every *Landwehr* soldier would in earlier years have served in the army.

Scharnhorst devised methods of evading Napoleon's limitation of the size of the Prussian army to 42,000 men. The so-called *Krümpersystem* allowed every company to release three to five men per month who were then replaced by the same number of *Krümpers*, as the recruits were called. In this way each company trained up to 60 additional men annually who were then available in case of mobilization. Also, following the French example, the Prussian army was restructured into brigades in each of which all divisions of the service were represented and which were capable of independent operation.

Changes in structure were accompanied by changes in the conditions of service and in tactical training. Except in a very few cases corporal punishment was abolished – almost half a century before this barbaric practice was abandoned by the British army. Considering that corporal punishment was and remained part of the sentences imposed by German criminal courts until well into the twentieth century, this measure was considerably in advance of its time. Exercises were no longer dominated by parade-ground drill, but included training in the field and on rifle ranges and the combination of *Tirailleur* tactics with the massive firepower of the line and the concentrated push of a column of battalion strength. Cavalry, artillery and infantry were trained no longer to look upon themselves as independent, but as achieving the maximum effect by their combined and integrated efforts.

As was the case with Stein's and Hardenberg's reforms, a substantial section of the Prussian nobility turned against Scharnhorst – yet another 'foreigner'. They rejected on principle the view that the collapse of Prussia had been caused by the failure of the *ancien régime*, and argued that the fault lay primarily with individuals, who had been soft or incapable or both. They argued that the Frederician army had been beaten because the old Frederician discipline and obedience no longer prevailed. Standards had been allowed to deteriorate. This may be true. A master of defence such as Frederick would hardly have been swept off the battlefield with one blow as was the army of Frederick William III. But it is more than doubtful whether in the long run he would have been capable of resisting a modern national army, and Napoleon's offensive strategy.

Scharnhorst and his fellow military reformers such as Gneisenau, supported by Stein, could see only one alternative: a thorough reform or none at all. Their opponents conceded that there was a need for reform but maintained that this could be carried out within the framework of the Frederician army. They were blind to the new and strong national currents which played so large a part in the motivation of new military forces, giving them their very dynamism. They failed to see the significance of the popular risings against Napoleon in Spain and in the Tyrol, and the long-term implications such new methods of warfare would have upon the conduct of war.

One of Scharnhorst's main opponents was General von Yorck, who had already moved to the fore as an opponent of the Prussian Reform Movement in general. That does not mean that he had closed his eyes completely to the need for military reforms. Even before 1806 he had recognized the importance of the new French tactics and begun to exercise his troops accordingly. Nor did he oppose in principle the introduction of compulsory military service for all. What he objected to was the erosion of the privileges of the aristocratic Prussian officer corps. The twofold purpose of the reforms, namely to break down the barriers which the predominantly agrarian social structure of eighteenth-century Prussia had erected around the army and, secondly, to provide within the framework of the Prussian state in general and the Prussian army in particular a place for an aspiring middle class infected with new nationalism, Yorck considered as evil, believing that by different means they would produce the same result as the French Revolution – a total social and political upheaval at the end of which there would be the victory of the mob.

Certainly the democratic tendencies evident in such practices as the rule that allowed the *Landwehr* to elect its own officers, and in the demand by the supporters of the Reform Movement for the introduction of a constitutional monarchy, were ultimately a stumbling block for the Prussian Reform Movement as a whole. It was the middle class who were most receptive to the ideas of the French Revolution, especially the younger generation, who before and after the overthrow of Napoleon vociferously expressed their opinion that the time had come to give not only Prussia but also Germany a new shape. This trend, and the fact that its main support came from the army, caused Castlereagh to write in 1815: 'I fairly own that I look with considerable anxiety to the tendency of their [Prussian] politics. There certainly at this moment exists a great fermentation in all orders of the state, very free notions of government, if not principles actually revolutionary are prevalent, and the army is by no means subordinate to the Civil authorities.'

Within that context the opening up of the officer corps to the middle class and the organization of the *Landwehr* were hardly conducive to calming the reactionaries. Therefore, while the reformers had tried to unify the nation and the state and to modify the traditional social structure to include the middle class and its aspirations, the gradual upsurge of reaction increased the gulf between nation and state once more. 'To arm the nation means merely to organize and facilitate opposition and dissatisfaction', argued Prince Wittgenstein. The *Landwehr* and its officers represented a potential army for civil war.

Yet the fear of the reactionaries that Scharnhorst planned to do away with the Prussian nobility was entirely without foundation. What he wanted was its rejuvenation by a blood transfusion. Noblemen entitled to commissions by birth had little interest in developing their faculties through education. The reformers believed in the principle of free competition between the nobility and the middle classes, and sought in that way to harness for the state new sources of strength which had hitherto been allowed to flow into the wasteland. But Scharnhorst rejected outright the notion that only the nobility had a concept of honour and of service: 'That the fundamental principles of love of honour can predominate among the bourgeoisie as among the nobility, is borne out by the French officers of the present day.'

What mobilized broad sections of the nobility in opposition to the military reformers was that with the required reduction of the Prussian army and its reorganization, famous old regimental names disappeared to be replaced by new units carrying only numbers and the name of the province in which they were garrisoned.

Just as the cabinet prevented Stein from having direct access to the King, the office of the Adjutant confronted Scharnhorst. As commander-in-chief of the army Frederick William III, like his ancestors and successors, tended by both training and inclination more towards military than civil affairs. Therefore as long as the Prussian monarchy existed a form of military cabinet continued to function. Scharnhorst's aim of institutionalizing the military leadership in the form of a ministry of war was cut short by his own death, but as long as he lived he combined a strength and broadness of purpose that maintained unity and direction in his reforms.

Frederick William III did not make things particularly easy for Scharnhorst. His reasoning powers clearly showed him that Scharnhorst was right, but emotionally he remained tied to the legacy of his grand-uncle, and this made him vulnerable to the arguments of those who opposed Scharnhorst. He, too, wondered what forces one would ultimately awaken by the introduction of military conscription. He saw the need for the abolition of the privileges of the nobility in the army and therefore approved of the introduction of examinations for ensigns and officers, but he obstinately refused to close down the cadet institutes, which Scharnhorst saw merely as training schools for the nobility and not conducive to producing the necessary national élite. In the long run, however, the pressure from the growing middle class proved too strong, even for the Conservatives in Prussia, and the cadet institutes were opened to all suitable applicants.

Scharnhorst also faced opposition from the civil service, which argued that it was not in Prussia's economic interests that able young men be suddenly removed from their careers for four years. It would have preferred the Napoleonic system whereby a conscript could buy himself out by providing a deputy to serve in his place. Scharnhorst objected vociferously to this idea because such a concession would have run contrary to the whole concept of his reform work. Nevertheless, he was compelled to agree to a compromise solution according to which every academic, and for that matter anyone able to pay for his own army equipment, had to serve only five months in the line whereas everyone else served for five years.

Unlike Stein's and Hardenberg's reforms, which can be listed edict by edict, Scharnhorst's can, with a few exceptions, be discerned only in the army regulations. For instance compulsory military service was never publicly proclaimed. *De jure* the old cantonal system of Frederick William I remained in force until March 1813, although *de facto* it had already been abolished for five years. Only the tactical reforms of the Prussian army found expression in a general revision of the military manual.

However, in the span of seven, or at the most nine, years basic attitudes established over a century can hardly be eliminated. After the death of Scharnhorst, which was followed later by the departure of Gneisenau and Boyen, the results of the military reforms were still visible on the practical level, but the deeper, spiritual and national current that had motivated them had already sunk into oblivion. As early as 1824 one observer, an Austrian general, noted that the Prussian army had returned 'to the old strict forms', that it had once again become accustomed to unconditional obedience, and that this army which perhaps had contained elements conducive to the destruction of public order, had once more become one of the firmest supports of the existing order.

Considering the far-reaching aims of the Prussian Reform Movement (within a purely Prussian context), particularly those in the educational and military sectors, then the net result was a very disappointing one. All that had ultimately been achieved in the military sector was the transformation of an army that had largely been based on mercenaries into one that was specifically Prussian and whose function in a sociological sense was that of integrating all its members into the Prussian state community. However, in the realm of education, Humboldt's influence attained international proportions, the extent of which lies beyond the scope of this work.

Chapter 9

The War of Liberation

The Treaty of Tilsit had reduced Prussia to the role of a buffer-state between France and Russia, its independence or freedom of action being severely limited. The indemnity levied by Napoleon upon Prussia was of such a size that even with the strictest of economies Prussia was not able to raise it. This caused Stein and later Scharnhorst to counsel the King to seek a rapprochement with Napoleon, a rapprochement designed only for tactical purposes until such time as Prussia could regain its freedom of action. But on this point the King was adamant; he rejected this counsel, and Stein's suggestion that Napoleon be godfather to one of the Prussian princesses found no hearing.

The French had set specific dates for the payment of the indemnity and made the withdrawal of their forces of occupation conditional upon their being met. Stein tried to negotiate with the French but his forthright character lacked the subtle manners of the skilled diplomat. Napoleon, who had first demanded 150 million francs, then 120 million and finally 100 million, insisted that the last sum be raised from the sale of royal domains, which of course would have been tantamount to vast annexations of Prussia's heartland. Actually this demand provided the very lever with the aid of which Stein was able to persuade the Prussian nobility to agree to a general income tax. But Napoleon was still evasive.

In that setting the Spanish rising against Napoleon erupted. Spain, perhaps besides France the only united nation on the European mainland, lit and carried the torch of national liberation, fighting the usurper as the very personification of evil, apostasy and atheism. Napoleon, in his own way a child of the Enlightenment, had calculated with measurable, empirically verifiable quantities. A rising which derived its impetus from a combination of national, religious and other spiritual forces represented an imponderable for which he had made no allowance and which therefore proved a very unpleasant surprise. Within a few months of its beginning, the widely distributed Spanish pamphlet literature inciting the population to resistance against the French had reached the German states. Here it served the same purpose, sometimes as a model, but more often directly adapted, any changes being made only to make it suitable for the specifically German situation. From Spain the pamphlet literature made its way in two major directions, to London and to Vienna, from where it found its way back into the German heartland. The Spaniards carried the torch and its sparks set aflame the emotions and passions of those suffering under Napoleon, who believed that the moment was near to overthrow Napoleonic rule in Central Europe.

The Austrian chancellor, Count Johann Phillip von Stadion, thought that moment had come provided that Prussia could be rallied to Austria's side, thus restoring not only unity of action but also continuity in German history by abolishing the recent Austro-German dualism. Stadion was, like Stein, the scion of an old German family of *Reichsritter* and found in Stein a man of the same mould and the same mind. Stein, who had failed to obtain any concessions from the French by negotiation, expressed himself in favour of conflict with them. Frederick William III was prepared to move but only if Russia would take the same course and of that there was no sign as yet. Spain now achieved by force what Stein had failed to obtain by negotiation: the events in Spain compelled Napoleon to move substantial forces from Central Europe into the Iberian peninsula, the oppressive occupation of Prussia by French forces was reduced to a minimum, Frederick William III could return from Königsberg to his capital Berlin.

Russia's Czar Alexander counselled Frederick William peace and quiet for the time being, then journeyed to Erfurt to participate in a congress to which Napoleon had invited him, France feeling the need to secure its back while engaged in Spain. In Prussia, too, the peace party (a party largely identical with the opponents of the Reform Movement) advised moderation. Stein advocated that Prussia join Austria against Napoleon, but whether he could have carried the King is doubtful. In any case a letter of his dated 15 August 1808 was intercepted by the French, apparently not without some help from Stein's Prussian opponents. The letter contained expressions of strongly anti-Napoleonic sentiment and Napoleon, who now realized the danger, demanded that Stein be dismissed and that Prussia accept France's final demands of the payment of 140 million francs and the occupation of three fortresses along the river Oder. Frederick William saw no other way but to sign and ratify the Paris Treaty, and finally to accept Stein's formal resignation of 24 November 1808. The forces of reaction among the Prussian nobility triumphed: 'one mad head has been crushed already, the remaining vipers will dissolve in their own poison' commented General Yorck.

Stein, now also publicly pursued by the French, found refuge in Vienna, from where he further endeavoured to achieve agreement between Vienna and Berlin. But his successor in Berlin Count Dohna, minister of the interior, and Freiherr von Altenstein, minister of finance, were not to be drawn in the face of Frederick William's refusal to act without Russia's support and their policy of appeasement towards the forces of reaction within the Prussian nobility.

Austria decided to use the favourable moment that seemed to have presented itself, hoping that by its example it would ultimately carry

Prussia as well. Never was the House of Hapsburg greater than in those moments of history when it represented, for better or worse, German interests. The year 1809 saw that dynasty at the head of the first attempt by the German nation – which once again was in the process of re-formation after its original unity and national consciousness had been ruptured by the Reformation and its aftermath – to obtain its national liberty by means of a national rising. The Spanish example was to be emulated in Germany. By the combined weight of popular risings both along the Danube and the Ebro Napoleon was to be forced down. Friedrich von Gentz, Friedrich Schlegel and a host of others penned pamphlets and proclamations appealing to German patriots every-where. Archduke Charles in a public proclamation to the German people and his troops announced 'Your victories will free them from their chains, and your German brothers, still in the ranks of the enemy are waiting for their liberation.' Vienna became the centre for a systematic propaganda campaign for the rest of Germany, with branches in Munich run by Stadion's brother Friedrich Lothar von Stadion, in Dresden by the Austrian envoy Buol and in Prussia by Adam Müller and the poet Heinrich von Kleist. The feeling of certainty that these efforts would result in a general rising of the Germans against Napoleon was the critical factor in Austria's final decisions to go to war, a decision already arrived at in principle towards the end of 1808. War began in April 1809 with an appeal written by Friedrich Stadion and Schlegel and signed by Archduke Charles addressed 'To the German Nation'. In Prussia Scharnhorst and Gneisenau were in favour of joining Austria and Queen Louise thought that if Prussia's downfall were inevitable, then it would be better if it were with honour.

In the Tyrol a well-planned mass rising of the peasants, inspired by Vienna and in part financed by London, led by the inn-keeper Andreas Hofer expelled the occupation forces of the Confederation of the Rhine, primarily Bavarian troops, from the capital of the province, Innsbruck, and from the province as a whole. The troops of Archduke Charles, however, moved too slowly, allowing Napoleon to concentrate his forces. Charles was pushed back into Bohemia and Napoleon advanced towards Vienna. Only on 21/22 May 1809 did Charles succeed in inflicting upon Napoleon the first defeat he had suffered, that at Aspern. But again this success was not followed up and Napoleon regained the initiative, defeating the Austrians at Wagram on 5/6 July 1809.

Although the Prussian government had been more sceptical about the chances of success, the example, especially that provided by the rising of the Tyroleans, was infectious for some. On 28 April 1809 the 2nd Brandenburg Hussar Regiment in Berlin under the command of Major Ferdinand von Schill, already distinguished in the defence of Kolberg, marched out of the city, ostensibly for an exercise. But Schill's plan was not to return to the city but to conduct his own campaign against the French troops and in this way to force King and government to join with the general effort. Once he had left the city he told his officers and men about his plan and gave them the opportunity to leave and return to Berlin. Only a handful did so, the vast majority of officers and men pressing to take action against the French forces at the earliest possible moment. Schill then marched south to Dessau which he entered with a public proclamation announcing the city's liberation and his intentions. He was enthusiastically cheered by the city's population, but public support did not go beyond that. He and his troops remained isolated and the popular uprising which Schill had hoped his action would incite did not materialize. Schill's intention had been to march to the kingdom of Westphalia to join up with the forces of Colonel von Dörnberg who had planned a similar rising to that of Schill against King Jerome. That rising, too, proved abortive and Dörnberg escaped to Bohemia. Schill, however, decided to move north to the Baltic in the hope that he and his men would be taken and saved by the British Navy. He surprised the garrison of the city of Stralsund and occupied it, hoping either to be able to turn it into another Saragossa, (where in 1808 Spanish soldiers and civilians under the leadership of Jose de Palafox y Melci had given a splendid account of themselves in defending the city against siege by the French) or at least to hold it until the Royal Navy should arrive. On 31 May 1809 Dutch and Danish auxiliary forces of the French stormed the city defended by Schill and his 500 men. Schill was killed in the action and the 11 of his officers who were captured were put before a French court martial at Wesel and later shot there on 16 September 1809. From Dörnberg's forces 14 officers were selected by lot and shot at Brunswick. The remaining prisoners were condemned to serve as French galley slaves, but those that survived regained their freedom after the fall of Napoleon.

Frederick William III condemned outright Schill's action as an act of mutiny. This was not simply in order to placate Napoleon but expressed his innermost convictions. Apart from that, the appeal to the masses, the attempt to incite an entire nation into a popular rising and a national war of liberation were actions totally alien to him.

The failure of the north proved a serious disappointment to Vienna. The Hofburg seemed to have been unaware that the north German plains were hardly the kind of ground on which a guerrilla war analogous to that of Andalusia and Tyrol could be fought. Kleist's resounding words

> Schlagt ihn tot, das Weltgericht
> fragt euch nach den Grüden nicht

> *Strike him dead, the council of the world*
> *will not ask you for the reasons*

were no compensation for the Austrian forces hard pressed by Napoleon. Frederick William III remained adamant in his decision not to act unless he had the support of Russia. Both Scharnhorst and

Gneisenau tried hard to persuade him, but to no avail. An embittered Gneisenau resigned his post and went to England hoping he could persuade the British government to land forces in northern Germany. But in the meantime the momentous events of Wagram had occurred. Six days after Wagram, on 12 July 1809, Napoleon and Emperor Francis decided to conclude an armistice. The Tyrolean peasants were left to their fate. They continued to fight on, at first very successfully, until finally in the autumn of 1809, forsaken by their Emperor, all their lines of communication cut, they were defeated by French and Bavarian forces. Their leader, Andreas Hofer, escaped, but his hideout was later betrayed. He was arrested, perfunctorily tried and then shot at Mantua in 1810. Other Tyrolean leaders like Speckbacher, who managed to evade the French, made their way to Vienna where they were treated by the Hofburg with considerable embarrassment and for the next few years sustained on a pittance hardly commensurate with their efforts in support of their dynasty.

On 14 October 1809 at Napoleon's headquarters, Austria signed the Peace of Schönbrunn, which reduced it to a second-rate power. It had to participate in the continental blockade and also reduce its armed forces to 150,000 men. Count Metternich, who had negotiated the treaty, now replaced Phillip Stadion as Austria's leading minister.

Yet the events of 1809, however unsuccessful and disastrous in their immediate outcome, proved to be the precursors of the War of Liberation. They accelerated a process of crystallization of anti-Napoleonic feeling in Germany as a whole, awakening new sympathies for the cause of liberation throughout the German states and focusing any future hopes particularly upon Prussia. In spite of a vacillating monarch, Prussia was now carrying through a programme of reform that was considered worthy of emulation throughout the country, especially since the leaders of the Reform Movement never obscured their ultimate aim, namely the reforging of a German union which over the preceding two centuries had broken asunder.

In order to mobilize the broad spectrum of middle class opinion a 'League of Virtue' had been founded in Königsberg in April 1808 which aimed at spreading and deepening liberal and national ideas. It had to be dissolved under French pressure in December 1809 but was quickly succeeded by the *Turnbewegung*, the gymnastics movement founded by Friedrich Ludwig Jahn in 1810 at Berlin. Ever since 1807 Jahn had spoken out publicly against French oppression, and he considered his gymnastics association as a political as well as physical preparation for the struggle of liberation. It provided the mass basis for the German League which he founded with Karl Friedrich Friesen and which from Prussian territory was to spread into the states of the Confederation of the Rhine.

Since 1809 the signs of crisis had further multiplied within the Napoleonic Empire. For over two decades France had conducted war continuously, the fruits of which, glory apart, never seemed to ripen.

Evidence of dissatisfaction increased; Napoleon's police minister Fouché, who had covered France with an elaborate network of secret informers, had ample work to do. Furthermore, in the following year basic differences between the French and Russians cracked the surface of official amiability. For the sake of its own economic interests Russia broke the system of continental blockade, while Napoleon retaliated by occupying the mouths of the rivers Elbe, Weser and Trave and by dissolving the duchy of Oldenburg whose ruling prince was the brother-in-law of the Czar. When Alexander then demanded from Napoleon an assurance that he would not reconstitute the kingdom of Poland with the frontiers of 1772 and met Napoleon's refusal, the fuse for the explosion between France and Russia had been lit.

Both powers set out to consolidate their position in preparation for the impending conflict. Prussia's position as a buffer-state made it virtually impossible not to take either one side or the other. In order to anticipate French measures designed to curtail Prussia's already severely restricted area for manoeuvre, Frederick William offered an alliance to the French while at the same time sending Scharnhorst to St Petersburg, which since the defeat of Austria had become the haven of Prussia's political emigrés, including Stein. Scharnhorst informed the Czar of Prussia's action and at the same time concluded a secret military convention. Hardenberg in Berlin, observing Napoleon's hostile attitude, favoured a public alliance with Russia, but Frederick William was not sufficiently convinced of the Czar's reliability to take the risk that such an alliance would involve. From St Petersburg Scharnhorst was sent to Vienna where Metternich blandly told him that it was not in Austria's interest to further the establishment of Russian hegemony in Europe at the expense of the French. In the face of this Hardenberg once again turned to the French who were now ready for an alliance, which was concluded on 24 February 1812. According to its terms Prussia was to supply one auxiliary corps for the French forces if war between France and Russia should break out. French troops were already massed on Prussia's frontier; had Prussia not signed they would have invaded Prussia instead of traversing it *en route* for Russia.

The ratification of the alliance on 5 March 1812 caused a serious upheaval among the military reformers. Scharnhorst and Gneisenau together with other generals submitted their resignation to the King. Gneisenau's second resignation within two years was accepted and he returned to England. Boyen and Clausewitz together with others went to St Petersburg. Scharnhorst moved to Silesia and retained his competency as the King's technical advisor.

Napoleon had by now massed his forces along the Russian frontier in the north, an army of 600,000 men, only 210,000 of whom were French. The second largest contingent, approximately 180,000 men, was supplied by the German princes. On the evening of 22 June 1812 Napoleon began crossing the river Memel, the Russian frontier. The Russian forces withdrew, leaving Napoleon in a situation he had never confronted before and to which he could not adjust. Counting on his superiority in numbers he had ignored Russia's major ally, its – sheer size – and his 600,000 men were absorbed in the Russian vastness as quickly as a platoon on Salisbury Plain. Exploiting their geographic advantage to the utmost, the Russians tempted Napoleon deeper and deeper into the country, by capturing Moscow he won a Pyrrhic victory ultimately symbolizing his strategic defeat. With a mass army which, in view of Russia's scorched earth policy, could not be fed off the land; with lines of communication cut or because of distance functioning badly; with an enemy who could attack and then withdraw at will into the boundless Russian space and who, therefore, could never be manoeuvred into a decisive battle; there was only one course of action for Napoleon – to get out of Russia and save of his army what could be saved. And precisely during his withdrawal Russian attacks became stronger and stronger, culminating in the disaster at the crossing of the Beresina. The campaign of 1812 was more than a lost campaign for Napoleon, it was the beginning of his end.

Napoleon's Prussian auxiliary corps numbered 20,000 men commanded by General Crawert, attached to Marshal Macdonald and covering the northern wing of Napoleon's advance along the Baltic. Crawert appears to have been an ardent and uncritical admirer of Napoleon's military genius, but when shortly after the beginning of the Russian campaign he fell ill and was replaced by General von Yorck attitudes began to change. Ordered by Macdonald to fortify, at Prussia's expense, the city of Memel, Yorck refused outright saying that there was no clause to this effect in the alliance treaty. In August, during skirmishes with the Russian garrison in Riga, Prussian prisoners were taken whereupon Yorck duly sent his plenipotentiary to the Russians to get his prisoners exchanged. But the prisoners had joined Russia's German Legion, a legion set up by Gneisenau and Stein, together with the Committee for German Affairs. During October and November the Prussian contingent was not seriously involved in battle. Yorck in his headquarters, however, was subjected to continuous bombardment, not by Russian artillery but by Russian letters pleading with him to join Russia's effort since Russian and Prussian interests were identical. The governor of Riga, the Marquis von Paulucci wrote:

Let us come to the core of the matter. The man who has covered Europe with wounds from which it will bleed for a long time, is approaching the end of his disastrous greatness . . . This circumstance puts Prussia in the position of the arbiter of Europe's future and you to become the liberator of your fatherland. There are two ways in which you could achieve this aim. Firstly, to combine your forces with mine, arrest Macdonald and march for the liberation of your King. The Czar would support you with all available means. Secondly, with reference to the retreat of the French you could declare that you wish to cover the frontiers of your fatherland, withdraw your forces beyond the Niemen and maintain neutrality . . .

Yorck was in a position where his action could give the lead for liberation, or it could evaporate almost into nothingness, leaving behind like Schill, only a messy residue of treason and mutiny. Yorck kept the King informed of the Russian approaches, wishing that his Supreme Commander would issue a firm decision one way or the other. Frederick William refused to be drawn. Then on 17 December 1812 a decision was made for Yorck – by the Russians. Russian forces under the command of General Diebitsch had made a breakthrough to the south of him and operated in Yorck's rear. Yorck consequently ordered the Prussian withdrawal to the Russo-Prussian frontier. The Russian forces observed his retreat, but not once took any of the ample opportunities for attack. General Diebitsch's adjutant was none other than Colonel Karl von Clausewitz, Scharnhorst's former favourite pupil. Shortly before they reached the frontier, Diebitsch cut off the rear of the Prussians and then asked for a consultation with Yorck. On Christmas morning 1812 the two generals met, but the conversation did not proceed satisfactorily. Diebitsch said that he had no interest in putting obstacles in the way of the Prussians, all he wanted was part of Yorck's ammunition supplies and pieces of his artillery. Yorck was uncertain; he did not want to take any step that might blemish his military honour. Furthermore, he was deeply suspicious of Clausewitz who was present during the talk – and Clausewitz equally so of Yorck, whom he considered an arch reactionary and whose influence he had experienced on many occasions when a supporter of and participant in the Prussian Reform Movement.

Yorck was in a situation that brought him into conflict with the principle which he had adhered to all his life, as had his forefathers before him: unhesitating, unquestioning obedience to his orders. What was asked of him now was something that had never been taught in the cadet institute or anywhere else in the Prussian army: he had to make an essentially political decision. Nevertheless, leaving the much-detested Macdonald was a treasonable act, and when Clausewitz asked for another interview Yorck refused to see him. Clausewitz was followed by Scharnhorst's brother-in-law, Count Dohna, sent by Paulucci, carrying a personal letter from the Czar. In it the Czar undertook not to lay down his arms against the French until Prussia's former position among the powers of Europe had been fully restored.

This letter was crucial. It decided Yorck to resume his personal negotiations with Diebitsch. At the same time he informed Frederick William of the developments. Clausewitz reappeared in Yorck's headquarters at Tauroggen, 40 kilometres from Tilsit, and during a night session Yorck and Clausewitz drafted a convention. Yorck had also sent a Major von Seydlitz to Berlin, expecting to receive definite orders from the King. But when Seydlitz returned he had no explicit orders from the King, only evasion, except that by word of mouth he was to forward the message that negotiations with the Austrians had already started and that Yorck should act according to the circumstances. Yorck was confused but then interpreted the phrase 'according to the circumstances' as a blank cheque for his action. On 30 December 1812 at the mill of Poscherun outside Tauroggen, Yorck met Diebitsch again and both signed the Convention of Tauroggen by which Yorck separated his Prussian forces from those of Macdonald and promised to maintain neutrality. The signature was greeted by enthusiastic cheering from the Prussian and Russian regiments. Turning to his officers Yorck said: 'Gentlemen I do not know what I shall say to the King about my action. Perhaps he will call it treason. Then I shall carry the consequences. I shall put my grey head willingly at the disposal of His Majesty and die gladly, knowing that I have not failed as a faithful subject and a true Prussian.'

Indeed, Frederick William III did consider Yorck's action treasonable and gave orders that he be relieved of his command. Since however, no formal order was given, except by publication in a Prussian newspaper, Yorck refused to hand over command. 'Up to now no general has received his orders via the newspapers' he said, and from then on he became one of the driving forces which tried to bring the Prussian army into the war against Napoleon. However detestable it was to him, for the time being circumstances forced him into a common front with the Prussian Reform Movement. But the charge of treason stayed with him for the rest of his life. Not only was it debated by the King and within the officer corps, Yorck debated it continuously within himself and for that reason refused the title of Field-Marshal, stating 'I must fear, having my anxieties raised by the events of the past, that on future occasions of state I may act against my own convictions, and therefore in one way or the other make a mistake at the decisive moment.' This was Prussia's military nobility at its best.

The French defeat at the hands of the Russians further fanned the flames of anti-Napoleonic sentiment in Prussia. Already, the day before the conclusion of the Convention of Tauroggen, the deputies of the nobility representing Prussia's eastern provinces had called for the conclusion of a peace treaty with Russia. No doubt besides patriotic motives, the fear of seeing their own property ravaged by war must have played an important part. But the French debacle had also activated many others and given increased influence to the 'Committee for German Affairs' founded in St Petersburg by German emigrés, Stein, Dohna, Clausewitz, and a host of Prussian officers among them. It was Stein's influence in particular which turned the Czar's romantically inclined mind towards thinking of the war against Napoleon in wider terms than that of national defence and looking at it instead as a war for the liberation of Europe from the Napoleonic yoke. Yorck's action played into their hands; Boyen was sent from St Petersburg to Prussia; Stein followed first to Königsberg and then to Breslau where he arrived towards the end of February 1813. By that time he had travelled only through Prussian territories which had been liberated from the French by the Russians, and no French soldiers were now left east of the river Oder. Yorck was already actively fighting alongside the Russians. Frederick William III on Hardenberg's advice had already left Berlin for Breslau in order to avoid being seized by the French. On 3 February 1813 he issued an edict calling to arms all citizens of the ages of 17 to 24, who had hitherto been exempt from extensive military service, and on the ninth of the same month removed such other exemptions from military service as still existed. For the duration of the war general conscription was thus introduced. On the same day alliance negotiations were started with the Czar. Prussia wanted the reconstitution of its frontiers of 1806. Russia was agreeable to this, insisting only that the formerly Prussian slice of Poland should go to Russia, while Prussia was to be compensated with Saxon territories. The King was not willing to accept this so negotiations were carried on for almost three more weeks, and only upon Stein's intervention in Breslau concluded on 27 February 1813 at Kalisch. The alliance was a risky venture for Prussia; it soon became apparent that the Russian forces were not as numerous as had been expected, while the French still held considerable contingents in Germany. Austria was in favour of the new coalition, but for the time being chose to adopt a 'wait-and-see' attitude before it made its own position clear.

On 10 March 1813, the birthday of the deceased and much beloved Queen Louise, Frederick William founded the 'Iron Cross' order. Five days later the Czar entered Breslau and on 16 March Prussia declared war on France. The following day the Prussian King issued his famous proclamation *'An mein Volk'*, to a resounding reception. Public collections to finance the war produced within a few days six and a half million thalers, those with least to give giving the most. Volunteers from all over Germany and from all social strata joined the Prussian colours in such numbers that in the 12 months from March 1813 to March 1814 the Prussian army received more than 50,000 volunteers. The poet of the War of Liberation was Theodor Körner, a Saxon. When he heard of the Prussian mobilization he immediately left his position at the Vienna Hofburg theatre and made his way to Breslau. There, as an ordinary soldier of the light infantry, he entered the Freikorps Lützow, one of several units which did not consist of regular or conscript soldiers but which made a point of being German rather than purely Prussian units. The colours of its uniform – black, with red piping and golden buttons – gave the men of 1848 their national colours of black, red and gold. Körner was in many respects the 'ideal' man of his time, a fighter and poet whose stature attained heroic proportions after his early death in action in 1813. His poems set to music remained among the favourite songs of Germany's youth for well over a century. Among the volunteers to the Prussian colours students played a prominent part, but it would be erroneous to consider the volunteers as an essentially middle class movement. On the contrary; students and grammar school pupils together amounted to no more than 7 per cent of the volunteers (students 4.9 per cent, pupils 2.1 per cent), while artisans, manual labourers and peasants represented a total of 59.5 per cent (artisans 41.2 per cent, manual labourers 14.7 per cent, farmers and peasants 3.6 per cent). The areas traditionally under the Prussian crown before the reign of Frederick the Great provided 53.7 per cent of the volunteers; the rest came from all parts of Germany including those states of the Confederation of the Rhine. Thus the youth which rushed to the colours to join the struggle against Napoleon was a cross-section of the younger generation, its representatives cutting across class barriers and geographical borders.

On 25 March 1813 the Proclamation of Kalisch was released from the Russian headquarters. It described the aim of the war against Napoleon as 'the restoration of the German Constitution, alone by the German princes and people and in accordance with the original spirit of the German people'. It was a careful, contradictory formulation out of which everyone could take just what he desired – the princes the restoration of all that they had been deprived of by Napoleon, the middle class the growing aim of a greater political unification of Germany and with it a greater political effectiveness of Germany in the councils of Europe. For the Prussian conservatives, however, it was a matter primarily of overthrowing the French usurper and restoring lost rights, be they the rights of the German princes or those of princes dethroned by Napoleon. This forged the link between the growing German national movement and the defenders of the concept of monarchic legitimacy; together these formed the theme that was to dominate German politics for the rest of the nineteenth century and eventually find its most contradictory expression in the Constitution of the German Empire of 1871.

By March 1813 Prussian and Russian forces had also joined up and on the same day on which Frederick William III issued the proclamation *'An mein Volk'*, Yorck and his corps entered Berlin to public rejoicing. Russian Cossacks ventured even as far as Hamburg where they were received enthusiastically.

Napoleon had also begun to rally his forces, to build a new army from the remnants that had returned from Russia. His depleted forces were replenished by new recruits and men supplied by the states of the Confederation of the Rhine. But Bavaria wavered in its support for Napoleon, for the Bavarian army had lost 30,000 men in Russia. Saxony too was undecided which attitude to take, its King fleeing to Prague while the Allies occupied his kingdom. The failure immediately to transform the war against Napoleon into a mass rising of the German people, as had been intended, proved a considerable disappointment to the Allies. In spite of his defeat in Russia, Napoleon still held sufficient sway to convince others of his invincibility, at least against the Prussians. Nor was the prospect of changing the French occupation for occupation by the Russians particularly alluring. Most important, however, was Austria's continuing indecision.

This allowed Napoleon to move his forces rapidly via Mainz and Frankfurt towards Saxony. He had drawn up his plan of battle but was unexpectedly disturbed by the Allies' attack at the village of Grossgörschen on 2 May. Tenaciously Napoleon fought off the attack and forced the Prussian and Russian forces to withdraw, but without taking any prisoners or booty because he was so short of cavalry that he could not pursue the Allied withdrawal. One thing this first engagement made clear to Napoleon was that the Prussian army at Grossgörschen was a different force from the one he had fought at Jena and Auerstädt. In a letter to his wife, Gerhard Leberecht von Blücher, who had been put in command of the Prussian forces, gives an idea of the fierceness of the fighting: 'Whatever news you hear, remain calm. Although I have been hit by three bullets and my horse has been shot from under me I am and remain in full activity. I have been shot in the back which pains me. I shall bring you the bullet. We are now facing the enemy again and are looking forward to the second battle, and in it Napoleon shall not fare any better.'

Blücher's chief of staff was Scharnhorst, but after he had been wounded at Grossgörschen he was replaced by Gneisenau. Disregarding the condition of his wound Scharnhorst made his way towards Prague to try to persuade the Austrians to join Prussia against Napoleon. The wound developed gangrene and Scharnhorst died in Prague on 28 June 1813.

As a result of the first battle the Allies withdrew from Saxony to the river Spree where they awaited Napoleon's attack in well-fortified positions near Bautzen. Blücher and Gneisenau were in favour of an attack, but being under Russian supreme command and Czar Alexander being sceptical of the chances of success for any such attack, they had to remain on the defensive. Napoleon attacked on 20 May and under heavy defensive fire secured a crossing of the river. He was about to trap the Prussians in a pincer movement when the Allies saw his plan and avoided the manoeuvre by retreating.

Two battles had been lost by the Prussians, but the fighting had been of such intensity that Napoleon concluded his opponents were rather stronger than they really were. Since he himself best knew the weaknesses of his own army he offered an armistice, which was accepted and concluded on 4 June 1813. Napoleon later described it as the greatest stupidity of his life. By overestimating the Allies he failed to see that they too were in deep crisis. The French were at Prussia's frontiers, and the Russians were already envisaging a withdrawal of their contingents to Poland. That the armistice was concluded at all was mainly due to Czar Alexander and Frederick William III. It was opposed by Hardenberg, Blücher and Gneisenau. The two months of the armistice were well used by the Allies. Apart from improving both the numbers and equipment of their forces, their main effort was spent in trying to persuade Austria to join the alliance. Metternich's initial aim was to put Austria in a position in which it could ultimately play the arbiter between the Allies and the French and by this means restore its former position in Europe. At the same time Austria armed heavily. Metternich's policy, however, was opposed by the 'Patriot's Party' under Count Stadion. But Metternich, who had been one of the driving forces in favour of the war of 1809, had learnt his lesson and did not wish to risk the vengeance of Napoleon nor to reduce Austria to dependency on Russia. By the early summer of 1813 Austria was sufficiently strong to claim the role of 'armed mediator' and so in effect dissolved its alliance with France. Castlereagh on behalf of Great Britain did his utmost at Reichenbach to keep Prussia and Russia in the field. Britain would pay a total of £2 million for the upkeep of their forces, and both powers agreed to Castlereagh's request that no separate negotiations should be opened with the French without prior consultation with the other allied powers. At the Treaty of Reichenbach of 27 June 1813 between Austria and the Allies, Austria took the position that if Napoleon was not prepared to accept the conditions of the treaty then it would join the Allies. Napoleon was asked to dissolve the duchy of Warsaw, to restore Prussia and the free cities of the Hanse and to return the Illyric provinces to Austria (although nothing was said about the dissolution of the Confederation of the Rhine). Much to the Allies' surprise Napoleon accepted these conditions, with the proviso, however, that the armistice be prolonged until 4 August 1813. Napoleon hoped in this time to win over the Czar by separate agreement, but for once the Czar proved immovable.

The armistice came to an end on 4 August 1813, and on the eleventh of that month Austria joined the Allies. Prior to this Sweden had also joined the alliance and landed an army on the shores of the Baltic. The Allies now numbered a total of 480,000 men against Napoleon's 450,000. This superiority in numbers was again in effect reduced by a lack of unanimity of purpose. Only Prussia and Russia were decided upon terminating Napoleon's days as Emperor; Austria, on the other hand, feared that Russia and Prussia might grow too strong, while Sweden wanted to annex Norway, which at that time belonged to Denmark.

The Allied autumn campaign of 1813 planned to encircle Napoleon's central position in Dresden. The main army in the south, under the command of the Austrian von Schwarzenberg and consisting of Austrians, Russians and Prussians, together with the Silesian army under Blücher, were to force Napoleon into a decisive battle. The Allies achieved initial successes at Grossbeeren and Bad Hegelberg south of Berlin, in which the *Landwehr* formations especially distinguished themselves. But the southern army suffered a reverse at Napoleon's hands near Dresden. Blücher, who also had been compelled to withdraw, decided to escape the shackles of a high command that shunned any risk. On 26 August 1813 he attacked Macdonald's forces at the Katzbach and inflicted a heavy defeat upon them:

Today was the day for which I have wished for so long. We have completely beaten the enemy. The fighting lasted from 2 o'clock in the afternoon until the evening. Not many prisoners have been taken; the troops were too embittered and killed everything. It rained the whole day and the rifles would not fire any longer. My infantry men fought with the bayonet. After the battle everyone wanted to rest, but I ordered that the men and horses summon their last reserves of strength in the pursuit of the enemy . . .'

As at Grossbeeren, Blücher's infantry men were mainly Silesian *Landwehr* men.

Napoleon continued to concentrate his forces around Dresden, seeking to defeat decisively one or other of his opponents. The question for the Allies was how to combine their armies while Napoleon still stood between them. Bernadotte declared himself ready to have the Silesian army move towards him and so join forces. The two armies met and moved on Leipzig while Schwarzenberg's army approached from the south. Napoleon now saw the danger that he might be cut off in the rear and have to fight with reversed fronts like the Prussians at Jena. To counter this danger he moved the bulk of his forces against Bernadotte and Blücher with the intention of beating them, or at least of forcing their withdrawal beyond the river Elbe. Bernadotte was in fact ready to withdraw but Gneisenau suggested that any withdrawal be carried out without crossing the Elbe, thus not only threatening Napoleon's rear, but also allowing the establishment of a quick junction with Schwarzenberg's forces. Napoleon's army, poised for attack, found no enemy they could attack. Near Merseburg the Allied armies joined and Napoleon now decided to force a battle, if only because a decision in his favour would then open for him the way to the west. He had to seek a battle in order to win an opportunity for retreat.

The battle raged at Leipzig from 16 to 19 October 1813 and was one of the greatest battles to be fought in the nineteenth century. Napoleon had positioned his army around Leipzig – 190,000 men in all against an allied force which at the beginning of the battle numbered 200,000, at the end when all reinforcements had arrived, 300,000. On 16 October the Allies fought their way in to the approaches of Leipzig, on the seventeenth the Prussians entered the suburbs of the city, and the following day began the battle for the city into which Napoleon had been compelled to withdraw. Heavy street fighting raged within the city, the French and their allied contingents trying to fight their way out to the west. When, however, a French corporal blew up the Elster bridge over the Elbe a vast number of French and Confederation of the Rhine troops had their escape route cut off. Some tried to swim to the other bank of the river. The Polish nobleman Marshal Poniatowski, Marshal of France, perished in the attempt. The French were defeated. In the market square at Leipzig the Allied armies, their commanders and their monarchs met. The possibility of cutting off the fleeing French forces existed, but the Allied troops were exhausted. Napoleon, attacked only once in his retreat, by the Bavarian forces whose King had joined the victors just a few weeks before Leipzig, managed to escape beyond the Rhine. The Confederation of the Rhine dissolved itself.

On New Year's Day, one year after the signing of the Convention of Tauroggen, Prussian forces crossed the Rhine at Caub and marched west. Since Leipzig, the subject of the discussion had been whether and how to continue the war. Within the Allied camp signs of serious dissension manifested themselves, the age-old rivalry between Russia and Austria flaring up again, and once again it was Castlereagh who successfully implored them to remain united in order to achieve a result that would secure the peace of Europe. Gneisenau spoke emphatically in favour of an immediate invasion of France via the Netherlands and Lorraine. Schwarzenberg, and others, thought that any invasion of France would precipitate a popular rising in France as in 1792. If anything operations should be directed via Switzerland into southern France and towards the Pyrenees to join up with the forces of the Duke of Wellington. This would also serve to isolate France and Italy from each other. Schwarzenberg's plan found support also within the Prussian camp, where General von Knesebeck pointed to the decrepit state of many of the Prussian units; many *Landwehr* contingents had no longer any boots and were marching in rags, and without re-equipping the army it would be impossible to conduct a winter campaign. Frederick William III shared Knesebeck's views and further stated that in any case the left bank of the Rhine was of no interest to him. Unlike the Prussian Reformers he did not wish to topple Napoleon but merely to contain him. Only after Napoleon had refused the terms offered him by Metternich was the subsequent conduct of the campaign decided upon with the purpose of forcing peace upon him.

When the Allied armies reached the plateau of Langres, they halted again and reiterated their terms for a peace to Napoleon, this time within the frontiers of 1792. The negotiations came to nothing, Blücher achieved the Allies first victory on French soil at La Rothiere and, encouraged by this, the Allied forces resumed their general advance, headed by Blücher's army. In the course of his advance, however, Blücher suffered three quick defeats which caused him to rejoin the bulk of the Allied forces. In the political councils of the Allies opinions as to the further conduct of the campaign still differed widely, with Czar Alexander and Metternich particularly in dispute. Metternich wanted peace negotiations, Alexander refused to participate in them. Napoleon finally resolved the differences by his refusal to negotiate. It was mainly due to Blücher's and Gneisenau's efforts that a withdrawal to the plateau of Langres was avoided, and on 31 March 1814 the Allies entered Paris. A few days later Napoleon abdicated and left for the island of Elba.

The hero of the day was without any doubt Marshal Blücher, 'Marshal Forward'. For the Germans he became the very symbol of the

War of Liberation, but not only for them. The British, who several decades before had cheered the successes of Frederick the Great, found equal and perhaps even more admiration for the old, forthright man, and his visit to London proved a personal triumph.

Yesterday I landed in England, and I cannot understand that I am still alive. The people nearly tore me into pieces, they removed my horses and carried me. This is the way I got to London.

How they go about with me in London is equally indescribable. The moment I show myself they start shouting and soon 10,000 are gathered. I cannot venture to appear in uniform. I am being fatigued inhumanly, am being painted by three painters simultaneously. I have not even had time to have a look around. I have to shake hands with everybody and the ladies virtually court me. They are the craziest people I know.

Towards the end of September 1814 the Congress of Vienna commenced. Its course soon showed that the popular emotions which had gradually given the War of Liberation its impetus, emotions engendered by various pre-war promises of constitutional changes (especially in Prussia), were to be ignored. The statesmen of Europe, representing one stratum of European society, confronted their respective social orders with a united front. Restoration was the *Leitmotif*, fears that liberal middle class influence could escalate developments similar to those that had taken place in France were predominant. On a practical level territorial questions occupied most of the discussion. For Prussia the main topics were Saxony and Poland. Czar Alexander wanted the whole of Poland to be turned into a kingdom in personal union with Russia. Prussia in turn demanded the whole of Saxony in compensation. Neither Great Britain nor Austria were agreeable to such territorial aggrandizement, and France, represented by the able Talleyrand, knew how to exploit these differences to advantage. At one point the tension reached such heights that Britain, Austria, France, the Netherlands, Hanover and Bavaria concluded a secret alliance against Prussia and Russia.

Into a tension-laden Vienna erupted the news that on 1 March 1815 Napoleon had landed at Cannes and that most of the French army had deserted the restored Bourbon King to join him. The war-time alliance was quickly restored. On 20 March Napoleon entered in splendour a Paris which had just been hurriedly vacated by the Bourbons. Among the Allies only the British and the Prussian forces were on an immediate war footing. The British army under Wellington was in the Netherlands, the Prussian army under Blücher in the Rhenish provinces. Once again Gneisenau was appointed Blücher's chief-of-staff, which to him was something of a disappointment since he had hoped for an independent command. But he obeyed the King's instruction and acted as the brain behind Blücher's military actions. In fact it is through Gneisenau that the office of chief-of-staff attained the role it has played ever since.

At first the Prussian campaign suffered a setback near Liège when Saxon formations mutinied upon hearing they were to be split up because of the territorial changes in their country. They were disarmed and the leaders of the mutiny executed by firing squad. Napoleon moved onto the offensive with the aim of splitting the coalition. While the centre of gravity of the Prussian army was Liège, that of the British was around Ghent, their vanguards meeting in the Charleroi region. Napoleon realized that these two armies could only fully join forces if one or the other gave up its main base. Therefore he believed that he could beat them separately. With surprising speed he attacked Blücher at Ligny on 16 June 1815. Blücher accepted battle because Wellington had promised aid, but the Prussian and British formations were still too far apart for this aid to come in time. Moreover once Wellington was himself under attack by Marshal Ney at Quatre Bras he was soon in need of all his forces himself. The Prussian lines became overextended; in one direction in order to cover their rearward communication, in the other in order not to lose touch with Wellington. For hours the battle raged in the hot June sun until as evening approached Napoleon used his Imperial Guard in the centre to capture Ligny. Blücher was wounded and only the onset of darkness put an end to the battle. Retreat was now unavoidable, with Wellington likely to do the same in the direction of Antwerp. At that moment Gneisenau issued the instruction that the Prussian retreat should not be in the direction of the Rhine but to the north-east towards the village of Waterloo, there to join up with the British. The Prussians had therefore made the sacrifice of their main base. This went against Napoleon's calculations and proved disastrous for him. It was beyond his reckoning that a defeated enemy would accept a second battle immediately, and he assumed that the British and the Prussians would retreat in different directions. Marshal Grouchy was despatched with his forces towards Liège to harrass the Prussians, only there were none to be harrassed. Believing he had only one enemy to face, Napoleon made ready to fight the British at Waterloo.

Wellington moved into defensive positions, and determined to hold them: 'Our plan is simple: the Prussians or the night.' Napoleon, in full view of the British contingents, calmly reviewed his troops and then attacked. Three major attacks collapsed against the defensive fire from Wellington's forces. Nevertheless the British position was becoming very precarious when towards the late afternoon the Prussian army, driven on by Blücher to the limit, reached the battlefield and from their marching columns immediately reformed for the attack, taking the French in their right wing and rear. At first Napoleon thought that it must be Grouchy, who had about one-third of the French army with him, but soon realized his error. Blücher's attack transformed the situation completely. The defensive battle now became an offensive one and the French, fearful of being taken between the British and Prussians, tried to escape *en masse*. With Wellington's forces in a state of near exhaustion the Prussians undertook the pursuit of the enemy.

Gneisenau told the troops: 'We have shown the enemy how to conquer, now we shall demonstrate how to pursue.' Almost all the French artillery was captured, as well as Napoleon's carriage.

Near a farm with the name of Belle Alliance, Blücher and Wellington met. Not much was said; both were too moved by the awareness of how close they had been to the abyss of defeat, too grateful that it had been transformed into victory. And victory was complete, for Napoleon had been toppled, his career had ended. The nemesis of power had taken him to St Helena, there to end his days.

Chapter 10

Restoration

The impact of Napoleon's return to France had caused the four great powers of Europe – Great Britain, Austria, Russia and Prussia – to temporarily bury their differences. Britain and Austria quietly nullified the secret alliance made at Vienna, and on the Prussian side Gneisenau and Boyen abandoned detailed plans they had drawn up for a German 'people's war'. Although in contradiction of the principle of monarchic legitimacy, this planned war was to solve the German question, if necessary at the expense of the princes; the plans caused Frederick William III and Hardenberg some misgivings, but they were not in outright opposition.

Prussia reduced its territorial demands and received the smaller northern part of Saxony, while from the grand duchy of Warsaw the province of Posen was detached, thus giving Prussia's eastern frontier a better defensive line. Furthermore the rest of Vorpommern, as well as the city of Danzig was acquired. Yet these territorial acquisitions were relatively minor when compared with the gains in the west, where along the Mosel, the Saar and in the central region of the Rhine Prussia received a consolidated territory, forged out of 150 individual territorial possessions – the Rhineland. Great Britain had been one of the main supporters of this cession, wishing to see a strong power established along the Rhine as a counter to France. Whilst Prussia now became more and more immersed in Germany, Austria, by ceding its own possessions in the Low Countries (from which the state of Belgium was formed), withdrew territorially into Germany's south-eastern corner, but was nevertheless still intent upon exerting the major influence in the German states. However, in spite of Prussia's territorial acquisitions, the state was still divided into an eastern and a western half, with Hesse and Hanover coming between the two parts.

It was at this time that the demand was first voiced for Prussia to assume the leadership of Germany. Boyen and even the arch-conservative Marwitz had already entertained similar ideas, or at least considered making Prussia the leader of the north. But Frederick William III and Hardenberg realized that this pre-eminence could not be achieved without conflict with Austria, and, on the whole, they preferred Austria's support rather than its opposition. What gave the demand for Prussian leadership in Germany its piquancy was that it did not originate from the leading Prussian politicians but from representtatives of the middle classes in south-western Germany, German patriots who had formed themselves into the so-called 'Hoffman League'. Frederick William III's promise of a constitution and a representative assembly answered the constitutional desires of many Germans and in effect formed part of that moral conquest of Germany which the Prussian Reform Movement had envisaged. But Prussia, although a great power, could act only within the framework of the other great powers, and in 1814/15 a demand of this nature was, though a first sign of the shape of things to come, still premature and unrealistic.

After Napoleon's return and subsequent defeat, the second Paris Treaty of 20 November 1815 caused France to lose additional territory. At the headquarters of the Prussian army the cession of Alsace and Lorraine was demanded, but Hardenberg and Humboldt, who represented Prussia in Vienna, were content to accept the cities of Saarlouis and Saarbrücken, to which was added an indemnity and the Prussian occupation of various French territories until France had paid.

The result of the Congress of Vienna was a work of restoration which in so far as the German states were concerned established a peaceful German dualism between Austria and Prussia, all within a 'greater German' context under the leadership of the House of Hapsburg. This solution was perfectly acceptable to men such as Stein who saw in the creation on 8 June 1815 of the German Confederation the restoration of the Holy Roman Empire of the German Nation under a different name, a framework within which the German national spirit could develop and prosper. However, this view ignored the current of national feeling in Europe which, travelling from west to east, had taken hold of the German middle classes. This current was flowing on still further east and south-east, effecting a renaissance of national feeling in the various peoples and ethnic groups in eastern central and south-eastern Europe. Out of that feeling arose the contradiction that the Austrian Empire could not be at one and the same time the leader of a 'greater German' national confederation as well as the head of an Empire embracing many different nationalities. The universalist roots and traditions of the old Empire were increasingly at odds with the new spirit of the age. Metternich realized this all too clearly and set himself the task of stemming the tide. His ultimate defeat was inevitable, but it is a measure of his ability that he managed to survive for so long until 1848.

The German Confederation was given the guarantee of the signatory powers represented at Vienna. It is doubtful whether the German representatives were fully aware of the implications of this guarantee in that it guaranteed the right of the other European powers to intervene at any moment when complications or changes within the Confederation were taking place.

The representative organ of the German Confederation was its diet in Frankfurt-am-Main, in which the Hapsburg Empire held the chair.

Other members were five kingdoms (Prussia, Bavaria, Saxony, Hanover and Württemberg), the electorate of Hesse, seven grand duchies including Luxembourg, twelve dukedoms, one Margrave and four free imperial cities, a total of thirty-seven hereditary dynasties and four city republics. As some Houses became extinct, ultimately thirty-four dynasties and the four free cities were left. Of the two major powers, Austria and Prussia, only parts of their territories were members of the Confederation. Neither East or West Prussia or Posen were part of it, nor were the Hungarian, Polish, southern Slav and Italian possessions of the Hapsburgs. The diet's main objective was to secure the principle of monarchic legitimacy and oppose the forces in favour of German unity – although this was not immediately appreciated by its contemporaries. To them it was an element of European stability, and for almost half a century it fulfilled this function. Wilhelm von Humboldt in his memorandum of 3 September 1816 argued that 'the entire existence of the Confederation was calculated to maintain equilibrium through innate gravity'. Germany as a conquering state was something which no real German could desire. But dissenting voices could be heard already, the ardent nationalist and major propagandist of the War of Liberation, Ernst Moritz Arndt, was demanding the unity of people and state. While accepting the Confederation, he thought it desirable that a new leadership should stand at its helm, because even the worst Emperor would be preferable to a group of ideal leaders who could not agree. Arndt's distrust was directed particularly at the selfishness of the German princes. Stein too, having second thoughts, found the lack of a common leadership potentially dangerous. Indeed this was one of the weaknesses of the German Confederation, the existence of an almost unlimited sovereignty for its member states. It lacked the institutions to conduct a common foreign policy, possessed no executive power, no unified judiciary and no common currency, let alone a common economic policy. Thus it was that the need for the reform of the German Confederation became a call that could be heard virtually at its birth.

The kingdom of Prussia after 1815 constituted two territorially unequal parts (its former southernmost possession, Ansbach-Bayreuth, remained with Bavaria). The eastern part was predominantly Protestant, the western part predominantly Catholic. The western acquisitions especially posed many new tasks for the Prussian state, for it was now necessary to integrate territories where the French influence had been strong and where Napoleonic reforms had been successful. Among the new territories acquired in the west, the Ruhr was still rural country of rich pastures covered by medium-sized farms although the Saarland on the other hand was already showing signs of industrial progress.

Because of the new territories, Prussia developed a new internal organization dividing its territories into 10 provinces (being later reduced to eight), each province having its corporate autonomy and being headed by an *Oberpräsident*. The provinces were Western

Prussia, Pomerania, Silesia, Westphalia, Brandenburg, East Prussia, Rhineland, Lower Rhine, Saxony and Posen. As a result of the territorial changes of 1815 Prussian territory now extended for 278,000 square kilometres and contained a population of 10.4 million. These changes also meant that it had become much more a specifically German state than it had been in 1807. The agrarian and municipal reforms of the Reform Movement also favoured capitalist and industrial development, and without knowing it in 1815, Prussia, thus enlarged, had laid the foundations upon which a few decades later Germany's industrial development was to take place. The effect of the military reforms was that for some years to come Prussia was to possess one of the most progressive and efficient military systems in Europe.

The year 1815 witnessed also the creation of the so-called Holy Alliance. On 26 September Francis of Austria, Alexander of Russia and Frederick William of Prussia concluded this alliance of 'Christian monarchs' to establish supranational co-operation for the maintenance of the political and social *status quo* and the consolidation of the anti-national forces in Europe. To many Germans, Prussians included, this caused their first awareness of the fact that the popular forces raised by the War of Liberation were now to be contained and that their ambitions were to be denied – by force if necessary. A new brand, a reformed brand of normalcy had returned, in which monarchy and bureaucracy were firmly aligned on the one side against a crumbling front of political and military reformers on the other, the latter being backed by sectors of the middle classes who were increasingly politically conscious. Disappointment at this development was voiced by many and is exemplified by the exclamation of the student Arminius Riemann at the Wartburg festival of 1817, the three-hundredth anniversary of the Reformation and the fourth anniversary of the battle of Leipzig: 'Four long years have gone by since this battle. The German people entertained bright hopes, but they have all come to nothing; everything is different from what we expected'.

In point of fact the Holy Alliance was of more symbolic than practical value. It was symptomatic of the counter-revolutionary spirit of the ruling classes after 1815; Metternich himself said that it was never used, nor was its use ever considered even. In terms of practical policy the concert of European powers (which after the readmission of France in 1818 consisted of the European pentarchy – Prussia, Austria, Russia, France and Great Britain), with its roots in the eighteenth century, proved a much more effective instrument than the vague formulations of the Holy Alliance – even at times when there was discord in the orchestra.

That not even these major European powers could prevent the questioning of the results of the Congress of Vienna was first demonstrated in Spain and then in Greece, then by the separation of Belgium from the Netherlands and by the abortive rising of the Poles. But in spite of these local upheavals the order constituted at Vienna prevented the outbreak of any major war between the European powers until the Crimean War.

Among the politically conscious population a feeling of deep resignation spread. Many who had participated prominently in the War of Liberation withdrew from public life and sought refuge in religious, historical and philosophic meditation. This refusal to face political life lay at the roots of the blossoming of the Romantic movement in Germany, roots that reached back to the eighteenth century. The movement achieved prominence in literature, music, painting (the most prominent Prussian painter of that period being Caspar David Friedrich), historiography, jurisprudence and philology. By turning their backs on the present, German scholars rediscovered the glory of the Middle Ages – no wonder that the drive to raise funds for the completion of Cologne cathedral, for centuries unfinished, now reached its height and finally achieved its aim. Literary folklore once again awakened a consciousness of the past, idealized perhaps, but in the process saving much that otherwise might have been consigned to oblivion. The brothers Grimm, Achim von Arnim, Clemens von Brentano, Josef von Eichendorf and E. T. A. Hoffmann were some of its more prominent protagonists.

Meanwhile the reorganization of Prussia continued apace. Much of the Stein–Hardenberg reforms were negated or reversed in their original intention. By 1816 the pressure of the landed nobility east of the Elbe was strong enough to force an amendment to the present liberation of 1811. While the reverse side of this emancipation had been the enlargement of the nobility's estates, the amendment, in force until 1850, resulted in the creation of a rural proletariat.

The situation was rather different in the western provinces where from the beginning a different economic structure had existed. There, trade, commerce and industry predominated and the social conditions were vastly superior to those prevailing in the Prussian heartland, not least through the influence of the French Revolution and Napoleon's reforms. One of the spokesmen for Rhenish liberalism, David Hansemann, summarized the differences in 1830 in a memorandum as follows:

The provinces of Rhine, these genuine Germanic districts upon which oppressive servitude had never been imposed through conquest as in the case of the eastern provinces – so that the French Revolution found here fewer remnants of the burdens of feudalism to abolish than in most parts of France itself – they (the provinces of the Rhine) *have not come to Prussia in order to determine how far the remnants of feudalism could coexist with a more advanced state of culture, but in order to demonstrate how this state could be attained in the eastern provinces once the freedom of commerce and the emancipation of the peasants have taken deep roots, and to show that with justice as an institution, exercised publicly and independently, with full equality before the law and the judge, good government can be exercised.*

Concomitant with the retardation of the ideas which had motivated the Prussian Reform Movement, there was a stagnation in constitutional development. Stein in 1806 had argued for a form of representative assembly, a cause which after his fall was taken up by Hardenberg who, however, had found it necessary to compromise with the forces of opposition, thus in February 1811 he had convened in Berlin an interim assembly of notables from Prussia's eastern provinces. It was a concession to the call for a representative assembly and for a written constitution, to which Frederick William III had committed himself by his public promise of 22 May 1815 and by further promises that each of the provinces would obtain its own representative assembly. Hardenberg took up this call in 1815, not because he was a liberal but because the process of the institutional reorganization of Prussia and the integration of the newly acquired territories into one state required uniform legislation and taxation. This he felt could not be done without the co-operation of those capable of paying taxes, and that co-operation could best be gained by means of representative assemblies. Stein's and Hardenberg's motivation differed: Stein had proceeded with the idea of creating a harmonious state, while Hardenberg, perhaps more practical, thought in terms of a more efficient state, a rationalization of its entire infrastructure. Already in his Riga Memorandum he had used the phrase of revolution from above, 'a revolution in the name of good sense'. Explicitly, his concept of the Prussian state consisted of democratic principles in a monarchic government: 'this seems to me to be the suitable form corresponding with the current spirit of the times', he said.

On 30 March 1817 Frederick William III issued a cabinet order calling together a constitutional commission consisting of civil servants. This commission was first to travel through the individual provinces, consulting opinion among the notables, in order to gain an impression of what remained of the old institutions of the estates and what reforms were desired. The commission comprised 22 members of which more than half were supporters of a written constitution, but general lack of unanimity, vague terms of reference for the commission and personal rivalries among its members ultimately caused its dissolution without it having produced any result. Metternich's influence upon Frederick William III also decided him not to move beyond the stage of provincial representative assemblies to which he had committed himself in the Teplitz Punctation of 1 August 1819. This document, drawn up by Metternich, envisaged a step-by-step approach towards popular representation, progressing from district assemblies to provincial diets to a central committee of national representation, every step being taken so slowly as to ensure that the final stage would never come. Hardenberg on the other hand had envisaged a two-chamber system of representation which was to have not only advisory functions but ultimately legislative functions as well.

The constitutional movement in the middle classes, which since 1815 had been spreading fairly rapidly found its most eloquent spokesman in the publicist Joseph Görres who had handed to Hardenberg the 'Coblenz Address' signed by 3,000 Rhinelanders. This, almost in the tone of an ultimatum, demanded from the King that he fulfil his constitutional promise of 1815. Frederick William III was quick to see the forces of revolution at work in his kingdom and became less than ever prepared to grant the 'Magna Carta' demanded.

But the constitutional movement also had its spokesmen inside the Prussian administration. Wilhelm von Humboldt had been recalled to the ministry of the interior to deal with the problems of the estates and, unlike Hardenberg, who although a constitutionalist himself always trod very carefully on dangerous ground, Humboldt demanded outright popular representation by direct elections. Not because of a difference of aims, but because of a difference over the means to be deployed in achieving them, a deep rivalry developed between the two men.

Outside the Prussian administration, in Prussia and in Germany as a whole, the constitutional movement gained ground. The disappointments caused by frustrated hopes led to public expressions of disgust with the existing *ancien régime*. Jahn's gymnastic associations, the newly founded student corporation, the *Burschenschaften*, and the assassination of the writer August von Kotzebue (who was also a Russian informer) by Karl Ludwig Sand in 1819, seemed to provide evidence of a revolutionary party at work. Prisons throughout Germany registered an increasing intake of 'political free-thinkers'. Youth kept on protesting and finally, clamouring for revolution, went to the barricades. It is in this context that Germany's academic youth gained real prominence. Having fought for the liberation of their country they now felt that they also had the right to determine its political future. Heinrich von Gagern wrote 'We desire among the individual states in Germany a greater responsibility for the common good, a greater unity in their politics, no politics at all to be conducted by the individual states ... we desire that Germany be treated as one country and the German *Volk* as one *Volk*.' All these were expressions of a potentially revolutionary fervour which Metternich sought to curb by the Carlsbad Decrees to which Prussia adhered; not to have done so would have entailed Prussia's leaving the German Confederation.

But when the conservative Adam Müller's suggestions for the supervision and investigation of the universities and the censorship of newspapers, journals and pamphlets were implemented, it gave rise to a fundamental disagreement within the Prussian administration which resulted in the resignations of the liberal minister Humboldt, the military reformer Boyen, and Beyme. Jahn's gymnastic societies were proscribed, Arndt was no longer allowed to give his lectures at the University of Bonn, and the lectures by Schleiermacher and other suspects were regularly monitored by police spies.

All this encouraged the Prussian nobility east of the Elbe, men mainly conscious of being Prussian rather than German, who feared losing yet more privileges and who felt that a constitutional assembly was likely to erode these privileges most effectively. Led by Duke Charles of Mecklenburg, they agitated against representative assembly considering it to be, as Marwitz put it, 'a demagogic invention'. Nobility and the majority of the Prussian bureaucracy combined to abort the constitutional movement, and finally, by a cabinet order of 11 June 1821, Frederick William III limited representation to provincial diets. Hardenberg, worn out by the struggle for a compromise between what was desirable and what could practically be achieved, died a lonely man in Genoa in November 1822.

By a decree of 5 June 1823 it was ordered that the historic estates of the provinces should form diets, the diet of each province to be constituted from representatives of the nobility, the burghers and the peasants. In practice this meant that the representatives of all three classes were the propertied men, property being the main qualification for membership. The diets of the Prussian provinces comprised 1,329 deputies of the towns, 2,207 deputies from the propertied peasants and 12,654 estate-owners. Thus was the constitutional promise of 1815, for the time being, buried in Prussia.

The ideological foundation for the process of restoration in Prussia had already been laid in 1816 by the work of the Swiss Karl Ludwig von Haller in his *Restauration der Staatswissenschaft*. His aim was to cleanse the political theory of the state from what he considered to be the evil influence of natural law and especially from the ideas of Rousseau and Hobbes. Government's function was to govern, and society was to be organized according to the aristocratic principle of nature. The state, in Haller's view, was an organic structure composed of families and corporations, the original cell of the state being the family and the property belonging to it. As the father was the head of the family so the sovereign was the head of the conglomerate of families making up the state, the 'patrimonial state' as Haller put it. The difference between the sovereign and the subject was that the sovereign had, other than God, no superior power over him. In contrast to the traditional maxim of Hohenzollern kings such as Frederick William I and Frederick the Great, who conceived their role as that of the first servant of the state, Haller argued that the monarch was neither representative nor servant of an abstract concept of the state but was the owner of the state which was his very property. His power derived from the land he and his forefathers had accumulated during the course of time, and the fact that they had succeeded in acquiring such territories as they possessed was evidence of the working of the divine will, because without it they would not have been successful. Haller applied the same principle to other property owners and heads of families, who he called upon to exercise sovereign rights within their own sphere. These, to Haller, were the foundations of a truly Christian state, a patriarchal unit, dependent upon the monarch and God and held together by mutually binding duties and obligations. In such an organic society based upon the Christian ethic, a written constitution was no more relevant than an attempt to intervene or regulate the organic process of nature by means of private or constitutional law. The power of the prince was not limited by the institutionalized authority of others or by the existence of a catalogue of human rights, but by the privileges which other corporations and other families enjoyed and by treaties. Haller summarized his views with the formula: 'Equality before the law, except where existing treaties demand exception.' This of course implied severe limitations on the legislative powers of the monarch, and at the same time affirmed the patrimonial justice of old. Taxation could not be sanctioned by popular representation, but only by the separate estates. And Haller rejected conscription as a fruit of revolutionary principles of state because 'excepting general human duties, subjects have to fulfil only obligations contracted; more cannot be demanded of them'.

Society consisted of a pyramid of treaties, privileges and liberties as had, according to Haller, been the case in the Middle Ages. Modern development had attacked these foundations, eroding them by sovereignty and centralization, putting the state above the subject, a general levelling process above which stood only the monarch. Haller's teachings were a protest against the modern state, in personal terms a protest against Hardenberg's policies; they amounted to a complete negation of any social contract theory.

Although Haller himself took the logical ultimate step in his thinking and became a convert of the Roman Catholic church, his influence was and remained most pronounced in Prussia, where the son of Frederick William III, Crown Prince Frederick William, and his friends the brothers Leopold and Ludwig von Gerlach became his ardent admirers, envisaging an ideal state of Christian–Germanic origin governed by a monarchy based on the estates, infused with Haller's patrimonialism. Haller supplied the ideological weapons for the Prussian nobility to use – in so far as it was actually capable of using them – against the constitutional state as much as against the centralizing tendecies of absolutism. They were a weapon against the tendencies inherent in the *Allgemeine Landrecht*, but nevertheless demonstrated that the Prussian nobility and monarchy did not form an organic entity but merely an alliance, virtually imposed by the forces of absolutism – and any alliance could be severed. The Prussian nobility had resented since their inception the reforms imposed upon them between 1807 and 1813; they resented revolution from above as much as revolution from below. This antipathy was not restricted to Prussia alone. After 1815 the reaction of the estates grew against the results of enlightened despotism, the continuation of reforms and what was called 'the spirit of the Confederation of the Rhine'.

While Hardenberg was still at the helm of the administration, the entire civil service apparatus and the territorial organization was subjected to a thorough overhaul. At first Prussia was divided up into

10 provinces, which were then, by joining the provinces of the Rhineland and East and West Prussia, reduced to eight. In place of the Napoleonic prefect system which Hardenberg had previously used as a model, he returned to the collegiate principle. At the head of each province was a *Oberpräsident* who shared power with the general commanding the army corps of the province. In place of the principle applied at first, namely the centralizing of all aspects of public life into one administration, necessity compelled a separation once again into various branches such as education, health, taxation, post, and mining. Basically each provincial administration divided into three branches: internal and police affairs; church and education; and direct taxation, domains and forestry.

The Council of State planned by the reformers was instituted in 1817, but not as a governing institution, as they, and particularly Stein, had desired. It was only an advisory body to give advice and submit suggestions concerning new legislation. Its members consisted of the royal princes and the heads of the civil service and it was by no means a substitute parliament; at best it was a body in which expert opinion was represented. In 1816 the ministry of the interior was changed by detaching its police functions, and a separate ministry of police was created. Owing to the territorial acquisition of the Rhineland the uniformity of the Prussian legal code, the *Allgemeine Landrecht*, was disturbed because in these territories the Code Napoleon was still operating. This necessitated the division of the ministry of justice into two branches, the new one having exclusive responsibility for the Rhineland as well as the job of devising ways and means by which the two different legal systems could be adjusted to one another and ultimately fused. While a newly created ministry of trade had only a short life, a contemporary creation, the ministry of culture, with Freiherr von Altenstein as the first Prussian minister of culture, was of lasting duration. This overhaul was not without its inner contradiction. On one side was Hardenberg in his position as *Staatskanzler*, chancellor of state, with his general ministry functioning on a collegiate basis, and on the other were the ministries with specific areas of responsibility. Ministers and their bureaucrats, aware of their own expertise and competence, increasingly challenged and obstructed policies initiated at the top, an example of which is the conflict between Hardenberg and Humboldt. Nevertheless the overhaul had furthered the unification of the Prussian kingdom. Unity in the religious sector increased through the union in 1817 of the Lutheran and reformed Protestant confessions into a state church of which the King was the supreme bishop.

One of the major aims of the Prussian reformers had been to create the *Rechtstaat*, the state based upon law, a demand not originated by them but implicit in the instructions which lay at the origin of the *Allgemeine Preussisches Landrecht*. The logical consequence of this demand was an independent judiciary, a judiciary outside the power of a royal cabinet order. The financial crisis of 1808 to 1818, which did not leave Prussia untouched, had only been mastered by the issue of credits; these credits, however, could not be obtained unless they were legally fully secured. They also entailed the risk of political demands by those who granted them. To avoid this risk, the Prussian bureaucracy decided to refrain from taking short-term loans from capital sources within the kingdom and instead took up a long-term loan from the House of Rothschild abroad. In an age of growing demands for a constitution and a representative assembly this deprived those who put forward these demands of the lever which in other countries had brought about liberalization and democratization: the question of taxation. Foreign loans also meant that cases of litigation involving money suits against the state could not be brought, and consequently the judiciary was given no areas in which its decisions could affect questions of an ultimately political character. The minister of justice, von Beyme, had in 1809 succeeded in halting the wave of complaints against the judiciary that had been submitted directly to the King. This eliminated the monarchy from continuously intervening in the legal process. But as the bureaucracy strengthened its position and increasingly monopolized expertise, it began to emancipate itself from the King. The only institution which could then exercise control over the bureaucracy was the judiciary and therefore the aim of the bureaucracy was once again to obtain control over the judiciary. If, for example, the ministry of justice refused to interfere with the independence of the judges, it could only appeal to the King, who likewise tended to refuse. Nevertheless, one of the themes dominating Prussian domestic politics from 1815 onwards was the attempt by the bureaucracy now it had achieved full tenure and, from 1820 onwards, also pensions by right to emancipate itself from the one remaining controlling body, the judiciary, by integrating it into its own institutions.

Like the ministry of culture the ministry of war was also a new creation. Founded in 1814 under von Boyen it was an institution which was the focal point of the struggles for and against the army reforms introduced between 1807 and 1813. Conscription had been introduced formally for the duration of the war only. By a cabinet order of 27 May 1814 it was lifted again causing anxiety among the reformers that a return to the cantonal reglement would take its place. Boyen's efforts prevented this, but he too had to pay his price, namely the *Landsturm*, a force secondary to that of the *Landwehr*. Thus before Hardenberg's and Frederick William III's departure for the Congress of Vienna the King signed, on 3 September 1814, the law making conscription a permanent institution, to be supplemented a year later by new regulations governing the *Landwehr*. From then on Prussia had a relatively small army of the line numbering approximately 136,000 men (whose members had to do three years' active service plus two years in the reserve) and a *Landwehr* of 163,000 (whose members did seven years' service) which met for a few weeks every year but in time of war was integrated into the army of the line. There was also a second line of the

Landwehr for purposes of teritorial defence, but this did not participate in peacetime exercises.

Conscription and the *Landwehr* were institutions viewed with immense hostility by Prussian conservative reactionaries such as Prince Charles of Mecklenburg and Prince Wittgenstein. The latter declared that 'Arming the nation means the organization of revolution.' Attempts were made to abolish both institutions. The minister of finance von Bülow argued that they resulted in a financial burden which the Prussian state was unable to carry. Boyen, in reply, demonstrated that the financial burden per head of Prussia's population was, considering its actual earnings and rising prices, lower than it had been when the old army, which had been basically ineffective, was in existence. In this he found the support of the King. The issue of the *Landwehr* itself was, however, more explosive. Through faults of its own it had allowed such standards as it has possessed between 1813 and 1815 to deteriorate and now gave cause for serious complaint. Up to the rank of captain it was commanded by its own officers, virtually elected by the men. Within each governmental district it had its own inspectors and, being a part time army, *Landwehr* soldiers and officers were naturally deeply involved in the life of their community. Only the general of the province was their direct superior officer. Boyen was emphatic in maintaining the militia-type character of the *Landwehr* because he considered it vital that it preserve its character as a people's army. Hence he insisted upon strict segregation between the regiments of the line and the *Landwehr*, which he feared would be put in jeopardy if the line regiments exerted greater influence upon it. The King, however, counselled by his generals who complained particularly about what they considered to be the lax discipline of the *Landwehr*, wanted the influence of the regular army to be greater and also desired the removal of the *Landwehr* inspectors and the combination of line and *Landwehr* regiments into divisional formations. The King's wishes prevailed. In 1819 the *Landwehr* was reduced in size and put under the direct command of the regiments of the line. Boyen resigned his post, as did the chief-of-staff Grolmann.[1] It was the beginning of that ministerial crisis which resulted from the reactionary policy of Frederick William III and culminated in the struggles over competencies and policy formulation that took place between Humboldt and Hardenberg, and the minister of justice Beyme and Hardenberg. To all intents and purposes the Reform Movement had come to an end. It remained a promise half-fulfilled that left behind only a sense of betrayal and bitter frustration.

Economic and financial reasons, however, ensured that in the economic sector such new freedoms as the freedom of commerce were not revoked, in spite of the pressure exercised by the guilds and various branches of trade. As the landed nobility and the propertied peasants of Prussia realized the advantages of free trade, they were not slow in also realizing their community of interest with the more commercially and industrially advanced western provinces of Prussia. It was the first sign on the horizon of that alliance that was to exert such profound influence upon the politics of the German Empire from 1875 onwards: the alliance between the agrarian capitalism of the great estate-owners east of the Elbe, and the forces of heavy industry in Germany's west.

Trades were no longer regulated, which meant that the guilds progressively decayed while the manufacturing interest's avenues of advance opened. Stein and Humboldt had already argued the case for a German policy in the matters of tariffs, trade, postal communications and coinage. That these wishes reflected the interests of German trade and commerce is shown by the foundation in 1816 of the *Deutscher Fabrikantenverein*, the German Manufacturers' Association, and in 1819 of the *Deutscher Handels- und Gewerbeverein*, the German Trade and Commerce Association. Both agitated for the abolition of all tariffs within the German frontiers. Friedrich List, who had founded the latter association tried to influence the diet of the German Confederation and in person petitioned the German monarchs for the greater liberalization of trade and commerce within Germany while at the same time protecting infant German industries from foreign imports. None of the monarchs had enough vision to recognize the potential in List's plans, but the growing danger of financial bankruptcy in Prussia after 1815, which had forced the Prussian state to take up the Rothschild loan, also compelled it to do everything possible to get the Prussian economy on its feet again. Within the Prussian administration supporters of the principles of Adam Smith, such as state councillor Kunth and the general director of taxation Maassen eventually won over the rearguard resistance of the mercantilists like the *Oberpräsident* of Brandenburg, von Heydebreck. They designed a draft bill, which became law on 26 May 1818, making taxes and tariffs uniform throughout Prussia, but attacking the enclaves within Prussia and those territories that divided the eastern from the western half with prohibitive tariffs, particularly against Hesse-Nassau and Hesse-Darmstadt.

By the late 1820s three blocs were in competition within the German Confederation. One was Austria, which saw the advantages in the removal of internal German trade barriers but at that time was not yet willing to apply a policy of this kind to its territories of other nationalities. The second was Prussia, which recognized that its potential economic power could ultimately win for her dominance in northern Germany. The third bloc was made up of the states of central and southern Germany which feared being swallowed by either Austria or Prussia. Only this last bloc was divided amongst itself, Hesse-Darmstadt soon beginning to turn towards Prussia, leaving Württemberg and Bavaria as one group, Baden and Hesse-Nassau as another. Bavaria and Württemberg gave the signal for the events that were to follow; on 18 January 1828 they concluded a customs union, whose institutions were eventually to become those of the German customs union. That left Hesse-Nassau, whose ruler thought that he could survive without associating himself with either Prussia or Bavaria-Württemberg. Only Hesse-Darmstadt, on 14 February 1828, joined the Prussian customs union.

The economic consolidation of Prussia in the north alarmed both Austria and Bavaria. Austria and Prussia now made their bids for the hitherto uncommitted German principalities. Prussia's relentless economic pressure on its central German enclaves was a strong enough warning. A central German association came into being whose most prominent feature was its aversion to Prussian and for that matter also to Bavarian aims, but which was quite incapable of putting forward any alternative policies. Metternich's endeavours to forge an economic coalition against Prussia also failed because he too was at a loss for a viable alternative. If anything, these obstructionist policies demonstrated to Germany's north and south that their interests were identical and provided the basis for those negotiations from which was finally to emerge the German customs union in 1833. The need for improved road communications from east to west and north to south was an instrument which the Prussian minister of trade, Motz, used masterfully to bring the central German states to Prussia's heel. In order to persuade the Bavarians of the advantages of Prussia's trade policy Motz sent Goethe's publisher Cotta to Munich, where his appearance and demeanour achieved their aim of convincing the Bavarians that Prussia did not correspond with its caricature image. As a consequence of this rapprochement between Prussia and Bavaria, Hesse too began to see things a little more favourably, especially after the trade treaty of 27 May 1829 between Prussia and southern Germany which left open the possibility of Bavaria and Württemberg joining Prussia's western provinces in a customs union. This was the decisive step in the final disintegration of the central German union that was directed against Prussia and Bavaria alike and was in favour of the economic exclusion of Austria from Germany.

Prussia and Bavaria together had brought new mobility into the entire German question. Motz was well aware of the political consequences of his policy; to him it was not merely a question of revising internal conditions of trade and standardizing tariffs, he envisaged a revision of the constitution of the German Confederation and the strengthening of Germany's national power externally, under the direction and protection of Prussia. When he died in 1830 he did not see the completion of his work in the form of the German customs union, the economic precondition of that work which Bismarck was to complete politically. Kingdoms, principalities and territories still uncommitted began to reconsider their position. Baden came to agreement with Bavaria in 1830, Prussia, Saxony and Thuringia in 1833. This culminated in the German customs union of 30 March 1833 which came into force on 1 January 1834. For the first time in modern German history the German states had given up significant parts of their sovereignty in the interest of the entire German community. The standardization of Prussia's tariffs had, unforeseen by its originators, led to the economic reunification of Germany.

The July Revolution of 1830 in France, except for seemingly confirming the prejudices of reactionaries everywhere, had few practical repercussions in Prussia. In a European context, however, it brought France closer to Britain where the Liberals had replaced the Tories. This in turn caused the Prussians to lean further towards Russia and Austria again and especially the former because with the death of Alexander, Czar Nicholas I, the son-in-law of Frederick William III, had succeeded to the throne. When the Poles attempted their abortive national rising Nicholas became the epitome of the despot defending legitimism and absolutism in Europe. Devoid of the subtle kid-glove approach of a Metternich, Nicholas preferred the immediate use of brute force.

In the main the Polish rising was restricted to the Russian-occupied part of Poland which now lost such independence as it had still possessed. On Prussian territory only in Posen were minor attempts at insurrection made, but too half-heartedly to bring success. One effect, though, was a change in the attitude of the Prussian administration towards its Polish subjects. When Posen had been annexed in 1815 Frederick William III in an address to his subjects declared that no one would expect them to change their nationality. Administrative practice conformed with the spirit of this declaration. The official languages were Polish as well as German, Polish noblemen were appointed as *Landräte*, and at the head of the province, administered by *Oberpräsident* Zerboni, was also Prince Radziwill, a Polish magnate and patriot married to a German. There were no signs of a Germanizing policy until after the rising of 1831. A new *Oberpräsident*, von Flottwell, renowned as an efficient administrator, was appointed, whereupon he discarded Polish as an official language and replaced the Polish *Landräte*.

The July Revolution in France also gave cause for the German Confederation to rethink what its military contingency plans should be in case of war with France. The initiative for this came entirely from Prussia and as the smaller German states felt that in case of war with France they were likely to get greater and more efficient protection from Prussia than from Austria, the Prussian line of thought prevailed. The plan was that in case of war three armies were to be mobilized. A Prussian army, to include other north German contingents, was to be positioned on the lower Rhine, a mixed Prussian and south German army on the Main and an Austrian army on the upper Rhine, all commanded by a joint headquarters.

Inevitably the July Revolution also injected the conservatives with new vigour, Metternich's fear of a liberal revolutionary tide being such that he suggested the abolition of all constitutions in Germany, a plan, however, which was thwarted by Prussia. But on 28 June 1832 the diet of the German Confederation, the *Bundestag*, did accept the introduction of the 'Six Articles' which subjected the constitutional life of the states of the German Confederation to its control, thereby hopefully maintaining the monarchic principle and restricting the liberties of such representative assemblies as existed. A month previously the Hambach Festival had taken place, when German liberals, young and not so young had tried to bring back into the remembrance of the public the ideals that had motivated them in 1813. One of their demonstrations was to unfold their black, red and gold banner alongside the white and red Polish national flag. In Prussia this again caused increased censorship and police supervision of suspected persons. The attempt on 3 April 1833 by 50 students of the universities of Göttingen, Heidelberg, Erlangen and Würzburg, aided by Polish émigrés and Alsatians, to seize Frankfurt-am-Main (the seat of the diet of the German Confederation) and proclaim a German republic failed. However, one of the consequences of the attempted coup was the setting up in Prussia of a commission of investigation. Between 1833 and 1836 it convicted a total of 204 students, 39 of whom were sentenced to death (although these sentences were all commuted to life imprisonment).

In spite of this wave of reaction, many advocates of political liberalism and moderation at that time still felt that Prussia remained the hope for Germany. The renowned historian Friedrich Christof Dahlmann, at that time still in Göttingen, wrote in 1832 that in Germany there was one state which, as he put it, 'possesses a wonderful spear', and that the fatherland had cause to look at it with admiration but also with anger. That state was Prussia, and Prussia should fulfil its historic mission. If the King of Prussia transformed his country into a constitutional monarchy from that moment it would lead the German Confederation and command the loyalty of every patriotic German. During that same year the south-west German jurist Paul Pfizer published his *Letters between two Germans*. He argued that Austria had developed policies that lay outside the healthy national interests of all Germans, and had therefore alienated itself from the German body politic. One could expect no more than that it would leave altogether and cede its leadership to Prussia. 'It was Prussia which, by the extraordinary exertion of all its physical strength and even more by the moral weight which its enthusiasm could place on the scales, decided the liberation of Germany from Napoleonic rule and has therefore rightfully assumed the claim for hegemony in Germany, lacking only its external confirmation.' Prussia was destined, historically, to become the protector of Germany, and for the sake of Germany it was imperative that the minor princes and kings of Germany should place a part of their power and sovereignty into the hands of Prussia.

In retrospect it can be seen that the achievement of a German customs union was a step in this direction; from that moment on one can speak of a German economy, which at that time had its source of power in Prussia, in the Ruhr.

When the French had been expelled from Germany Ludwig von Vincke, a close associate of Stein, became general commissioner for the liberated territories. Vincke was a widely travelled man who had stayed in Great Britain on several occasions and was the author of an important book on Britain's internal administration in which he particularly praised British self-government. Like most of the Prussian reformers he was also a disciple of the principles of Adam Smith. In 1815 he became *Oberpräsident* of Westphalia, then still a conglomeration of scattered territories that had still to be welded into a united province, and during his administration Vincke succeeded in doing just that. At first he was hampered by the sorry state of Prussia's finances, but after the Rothschild loan of 1822 things changed in Prussia in general and for Vincke in Westphalia in particular. From that time dates the transformation of the agrarian region of the Ruhr into an industrial basin whose newly discovered coalfields became the backbone of Prussia's economic strength in Germany. Vincke realized that communications, especially an improved network of roads, was the best way to promote industrial development; this was to be supplemented by a network of canals, serviced by docks and storage facilities.

The road-building programme in Prussia as a whole reflects the improvement in Prussia's economic position. In 1816 Prussia had a total 3,162 kilometres of state-owned roads, with 1,798 kilometres in the Rhenish provinces and Westphalia, 679 in Silesia, 466 in Prussia's part of Silesia and 209 in Brandenburg. By 1831 the total length of state-owned roads had increased to 6,794 kilometres; by 1838 to 8,632 kilometres; and by 1848 11,852 kilometres. The introduction of the railway crowned this revolution in Prussia's transport system. The first Prussian railway-line was opened between Berlin and Potsdam in 1838, an event not particularly cherished by Frederick William III who wrote: 'Everything is in a hurry; peace and *Gemütlichkeit* are suffering. I cannot expect for my part any great blessings from being a few hours earlier in Berlin.' The poet Heinrich Heine, however, commented: 'The railways are again a determining event, a turn in the history of mankind, changing the colour and form of life; a new era of world history is beginning and our generation can be proud to have witnessed it. What changes there will be in our view of life, in our imagination! Even elementary concepts like time and space are shaken. By the railways space will be killed and what remains for us is time!'

By 1844 Prussia possessed 861 kilometres of railway-line and only four years later 2,363 kilometres. Railways led to the expansion of Prussia's steel works. In 1847 Prussia already possessed 60 steel rolling mills, and in 1841 the firm of Borsig had built the first locomotives in Prussia. Railways also proved an incentive for private investment, because in contrast to other industries the railways faced no competition. Since they also accelerated development in the entire steel and iron industry and an increase in the number of workers, the creation of a specifically industrial working class corresponded with the general rapid economic development. Prussia's economic advance in relation to other German states is illustrated by a simple comparison with Saxony, which in 1838 produced 100,000 Zentner of pig iron while Prussia during that same year produced 1,817,000 Zentner. The names of Alfred Krupp and August Borsig now became the first luminaries in Prussia's economic skies. Krupp's ancestors had been wealthy merchants and the family fortune provided the capital for the founding of their steel factory. August Borsig a joiner by trade, was more adventurous; of 59,000 Thalers capital only 5,300 came from his own savings, while the rest he had borrowed from anyone willing to be persuaded by his vision of an industrial empire.

The advance of the steam engine in manufacturing industries provides a graphic picture of industrial advance. Whilst the Newcomen engine had already entered Germany (in Prussia's westernmost province) in 1753, Watt's engine was introduced near Magdeburg in 1779. By 1796 the Silesian mines and forges all had steam engines. By 1830 Prussia had 245 steam engines with a total of 4,485 horsepower, by 1837 419 engines with a total of 7,355 horsepower, and by 1849 1,445 steam engines with a total of 67,149 horsepower. The output of coal provides another indicator of Prussia's industrial advance. In the newly acquired Saar provinces, in which mining had already been long established, the annual output of the state-owned mines rose from 113,689 tons in 1816 to 408,377 tons in 1844, while in those of the Ruhr, industrially only on the brink of development, output increased from 388,000 tons in 1815 to 956,000 tons in 1840.

Needless to say, such industrial expansion required not only a labour force of sufficient size, but also skilled engineers and technicians. Peter Christian Wilhem Beuth, a native of Clèves and, as head of the Technical Commission, once a member of Hardenberg's staff, drew attention to this need especially after a visit to Britain in 1826. But already nine years before that he had founded in Berlin a learned society to promote the progress of industry. It numbered at that time 367 members, half of them living in Berlin and included 110 civil servants (among them university teachers) and 66 merchants and bankers. The remainder was made up of representatives of about 30 different crafts. Shortly after the foundation of the society Beuth submitted to the Prussian government a plan for the establishment of a Technical Institute in Berlin, arguing that the existing educational system was inadequate for teaching the acquisition of skills required by modern industry. In November 1821 the first such institute later to become the Technical University of Berlin, opened its gates. The government provided money for scholarships, and private endowments also helped it considerably. Its numbers rose from 13 students in 1821 to 101 by 1845, and by that time similar schools and institutes had been founded throughout Prussia. To spread technical knowledge and to show to an international public the progress made by Prussian industry Beuth organized exhibitions in Berlin in 1822, 1827 and 1844. At the first 176 manufacturers were represented, at the second 208 and at the third 3,040.

While at the turn of the century in Prussia the average working day was 12 hours, with night-shifts and Sunday work being very exceptional, that had changed profoundly by the mid-1820s. Already in 1816 a Prussian government report concerning the Rhenish departments, after praising the industrial achievements so far attained and the changes such inventions as the steam engine had brought about, went on to say 'These in outline are the technical and commercial results. . . . Less enjoyable are the moral ones. These are common to all factories, but in particular . . . it is already noticeable . . . that the more machines and the division of labour increase, the more human beings decline to the state of an engine, especially . . . as very little is done still for the development and the maintenance of all that is human.' The report found this very pronounced in the provinces on the left bank of the Rhine, less so to the east of it, It also records complaints from manufacturers who are compelled to do without child labour for a few hours each week when the children have to attend school. Already the first voices could be heard warning of the dangers of adopting wholesale the English factory system and its methods of production. Inevitably it would cause dissatisfaction among a large part of the population and it was seen as the duty of the state to legislate against such abuses as were practised by industry, and thus to ameliorate and improve the condition of the labouring classes.

Most of the workers of that period came from the peasantry who, in the wake of the Stein–Hardenberg reforms, had lost their smallholdings; they were supplemented by artisans who could no longer reach the professional peak of trades swallowed up by the capitalist factory system. But the same reforms which had given birth to a reservoir of labour for industry also helped to transform agriculture by introducing capitalist methods of production. Alongside the landed nobility east of the Elbe emerged the bourgeois estate-owners. In 1828 in areas such as the Niederlausitz 25.9 per cent of the estates were in middle class possession; in 1853 already 54.8 per cent. Estates and large peasant holdings prospered at the expense of those who had smallholdings, a large proportion of whom were unable to make a living so had to give up their land and become factory workers. They worked 16 to 17 hours a day, six days a week. In Berlin the average weekly wage for an unskilled labourer amounted to $3\frac{1}{2}$ to 4 thalers, that of a railway worker only to 2 or $2\frac{1}{2}$ thalers; the minimum subsistence level for a family of four was 4 thalers per week. Children went to work from an early age until in 1839 the Prussian government decreed a minimum age of 9 for working children. The reason for this decree was the growing number of recruits who failed to measure up to the health standards required for military service.

While industry prospered in Prussia, so did the arts. Gottfried von Schadow, the sculptor of the Quadriga on the Brandenburg Gate, had a number of able pupils, the most prominent of whom was Christian Daniel Rauch. His mausoleum for Queen Louise in the garden of the

Charlottenburg combines classic simplicity of line with the austere serenity that gave the Rococo in Prussia its unique character. Rauch created monuments to such popular heroes of the time as Blücher and Scharnhorst, and also the statue of Frederick the Great on horseback, now recovered and restored by the authorities in East Germany and moved to a prominent position at the Sanssouci at Potsdam. His work also took him outside Prussia to work for the Czar and for Ludwig I of Bavaria. Among Rauch's contemporaries Karl Friedrich Schinkel is well known by virtue of his classicist architectural work such as the *Neue Wache*, Unter den Linden (today the Monument for the victims of Facism and Militarism in East Berlin) and the Berlin playhouse.

Painting also prospered, mainly in Prussia's western provinces, where at the Düsseldorf Academy Wilhelm Schadow became famous, although perhaps the Academy's most distinguished pupil was Alfred Rethel. In Berlin music also occupied a prominent place, Felix Mendelssohn-Bartholdy having Berlin as his home and birthplace. The forces of restoration after 1815 had reasserted themselves but had not been able to silence the intellectual life to which Wilhelm von Humboldt and his brother Alexander von Humboldt had given such vigorous impulses. Women began to move to the fore of Berlin's intellectual society, women such as Bettina von Arnim and Rahel Varnhagen. The new universities of Berlin, Breslau and Bonn demonstrated the impact of the educational reforms of Wilhelm von Humboldt and his successors and thus exerted their influence far beyond Germany. Ranke, Savigny and above all Friedrich Hegel reached the height of their powers in Prussia, as did Hegel's opponents such as Ludwig Feuerbach and David Friedrich Strauss. Karl Marx might have done so too, had he not been rejected for a lectureship at Berlin University.

The July revolution of 1830 in France reveberated through Prussia where the unfulfilled promise of a constitution remained a live issue. In opposition to the representatives of the German liberal cause – which was firmly suppressed by Prussian censorship anyway – Protestant and Catholic intellectuals and politicians like Jarke and Radowitz founded the *Politische Wochenblatt*, the mouthpiece of the romantic conservatives whose members, including the brothers Gerlach, were close to Crown Prince Frederick William. Their literary opponents were writers such as Theodor Mundt, Karl Gutzkow, Heinrich Laube and, from beyond the frontiers of Prussia and then Germany, the poet Heinrich Heine, who preferred self-imposed exile abroad, ultimately in Paris. Heine had come to Berlin from the Rhineland, and in 1822 visited Munich from where he wrote to Varnhagen von Ense: '. . . I am in the process of becoming very serious here, almost German; I believe this is caused by the beer. I am homesick for Berlin. If I stay in good health I shall see whether I can move there. In Bavaria I have become a Prussian'. A decade later Heine together with Ludwig Börne and Georg Büchner represented the revolutionary-democratic representatives of German literature. Unfortunately in the main they were united only in what they rejected, particularly the *Obrigkeitsstaat*, while lacking in concrete alternatives. Theirs was an abstract demand for liberty, almost totally blind to social questions. Men like Phillip Jakob Siebenpfeiffer, another radical writer, or Friedrich Seybold, whose interests went beyond the attainment of bourgeois liberties but whose speeches and writings focused upon the mass of the people, were strangers to them. Nor, in the light of Prussia's (or for that matter Germany's) recent experience at the hands of France, could representatives of 'Young Germany' like Heine expect wide public attention when their appeals, their polemics and their trenchant satire came from Paris.

One major problem still to arise in the 1830s, if only for a short time, was the conflict between the Roman Catholic church of Prussia's western provinces and the Prussian state. The conflict did not touch theological issues at all; Prussia had learnt to live with its Catholic citizens as the example of Silesia had demonstrated. But when in 1835 a new archbishop of Cologne was appointed conflict promptly ensued because of his immediate prohibition of mixed Catholic and Protestant marriages, which had previously been accepted by the Catholic church provided that the children of that marriage were brought up in the Catholic faith. Also, Catholic students at the university of Bonn were forbidden to attend lectures delivered by any professors known to be firm supporters of the Prussian state. The state reacted vigorously, removing the archbishop and imprisoning him in Minden fortress. The Curia of the Roman church reacted with equal vigour by appointing a new archbishop who supported the policies of his predecessor. He too was imprisoned and brought to Kolberg. Only after the death of Frederick William III was the proper working relationship between Catholic church and Prussian state restored. Frederick William III died on 7 January 1840. He left a political testament which he had written in 1827 and in which, not untypically, he expressly warned his successor equally of the twin dangers of following every political fashion of the day or displaying excessive love for what was old and obsolescent. In Frederick William's view, if these two extremes could be avoided, the introduction of useful and beneficial innovations should be possible. Externally Prussia's future would lie in close support of Russia and Austria. The question of a constitution he did not mention at all; together with his civil service he shared the opinion that a good administration was superior to any constitution whatever its intrinsic worth might be. To the surging force of constitutionalism he had remained blind to his deathbed.

Notes
1. With their departure the spirit of the officer corps of the regiments of the line began to determine the development of the Prussian army.

Chapter 11

Frederick William IV

Frederick William IV who succeeded his father was born on 15 October 1795 and had been Queen Louise's favourite son. After Jena and Auerstädt he accompanied the family to Tilsit and Memel and only in December 1809 did he, together with his parents, return to Berlin. Unlike his father he was characterized by a restlessness which caused him to begin many things without ever completing any one of them, his impulsiveness driving him from one project to another. He displayed true talent in drawing and in architecture, so much so that his tutor Jean Pierre François Ancillon, a theologian and historian of Huguenot descent, commented to him: 'I can see you spending your entire time with the pen in your hand; for a future Schinkel this would show very good application. But since the state does not consist of a Gothic temple and since no people have ever been governed by Romantic pictures, your eternal drawing is a true waste of your valuable time.'

His coming to the throne was cheered by the population at large. It was to be a new era, of which they had great expectations. And Frederick William's first actions seemed to bear out these expectations. Ernst Moritz Arndt was restored to his chair at the University of Bonn, the police supervision of Jahn was lifted, the Brothers Grimm were called to be members of the Prussian Academy of Sciences and Alexander von Humboldt appointed state councillor.

This dose of liberalism, however, was counteracted by the appointment of the King's close friends to important posts, men such as Leopold von Gerlach and General Thile who were conservatives imbued with Haller's organic concept of state and with the religious fervour of Pietist revivalism. Contemporaries began to wonder what the King's real policy was to be: a liberal or a Pietist one. True to his character, Frederick William wanted both. If his father had suffered from an impediment of speech, his son had the impediment of speaking too much. Public speeches from the throne had hitherto been unknown. Frederick William's were speeches of little political content but rather more religious sermons, which led liberals like Friedrich von Gagern to the conclusion that they were not characteristic of a man of action.

His concept of monarchy was fundamentally different from that of the early Hohenzollerns. If they declaimed themselves as the first servants of the state, Frederick William IV emphasized that he held his crown by the grace of God, that his office was of divine origin; 'I and my house – we wish to serve the Lord', he said. Or he maintained that God had furnished the King with supernatural powers, which, like a miracle, put him intellectually and spiritually far above anyone else, even the highest official and the closest confidant. His trust in the power of divine will was responsible for his inactivity at decisive moments; the Lord would make the decision for him.

Upon his accession the government and administration remained for the time being as it had been after Hardenberg's death. His cabinet minister was General von Thile, a conservative but efficient administrator. As successor to Altenstein as minister of culture Eichhorn was appointed, another Pietist. Another conservative was the minister of the interior, von Rochow, a man passionately committed to fighting the influence of 'free-thinkers' in Prussia. This passion led him into an immediate quarrel with one of the remaining members of the Prussian Reform Movement, the liberal *Oberpräsident* of East Prussia in Königsberg, von Schön. Boyen was recalled to head the ministry of war, but wasted by past struggles, his second tenure left no great mark on Prussia's military development. In the ministry of justice Kamptz, the persecutor of the so-called 'demagogues of the 1820s' remained in his post until he was replaced by Savingy in 1842. Of significance also was the minister of the exterior, von Canitz, appointed to office in 1845. But Frederick William IV left his ministers in no doubt that they were only executive organs of his very own personal rule, inspired as it was, so he was convinced, by divine will.

Hence his political views were more the product of his fanciful imaginings than assessments of the political reality around him. His romantic world view looked at the state as a product of organic growth; he admired the ancient German constitution (whatever he took that to be), with its institutions and differentiation according to estates, a constitution based upon mutual trust and duties. He was the first Prussian monarch to display active interest in the 'German' cause, meaning by this the restoration of Germany to its medieval splendour. That this could eventually mean that either Prussia or Austria would have to give way in the bid for leadership did not occur to him. He was and remained not only a Prussian but also a 'greater German', the first of the brand in the House of Hohenzollern. To him a German Empire without a ruling ancient dynasty such as the House of Hapsburg, without dominance over specifically non-German territories, seemed unthinkable.

One of his first actions as monarch was the termination of the struggle with the Roman Catholic church by the reinstitution of the rebellious bishops. He believed this to be the beginning of a process by which the Protestant and Catholic denominations would ultimately be united again. And a first step in this process was the continuation of the building of Cologne cathedral, which he inaugurated with a festive speech. In practical terms his way of proceeding in the Roman Catholic question left the impression among Catholics that *de facto* he had confirmed that bishops were subject only to the instructions of the Roman Curia, and that in case of conflict the state would have to bow to papal command. It was a misunderstanding that ran deep and was to be one of the root causes of the *Kulturkampf* 30 years later.

Frederick William IV completely reversed Frederick William III's Polish policy, that is to say that policy inaugurated after the Polish rising in 1831. Flottwell, the *Oberpräsident* in Posen for the past 10 years, was transferred in 1841 to Saxony; the policy of Germanization ceased. In 1841 Frederick William IV declared in Posen that he loved all his subjects equally, irrespective of whether they spoke German, Walloon, Lithuanian or Polish. They were all children of Prussia, and under his rule no nationality should suffer any disadvantage. All civil suits in the courts had now to be conducted in the language of the plaintiff, all official decrees had to be accompanied by a Polish translation. The Catholic archbishop of Gnesen, a true Polish patriot, appeared to be the political leader and the ultimate arbiter rather than the representative of the Prussian civil service. But instead of winning the loyalty of his Polish subjects by these measures, in an age of national *risorgimento* Frederick William found that the Poles interpreted the concessions as no more than signs of weakness at the centre of the Prussian state.

The unresolved question which Frederick William IV had inherited from his father was that of a constitution for Prussia. Time and again the demand was heard that the promise of 22 May 1815 should be honoured. At first Frederick William IV adopted a very negative view. On 4 October 1840 he clearly stated that he did not intend to solve the problem in the spirit of the promise given in 1815. He did not wish that between himself, King by divine right, and his people 'a piece of paper would intervene as a kind of second providence, to govern us with its paragraphs'. To him a constitution was directly associated with the event he hated most, the French Revolution.

But neither could he ignore the opposition, which came primarily from liberals in the civil service in East Prussia, like Schön, and from representatives of the prosperous middle classes of Prussia's western provinces, like David Hansemann, Ludolf Camphausen and Gustav Mevissen. In Königsberg the General Practitioner Johann Jacoby published in 1841 a pamphlet under the title 'Four Questions Answered by an East Prussian'. In it he demanded the participation of the people in affairs of state not as a favour but as a right. Jacoby made contact with all the prominent representatives of the opposition. This was cause enough to institute criminal proceedings against him and he was sentenced to two and a half years imprisonment, but he appealed and the Chamber Court acquitted him.

One of Jacoby's most fervent allies in public was a newspaper founded, financed and edited by a group of Rhenish industrialists and intellectuals which became the mouthpiece of the Rhenish upper middle class, the *Rheinische Zeitung für Politik, Handel und Gewerbe*. Its editor was for a time Karl Marx. Only in 1844, when Silesian weavers began to protest against their working conditions, did the Rhenish middle class realize the potential force of the proletariat and withdraw its support from the increasingly socialist-inclined *Rheinische Zeitung*. That the press could play such an important role in public protest was due to Frederick William's relaxation of censorship. Pictures, drawings and books were exempt from censorship, and a censorship court, the *Oberzensurgericht*, was founded in 1842 as a protection against the arbitrary rulings of individual censors. But when immediately after this relaxation the King found himself confronted by a tidal wave of caricatures and satire he soon changed his mind and censorship, though in a less severe form, was reintroduced.

The general political developments in Prussia were not without their influence in this decision. Increasing discontent was articulated in those areas of the kingdom which did not share in the general social and economic prosperity of the period, or had been affected by any sudden slump in economic activity. One such area was Silesia, the largest centre in Prussia and in Germany for textile production. The weavers were as yet not concentrated in the factory system but worked at home. The annual income of a weaver amounted to 60 thalers and that of a spinner to 30 thalers, while subsistence level in 1843 for a family with three children required an annual income of 100 thalers.

Devoid of all means, the weaver had to buy his yarn from the manufacturer and then supply him with the finished cotton. As the yarn was bought by payment in the form of an advance on his wages the weaver was in the hands of the manufacturer . . . I have often met these poor during the winter, in terrible weather, hungry and freezing, carrying their finished cotton many miles to the manufacturer. At home wife and children were waiting for the return of the father; for a day and a half they had eaten nothing other than potato soup. The weaver was shocked by the low offer made for his product, but there was no mercy . . . he took what was offered to him and returned full of despair to his family.

Thus wrote Wilhelm Wolf, born in Silesia and later to become a close associate of Marx and Engels. When between 1843 and 1844 the market for cotton was depressed, affecting the German cotton industry in the same way as it did that of Britain and the United States, utter despair drove the Silesian weavers into the streets where they protested in front of the houses and factories of those owners who were particularly hated. On 4 June 1844 at Peterwaldau a number of weavers marched through the village calling upon bystanders to join them. The response was enthusiastic and they marched to the house of the local manufacturer where they demanded an increase in their wages. The manufacturer replied in tones of derision which so incited the crowd that they stormed the house and destroyed it along with all the manufacturing equipment. The manufacturer just managed to escape and made his way to Breslau where he called for intervention by the military. The following day a military detachment on their way to Peterwaldau arrived at Langenbielau, another centre of the weavers' revolt. Protesting weavers met them; the soldiers opened fire killing 11, among them women and children, and wounding another 24. But the resistance of the weavers did not cease. Time and time again they attacked the troops with sticks and stones, forcing them to withdraw to wait for reinforcements. On 6 June four companies with four pieces of artillery arrived, supported by a detachment of cavalry, and occupied Peterwaldau and Langenbielau. Over 100 weavers were arrested and transported to Breslau. There 80 of them were put on trial and sentenced to a total of 203 years forced labour, 90 years imprisonment and 330 lashes with the whip. The alliance between the industrial middle class and the state had been demonstrated for the first time in Prussia. It was the beginning of the political activity of the German proletariat.

Yet this alliance was far from universal. Bettina von Arnim published a book under the title *This book belongs to the King* in which she vividly described the suffering of the working class in Berlin. August Heinrich Hoffman von Fallersleben, professor of German language and literature at the University of Breslau, published a book of satirical poems entitled *Unpolitical Songs* for which he was deprived of his university chair. In exile he wrote what was to become the German national anthem, 'Deutschland, Deutschland über alles'. Another prominent writer and poet, Ferdinand von Freiligrath, in 1844 refused a royal pension from the Prussian King and emigrated to Brussels, while Heinrich Heine wrote his most famous poem 'Germany – a Winters Tale'.

A crisis in trade and commerce, accompanied by a series of bad harvests, kept the popular unrest aflame. During 1847 there were several revolts in Germany, generally caused by severe economic suffering. In Berlin, market stalls and food shops were stormed by the crowds. Moreover the general economic crisis led once again to a crisis in Prussia's finances. The need to float public loans forced Frederick William IV to make a concession towards greater constitutionalization. At first, in 1841, he had thought he could circumvent the problem by supporting the greater development of provincial diets. These were to be advisory bodies meeting every two years to discuss affairs, partly in public. They were also to create committees which were to meet while the provincial diet was not in session. On 18 October 1842 these committees were called to Berlin as 'United Committees', a kind of substitute for a general parliament. But Frederick William still refused to go the whole way towards a parliamentary system. Membership of the provincial diets as well as of their committees was to be a system of representation of the estates. Thus the United Committees comprised a total of 98 members, consisting of 46 nobles, 32 burghers and 20 propertied peasants.

Finally, the King could no longer resist political and economic pressure and on 3 February 1847 published a decree which called into being a Prussian diet, the United Diet, while still maintaining the United Committees as well as a permanent Delegation for the State Debts responsible, naturally enough, for the state debts. The United Diet was to meet as often as the requirements of the state called for it, such as when there was a need for new loans, the introduction of new taxes or the increase of existing taxation. The United Committees were, in the absence of the United Diet, to meet every four years. Both diets and committees had the right to agree to or refuse loans and taxation as well as to participate in the legislative process, but only inasmuch as did the provincial diets already. This of course meant that as far as legislation was concerned their function was still restricted to a purely advisory and consultative role. While the United Diet was to represent the three estates, the higher nobility such as princes were to deliberate separately as a kind of upper house, the *Herrenhaus*.

Frederick William's decree proved too little too late, but was better than nothing. On 11 April 1847 the United Diet was opened in the White Hall of the Berlin Palace. An important novelty of the gathering was that its proceedings could be fully reported by the press, something hitherto unknown in Prussia. But more importantly the members of the diet, under the protection of the law and irrespective of social standing, could and did speak out and criticize their King. The diet comprised 237 members of the nobility, 182 representatives of the towns and 124 representatives of the propertied peasants, while the upper house was made up of 70 princes and counts.

The King's opening address caused a furore: 'no power on earth will succeed in causing me to change the powerful relationship between the prince and the people for a constitutional one, existing as it does because of its natural origin and by virtue of its inner truth'. The members of the diet immediately demanded full constitutional rights.

Revolutionary tidings continued to spread throughout Germany and Europe during 1847. In France dissatisfaction at the existing corruption made it only a matter of time until revolution broke out, and when in February 1848 the Second French Republic was proclaimed, the flame of revolution spread over the entire European mainland, in Germany giving rise to a broadly liberal, popular movement. In Prussia it began on 3 March 1848 with a mass demonstration of workers in Cologne which spread throughout the Rhineland. Three days later similar demonstrations were taking place in Berlin and other German cities and provinces. Frederick William IV was forced to act. To prevent outright revolution, as was taking place in France, David Hansemann advised the King to turn to the people and to introduce moderate reforms, espousing the cause not only of Prussia but giving a lead to the liberal middle classes of Germany as a whole by supporting German national unification, in other words reform of the German Confederation. In Hansemann's words: 'I beg your majesty to understand the momentous importance of the time and to put yourself at the head of German liberty and independence'.

Afraid of revolution, Frederick William at first concentrated troops in Berlin while demonstrators demanded their withdrawal. Then on 18 March 1848 he published a new decree in which he called a meeting of the United Diet for 2 April, promising in place of a German Confederation a German federal state, a German military constitution, a German navy, a Prussian constitution and the freedom of the press. But Frederick William's confidant and Prussia's envoy at the diet of the German Confederation in Frankfurt, Joseph von Radowitz, had already tried for some time to get some action on the German question. It had become more and more apparent that the call for reforms of the German Confederation could not be ignored in the long run. Late in the previous year Radowitz had drafted a memorandum concerning the future of Germany which in its conception was 'greater German' but which in practical terms suggested what amounted to a division of power between Prussia and Austria. In case of obstruction by other members of the Confederation, Radowitz thought a suitable alternative would be to have a bilateral agreement between Prussia and Austria (the way in which the existing customs union had been negotiated). According to his plan the House of Hapsburg would retain the imperial crown while Prussia would be given the supreme command over the military forces of the German Confederation. Austria was to be coerced by moral arguments to adopt a more positively German attitude. Radowitz had travelled to Vienna to discuss the matter with Metternich, but the latter's reception of the plan was less than lukewarm. All that was agreed upon was to convene a ministerial conference in Dresden; but before this could meet revolutionary events had overtaken it.

Partly in response to the wide popular movement which was expressing itself in the form of numerous demonstrations, liberal members of the German intelligentsia who were meeting in Heidelberg during the first week of March 1848, resolved to press publicly as well as in the diet of the German Confederation for the convening of a German national assembly, for a German constitution and, in preparation for that, for a preliminary parliament, the *Vorparlament*, to be convened in Frankfurt-am-Main on 30 March 1848.

Frederick William IV's proclamation of 18 March coincided with the diet of the German Confederation recommending to its member states the liberty of the press and the adoption of the colours of black, red and gold as German national colours.

As with his previous measures, Frederick William's proclamation was again too little too late. Berlin's population, clamouring for the withdrawal of the troops, roamed through the streets and outside the Palace. During a mêlée with the troops two shots were fired, allegedly by accident. Though no one was hurt, the masses felt betrayed by the King and the shots were the signal for the revolution in Berlin. Hundreds of barricades were erected in the city and bloody street battles ensued. 'Between four and five o'clock the first artillery shot came from the Kurfürsten bridge down the Königstrasse; it fails to destroy the barricade. Shot follows upon shot, the barricade is shaking, torn corpses lie everywhere at the street corners. Between five and six o'clock infantry pickets come. They are fired upon from the windows and met with a barrage of stones'.

For more than a century in German historiography the tale has been peddled that the masses were mobilized by 'foreign agitators'. This has never been substantiated. The barricades were manned by students, artisans and burghers. The locksmith journeymen Glaswaldt and Zinna defended a barricade in Berlin's Jägerstrasse. When a platoon of infantry approached from the direction of the Friedrichstrasse, Glaswaldt fought them with an ancient rifle until he was hit by a bullet. Then Zinna, armed only with a rusty sabre, attacked the platoon alone, injured its officer, and then used paving stones against the soldiers until he was hit. He subsequently died of his wounds. Workers of the newly established Borsig factory in Berlin joined the revolutionary movement *en masse*. In Berlin in particular the revolution was carried by the exploited and therefore dissatisfied working class, a fact confirmed by the young Rudolf Virchow, then a doctor, in a letter of 1 May 1848 to his father: 'You are quite right, essentially it has been the workers who have decided this revolution, but I also believe that you in the provinces do not fully realize that this revolution was not simply a political one, but essentially a social one.'

At first Frederick William IV was at a loss to know what to do. He found the bloodshed repellent, and his wife and several of his advisors pressed him to relent and concede to the demand of several deputations of burghers to withdraw the troops from the city. He was aware that the stance he had adopted as the reformer of the German Confederation was hardly compatible with the suppression by force of his fellow Germans. At midnight on 18 March he drafted a new proclamation appealing to his 'dear Berliners' to return to normal life and to clear away the barricades, in return for which he gave his royal word that he would withdraw the troops. Frederick William found considerable opposition to this course from the military party led by General von Prittwitz, commander of the Berlin garrison. His suggestion was for the King and family to leave Berlin and then put down the rising from without. But Frederick William rejected this advice.

When, on the morning of 19 March, news arrived that several barricades had been cleared, the King ordered that troops should be withdrawn wherever the barricades had been removed. Confusion ensued, resulting in a total withdrawal of the troops that left the King alone in the palace without any military protection. The masses followed close on the heels of the withdrawing troops into the city, and the military party, as a rejoinder to the King's refusal to take its advice, decided to let him stew in his own juice.

Jubilation and rejoicing echoed through the streets of Berlin; the **revolution had won**, or so it seemed. The King's brother, Prince William of Prussia, the future Emperor William I, was held responsible by the masses for the bloodletting and had to flee the city on a 'temporary mission' to England. In accordance with the example already established in Paris, during the morning of 19 March a mourning procession carrying the coffins of the victims arrived at the inner courtyard of the palace. King and Queen were forced publicly to pay their respects to the fallen revolutionaries. For the first time the Prussian monarchy had been humbled by its own subjects and when the 216 dead were buried the King again had to pay his respects from his balcony. The revolutionaries now formed a militia which provided protection for the King in place of the army. The militia was quite successful in re-establishing order. But further concessions by the King were necessary. On 20 March a general amnesty was declared for all persons convicted of political crimes. One of the King's ministers, Heinrich von Arnim, advised him to divert public attention to the German question by publicly supporting the German national cause. By that he could be sure of winning the support of the masses. Hence on 21 March, draped with a black, red and gold sash, Frederick William rode through the streets of Berlin delivering speeches to the citizens' militia, the university and the city deputies. He promised to put himself at the head of the movement for German unity without any ambition towards ruling Germany himself. He then issued a manifesto containing the famous sentence: 'Prussia henceforce merges with Germany.'

It was rhetoric, no doubt well-intentioned but devoid of any basis. The Prussian government was in such a shambles that for a time it was incapable of significant action within Prussia, let alone on a German national level. To re-establish some semblance of order at the top of the government a new group of ministers was appointed, headed by Ludolf Camphausen, a Rhinelander, and including as minister of finance David Hansemann, another Rhenish liberal. The ministers were to discuss the drafting of a Prussian constitution and one of the early results was the convention of a Prussian national assembly elected by general and direct elections. It met for the first time on 22 May 1848. At the same time the diet of the German Confederation in Frankfurt had decided to call on all German governments to hold elections for a German national parliament. That parliament convened in Frankfurt's Paulskirche on 18 May 1848 to discuss and decide a German constitution. That university professors were more than adequately represented ensured that the discussions were lengthy, frequently (under the guise of academic detachment) extremely partisan and doctrinaire, and very often irrelevant to the issues in question. A provisional central authority was established with Archduke Johann of Austria being appointed as *Reichsverweser*. With that the revolutionary enthusiasms at the national level began to evaporate.

In Prussia another issue had gained temporary dominance. In 1846 a renewed Polish rising had taken place with its centre in Cracow and affecting mainly Austrian Galicia. The intention was to spread the rising to Posen, but the attempt was anticipated by the Prussian authorities who arrested the leader, Mieroslavski, and others. They were tried for high treason and sentenced to various terms of imprisonment. In the wake of the political amnesty of 1848 Mieroslavski was freed and renewed the attempt that had failed two years before. The German population in Posen now faced the threat of being submerged by the Poles. To prevent this, German districts were put exclusively under German administration with the intention of annexing them to the German Confederation. The result was uproar and revolt among the Poles, which in turn caused very adverse comment on Prussia and Germany from outside Germany's frontiers. During the course of the spring and summer of 1848 Prussian military forces quelled the rising and Mieroslavski escaped abroad. This put an end to the planned reforms in the province of Posen.

The other prominent issue at the time was that of Schleswig-Holstein. A popular Danish movement had demanded the incorporation of Schleswig into the Danish monarchy and Danish troops had occupied the territory. The Germans in Schleswig insisted upon their independence and formed a provisional government. Berlin was asked for aid and Prussia's King, after having proclaimed himself at the head of the movement for German unity, could do little other than comply with the request. He turned also to the diet of the German Confederation and to the German princes for aid. At first he attempted to resolve the problem by peaceful means but Danish obstinacy made this impossible. The diet of the German Confederation fully supported the Germans in Schleswig and war broke out conducted by the German Confederation with predominately Prussian troops under the command of General von Wrangel. But when Russia, Britain and France threatened to intervene on the Danish side, an armistice was concluded on 26 August 1848 and Prussian troops were withdrawn from Schleswig. The provisional government was replaced by a mixed commission made up of Germans and Danes. Public disgust in Germany over this capitulation was widespread. The radical Republican Party called for public opposition to the Frankfurt parliament, and renewed uproar and street fighting ensued in various parts of Germany. Although these new attempts at popular risings were quickly quelled, the fact could no longer be ignored that the population at large now played a role which sooner or later would reach decisive proportions. In the meantime on 19 October 1848 the national assembly convened again, this time to tackle the question of a German constitution; the task was concluded by 28 March 1849.

As by the autumn of 1848 the revolutionary fervour had begun to evaporate and it became apparent that the discussions about a Prussian constitution had brought forth little that was of any practical use, Prussia's conservatives began to reassemble and form the Conservative Political Party. Their mouthpiece was the newly founded *Neue Preussische Zeitung*, carrying as its symbol the Iron Cross and therefore popularly referred to as the *Kreuzzeitung*. The founder of the party,

Ernst Ludwig von Gerlach, represented a conservatism that was aware of the social problems confronting Prussia as a whole, and of the social responsibility which rested on the state and its prosperous and propertied members. By late 1848 he had also come to the conclusion that the time was ripe for counter-revolutionary action. He urged the appointment of a military prime minister. After renewed outbreaks of violence in Berlin the Camphausen ministry had resigned in June 1848, followed by the Auerswald–Hansemann ministry, Gerlach suggested the general commanding Breslau, Count Friedrich Wilhelm von Brandenburg (the son of Frederick William II and Wilhelmine Enke) as prime minister. The Prussian national assembly protested, but the King replied by proroguing it, knowing that the military balance was now in his favour. On 10 November 1848, 40,000 troops under the command of General von Wrangel entered Berlin and disarmed the citizens' militia. The events in Berlin had their repercussions throughout Germany, where many expressed sympathy with the Prussian national assembly. But such expressions were of little value when not followed up by deeds. Attempts by workers at disrupting lines of communications to Berlin to prevent further troop transports were too sporadic to have any practical effect. When the Prussian national assembly refused to consent to any taxation, Frederick William IV dissolved it, without having any right to do so. And on the same day, 5 December 1848, he imposed his constitution upon Prussia. The method itself amounted to a rejection of the principle of popular sovereignty; again it was a reform from above, a reform which included many features which liberals had been demanding for decades. General and representative elections were planned and two chambers were to convene to discuss the final version of the constitution. But the full executive powers of the crown were retained, though within a framework of constitutional limitations. A vital feature omitted from the constitution was that the armed forces should be sworn in on it; a clause was included which stipulated that civil servants should swear loyalty and obedience to the King.

It has been said that even the 'imposed' constitution had been framed under the pressure exercised by public opinion in Berlin, particularly by the 'mob in the streets'. This is indeed a serious qualification. By the end of 1848 the revolutionary impetus in Prussia had run its full course and exhausted itself. Indeed the temporary 'rule of the mob' had caused the old supporters of the Hohenzollern dynasty to range themselves more firmly behind it. And not far behind them in supporting the monarchy was the liberal middle class, petrified by the mob's appearance as the sorcerer's revolutionary apprentice. Unable to agree among themselves, many seem to have viewed the King's dissolution of the Prussian national assembly and the imposition of his own constitution as the lesser of several evils.

In Frankfurt, in the meantime, the deliberations over a German constitution proceeded. The main underlying problem was of the relationship which Austria and Prussia were to have within the German body politic in general. The majority of the members were in favour of a strong central government in place of the existing loose confederation. That of course meant that Austria could participate only with its German territories, while its non-German lands had to have a separate constitution and administration. This was opposed in Austria by the supporters of an Austro-Hungarian unitary state. That opposition led to the resignation of the president of the Reichsministry, the Austrian minister Schmerling, who was replaced by the president of the assembly, Heinrich von Gagern. He opted for a 'little German' solution supplemented by some form of treaty of union with Austria. Austria's reaction was unfavourable and the Frankfurt assembly now divided itself into three major groups: the 'greater Germans' holding on to Austria; the Catholics the radical left and the liberal centre, mainly the professors; and lastly those who advocated a 'little German' Empire with an inheritable imperial title, these concentrating their efforts on Prussia. The last group contained all shades of right-wing opinion but also found strong support, in spite of some reservations, from among the liberal centre. Von Gagern travelled to Potsdam in November 1848 to discuss the matter with Frederick William IV and to find out whether he would be prepared to accept the imperial crown. The King stated that the acceptance of such an honour without the agreement of the princes in Germany would be a revolutionary action; he refused to recognize the principle of popular sovereignty. But he would consult with the princes. This he did but was told by Austria that it had its own plans for an Austrian unitarian state and that it could not accept a German federal state with a unified central government. Moreover, the Austrians tried to persuade him to join their cause and overthrow the Frankfurt parliament. Frederick William refused to sanction such an action.

He looked for alternative solutions such as the creation of a German federal state of which the German-Austrian provinces were to be part and with which the Austro-Hungarian monarchy was to be closely associated. At the apex of that creation was to be a Chamber of Kings. But Austria would not have any of that and rejected the entire Frankfurt constitution demanding at the same time that the assembly accepted the constitution which the Hapsburgs had just forced upon their lands. This put an end to the endeavour of the 'greater Germans' in Frankfurt. On 27 March 1849 a new constitution was accepted with a small majority by the Frankfurt assembly. It was the 'little German' solution and included the inheritable imperial title. A day later 290 representatives declared themselves for Frederick William IV of Prussia as German Emperor.

At the court of Berlin embarrassment was considerable. The question was how to receive the Frankfurt delegation. General von Wrangel advised simply 'Don't let them in'. The delegation included Ernst Moritz Arndt, the historian Dahlmann, and a German of the Jewish faith, Gabriel Riesser. On 3 April 1849 it was received by Frederick William IV. The president of the national assembly, Eduard Simson from Königsberg, addressed the King, emphasizing how enthusiastically the fatherland welcomed the Hohenzollern dynasty as Germany's future imperial family. The King himself was torn between dynastic ambition, national sympathies and his legitimistic principles, but again he repeated his previous point of view, namely that acceptance of the imperial crown was dependent on the agreement of all other German ruling houses.

The Frankfurt delegation was deeply disturbed, for the King's refusal also implied that he rejected the entire constitution. Their fears were confirmed a few weeks later when the King dissolved the lower chamber of the Prussian diet on 27 April because it had recommended the acceptance of the German constitution. As a palliative to the decision voiced to the delegation, Frederick William issued a circular note to all German courts in which he declared his readiness to lead a German federal state comprised of those states who wished to be members. Its shape and constitution would be determined at a later date. This immediately brought forth Austrian protests against a federation under Prussian leadership while the Frankfurt parliament insisted on adhering to the new constitution and began to negotiate with the individual German states. Twenty-eight of them were prepared to accept the constitution and Prussia's leadership. But in addition to Prussia, Bavaria and Saxony were also against the constitution. Of the German kingdoms only the King of Württemberg, virtually forced by a massive popular demonstration in Stuttgart, finally declared his adherence to the constitution. The Saxon King, also under public pressure to do likewise, received Frederick William's assurance of aid if pressure were to become too great. A new series of popular risings began, the first in Dresden on 3 May 1849, then others on 7 May in the Rhineland and in Westphalia, and on 11 May in Baden, while on 17 May a revolutionary government established itself in the Palatinate. True to the motto which Frederick William had once written in a letter to Bunsen, his ambassador in London – 'Against democrats only soldiers can help' – Prussian troops intervened in Dresden, in the Palatinate and in Baden and suppressed the revolution bloodily, re-establishing the authority of the individual states of the German Confederation. The revolution of 1848 had come to an end.

Lenin once described as an essential precondition for a successful revolution the coincidence of a crisis in the ruling classes and revolutionary pressure from the lower orders of society. The dynastic houses of Germany were rattled by the events of 1848/9 but not fundamentally shaken. The revolution produced serious anxiety among the upholders of the political and social *status quo*, but really no more than that. The revolution, as a result of Germany's particularist traditions, lacked a real epicentre. As it was, a number of local revolutions had occurred independently of one another, in isolation from one another, and not co-ordinated into one major revolutionary effort. Furthermore the honourable men who assembled at Frankfurt lacked one important instrument – power. In many respects the revolution was a sad epilogue to the high expectations of the Prussian Reform Movement of 1807–1815, a movement which in its composition had been less Prussian than German and had found itself in possession of real power, though for fear of releasing those forces which led to the excesses of the French Revolution it proved too reluctant to use it for change at a national level.

Nevertheless the revolution of 1848 demonstrated the process of politicization of the German nation as a whole. In the place of abstract theoretical discussions was now concrete political experience. That the outcome was failure again underlined the different patterns of political development in Germany and Western Europe. The disappointment in Germany ran deep, leading to the disillusionment of many with politics. Some went into radical opposition, an opposition of negative criticism and refusal to co-operate, an attitude which was to be maintained until 1918. Others accepted their fate and adapted their political consciousness to the prevailing political situation, regressing from 'citizens' back into 'subjects' of their respective dynasties. Still others ignored politics altogether, moving back into the lofty heights of the intellect and condemning politics as 'dirty business'. Yet to consider a triumph of the revolution as a victory for democracy would be to read history backwards, so likewise to consider its defeat as a triumph for militaristic forces that in the future would threaten the peace of Europe would also be wrong. In 1848/9 Western Europe thought differently. In France Thiers considered the German unification aimed at by the revolutionaries as the greatest danger for France, and, invoking the traditions of Frederick the Great, urged Prussia to resist the spirit of Frankfurt with all her might. France's foreign minister Bastide declared to the Prussian envoy in August 1848: 'We shall fight the triumph of democratic and unitary tendencies in Germany. By our moral support we shall maintain the German princes in their places and for that reason we refuse to receive officially any envoy of the central authority.' Two months later Cavaignac, as president of the Second Republic, stated that German unification under the auspices of the German liberal national movement would be opposed by France, if necessary in alliance with Russia. Some observers already envisaged Germany becoming involved in a two-front war. In Great Britain opinion was more sympathetically inclined towards the revolutionaries, but the Frankfurt parliament was nevertheless considered a doubtful venture contradicting actual political realities; 'a German romance' as Disraeli called it. The episode in Schleswig-Holstein, the call to create a German navy, the threat of economic competition from a united Germany were all factors adversely influencing contemporary judgement by others of the revolution. The peace of Europe seemed to be more threatened by the Frankfurt parliament than by the head of the Hohenzollern dynasty in Berlin. Expansionist aims loudly voiced by representatives at the Frankfurt assembly alarmed Europe, aims proclaimed not only by liberal opinions but by representatives of the nascent socialist movement such as Ferdinand Lassalle. Friedrich List had propounded an economic union from the North Sea to the Black Sea; the Austrian deputy at Frankfurt, Moring, a 'greater German' Empire with German economic hegemony from the Rhine to the Volga; and the Austrian minister of trade and finance, von Bruck, the creation of *Mitteleuropa*, a customs union to include the Netherlands, Scandinavia and the Balkan states. Constantin Frantz, so often referred to as the epitome of a healthy European federalism, dreamt of a pan-Germanic union which included the annexation of Holland, Switzerland, Denmark and Sweden. No doubt the German revolution of 1848 was very ambitious, but it lacked the power to realize those ambitions. The attempt at their realization was left to a later generation.

The middle classes had been defeated in their political aims, so they now set about transforming political defeat into economic victory. In the next 20 years economic development in Prussia alone took greater strides than in the entire preceding century. While in 1846 Prussian industry deployed 1,139 steam engines with a total capacity of 21,715 German horsepower, by 1866 the number had increased to 6,669 steam engines with a total capacity of 137,377 German horsepower. The landscape changed accordingly, especially in the Rhineland and in Upper Silesia. Railways made similar advances. In 1850 Prussia's railway network totalled 3,869 kilometres; by 1860 it had grown to 7,169 kilometres; by 1870 to 11,523 kilometres. In the factories mechanization replaced the artisan. In 1846 in 2,529 Prussian cloth factories, 78,423 hand-operated looms were used and 4,603 mechanized ones. By 1861 the number of cloth factories had been reduced to 1,900 employing 15,258 mechanically operated and 28,012 hand-operated looms. In the iron and steel industry in Prussia the number of workers employed per factory increased from 18 to 40 between 1849 and 1861, while in the engineering industry over the same period it rose from 18 to 40, and in the railway yards from 27 to 70. This process was accompanied by greater industrial concentration. The number of companies operating cotton mills decreased between 1846 and 1861 from 616 to 351, those operating steel mills from 913 to 655. Only the engineering industry still showed an increase in the number of companies. Shareholding companies began to spread. Between 1826 and 1850 a total 102 shareholding companies were founded in Prussia with a total capital of 638 million marks. From 1851 to 1870, 295 further companies were founded with a total capital of 2,400 million marks. Ninety per cent of the investments of the shareholding companies were made in railways, mining, steel and iron, banks and insurance. Between 1850 and 1870 new industries emerged, particularly the electrical and the chemical industries. Early in 1859 Karl Marx wrote: 'Whoever last saw Berlin 10 years ago would not recognize it again. A stiff parade ground has been transformed into the powerful centre of German engineering. When one travels through Rhenish-Prussia and the duchy of Westphalia one is reminded of Lancashire and Yorkshire.'

This industrial development of Prussia was immensely aided by the legislation of the Prussian state. Since December 1848 the ministry of economics had been headed by August von der Heydt, a man of Rhenish origin and liberal free trade convictions. Industrialists were kept happy by tax concessions, which diverted their attention from political demands. However, because of its strategic importance the expansion of Prussia's railway network was subject to a considerable degree of state direction.

With full justification the nineteenth century has been called the Age of Iron. There were two main phases, the first marked by the ultimate victory of coal over charcoal, the second by the replacement of welded steel by rolled steel. The patenting in 1856 of Sir Henry Bessemer's steel-making process, which facilitated turning iron into steel, marks the beginning of the second phase. Ten years later the process was further refined by Siemens, and from then on began the Age of Steel. But the advances in the iron industry, advances concentrated mainly in Germany, could not have been made without the contribution of the natural sciences, especially chemistry and physics. As the report on the Industrial World Exhibition in London in 1851 shows, the German chemical industry was far ahead of its British and French competitors.

Coal production in Prussia increased by leaps and bounds. The output of the Saar coal mines increased from 674, 860 tons in 1850 to 2,179,758 tons in 1860, that of the Ruhr fields from 1,961,000 tons in 1850 to 4,276,000 tons in 1860. The Upper Silesian coal mines, to a large extent state-owned, remained fairly static in their output until 1851, when the increasing demand for coal, iron and steel forced the Prussian administration to develop the area as it had the Saar and the Ruhr. Since Silesia was lacking in the widespread system of waterways which characterized Prussia's western provinces, the introduction of a railway network gave great impetus to its industrial development. Towards the end of the century Silesia alone produced nearly 40 per cent of Germany's coal.

This development created other problems, mainly affecting labour. The rationalization of agriculture on the vast estates of the German east had resulted in an available reservoir of labour which first migrated to nearby towns and then further westward to the industrial regions. For example, on the eve of the First World War the number of Poles, or Prussian subjects of Polish origin, living in the Ruhr area is estimated at between 350,000 and 450,000. Conversely the industrial expansion of Upper Silesia during the second half of the nineteenth century led to a vast influx of Poles from Russia's and Austria's Polish provinces. In addition Prussia's annual birthrate increased by between 2 and 3 per cent from the middle of the century.

Capital, coal and the railways were the triple foundations of the new industrial age. But the railways made not only the transport of goods easier and quicker, they also accelerated the spread of news, a process further enhanced by the introduction of the electric telegraph. 'One must not forget that it was the railway which was the first to call electric telegraphy into being; it was its cradle and school' as one British observer noted at the time. In 1851 in Prussia 39,872 telegraphic messages were transmitted; five years later the number was 221,411. But that new age also had its critics. It gave rise to propagators of a social liberalism who tried to approach social problems empirically, observing the changing environment and modifying their theories accordingly. Some of them were themselves industrialists, most of them had travelled extensively in England and who were dominated by the determination to avoid the worst consequences of industrialisation. Marx and Engels dismissed most of their writings as the work of 'economists, philanthropists, humanitarians, improvers of the working-class, do-gooders, members of societies for the prevention of cruelty to animals, temperance cranks, hole-and-corner reformers of every imaginable kind'. Such derision can hardly apply to industrialists like Friedrich Harkort and Gustav Mevissen, both of whom were intimately familiar with the industrial scene in England. In 1846 during a visit in the Midlands and the North Mevissen wrote in a letter to his wife: 'This Leeds is the filthiest spot in all England. Hardly a ray of sunlight comes through the smoke-blackened windows. All the misery of modern industry is heaped up here. Magnificent factories in which thousands of human beings waste away physically and spiritually . . . What a bright future there will be when one day the grandchildren of these ragged workers demand compensation for the sufferings of the present'. Mevissen in his later years was to play an important role in drafting Bismark's social welfare legislation. And Harkort wrote: 'Although I personally am one of the leaders of industry, I despise from the bottom of my heart that creation of value and wealth which is based on the sacrifice of human dignity and the degradation of the working class. The purpose of the machine is to free man from animal servitude, not to fashion a more terrible bondage.' Therefore he became a fervent and successful advocate of government intervention to provide better education for the workers and guarantee their livelihood. Or as another one of that group, Wilhelm Schulz, argued, 'The initiative for these laws and regulations can come only from the state which represents society in its unity. So we see how we are again and again brought back from the field of socialism into the field of politics.'

Karl Heinrich Brueggemann may have been overstating his case considerably when, in 1842, comparing industrial conditions in Prussia with those of other industrializing countries he said that 'The Prussian government, for example, thought of a Factory Bill for the protection of working class children as soon as it thought of factories themselves. And our German conscience finds in this concern not a limitation, but an affirmation, of our national idea of freedom.' – but there is a germ of truth in the statement. For a Krupp worker to live in the Krupp settlement founded by the family was not a sign a dependence, for to be a *Kruppianer* was a point of pride. The aberrations of *laissez-faire* capitalism never developed to the extent they did in Great Britain and the United States, not for want of trying, but ultimately because of the existence of an *Obrigkeitsstaat*, irrespective of the adverse consequences this kind of state may have had in other ways.

Economic growth and prosperity did not proceed without set-backs. A financial crisis which began in Paris in 1856 and spread to the United States in 1857 and then to Britain, also affected Prussia seriously. The result was numerous bankruptcies, the weaker units of production collapsing while the stronger, better financed and more efficient ones became consolidated and concentrated. Almost 10 years later a similar, though not as far-reaching, crisis affected the Prussian economy again. But these were temporary set-backs which did not stop the overall upward trend of the Prussian economy.

Growing prosperity, however, could not resolve the political problems confronting Prussia, especially since Frederick William IV in spite of his adverse attitude to the constitutional experiment of 1848 in Frankfurt continued to believe in the need for reform of the German Confederation and a greater degree of German unification. As an initial stage of this process he envisaged the creation of a federation of the north German states under Prussia's leadership.

On 26 May 1849 Radowitz concluded a treaty with Saxony and Hanover which was joined by 28 of the smaller German states, but not by Württenberg and Bavaria. It amounted to the furtherance of the aim he had already pursued prior to 1848: the creation of a federal state under Prussian leadership associated closely with Austria by a treaty of union. Radowitz worked out a constitution in great detail, making provisions for a parliament with an upper house consisting of German princes and a lower house. In March 1850 a *Unionsparlament* convened in Erfurt in Thuringia to discuss the new constitution. Radowitz was now appointed Prussia's minister for foreign affairs. But neither Frederick William IV nor Radowitz was in a position to dispel Austria's suspicions. Austria's prime minister Prince Schwarzenberg demanded that the diet of the German Confederation be convened under Austria's presidency. It was boycotted by 22 members of the new union. The ensuing struggle for supremacy in Germany between Prussia and Austria was further complicated because it had begun to involve the Schleswig-Holstein question as well as a constitutional conflict in Hesse, where the ruler's taxation was challenged by the population. The German Confederation was preparing to support him with armed intervention when Prussia mobilized in response. Austria, supported by Czar Nicholas, issued an ultimatum to Prussia demanding the end of the mobilization and the dissolution of the union. Opinions were divided among Frederick William's ministers and advisors. Radowitz and Prince William of Prussia were in favour of accepting the risk of war in order to maintain the union. Brandenburg and the minister of war Stockhausen declared that Prussia was not prepared to take on both Austria and Russia. In the end Frederick William decided in favour of the view of Brandenburg and Stockhausen, but, typically, said to them that he hoped that they would not come to regret their decision. Radowitz resigned and Brandenburg communicated to Vienna Prussia's decision to demobilize. When on 6 November 1850 Brandenburg suddenly died, Otto von Manteuffel took over his offices as well as that for foreign affairs. In the Prussian diet Manteuffel declared: 'The strong is taking a step back but is keeping its aim firmly in mind and is looking for ways and means by which it can be achieved in a different way.' On 29 November 1850 Manteuffel and Schwarzenberg signed the Ölmütz Punctation which agreed upon the demobilization of Prussia's troops and those of the German Confederation and for the time being put an end to Prussia's bid for supremacy in Germany. The *status quo* in Germany was restored; Russia had become the umpire in Central Europe. Prussian conservatives like Ernst Ludwig von Gerlach argued: 'Unity between Prussia and Austria is German unity. Prussia's and Austria's disunity amounts to the tearing up Germany and the downfall of Prussia, Austria and Germany.'

Prussia returned, in the words of Marx, as a 'rueful sinner into the fold of the reconstituted diet of the Confederation'. From 15 July 1851 Prussia's representative in Frankfurt was Otto von Bismarck, from which position he did all he could to obstruct Austrian policy, saying 'If they put a horse in front, we put one in the opposite direction.'

After Frederick William IV dissolved the Prussian diet in 1849, conservative voices in Prussia could be heard calling for the complete abolition of the constitution, but Frederick William wisely decided to retain it and, with a newly elected diet, to revise it. This revision was carried out with liberal support, and replaced universal franchise, the achievement of 1848, with the three class franchise. For the time being this ensured a conservative majority in the diet. This return to conservative domination had been inaugurated the year before by a publicly little-noticed measure affecting the judiciary in Prussia. Since 1805 it had been the practice that it was up to the courts themselves to decide whether to institute court proceedings or not. As long as the judiciary was independent of the administration this ensured a liberally orientated legal process. But in times of political upheaval this degree of judicial independence was considered potentially dangerous, and so on 3 January 1849 a decree had been issued which transferred the decision to initiate proceedings from the courts to the state prosecutor's office which in turn was directly dependent on the ministry of justice. Thus the Prussian bureaucracy regained a position of power which had once been the domain of the absolute monarch, the loss of which had signified the emancipation of the middle class and which now signalled the ascendancy of the bureaucracy over the judiciary. It was now entirely in the hands of the bureaucracy as to what issues should come to court and which should not, the judiciary being empowered only to decide on those cases submitted to it by the ministry of justice and its adjunct the state prosecutor's office. The potential for direct intervention by the judiciary into public and administrative questions was removed; the bureaucracy could now take all its own administrative decisions and prevent problems from coming to court by referring to the lacking expertise of judges in any specific area of public interest. However, until the early 1880s the Prussian judiciary remained, as far as the restrictions imposed upon it allowed, an instrument of the liberal forces in Prussia, the only means available to the middle class to defend itself against the encroachments of the bureaucracy.

On 31 January 1850 Frederick William IV had accepted the revised constitution and sworn an oath on it. Executive power, appointment of ministers, supreme command of the armed forces and the conduct of foreign policy remained in his hands. The three-class franchise was converted into a system of equal representation for all three classes, which meant that the small group of rich tax payers had the same number of representatives as the bulk of the people in the third class. For instance in 1852 the Conservatives, representing the land-owners, had 196 deputies, while the opposition, representing the bulk of Prussia's population, had 152 deputies. The Conservatives, however, did not represent a homogeneous group, and those from Prussia's Rhenish provinces in particular, under the leadership of the Bonn jurist Moritz August von Bethmann Hollweg, shared many of the views of the liberals, especially the desire for German unification.

But what again united conservatives and liberals was the fear of the growing working class movement, the first signs of which were seen during the economic crisis of 1857 when there was a wave of strikes and lock-outs in the Rhineland, the Ruhr and Silesia. Demands for social improvements began to be articulated by the spokesmen of the masses for the first time. Berlin experienced its first demonstrations of the unemployed who demanded state support.

While Manteuffel was still minister of the interior, the emancipation of the peasants was completed. The decree issued on 2 March 1850 took considerably more account of the peasant smallholder than had previous legislation. No longer was he compelled to pay off services owed to the lord with land, but could now keep his land by paying for it over a 41-year period. In spite of strong opposition from the Junker nobility, who had the ear of Frederick William IV, Manteuffel succeeded in having the measure passed and executed.

During the last phase of the reign of Frederick William IV foreign policy issues once again moved to the fore. The conflict between Great Britain and France on the one side and Russia on the other, culminating in the Crimean War, threatened to involve Prussia as well. Due in no small measure to the King's own personal insistence, Prussia pursued a course of active neutrality, one rather resented by Great Britain and France, and for that matter by liberal opinion in Germany as well. Originally the temptation was great for the King to participate in Austria's attempted policy of mediation, but it soon became clear that this policy would lead to Prussia's isolation. Prussia now exerted pressure to stop Austria from drifting into a policy hostile to Russia. To that end an alliance of neutrality was concluded between Prussia and Austria on 20 April 1854. Russia at first saw in this alliance a hostile act, so by way of appeasement Frederick William removed the Russophobe elements, such as Bunsen, from the foreign office. Friedrich Julius Stahl defended Prussia's policy of neutrality in the Prussian diet:

I and my friends wish for Prussia's non-participation in the present conflict and desire that our old relationship with Russia is preserved without hostility towards the western powers. I must reject outright the so-called European standpoint in judging this question, because in the final analysis this standpoint is that of England and France or of Russia. I vindicate our right to judge solely and alone from a Prussian, from the German standpoint. We do not want to serve Russian interests – but neither do we wish to support the rivalries of the western powers and their view of the condition of Europe. We are not very anxious for a European concert in which England and France lead the orchestra while the Germans are the musicians. It is not in Prussia's interest that Russia enlarges her power, but it is the self-evident interest of Prussia and Germany that Russia's present position of power remains, along with her existing relationship with Prussia.

Bismarck endorsed this policy fully, for the backing of Russia was essential to Prussian policy as he envisaged it. Even at that early stage in his correspondence with Frederick William's close confidant and adjudant Leopold von Gerlach he rejected the notion that policy would have to be conducted on the basis of unalterable principles. Even the principle of monarchic legitimacy was not sacrosanct to him. Principles would have to be subordinated to the *raison d'état*; even a usurper like Louis Bonaparte would have to be treated according to that theory because, as Bismarck put it, he was not prepared to have ideological taboos occupy 16 of the 64 available places on his political chessboard. He recommended a rapproachement with France in order to deprive the southern German states of any opportunity to resurrect the Confederation of the Rhine. It would give Prussia the opportunity to become more active in the German Confederation and break the old Austro-Prussian dualism which ultimately could only be broken by war. He was proved right. The Crimean War was the last of the European cabinet wars.

However, many contemporaries condemned Prussian policy during the Crimean War as weak and indecisive. In the long run, though, it paid dividends, for 10 years later Bismarck was able to count on Russia's goodwill while he set about resolving the German question.

In July 1857, while returning from a visit to Emperor Francis Joseph in Pillnitz, Frederick William IV suffered a stroke. Several others followed which impeded his speech and caused partial paralysis of his limbs. His illness had nothing to do with mental disease as is often asserted; his growing mental incapacity was a result of the strokes. After long suffereing he died at Sanssouci on 2 January 1861.

Chapter 12

Prussia and Germany 1860-1871

During his illness Frederick William IV's brother William, Prince of Prussia, deputized for him, always for three-monthly periods which were then renewed. As Frederick William IV's marriage had remained without issue, William was the heir apparent of the Prussian monarchy as indicated by the 'Prince of Prussia' title. Frederick William's ministers remained in office during that time. But when after a year it became clear that the King's incapacity was irremediable it was necessary to transform William's office into a formal regency, which it remained until the King's death when William became King of Prussia.

William was the second son of Frederick William III and Queen Louise. Like his elder brother he had been deeply affected by the misfortunes Prussia and its royal family had suffered at the hands of Napoleon. Since those days he had never discarded his uniform and throughout his life considered himself first and foremost a soldier. When he was 17 he received his baptism of fire in the France of 1814. He seems to have taken little interest in the Prussian Reform Movement except for one of its important aspects, that of military reform.

His early life was marked by a deep emotional attachment, beginning in 1820, to the charming daughter of the Polish magnate Prince Anton Radziwill and his wife Princess Louise of Prussia. The couple were engaged in 1822, but Frederick William III hesitated to give his consent to the marriage. When finally his advisors decided that the Prince would be marrying a person considered to be of inferior rank, consent was formally withheld and William was held to the duties and obligations of his office because of his close proximity to the succession to the throne. Deeply hurt, he obeyed. Three years later he married Princess Augusta of Saxe-Weimar-Eisenach and from that marriage issued two children: Frederick, who was to become the 100-day Emperor, and Louise, later to be the wife of the Grand Duke of Baden, Frederick I.

His political views were coloured by the consequences of the French Revolution. Throughout his life he remained hostile to revolution and an adherent to strictly legitimist principles.

His reputation was tarnished early in 1848 when he was alleged to be responsible for the first shots to be fired into the crowd in front of the Berlin Palace. From then on he became widely known as the *Kartätschenprinz,* (Prince of Cartridges) although he had had nothing to do with the affair. Nevertheless at the time he was prepared to step down in the line of succession in favour of his son, but his elder brother prevailed upon him not to do so. William was a firm supporter of the movement for German unification, but, more than conscious of the value of his Prussian heritage, envisaged it only under Prussia's firm leadership. Therefore he rejected the endeavours of the delegates of the Frankfurt parliament; Prussia must never allow itself to give even the little finger of one hand to anything even remotely connected with revolutionary forces. His anti-revolutionary attitude was put into practice with severity when in the summer of 1849 he commanded the army, consisting mainly of Prussians, which defeated republican and anarchist risings in the Palatinate and Baden.

'Whoever wants to govern Germany, must conquer it first; *à la* Gagern it won't work. Whether the time for this unification has come God alone knows: but that Prussia is destined to stand at the summit of Germany, that underlies our entire history. But when and how? That is the question.' This utterance of 1849 summarizes his attitude to the German question. As military governor of the Rhenish provinces of Prussia, residing in Koblenz, he gathered those liberals around him who supported the 'little German' solution under Prussian leadership. He warmly welcomed Frederick William's policy of union, equally so the Erfurt parliament, and rejected any notion of a peaceful dualism between Austria and Prussia in the leadership of Germany. The Ölmütz Punctation came as a severe shock and deep disappointment to him.

Already his period as Prince Regent had indicated that departures from the policy pursued by his brother could be expected. Manteuffel had to resign in 1858 and was replaced by Prince Karl Anton von Hohenzollern-Sigmaringen as prime minister and Rudolf von Auerswald as minister of state. The cabinet represented moderate Conservatives and right-wing Liberals. On 8 November 1858, in his first address to his cabinet ministers, William emphasized that 'in Germany Prussia must make moral conquests by wise legislation, by elevating ethical elements and by controlling elements of unification, such as the customs union which is in need of reform'. This was clearly an appeal to the centre-to-right middle class opinion in Prussia and in Germany as a whole. That he had rightly assessed the growing strength of the Liberals was borne out by the elections to the Prussian diet of 27 November 1858, when the Liberals increased their number of seats from 36 to 147 while he Conservatives were reduced from an impressive 224 seats down to 60.

Outside Germany, especially in the west, the political horizons darkened. Napoleon III, 'the champion of nationalities and the guardian of German disunity', in an effort to ward off threatening domestic instability ventured forth to seek glory in the realm of foreign policy. His claims to the upper Italian provinces of the House of Hapsburg he justified by referring to the need to restore 'France's natural frontiers'. It fanned to full flame again the forces of Italian unification culminating in the war of 1859 of Austria against Italy and

France. It was the first 'modern' war in European history, conducted as it was because of a popular nationalist movement. But the justification used by Napoleon posed a serious threat to Germany because by the same token France's claims to the left bank of the Rhine could be justified. Fear of a Bonapartist policy of territorial annexation gave added impetus to the movement for German unification. Liberals and Democrats again began to argue in favour of a central government in Germany, a national parliament and a national army, but insisted that the most effective steps in this direction could only be taken if Prussia were to take the initiative. With that in mind Liberals and Democrats founded in Frankfurt the *Deutscher Nationalverein*. Its agitation for German unification under Prussian leadership met strong opposition from the representatives of the landed nobility in Prussia, who feared the political and social consequences unification would have for them. Upon William's accession to the throne on 2 January 1861, the question remained precisely as he had first put it in 1849; the 'when and how' of the unification. The fact was that, other considerations apart, Prussia was militarily no longer in a position to accept the risks such initiatives involved: the Prussian army had been allowed to deteriorate seriously and that had been a vital factor bringing about Prussia's decision to sign the Ölmütz Punctation. Laurels gained in the past had been lost by 1860 when *The Times* wrote:

Prussia is always leaning on someone, always getting somebody to help her, never willing to help herself; always ready to deliberate, never to decide; present in congresses, but absent in battles; speaking and writing never for or against but only on the question; ready to supply any amount of ideals or sentiments but shy of anything that savours of the actual. She has a large army, but notoriously one in no condition for fighting. She is profuse in circulars and notes, but generally has little to say for both sides. No one counts her as a friend, no one dreads her as an enemy. How she became a great power history tells us, why she remains so, nobody can tell . . . Prussia unaided would not keep the Rhine or the Vistula for a month from her ambitious neighbours.

This was written at a time when the liberal tide in Prussia in favour of German unification by 'moral conquest' reached its heights and when William decided to avoid the consequences of the existing military weakness by carrying out a thorough programme of military reform. To the memory of Ölmütz, still strong, was added the French military success in Italy in 1859. It so happened that military reform also provided the occasion for the beginning of the absorption of the liberal middle class into Prussia's social structure.

Already in February 1860 draft legislation for the reorganization of the Prussian army had been submitted to the Prussian diet for discussion and for the granting of the necessary expenditure, which amounted to an additional 9.5 million thalers. In the face of opposition from the Liberals, who feared that the Prussian army might be used eventually to do away with Prussia's constitution, the government withdrew its bill and the diet granted a provisional 9 million thalers upon the assurance that the money would not be used to implement controversial points of the army reform. Thus the government had achieved its main aim while at the same time leaving an escape hatch for the Liberals to withdraw through without coming to a firm decision.

Indeed the bill contained controversial aspects. William's minister for war, General von Roon, considered one of the primary reasons for the deterioration of the quality of the Prussian army between 1820 and 1860 to be the influence of liberal ideas which had weakened the *esprit de corps* among the officers in particular, as well as the morale of the army as a whole. Consequently, what the implications of the proposed reforms amounted to was a reversal of the policy of the Prussian Reform Movement: instead of basing the army broadly upon the people, making it an integral part of the nation, the relationship was reversed by turning the people into an integral part of the army. The army, so it was argued, needed not only to be more professional, it must be the nation's example; indeed it must be the school of the nation. The patriotism of the Jacobins must be replaced by a military patriotism. Prussia's greatness in the past had rested upon a strong army so the army must once again become the base of the nation. This in turn meant that the *Landwehr*, due to its lack of military indoctrination, could not form a part of that base. In fact the army reform of 1860 did away with the *Landwehr*, a force which so far had been led by its own elected officers, who in most cases represented the small town gentry, politically inclined towards liberal ideas and therefore the core of the opposition to the restoration of the *ancien régime*. The recruits of the regular army, however, were in the main still provided by the Prussian peasants, steeped in loyalty to the crown and their landlords, a countervailing power of conservatism to the liberal middle class (and one of the reasons why Bismarck introduced the principle of universal male franchise in the North German Confederation and later in the constitution of the German Empire of 1871).

In spite of the compromise solution the conflict over the army reform escalated, because the ultimate issue was whether the army should be the army of the King or of parliament. William I was not prepared to hand over his powers as supreme commander to parliament. But within the opposition the compromise solution had left its mark. On 6 June 1861 the German Progressive Party was founded, having among its membership Virchow, Mommsen, and Schulze-Delitzsch. Its platform was the transformation of Prussia into a parliamentary democracy, the national unification of Germany under Prussian leadership, and military service for two years instead of the customary three. But, significantly for liberal opinion at the time, it did not demand the introduction of universal male franchise. In the Prussian elections held in December 1861 the Progressives gained an impressive victory with 109 seats, while the other liberal factions gained 141, the

Conservatives only 14 and the Catholics 54.

Now open conflict erupted between King and parliament. Adolf Hermann Hagen, a Progressive, demanded a more detailed specification of the budget in order to prevent the government's uncontrolled use of funds for military purposes. His resolution was accepted by a majority in the diet. This now compelled the Liberal members of the government to submit their resignations and the King dissolved the diet on 11 March 1862. New elections were held on 6 May in which the Progressive Party gained 133 seats while the total of the opposition was 230, the Conservatives dwindling down to 11 seats and the Catholics to 28. On 17 September William I rejected attempts at a renewed compromise of reducing military service from three to two years in return for the acceptance of the budget. For the first time the King thought of abdication. Now Hohenlohe and another minister, von der Heydt, resigned. Roon had another candidate for the office of prime minister: Otto von Bismarck, or the 'mad Junker' as he had once been called.

Yet the picture of Bismarck as the epitome of the typical Prussian Junker is a caricature – in spite of ample evidence of his occasionally exaggerated projection of his Junker status – for no German politician of his standing has had more bitter words to say about the Prussian landed nobility. He was the product of two different social and political cultures – the Junkers on his father's side and the German liberalism of the early nineteenth century on his mother's. His mother was of middle class origin, and was the decisive voice in the determination of his education. He did not go through the cadet institutes but went to a bourgeois *Gymnasium* to be imbued with the ideals of a humanist culture. The finished product of these dual influences was a politician who had a sharper eye for the strengths and weaknesses of both conservatives and liberals than had most of his contemporaries. Precisely that insight gave him the ability to handle them both effectively.

One major element crucial to his thought and action in the realm of politics was his fear of revolution, of bringing forces into play which ultimately could no longer be controlled. To Bismarck the French Revolution had been an event of this nature. His suspicion and distrust of ideologies of any kind – whether liberalism, socialism or nationalism – became almost tantamount to a counter-ideology. Only the true statesman, which (not without justification) he considered himself to be, could use elements of these forces towards ends beneficial to the state; but the risk of finding one's self in the position of the sorcerer's apprentice was forever present. He fully realized that the revolutionaries of 1848 did not fail in their aim of unifying Germany simply because they lacked a monopoly of power and were opposed by military force, but rather because they lacked the backing of the princely governments who had vested interests in the maintenance of German particularism. Even limited progress by agreement between the several princes had, as the result of Austria's attitude, become impossible without war. Prussia could make good its vulnerability to external pressure only in part, and that was by the reform of its military apparatus. The conflict in Prussia between the forces of conservatism and liberalism, exemplified in the conflict over the army reform, at first did little to close the gap between them. Yet the very existence of this gap was diametrically opposed to the entire concept of the Prussian state. To personalities as different in their views as were Dahlmann and Stahl, the state was nevertheless something sanctified, a divine institution. A state such as Prussia could not afford to expose itself to the internecine strife of political factionalism. That, rather than the notion that the comprehension of military affairs exceeded the capacity of mere civilians, was the reason for Bismarck's successful endeavour to preserve the autonomous position of the army.

Under Bismarck the interaction of administrative measures and outside events helped to narrow the gap between liberals and conservatives and ultimately almost closed it. He was aware that within Germany there were still forces strong enough to obstruct a policy of moral conquest; that Europe also was not too anxious to see the formation of a new powerful national state in its midst. Hence Bismarck's phrase about the questions of the day having to be decided by 'iron and blood', a phrase used as a weapon against his opponents in the diet rather than as a proclamation of his political course.

Instead of letting the conflict continue to simmer, Bismarck decided to bring it to a head immediately. Since the diet objected to the military appropriations of the budget and since there was little chance that the measure would fare any better if submitted to the new session in January 1863, Bismarck had the entire budget voted down in the Prussian upper house. The parliamentary session was thus closed for 1862 and the Prussian government declared that it would continue the army reorganisation and make the necessary expenditure available, in the hope that the diet would finally confirm it *post factum*. Bismarck ingeniously argued that there was a loophole in the Prussian constitution because it did not say what should be done if government and diet could not agree on the budget. He refused to accept the point that this effectively meant open conflict between monarchic prerogative and parliamentarian democracy, and instead made it clear that the fundamental powers residing in the crown compelled it to continue in the execution of its duties until the moment when agreement between crown and diet was reached.

Bismarck's minister of war was Roon, his minister of the interior Count Friedrich von Eulenburg. Another person close to Bismarck, and as important in his own sphere of influence, was Gerson Bleichröder, the Berlin banker, Bismarck's 'court Jew'. Apart from acting as investment and business manager for Bismarck's private fortune, he was instrumental in raising the funds required for the wars with Denmark and Austria. Also, Bleichröder's international connections, particularly those with the Rothschilds in Paris and in London, proved extremely useful for Bismarck and supplemented his diplomatic connections. However, while Bleichröder's counsel remained cautious and conservative at all times, those of Roon and Eulenberg divided opinions in Prussia and also within the royal family itself. William I accepted Bismarck's hard line only very reluctantly; his wife Queen Augusta disliked Bismarck in any case, while the Crown Prince Frederick and his wife Princess Victoria, Queen Victoria's daughter, renowned less for her charms than her tactlessness, opposed Bismarck's course outright.

The new session of the Prussian diet was opened on 14 January 1863. The debate which followed the King's speech from the throne was dominated by Virchow's charge, as spokesman for the Progressives, that the government had broken the constitution. A delegation was to hand Virchow's address over to the King, but William I refused to see them. This incident set the mood for the rest of the session, each side continually provoking the other, the government refusing to yield an inch in order to demonstrate that the opposition could gain nothing. The fact was that irrespective of successes the parties could gain at the polls, a government that enjoyed the complete confidence of the King, in control of a reliable army and an equally reliable civil service, could not be toppled, particularly when it was led by a man utterly convinced that his policy would triumph. William I also made his position quite clear when a day before the parliamentary session was closed on 26 May 1863 he stated in a message to the diet: 'My ministers possess my confidence, their official actions have been taken with my agreement and I owe them thanks for opposing the unconstitutional endeavours of the house of deputies to seek the extension of their powers'.

As public opposition continued to increase, Bismarck issued a decree which gave the police power to suppress any newspaper after it had received two warnings, a measure in practice in France under Napoleon III and therefore all the more resented in Prussia. It raised a storm of opposition. Heinrich von Treitschke, the historian and then editor of the *Preussische Jahrbücher*, expressed his anger publicly and then decided to ignore all political aspects in his journal. Other newspapers, journals and periodicals followed suit. Crown Prince Frederick declared in Danzig that he had not had a hand in this measure. Town councils which requested the withdrawal of the measure were blandly told that their request was outside the field of their competency.

The new elections of 28 October 1863 increased even further the number of opposition seats. In his speech from the throne William I tried to be conciliatory. The measures regarding the press were revoked, but he insisted that the three-year period of conscription and the reorganization of the army be continued. The remainder of the speech concerned itself with the major items of Prussia's foreign policy.

Three questions in particular preoccupied Bismarck's foreign policy during his early years as the King's chancellor. First of all there was the news of an impending attempt at revolution in the part of Poland annexed by Russia. The Polish cause had enjoyed wide popularity in Central and in Western Europe, Austria doing nothing to stop any aid being given to the cause from supporters living in its Galician part of Poland. Bismarck, however, thought that the 'Greater Polish' ambitions would eventually be as dangerous to Prussia as they were to Russia. Moreover Prussia could use the Polish question as a way of establishing the closer relationship with Russia that was essential if Prussia was one day to act decisively on the German question. (Its actions had previously come to nought because of the joint intervention of Russia and Austria.) Bismarck therefore sent General von Alvensleben to Czar Alexander with a personal letter in which Bismarck emphasized their identity of interests in the Polish question and offered Prussia's support against any Polish insurrection. A treaty was drafted but not ratified. Nevertheless the friendly relationship, particularly between King William and Czar Alexander, was established, and without being obliged to do so Prussia closed its eastern frontier to prevent Polish insurgents from withdrawing into Prussian territory or volunteers entering Poland from Prussia. The fact that Great Britain, France and also Austria intervened on behalf of the Poles at St Petersburg (the possibility of war only being avoided because of Great Britain's reluctance to take that final step) was considered by Alexander to be foreign interference in Russia's domestic affairs, and this brought Russia and Prussia even closer together.

At the same time an issue which deeply stirred German national sentiment, that of Schleswig-Holstein, again came into the public eye. King Frederick VII of Denmark, yielding to the pressure of Danish nationalists and contrary to the London Protocol of 1852, separated Schleswig from Holstein, annexing the former and introducing a new constitution for the latter. The diet of the German Confederation called upon Frederick to stop this policy. When the Danish government refused the German Confederation decided to intervene. Two civil commissioners supported by 6,000 troops were to take over the administration in Schleswig-Holstein. But the Danes stole the march by accepting a constitution applicable to Schleswig as well as Holstein, which meant Schleswig's annexation and its separation from Holstein. Frederick died on 15 November 1863 without having been able to sign the constitution. The following day, on the basis of the London Protocol, Prince Christian of Glücksburg was proclaimed as King Christian IX, while at the same time Prince Frederick of Augustenburg released a proclamation in which he announced his succession in Schleswig-Holstein as Duke Frederick VIII. Frederick found immediate support in Holstein and among national and liberal opinion in Germany. Both Prussia and Austria decided to ignore the national support in Germany, though for different reasons. Austria's policy was the result of Napoleon III's plan to revise the treaties of 1815 according to the principle of nationality, a plan which the events in Denmark had given him occasion to voice again. This particularly threatened Austria's legitimist position, especially in her restless Venetian province. In practical terms what Austria aimed at in the Schleswig-Holstein question was the restoration of the previous personal union between the duchies and Denmark. Bismarck, however, thought in terms of their annexation, a course on which William I was initially very reluctant to follow Bismarck's advice, arguing that Prussia possessed no rights to claim these duchies. Bismarck pointed out that Augustenburg's claims were equally doubtful, and that there was also another possible outcome to the situation, namely the creation of a new small state, which as far as Prussia was concerned would offer no guarantees as to its future political direction. The wishes of German public opinion would best be met if Prussia, with the agreement of the German Confederation excepting Austria, declared war on Denmark and then placed Augustenburg on the throne. However, that policy would not only result in the opposition of Austria but was more likely also to risk the opposition of the western powers, particularly France who was eager to gain the left bank of the Rhine – Ölmütz could be repeated. To act jointly with Austria would be the course most likely to prevent the formation of a European coalition. Although William was convinced by Bismarck, neither Queen Augusta nor the Crown Prince and his wife were; on the contrary they supported the Augustenburg cause. Bismarck pointed out that the supporters of the Augustenburg cause in Prussia were those who were causing so much obstruction in the Prussian diet, another point which rallied William in favour of the policy pursued by his chancellor.

Therefore Prussia, jointly with Austria, pressed for action by the German Confederation against the Danish breach of the London Protocol. By the end of 1863 almost the whole of Holstein was in the hands of the forces of the German Confederation. In the meantime Great Britain and Russia tried to mediate; King Christian IX was ready to revoke the new constitution, but because of the nationalist fervour prevailing in Denmark he could find no support among his ministers and the mediation therefore failed. Prussia and Austria now asked the diet of the German Confederation to demand that the King of Denmark revoke the constitution or else the forces of the German Confederation would occupy Schleswig until their demands were met. This the diet refused to sanction and in spite of an English warning Prussia and Austria decided to go it alone, concluding an alliance for the purpose on 16 January 1864. They issued an ultimatum to Denmark and after its rejection Prussian and Austrian forces under Prussian command took the offensive, entering Schleswig on 1 February 1864. With the assault upon the *Düppeler Schanzen* of the Danes, the main weight of which was carried by the Prussian troops, the Danes lost their last position on the Schleswig mainland. The Danish government first sued for an armistice and then for peace. Preliminary peace was concluded on 1 August, the final peace on 30 October 1864 in Vienna. The duchies of

Schleswig, Holstein and Lauenburg were ceded by Denmark to Prussia and Austria, in whose joint possession they were at the time. This was hardly a completely satisfactory solution for either of the powers, but one which had taken the problem out of the framework in which the European powers could intervene and narrowed it down to a question concerning solely Prussia and Austria.

That Prusso-Austrian relations had reached a critical stage had already been demonstrated a year before when Austria convened a meeting of the German princes in Frankfurt on 13 August 1863 to discuss yet again plans for the reform of the German Confederation. All depended on the attitude taken by Prussia. Emperor Francis Joseph met William in Bad Gastein to ensure that the Prussian King would be present in Frankfurt and William was indeed in favour of attending. But Bismarck advised him against participation since the situation could possibly arise of the Prussian King being outvoted by the other princes. Thus 31 German kings, princes and dukes and their politicians gathered in Frankfurt amidst a splendour which recalled the days of the Empire past. But one was missing: William. Without him the other German princes were no longer greatly interested in any deliberations. Prussia had become the key factor in any German reform. And on 22 September 1863 William declared his agreement to any reform of the German Confederation and the extension of any of its competencies provided that Prussia's influence in the Confederation and German national interests in general received adequate consideration.

After the Peace of Vienna in 1864, the territories in the joint possession of Prussia and Austria were a new point around which Prusso-Austrian differences could crystallize. The suggestion was made that Prussia in return for the duchies should cede the county of Glatz to Austria. This was unacceptable to William, and neither was he willing to have the Augustenburg family installed in Schleswig-Holstein. When the diet of the German Confederation voted in favour of this, supported by the Austrian vote but against that of Prussia, Bismarck envisaged war. But conditions were not favourable, and neither was William. On 21 July 1865 Austria was asked by Prussia to suppress, jointly with Prussia, the Augustenburg agitation; the alternative offered was that Prussia would look after its own interests. Austria, engulfed by an economic crisis and internal political instability, did not wish to risk a conflict and in accordance with a suggestion from the Austrian envoy in Munich, a plan for partition of the administration of Schleswig-Holstein was drawn up which provided a basis for discussion. The Convention of Gastein of 14 August 1865 brought Holstein under Austrian administration, Schleswig under that of Prussia.

To most statesmen it was clear that this was only a temporary arrangement, and that the Prusso-Austrian dualism would have to be resolved sooner or later. First of all Bismarck secured his flanks – Russia in the east and France in the west. A trade agreement between Prussia and France had existed since 1862, concluded outside the

customs union.¹ Napoleon III believed he could exploit a Prussian–
Austrian conflict for the good of what he saw as the French national
interest. In the same way as he had supported the movement for Italian
unity for a price (Savoy and the Côte d'Azur), so he thought he could
profit by taking Luxembourg, then still a customs union with Germany,
or the Walloon part of Belgium. Bismarck raised no objections, willing
to sacrifice the territories as diplomatic bait, in the vital cause of French
neutrality. By an alliance of Prussia with Italy of 8 April 1866, Italy
agreed to declare war on Austria once military conflict between Prussia
and Austria had begun.

The following day Bismarck demanded in Frankfurt a reform of the
German Confederation. The wind was taken out of everyone's sails by
Bismarck's startling demand for a federal parliament elected by
universal male franchise. It was one of Bismarcks's most brilliant
moves. The three-class franchise had so far favoured the opposition in
the Prussian diet, and plans of utilizing the peasant and working class
vote in the support of conservative aims had already been aired in 1848.
In a still predominantly agrarian society the rural population could be
expected to be a bulwark of conservatism. Already in 1863 Bismarck
had made contact with Ferdinand Lassalle, the leader of the working
class movement, and Lassalle had responded favourably. But this new
move also had the appearance of being the first step towards a genuine
parliamentary system in Germany as well as Prussia and was therefore
bound to appeal to the middle classes throughout Germany. Precisely
those who for the past four years had opposed Bismarck found that
perhaps a first step in their direction was being taken. The ultimate aim
was the creation of a German federal state under Prussian leadership,
though because of Napoleon this could not be publicly proclaimed. Yet
in the immediate future Bismarck's expectation was not fully realized.
The suspicions which he had engendered over the previous four years
were too deep-seated to be quieted by one gesture. National liberal
opinion throughout Germany remained extremely sceptical.

William too was not completely resolute in his attitude, but the fear of
facing another Ölmütz, which to him as a soldier was simply unbearable
proved decisive – rather armed conflict than that. Any thought of
Russia and Great Britain mediating between Austria and Prussia was
quashed by Bismarck's proposal for a reform of the German
Confederation. Since the Prusso-Italian agreement the Italians had
been arming frantically on Austria's southern frontier. Austria armed
but declared that this was not for aggressive purposes. Prussia
demanded that all further rearmament be suspended and that Austria
should take the initiative. And Austria did. This proved a serious
embarrassment to Bismarck's policy, even more so as the King seemed
to be relieved that peace had been preserved. But this embarrassment
was soon dispelled because the Italians continued to arm. Austria, no
longer in doubt of being the object of a combined attack from the south
and the north, mobilized its southern army and stopped demobilizing

against Prussia. Bismarck could now demonstrate to William that Austria's reassurances of peace had been no more than deception.

There remained the problem of the states hitherto uncommitted to either Prussia or Austria. In the diet of the German Confederation, in order to avoid showing the nature of their response to Bismarck's reform proposals, as well as to gain time, the smaller German states asked that before they examined Bismarck's reform proposals he should submit them in greater detail and indicate in what ways these reforms should be carried out. These delaying tactics were not appreciated by Bismarck who demanded, as he had done previously, that a German parliament be convened before any discussion of the reform of the Confederation. If this demand was not met then Prussia would consider its own reform proposals as having been rejected. That was on 27 April 1866. The day before Italy had mobilized; Prussia followed suit on 3 and 5 May.

Quite unexpectedly Napoleon now entered the fray. He made contact with Austria with the aim of persuading it to hand over Venetia to France, in return for which he would not enter the war against Austria. Bismarck had not expected this. It delayed his schedule. A new compromise solution was submitted as an alternative to German unification which involved dividing Germany between the Hohenzollerns and the Hapsburgs. Bismarck found the plan acceptable, but not so Vienna. But Napoleon's intervention failed because the Italians did not want Venetia from his hands. They had had occasion to notice previously that gifts from Napoleon came to be rather costly in the end. In the meantime Saxony, Bavaria and Württemberg had also mobilized. Napoleon put forward another proposal, that of a European congress, to resolve the whole problem on the principle of nationality. Austria made it a precondition that all territories of its state be guaranteed beforehand. That put an end to the proposal. In the diet of the German Confederation Austria as well as Prussia declared that their respective suggestions had been rejected and Austria added that it would submit the Schleswig-Holstein question to the diet and to the estates of Holstein. Prussia declared this a breach of the Convention of Gastein, and General Manteuffel moved his troops into Holstein which the Austrians evacuated. Prussia then declared itself prepared to discuss the Schleswig-Holstein issue but only in connection with its plans for the reform of the German Confederation, which now included the explicit exclusion of Austria from it. To placate Bavarian feeling, Bavaria was to retain its own military high command, but Bavaria, fearing for its independence, joined Austria. Austria now demanded the mobilization of all the forces of the German Confederation. On 12 June the diplomatic relations between Prussia and Austria were severed and Bismarck declared that Prussia considered every vote in the diet for Austria as a declaration of war. On 14 June four Kingdoms voted for Austria: Saxony, Hanover, Bavaria and Württemberg; then came Hesse and Nassau, Frankfurt and Meiningen. In southern Germany only Baden voted for Prussia. Luxembourg too, took Prussia's side, as did most of northern Germany. The Prussian army received orders to enter Saxony, Hesse and Hanover. War began formally on 18 June 1866.

Thanks to Bleichröder's efforts, which not without recourse to some unconstitutional methods filled the coffers of the Prussian war chest, a war with Austria was now financially feasible, but nevertheless the available funds were limited and therefore the war had to be short and decisive. Militarily Prussia had the advantage of being the first power to have introduced in its infantry the Dreyse breech-loader as opposed to the muzzle-loader still in use among the Austrians. No longer was the bayonet attack considered the decisive part of the battle but rather the attack with accurately aimed fire.

Hanover and Saxony were quickly occupied. The King of Hanover and his Crown Prince, the Duke of Cumberland, were allowed to go abroad; the Hanoverian troops were disbanded. The Saxon forces joined those of Austria in Bohemia. The first major battle at Gitschin was decided in favour of the Prussian forces. William now took over supreme command from his headquarters at Gitschin were he was joined by Moltke, Roon and Bismarck. In view of the Prussian pressure the Austrian commander Benedek found himself compelled to withdraw towards Königgrätz, and advised peace with Prussia as soon as possible. But Austria tried to get Napoleon to mediate, hoping to use the time thus gained to move the Austrian southern army, which had just won a victory against the Italians at Custozza, to the north. In view of that plan Benedek decided to risk a decisive battle at Königgrätz on 2 July. It ended in a triumph for Prussian arms, the personal leadership of William I and the impeccable staff work of Moltke. The forces had been almost evenly balanced, with about 220,000 men on each side, of which the Austrians lost 44,000 and the Prussians 10,000. The Prussian armies now advanced in the direction of Vienna. By 18 July the Prussian headquarters were at Nikolsburg, 19 kilometres from Vienna. Actually Prussia's military situation was not as strong as Königgrätz might have suggested. It was not a decisive victory, and though beaten, Benedek's armies were still able to extract themselves from the threat of encirclement and cross the Danube at Pressburg in order to join up with the forces of the victor of Custozza, Archduke Albert. At the same time a cholera epidemic raged through the Prussian armies taking heavier tolls than the actual fighting. The lines of communication also favoured Austria rather than Prussia. And what if the Austrian army withdrew beyond Vienna? Bismarck with his own brand of sardonic humour suggested that in view of the difficulty of maintaining communication with Prussia it would be best to leave Prussia behind and march upon Constantinople to found a new Byzantine Empire. In short Prussia was as much in need of a speedy settlement as was Austria.

The Prussian advance in southern Germany was equally as rapid. But before it came to a conclusive victorious result for the Prussians peace negotiations had begun. From Prussia's point of view, the longer the war lasted the greater was the danger of the other European powers becoming involved, something which would hardly be in Bismarck's interests. Francis Joseph had already appealed to Napoleon, now offering to cede Venetia to Italy. Prussia and France negotiated in Paris, Prussia aiming at the creation of a North German Confederation under Prussia's leadership and the annexation of Schleswig-Holstein excepting its Danish districts. It was prepared to guarantee Austria's territorial integrity, apart from Venetia. In the Prussian headquarters, however, the appetite for victory had been whetted. The military party, including the King, wished to annex Ansbach-Bayreuth and other territories which had once been in the possession of the Hohenzollerns, plus parts of Saxony and Bohemia. But Bismarck argued the need for an agreeable relationship with Austria in the future, a relationship which would be jeopardized by such territorial acquisitions. His arguments prevailed and an armistice was agreed upon, but for a final peace additional acquisitions would have to be made in northern Germany. William I was determined to put an end to Saxony while Francis Joseph was prepared to fight on behalf of his most faithful ally. The future of Saxony was an issue which almost caused the break between the King and his prime minister, avoided only by Crown Prince Frederick who persuaded his father to accept the territorial integrity of Austria as well as Saxony. This was the basis of the preliminary Peace of Nikolsburg in which Austria also agreed to the formation of a northern as well as a southern confederation and a workable relationship between the two. Saxony was compelled to join the north. Austria was not occupied; the costs of the war for Austria were reduced by half to 20 million thalers.

The preliminary peace came just in time: Russia had called for a peace congress and Napoleon began to press demands such as Landau and Luxembourg as compensation for Prussia's gains. Bismarck rejected any French territorial gains at the expense of German territory. But the French clamoured to add Saarbrücken and Saarlouis to their demands as well as all the territories of Bavaria and Baden on the left bank of the Rhine. Prussia's response was one of outright refusal. Napoleon, unable to support his demands with military action, withdrew his claims to German territory and instead demanded the annexation of Belgium. Bismarck let it be known that he was prepared to consider Belgium. But the French envoy in Berlin, Benedetti, was careless enough to submit in writing a draft treaty which included this demand, and this Bismarck was able to use at the appropriate time to bring the other powers, especially Great Britain, into play. Napoleon let the matter rest.

The negotiations for a final peace between Prussia and Austria came to their conclusion in Vienna on 23 August 1866. On the following day the German Confederation was formally dissolved. Prussia gained Schleswig-Holstein, Hanover, Kurhesse, Nassau and other Hessian territories as well as the city of Frankfurt.

The victory of 1866 had immense repercussions upon Prussia's domestic situation. The inability of the Liberals to present an independent constructive political alternative proved disastrous. The Prussian liberals now turned towards Bismarck's camp; after all if the proof of the pudding lies in the eating then Bismarck had eloquently demonstrated that he pursued a policy of gradual unification of a Germany. The Liberals in the other German states did not adopt quite the same attitude, opting for a neutral course. In Prussia Bismarck was not slow in introducing an indemnity bill to the diet in which all the expenditures incurred since the constitutional conflict were to receive parliamentary approval *post factum*. The Prussian diet passed it by 230 votes to 70. Those Liberals supporting the bill formed themselves into the National Liberal Party under the leadership of Rudolf Bennigsen while the dissenters joined the ranks of the Progressive Party. Nothing was heard any more of transforming Prussia into a parliamentary democracy. The Conservatives also divided themselves, leaving behind the opponents of Bismarck's policy, the old Conservatives, while the majority founded the Free Conservative Party, representing agricultural interests as well as heavy industry. Predominance of Prussia had been achieved. Bismarck's major triumph, however, was that between 1864 and 1871 he had managed to isolate the German question from its European context and get it solved by the Germans themselves, without the intervention of any of the other European powers. Nor should it escape the attention that the role which the London Rothschilds had played in 1815, preserving Prussia's powers of restoration by their loans, was played by Bleichröder in 1866 when his efforts provided the finance for the war against Austria.

After the conclusion of hostilities a policy aiming at German unification based on a *Kleindeutsch* ('little German') solution had three alternatives. Firstly to win over a broad majority of the southern German population to join the North German Confederation and thus, much to Napoleon III's discomfort, implement the principle of national self-determination which he had so fervently advocated. Secondly, an arrangement with Napoleon over the Walloon parts of Belgium; or thirdly, a military conflict with France over dominance in Central Europe. As far as the first alternative was concerned the anti-Prussian mood in large parts of southern Germany engendered by the war would have led to certain failure, at least in the immediate future. The second alternative immediately touched the interest of Great Britain, which Bismarck was anxious not to alienate. Nor, unlike the situation in Italy in 1859, were there any German territories which Bismarck could offer without raising the wrath of German public opinion, even if he had had any inclination to make such an offer. It was the third alternative which was most favoured by the Liberals as well as the Prussian general staff – the idea of a preventive war. Bismarck successfully opposed this, chiefly because it would have led to the Liberals gaining an important voice in military matters, the prerogative of the crown, and thus opened the gates to further parliamentarization. His reply to the generals was that superior military strength was not a valid enough reason for a preventive war. Moreover German unification brought about in this way would be interpreted as an act of force by which Prussia imposed its will upon the south German states. As far as he was concerned he preferred a slower, more natural process by which the population of southern Germany would gradually be converted to the cause of German unification under Prussian auspices. Moreover, a preventive war would be very likely to lead to the involvement of the other great European powers.

The Peace of Prague was followed by a period of extensive negotiation with the other north German states concluded on 7 February 1867 when the constitution of the North German Confederation was submitted. On 12 February 1867 the elections for the Northern German diet took place. At that diet the small socialist party represented by August Bebel raised its objections. Bebel said that he protested 'against this confederation which proclaims not the unity but the division of Germany'. It was one of the many signs indicating a change of attitude by the socialists to Bismarck. With Ferdinand Lassalle Bismarck had shared some common ground. It had been Lassalle's dream to see the aims of socialism achieved within a German national state. After his death in 1864 the Marxist gospel of the proletarian world revolution gained in influence. With it also changed Bismarck's assessment of the character of German social democracy.

The constitution of the North German Confederation was accepted on 16 April 1867 by 230 votes to 53. It became legally effective on 1 July of that year. The Prussian crown was granted the presidency as an inheritable office, and it retained supreme command of the armed forces, control of the conduct of foreign policy, the right to make and to end wars, and the prerogative of appointing the federal chancellor. But all the president's actions required the chancellor's counter-signature. Prussia had achieved predominance in the *Bundesrat*, with 17 of the 43 votes. The chancellor could not be dismissed by the diet. The diet had legislative powers in granting the budget and economic legislation.

In the wake of the war of 1866 followed another economic depression which caused severe unemployment in Prussia and acted as an incentive for the creation of trades unions and the setting up of political workers' associations of many colours. One of their first political victories was the right, granted by the North German diet on 29 May 1969, for workers to combine and to strike. In principle they did not object to the state of contractual dependence into which the new factory system had pressed them. That came later. They advocated greater educational opportunities for workers and equality of opportunity, because industrialization inevitably reduced the value of individual craftsmanship. Prominently represented in the early workers' organization were the journeymen who could no longer expect to become masters of their trade because the masters, themselves threatened by the factory system, had closed ranks against what they considered might become excessive competition. They did not consider themselves at that time as the 'proletariat', since the term had a quite different connotation from that of later decades. A proletarian at that time meant someone who had not learnt a trade, a vagabond, a person of uncertain origin, unsteady pursuits and no means of support. It included journalists!

Marx and Engels dominated from London splinter groups which claimed to represent the workers. In Germany, however, the dominant personality was the writer and journalist Ferdinand Lassalle who in 1863 founded the *Allgemeiner Deutscher Arbeiterverein* in Leipzig. Its demands included universal male suffrage and the creation of workers' co-operatives which would manufacture goods on a profit-sharing basis. These enterprises were to be state-financed. Six years later in 1869 August Bebel and Wilhelm Liebknecht founded in Eisenach the *Sozialdemokratische Arbeiterpartei*, which was Marxist, internationalist, anti-Prussian and explicitly revolutionary in its aims. Lassalle, who had been the driving force behind the *Arbeiterverein*, was killed in a duel in 1864 and under a leadership less dynamic than that which he had provided the *Arbeiterverein* soon followed in the wake of revolutionary social democracy and fused with it in Gotha in 1875 under the name of the *Sozialistische Arbeiterpartei Deutschlands*. Seriously underestimated by Bismarck, this internationalist party organized on a national basis gained in workers' support, as fast as industrialization increased and Bismarck managed to draw other German states into the fold of the North German Confederation.

On 1 January 1868 the customs union had been extended for another eight years and a so-called customs union parliament was called into being consisting of the deputies of the North German Confederation and 85 south German members. For Bismarck this was a major step in the direction of gradual German unification, but further progress was obstructed by the south German deputies, the Prussian Progressives and the Conservatives.

The south German states which had concluded separate peace treaties with Prussia were incapable of putting up an institutional equivalent to the North German Confederation. Therefore, with the exception of Bavaria, they began increasingly to lean on Prussia. The Württemberg minister von Varnbuhler gave the initiative to the south German states to conclude mutual alliances with the North German confederation, and in case of war to hand over supreme command of the armed forces to Prussia. The practical consequence of this was the streamlining of the other German armies according to the Prussian pattern.

In face of this increasing process of German national consolidation Napoleon III was again under pressure to ensure that France too received its 'compensations'. Again he raised the question of the duchy of Luxembourg, which while in personal union with the Netherlands was also a member of the German customs union. Prussian troops were garrisoned in the Luxembourg fortress. Napoleon tried to purchase the duchy and in his negotiations assured the Netherlands that he would obtain Prussia's consent. The Netherlands agreed but this caused an outcry particularly among the German liberals and nationalists. Bennigsen asked in the North German diet whether the rumours regarding Luxembourg were correct. Bismarck replied evasively, but the Dutch current of opinion was strong enough for the Netherlands to withdraw from the negotiations. Napoleon believed that he had lost face, but he was inadequately prepared for war so he continued instead his military preparations while on the diplomatic level aimed for a triple alliance between France, Austria and Italy. Italy was to receive Rome, then still in the possession of the papacy. The projected alliance proved a failure, for Austria was too preoccupied with its own national problems that had resulted from the creation of Austria-Hungary in 1867, and the Italians found the assurances of Napoleon too vague to be trusted. But as late as February 1870 Archduke Albrecht visited Paris to discuss co-operation between the Austrian and French armed forces, discussions which in June of that year were continued in Vienna supported strongly by Austria's foreign minister Beust, who had held that office in Saxony until forced out by Bismarck. But Emperor Francis Joseph put an end to the negotiations; all he wanted was peace, and would only enter into a war if forced.

William I too was in favour of maintaining peace. But Bismarck did not delude himself that the process of German unification could be carried out without French opposition. He expected that French territorial demands would bring about the necessary consolidation among the south German states to bring them firmly onto the Prussian side. Moreover he was in a predicament; there was nothing that he could offer to the French. Prussian territories were out of the question, while if any other German territory were to be handed over to France there would have been a public outcry in Germany among those forces with which he had just managed to make peace. He was not in the favourable position that Italy had been in, of possessing territories which ethnically were French and which therefore could have been easily sacrificed.

Napoleon III, in the face of successive failures at home and abroad – the French diplomatic defeat of 1866, the abortive Mexican venture which had not yet been erased from the public memory – had to contend with an increasing opposition at home which was not reduced by a greater degree of liberalization. Then suddenly a new affair was sprung on France: the Hohenzollern candidature. In 1869 Prince Leopold von Hohenzollern-Sigmaringen had been asked by representatives of the Spanish Cortes to assume the vacant Spanish throne. Initially the Prince showed little enthusiasm, but Bismarck encouraged him in the hope that Prussia and Germany might profit because of the spread of the Hohenzollern influence. He treated it as a purely dynastic problem, hardly expecting that German national feeling would be aroused over the issue of a Hohenzollern candidate for the Spanish throne.

However, things did not develop as either Bismarck or the Spanish Cortes had expected. In Spain there was a misunderstanding in the decoding of the decisive message from Berlin, which in turn caused the Cortes to be prorogued. The affair had so far been conducted in secret, but that no longer seemed possible and Spain officially informed France of the intention of the Cortes to elect a Hohenzollern to the Spanish throne. France was naturally alarmed. The spectre of the Empire of Charles V and the position in which Francis I had found himself was all too readily remembered. To the French it was a Prussian intrigue. But the matter also had its tempting aspects. During the previous conversations with Austria the latter had indicated that if it were to participate in any war against Prussia, the cause could not be the German question. The French foreign minister, the Duke de Gramont, was the leader of the French 'Hawks'; in contrast Napoleon III, tired and ill, would probably have been prepared to let the matter pass. In the French chamber Gramont declared that France would not suffer a foreigner on the Spanish throne who would thus be able to disturb the balance of power in Europe to the detriment of France. He threatened war if the candidature was pursued. Initial French enquiries in Berlin brought the reply that the Prussian government had had nothing to do with the candidature and that this was a purely dynastic affair. Strictly speaking this was true. Gramont had been the first to threaten war, a call which the French press took up with vehemence before the German press was aware what was actually happening. Bismarck publicly interpreted the French attitude as a challenge to Germany's honour and subsequently instructed both Prussia's envoys and the press accordingly.

In the meantime the French envoy in Prussia, Benedetti, negotiated with William I in Bad Ems. William suggested that France should press Spain to drop the candidature; he had no objections himself if the Hohenzollern prince withdrew. In fact the Hohenzollern-Sigmaringen family withdrew the candidature on 11 July 1870. Whatever plans Bismarck might have had, they would have ended at that point had the Duke de Gramont not insisted on obtaining a major public diplomatic victory by humiliating Prussia. Gramont instructed Benedetti to demand an assurance from the Prussian King that he agreed with the withdrawal of the candidature and that he would not permit it to be put forward again in the future. Furthermore the Prussian envoy in Paris was asked that William I send a letter to Napoleon III which amounted to a personal apology for the matter. On the morning of 13 July Benedetti spoke to William I on the Ems promenade, who in a friendly manner rejected the notion of giving assurances for the future. During the course of the day William received the news of the withdrawal of the candidature and therefore sent his adjutant to Benedetti to inform him that the matter was closed. Benedetti insisted upon a further interview which William refused, saying that he had given his views in the morning and that he had no further comment. France's attitude was determined by a mistaken attitude of her own position among the European powers. She was a state among states with no right to demand a special position within the European community. The fact that she made that demand, culminating in the disregard of norms and conventions ruling the relationships between equal states, led to war.

Bismarck himself was disappointed about the withdrawal of the candidature, for it had seemed to him an intrigue good enough to match the French intrigues with Austria. On the evening of 13 July Bismarck, having returned from his estate at Varzin, was in the company of Moltke and Roon when a telegram arrived from Ems in which the Emperor informed him of his encounters with Benedetti, leaving it to Bismarck as to whether this telegram be published in the press or not. Its contents dejected its readers, who all too quickly saw in it another Olmütz. Moltke in particular was angry because the war 'den er schon fest ins Auge gefasst hatte' (which he had firmly envisaged) had receded into the distance again. As it stood it was very long, and more important it conveyed the impression that Prussia was giving way to French threats. Bismarck therefore sub-edited the document into publishable form, reducing it by half which made it brisker in tone and more readable, while at the same time eliminating any impression that Prussia had accepted humiliation at the hands of France. It has been said that 'by a tragic combination of ill-luck, stupidity and ignorance France blundered into war' (Michael Howard). This comment, however, does not fully appreciate France's role in the context of international relations at the time nor the way in which she acted. Up to the point of Benedetti's last intervention everything had taken place within the framework of relationships between equal states. France's insistence on occupying a higher rung on the status ladder by demanding additional extraordinary guarantees was the straw that broke the camel's back. She carried matters further than was necessary and mobilized. The Ems despatch also rallied German national feeling. For the time being south German particularism was swept away and when on 19 July the French declared war, not Prussia alone but Germany as one nation rose to the occasion. France's attitude had infused the German unity movement, which in the spring of 1870 was stagnating in south Germany, with new vigour.

Austria armed but remained neutral; it could not ignore the tide of German nationalism. Any possible threat from England was neutralized by Bismarck's leaking of Napoleon III's plan to annex Belgium. Russia maintained benevolent neutrality and kept Austria in check.

Both of the belligerents thought in offensive terms. The French planned an offensive across the Rhine in the vicinity of Strassburg which was to separate north from southern Germany. But logistical deficiencies, general lack of organization and serious shortcomings in the quality of the officer material, more than removed any advantages the French had (such as a long-range Chassepot rifle). The offensive never took off. By comparison the Prussian army reform now bore fruit. Military plans that had been drawn up in response to the Luxembourg crisis were utilized. They envisaged conquering Paris while at the same time the Prussian army would force the bulk of the French forces away from the southern regions of France, rich in agricultural produce, into the agriculturally poorer north-east. Moltke's principle was to attack the enemy and defeat him wherever he was met. The German forces divided into three armies. The 1st Army, under General von Steinmetz, comprised Rhinelanders and West-phalians supplemented by East and West Prussians. It represented the right wing, positioned around Wittlich near Trier. The 2nd Army, under the command of Prince Friedrich Karl, consisted of the Prussian guards, Brandenburgers and Saxons, Hanoverians and Holsteiners. They were in the centre between Homburg and Neunkirchen. The 3rd Army, under the command of Crown Prince Frederick William was made up of the south German forces supplemented by those from Silesia and Posen. They represented the left wing between Landau and Rastatt and were to advance into Alsace. The first major battles were fought on 6 August by the 1st and 3rd Armies respectively. The 3rd Army encountered the forces of Marshal MacMahon in Alsace and at the battle of Wörth the Bavarian forces gained their first victory which compelled the French to withdraw from Alsace in the direction of Chalons. The 1st Army met the bulk of the French forces at Spichern, captured the heights it was commanding and forced the French back upon Metz. Alsace was captured with the exception of Strassburg which was besieged. Now the 1st and 2nd Armies were to advance upon Metz, while the 3rd was to penetrate to the rear of Metz, cutting off the French retreat. In three days of battle, on 14, 16 and 18 August, which cost the German forces 50,000 men, the objective of encircling the French armies was achieved. This encirclement of Metz had originally not been envisaged in the German war plan since it tied down the bulk of the German forces in Lorraine while at the same time MacMahon was able to advance from the direction of Rheims to relieve the French armies there. Moltke now detached the 3rd Army to give battle to MacMahon's forces, which included Napoleon III. On 30 August the French were attacked and beaten by the forces of the Crown Prince of Saxony and compelled to withdraw towards Sedan. There, on 1 September, they were attacked again, beaten and had to surrender. Napoleon declared that he was ready to surrender personally. On 2 September 1870 more than 100,000 French soldiers and their Emperor capitulated.

But it was not, as many had hoped, the end of the war. The defeat at Sedan was the signal for revolution in Paris, Lyons, Bordeaux and Marseilles. Napoleon was deposed and a provisional government put into office under General Trochu, with Jules Favre as minister of the exterior and Leon Gambetta as minister of the interior. As the German armies advanced upon Paris and encircled it, the new government organized national defence anew. At first the siege war dominated;

Metz surrendered on October 27. Then the French took the offensive again but were repelled by the German forces. The main effort from December 1870 to January 1871, until the capitulation of the French capital on 24 January, was concentrated on the siege of that city.

Since the victory at Sedan Bismarck had been anxious to convert military victory into political capital by creating a unified German federal (but not unitary) state, as was the wish of the Liberals. From October onwards south German politicians visited the headquarters at Versailles to discuss their entry into an extended North German Confederation, or the creation of a new federal state. Bismarck possessed enough historical consciousness to make allowances for the particularist traditions of the German states. He was therefore ready to make special concessions, especially to Bavaria which in time of peace was to retain its own military supreme command and its own postal and railway administration. But what was the title of the president of that new federation to be? Was it to be German Emperor or Emperor of the Germans? Weeks of debates ensued over this particular aspect, particularly among the Liberals. But of far greater importance was the reluctance of William I to be any such thing. Only the written appeal by Bavaria's Ludwig II persuaded him to accept the title German Emperor. What William did not know was that Bismarck himself had drafted Ludwig's letter, and that Ludwig had received from Bismarck substantial financial contributions from funds acquired by Prussia as a result of the annexations of 1866. The diet of the North German Confederation sent a delegation of three under the leadership of Eduard Simson to ask William to accept the imperial dignity. On the surface continuity with 1849 had been re-established. The formal proclamation of the German Empire took place in the Hall of Mirrors of Versailles, 170 years exactly after Prussia had become a kingdom. Among those present no civilians were to be seen; Bismarck had donned a uniform, the delegates of the diet were not present. It was a moment of exultation for all except the man who became Emperor, who privately shed tears because he foresaw the dilution of Prussia and nearly refused to attend the ceremony of proclamation. During the day of the proclamation he virtually ignored Bismarck. A preliminary peace between Germany and France was signed on 26 February 1871, followed by the final peace settlement of 6 May in Frankfurt. France, in addition to having a sizeable indemnity levied upon it which it managed to pay within three years, also lost Alsace, of which Germany had been deprived two centuries before, and half of Lorraine. No doubt the recovery of these 'lost territories' cheered the hearts of the old Liberals of 1848; however as far as Bismarck was concerned the decisive influence was that of Moltke and the general staff, who stressed Germany's need from a military point of view for a more favourable frontier with the country that for centuries had exploited to the full Germany's weakness to its own advantage. The indemnity, besides keeping France weak for some time to come, was also expected to provide the funds in case the

Reichstag should prove as intractable about military appropriations as had been the Prussian diet between 1860 and 1866.

In Germany it was a moment of national rejoicing. 'Through what has one deserved God's grace, to experience such great and powerful events?' asked the historian Heinrich von Sybel. Previous critics of Bismarck like Treitschke, Gustav Freytag and Berthold Auerbach, were won over. The majority of the German people saw in the foundation of the German Empire the fulfilment of their national wishes and of German history.

Yet Bismarck's policy had been consistent with the Prussian tradition of putting the security and internal stability of the state above all other considerations. This is best shown in the Bismarckian constitution adopted by the German *Reichstag* on 16 April 1871. As an instrument of government it was as much a creation of statecraft as it was legislation. Hence to approach it from a narrowly constitutional angle would tend to confuse rather than elucidate the complexity of its structure. The peculiarity of this structure is immediately evident in its preamble, which speaks of 'the eternal union for the protection of the federal territory and the law within it, as well as for the care of the welfare of the German people'. This seems a legal paradox, because either the constitution is the product of a union of equal partners and in consequence a treaty, or the constitution is a law in which case no room is left for a treaty. Theoretically at least, the two approaches are mutually exclusive. But that such a situation is not unique is more than amply borne out by the constitution of the United States of America. The German constitution can be understood only by recognizing that it did in fact embody the two mutually exclusive structures of federalism and the unitary state, of treaty and of law. The fundamental question which this left open at the time was whether the principle of democratic legitimacy had overcome that of monarchic legitimacy – and it is precisely in this ambiguity that part of the Bismarckian compromise lies. Only conflict could produce a definite answer, that is when the exponents of the different principles disagreed instead of co-operating. However, Prussia's major advantage in 1871 lay in possessing precisely those traditions, that framework of institutions, both administrative and military, which very largely integrated the two classes upon which the Empire was built: aristocracy and middle class. The rapid rise of the working class was not then anticipated by Bismarck and therefore, for the time being, class conflict was not to be expected. The constitution of 1871 was the product of the desire for German unification and the aims of the German middle class as exemplified by the representation of the German people in the *Reichstag* on the basis of universal male franchise. The *Reichstag*'s essential function was participation in legislation. Any proposed piece of legislation had to have the consent of both the *Reichstag* and the *Bundesrat* before it could be enacted, and the *Reichstag* could also initiate legislation. However, unlike parliaments of today, the *Reichstag* was not overburdened by this task. Consequently in practical terms its main function was the exercise of those rights which allowed it to influence the imperial administration, its main power resting in its control of the purse. From the point of view of the *Reichstag* the constitution was unitary and took the form of law. But at the same time, looked at from the point of view of the *Bundesrat*, the constitution was federal. Here several German states were represented, the monarchic principle was the important part of the constitution, and the legal aspect was that of a treaty. In order to prevent potential party strife from cracking a structure formidable no doubt to the outside world but highly fragile to the experienced eye of Bismarck, neither foreign policy, nor the army, nor the government in the person of the chancellor were made subject to direct parliamentary control. By excluding so large an area from the direct interference of the *Reichstag*, its role (apart from that of controlling the budget) was restricted to that of a safety valve for potential discontent and an indicator of public opinion, both of which, if necessary, could be taken into account by suitable action from above.

Notes
1. By this agreement Prussia had gained access to the western European system of trade.

Chapter 13

Prussia in Germany

The role of Prussia in Germany was not one-sided but reciprocal. If Prussia Borrussified Germany, Germany Germanized Prussia. 'Prussia is more in need of Germanization than Germany is in need of Borrussification . . . In view of the obligations we have towards the Reich I consider it . . . a duty first to aim at the strengthening of the power of the Reich, rather than of a greater Prussia.' These words of Bismarck's both summarize his attitude and indicate the severity of the struggle he had with the Prussian Conservatives.

From Bismarck's point of view the dangers facing the new state were several. There was the French hostility as a result of the annexation, which he had opposed, of Alsace and parts of Lorraine, and furthermore for the first few years Austria-Hungary's attitude was an unknown quantity. From within he faced the threat of anti-Prussian political Catholicism in southern and western Germany, the traditional centrifugal forces of particularist sentiments, and the growing demand for the full parliamentarization of German government. That the *Kulturkampf* (which aimed at the complete elimination of ecclesiastical influence from Prussia's and Germany's political life) had nothing to do with any fundamental enmity of Bismarck towards the Roman Catholic church needs no great substantiation. As late as 1870 he had been prepared to grant the Papacy asylum in Berlin if it were forced to leave the Vatican, not out of any altruistic motives but in order to prevent a Catholic coalition against Prussia *à la* Kaunitz. Militarily the particularist forces had been defeated in 1866, but now they were able to continue their struggle on a parliamentary basis by joining and supporting the Catholic Centre Party. That, after 1871, applied to the Alsatians as much as to the Poles and Protestant Hanoverian Guelphs. Additionally in Bismarck's view the Centre Party '. . . represents the Catholic church in the service of parliamentarianism' (by which he meant the forces of parliamentary democracy). Bismarck's aversion to the uncontrolled intrusion of popular ideologies and emotion into politics needs stressing, because this aversion in itself became tantamount to an ideology: 'Liberalism is bound to move beyond the actual intentions of its carriers. They cannot hold back the powerful surge of 40 millions on the move.'

Particularism and parliamentarianism were the targets of the *Kulturkampf*, a struggle which brought no victory to Bismarck, but neither took him to a political Canossa. Bismarck, as well as many of his opponents, was quite suddenly forced to recognize the growth of a political working class movement which in 1871 he had considered a *quantité négligeable*. This movement was socialism, international in its aims and outlook (rather than national like the followers of Lassalle, with whom Bismarck had sympathized in the past) and revolutionary in its goals as well as in its proclaimed methods. It ranged the defenders of the social, political and economic *status quo* with the defenders of the principle of monarchic legitimacy everywhere, including the churches, on one side of the political fence facing the forces of revolution on the other. Bismarck had in fact failed to gauge the dynamics of the Industrial Revolution accurately; the transformation of the German economic and social scene between 1871 and 1890 was of a degree which even to Bismarck came quite unexpectedly. Added to this came the world-wide agrarian crisis and the problems of a growing urban proletariat, which alone would have been reason enough to abandon the *Kulturkampf*. The Industrial Revolution, the agrarian crisis and the rise of the proletariat resulted in a threefold body of legislation: a protective tariff policy, the anti-socialist laws, and substantial social measures.

Bismarck's protective tariff policy cannot be viewed in isolation from its international context. The agrarian depression caused by over-production by all major agricultural producers resulted in a virtually universal demand from the countries concerned, including the United States of America for the introduction of tariffs to keep out cheaper imports and guarantee the agricultural sector an income on a par with that of the industrial sector. One need only look at the rise of the Populist Party in America and at their demands to realize that they were in an identical predicament and had similar aims in many respects to the Socialists in Germany. Prussia's agriculture was extremely hard-hit by the import of cheap Russian grain, soon to be followed by severe industrial tariffs.[1] It is also an indication of the gradual erosion of the political position of the Junkers that they were no longer strong enough to push through tariff legislation in the *Reichstag* unsupported. To do so successfully they needed an ally, and that ally was that other sector of the German economy affected by Russia's tariffs: German heavy industry. Consequently the old agrarian order, in order to ensure its own economic survival, was compelled to take the helping hand offered by industry, thus accepting a capitalist industrial society and all it stood for. Thus agrarians and industrialists became the combined force that stood behind the successive pieces of tariff legislation in Germany after 1879.

The core of the matter was whether Germany, especially Prussia with its base of heavy industry, bureaucracy and social structure pre-industrial in outlook and character, was capable of mastering the problems posed by a new industrial economy, an urban working class and the agrarian crisis, and of coming to terms with their social consequences. Again, from Bismarck's point of view of the primacy of the state, it appeared imperative that neither state nor society should become the helpless object of the particularist forces of parties here and the economic interests of big business there. Instead society should receive its shape and character from the state, while the state itself should be based on an integrated and not a divided social structure. The concept of the natural harmony of social forces and the aim of realizing that harmony was, more than the class struggle, the determining feature of Bismarck's domestic policy. The principle of harmony, of solidarity between state and social structure, formed the foundation of Bismarck's 'state socialism', at its core identical with the concept of the function of the state held by Frederick William I and Frederick the Great.

Prussia's bureaucracy throughout the nineteenth century had followed the general trend of free trade and non-interference by the state in economic affairs. Bismarck, conceiving the role of the state as an integrator of society, an educator and a regulator, neither shared this attitude nor was prepared to tolerate it when faced with industrial and social upheaval. As early as 1863 he gave expression to his opinion that economic legislation was too important a subject to be left to the impersonal forces of the open market or to party agitation. The Paris Commune offered one of many examples of the need for preventive state intervention in order to reduce social discontent and capitalist abuse.

Diverging attitudes inevitably resulted in clashes with traditional Liberals. One of these was with the Prussian minister of trade, von Itzenplitz, who maintained that state intervention in wage and price regulation was tantamount to the victory of socialist principles. Bismarck replied that because social democracy denied the existing order of the state, the state's intervention alone could halt the socialist movement, 'channel it into beneficial directions and realize those parts of the socialist demands which appear justified and which can be carried out within the framework of the present social and state order'.

Bismarck was not alone in recognizing that orthodox Liberal doctrine of *laissez faire* could not cope with the consequences of the Industrial Revolution. In his later years he frequently referred to a passage in the work of a church historian which reads:

The third estate itself has originated the ideas which now carry the torch to mobilize the masses of the fourth estate against the third. What is now preached in public is nothing other than what has been written in the books of the learned . . . It is the education of the nineteenth century which preaches its own downfall. As was the body of ideas of the eighteenth century, the ideas of the nineteenth century are revolutionary at their core. What they will bear, the progeny they will have from their own blood, will kill their own mother.

The forces of revolution could not be met by the principle of *laissez faire,* nor by general repression, but rather by recognizing the practical and real issues underlying them and at the same time giving qualified support to the upholders of the social and political *status quo*. This policy produced some very odd results. Both Roman Catholic church and the Protestant churches responded quickly to the changes in the social conditions. Especially among the latter, Stoecker's anti-Semitic movement in Berlin, feeding primarily on the misery and psychological dislocations caused by the Industrial Revolution, at first appeared to attract proletarian elements. Bismarck took as serious a view of the appeal of this court preacher to the base emotions of the lower orders of society as he did of any other political emotionalism; against the spectre of a populist social revolution he recommended the application of the anti-socialist laws and the removal of Stoecker from the Prussian court.[2]

Bismarck's response to the forces of emotional mass politics epitomized by Stoecker was typical. When in terms of actual votes Stoecker turned out to be a negligible quantity, Bismarck ignored him and his movement. More important to him was the threat of social revolution, and this was one of the determining factors in his decision to end the struggle with the church. After this the churches became one of the main supports of the Bismarckian state against the alleged threat of socialist revolution. The Liberal Prussian minister of culture, Falk, who had been one of the main exponents of the *Kulturkampf* was replaced by Robert von Puttkammer, an orthodox Conservative of deep religious convictions which he carried to such extremes that he saw a direct connection between Prussia's fortunes and the grace of God. Prussia was 'God's own darling'. The course of his career, first as minister of culture and then as Prussian minister of the interior up to 1888, was characterized by his endeavour to restore religion as a vital and integral part of the machinery of state and a defensive weapon against the forces of materialism.

But religion alone was still deemed insufficient to secure the base of the German *Obrigkeitsstat*. To a large extent each new nation is shaped by that class or caste which makes the most important contribution to its actual creation and upon which its consolidation and security rests. In Prussia and Germany that was obviously the army in general and the Prussian army in particular – which the aristocracy still dominated. The middle classes needed to be drawn further into its mesh and firmly onto the side of the defenders of the social and political *status quo*. Of course the military victories of 1864, 1866 and 1870/1 had done much to win over liberal opinion to Bismarck's side both inside Prussia and elsewhere. But Roon's army reforms had already included a measure of great long-term significance from the point of view of the institutional absorption of domestic conflicts. This was the creation between 1861 and 1880 of the 'officers of the reserve', the reserve officer corps which became one of the ways in which the middle class was assimilated into the aristocratic and monarchic character of the Prussian state and the German Empire. (Though naturally the expansion of the officer corps was also partly the result of the realization that the old aristocracy was not numerous enough to supply officer material for the modern mass armies upon the mobilization of which military planning was now based.) Instead of extending the officer corps into the middle class, the middle class candidates for commissions were taken into an existing officer corps with an unbroken tradition and historic consciousness which gradually transformed the value system of the newcomers to conform with that of the Prusso-monarchic order. Against a background of industrial revolution and the rise of an urban proletariat Prussia's and Germany's middle class, constantly fearful of a potential revolution of the 'dispossessed', clung tightly to the security provided by the existing institutions. The social consequence was not the absorption of the army into the nation, but the militaristic indoctrination of the reserve officer corps and the militarization of the German nation as a whole, with an associated shift of the power base from the landed nobility east of the Elbe to the German middle class as a whole.

No doubt there are many reasons why this shift was possible. Many of the Germans who had warned of Prussian dominance in Germany were converted overnight by the war against France. With it the army had become Germany's venerable treasure and the resentment against Prussian militarism faded, especially in the face of the events of 1871, which resulted, among other things, in Germany having an apparently irreconcilable enemy on her western frontier. Germany's fundamental geographic vulnerability, the incompleteness of internal German unification (to many Germans the Bismarckian 'little German' solution represented only a half-way house), the heterogeneity of its historic traditions, national and yet ideologically transcending the national, as the concept of the *Reich* shows, all these seemed to give weight to the arguments in favour of a standing army removed from the fickle influences of parliamentary politics. Little more than 20 years later the Franco-Russian alliance raised the spectre of the *Einkreisungspolitik*, which was simply another sympton of the endemic insecurity that had afflicted Prussia for over 200 years and that had now been superimposed upon the entire German Empire. The Schlieffen Plan, Germany's Far-Eastern policy and ultimately the building of a German battle fleet, were its direct progenies.

The absorption of large parts of the German middle class by the military aristocratic value system of Prussia was not a major problem because the divisions between aristocracy and middle class in Prussia were far less rigid than is commonly assumed. The greatest influx of fresh blood into the aristocratic elite had came from the middle class, whose representatives within a few generations were themselves ennobled. The magnetism of the Prussian state and its nobility was strong enough to attract the most talented from wide circles of the middle class. Generally speaking, the pattern of the rise of Prussia's middle class was slow and steady enough to produce in it attitudes which did not differ significantly from those that had shaped the tradition, the culture and the way of life of the aristocracy. A common pattern of social advancement began at the level of the property-holding peasant or artisan and progressed via a profession such as teacher or clergyman to administrator or military subaltern and finally to a high administrative or military office. Well-known examples of families who followed this pattern are those of Humboldt, Scharnhorst, Gneisenau, Clausewitz, Schrötter, Schön, Yorck, Boyen, Grolman and Steuben. Moreover the marriage conventions were far from exclusive; the mothers of Bismarck and Bülow were of middle class origins as were those of Moltke the elder and Hindenburg. By comparison with the aristocracy of other German territories the figure of slightly less than 30 per cent of Junker marriages being to members of the middle class represents an extremely high proportion. As has been pointed out, one of the major factors making for an integrated state was 'that the middle class marriage did not necessarily mean a permanent deviation from Junker stock. The spouse might adopt the Junker code and viewpoint and the children frequently went back into the Junker fold' when their turn came to marry. But the marriage traffic did not all go one way; the scions of rising middle class families not infrequently married daughters of the nobility. Of the Prussian generals on the eve of the First World War who had middle class origins, 43 per cent had married into the nobility. The proportion of top jobs in the Prussian bureaucracy during the nineteenth century that were held by members of the middle class amounts to 22 per cent; 34 per cent of all ministers of the interior were members of the middle class. Between 1871 and 1918 32 per cent of the Prussian diplomatic service was middle class as was 26 per cent of the imperial German diplomatic service. In the Prussian lower house 78 per cent of its members were of middle class origins. As a comparative analysis of the political and military leadership in Austria and Prussia between 1804 and 1918 has demonstrated, Prussia provided the middle class with greater opportunities for personal advancement while its aristocracy made a greater contribution than its Austrian counterpart in all spheres of life outside the army and politics, especially the arts and sciences. Consequently, when considering the growing links between a middle class and aristocracy united in the effort to maintain the existing social and political structure, it must be borne in mind that in spite of differences past and present the necessary preconditions for this process already existed, especially in Prussia. The growing economic vulnerability of the landed nobility as a result of the agrarian depression aided the rapprochement between the two classes. But it was the institution of the reserve officer that was the major contribution to the process by which that part of the middle class in Germany that owed its rise very largely to the economic and industrial transformation of the country was assimilated into a pre-industrial social order and corresponding value system.

Side by side with this process, fundamental changes were taking place in the personnel of the Prussian administration, changes emulated in the other federal states of the Reich. Older members with an essentially liberal outlook were prematurely retired and replaced by younger members of the civil service who rivalled their colleagues in 'the exercise of a convinced conservative attitude. Those who are familiar with the personnel policy of the Prussian government during the last quarter of the last century will know that liberal political views among the administrative officers were virtually non-existent. The rising generation adhered to an entirely conservative concept of state.' In 1794 the members of the Prussian bureaucracy had obtained their security of tenure. Now, in order to ensure loyalty and conformity, William I issued a proclamation in 1882 which compelled Prussian civil servants to swear an oath of loyalty to the monarch and 'to represent the policy of my government at elections'. And, of course, a *conditio sine qua non* of entering the higher echelons of the bureaucracy was one's election as an officer of the reserve by the *Reserveoffizierskorps*.

By a drastic rationalization of the Prussian judiciary from 1879 onwards the judges between 50 and 60 years of age were retired and pensioned off – precisely that generation which had opposed Bismarck so strongly during the constitutional conflict. At the same time advocates and lawyers gained their independence from the ministry of justice, which at least gave to younger judges who wished to escape the stifling conservative pressure the opportunity to opt for a free professional existence. In spite of a continuing and increasing need for additional judges throughout the 1880s no further appointments were made, which together with the retirement of the more senior age groups was part of the policy fostering social and ideological conformity.

This refeudalization of the bureaucracy was particularly pronounced in Prussia, where it was all the more important because Prussia contained not only the main base of German industry but also, in terms of territory and population approximately two-thirds of the Empire. The relative uniformity of Prussia's social structure was one of the ways of achieving the desired stability and security, the fight against potential revolution in the form of the socialist movement and the institutional absorption of Germany's industrial revolution was instrumental in the relative success of this policy.

Bismarck could hardly have ignored the Social Democrats' public committment to international revolution. The Social Democratic deputy Georg von Vollmar put it in a nutshell when he wrote that the question between Social Democracy and the German state was solely one of power, a question to be decided in the streets and on the battlefield, a question that could be decided by the sword only. 'We want to annihilate you. Yes, we are the enemies of your property, your marriage, your religion and your entire order. Yes, we are revolutionaries and Communists.'

Two attempts on the life of Kaiser William I gave Bismarck the pretext to introduce his anti-socialist laws that were intended to break up and destroy the socialist leadership. 'The nature of Social Democracy is to negate the existing order of the state. From that follows the right and the duty of the state to combat not only the effects of Social Democracy but to deprive it of its right of existence within the state. It is at war with the state', wrote Bismarck in 1888.

But he accepted many of the substantive grievances which the industrial proletariat voiced. He frequently emphasized that Germany could not exist without a certain amount of socialism, indeed the state would have to accustom itself to practising more socialism, a 'state socialism', which amounted to 'practical Christianity'. The aim of this would be to provide 'not alms but the right to be provided for where the good will to work is no longer enough'. The practical result was his social legislation, unprecedented in scope for its time.

Bismarck's anti-socialist laws defeated themselves; Social Democracy was not so much a party as a way of life providing for its members educational, cultural and recreational facilities. The party was deprived of its leadership, but not of the nucleus ready to supply new leaders who would adhere to the doctrinaire party programme. Instead of destroying it, Bismarck helped to consolidate the party, and in his failure to eliminate the ideological revolutionary ferment – as opposed to legitimate social grievances – he looked for suitable alternatives to the existing constitution and the method of representation in the *Reichstag*. These ideas if put into practice would have amounted to a *coup d'état*, while the method of representation which Bismarck had in mind would have abandoned the principle of the numerical majority and replaced it by a system of representation of interest groups. Material interests would, in Bismarck's view, have represented a sounder political common denominator than the ideologies of the existing parties.

Christopher Dawson, Thorstein Veblen and others have drawn attention to the peculiar nature of Germany's Industrial Revolution, a view restated recently by Ralf Dahrendorf, emphasizing the importance of the speed and thoroughness with which it was carried out. What in Britain, for instance, was achieved over a period of 150 years, took in Germany barely one-third of that time. The index of industrial production (1913 = 100) rose in Britain from 34 in 1860 slowly but steadily to 53 in 1880 and 79 in 1900; by comparison the figures for Germany are 14 in 1860, 25 in 1880 and 65 in 1900. A transformation of that magnitude was bound to cause serious dislocation, especially in the social and political sphere.

This economic transformation was the result of several factors. Firstly there was the rise of industrial combines. A comparison of German public shareholding companies of limited liability with British companies of the same type aptly illustrates this. In 1910 Germany had 5,000 such companies with a total capital of 16,000 million gold marks, while Britain had 50,000 such companies with a total capital of 44,000 million gold marks. Thus the average capital of the British companies was less than 1 million gold marks, compared with 3 million gold marks for the German. Similar observations also apply to other spheres of industrial and financial activity. The growth of syndicates, trusts and cartels was state-supported in Germany, and it is true to say that from the very outset of industrialization medium-sized middle class enterprise played a smaller role than did the economic giants. Secondly, of course, industrialization as a whole enjoyed the active support of the state, a state whose social structure was dominantly pre-industrial in composition and attitudes. Thirdly, the state not only supported the Industrial Revolution but directly participated in industrial enterprise by the creation of nationalized industries such as railways and canals. For example in 1913 Prussia owned, in the mining and iron industry alone, 14 mines and 12 blast furnaces and forges. Since local government authorities administered and owned the electricity, water, gas and public transport businesses, and as both the state and the private sector participated in enterprises such as state banks, this amounted to a considerable part of industry and finance being state-owned and therefore state-managed, as compared with the domination by private enterprise in Great Britain. The primary objective of the state was not profit, but what it considered to be the common weal or the public interest. Imperial Germany in general and Prussia in particular had created 'an economic order consisting of a mixture of private and public property'.

Fourthly, parallel with state capitalism we find a developing state socialism. Again the Prussian impetus is of fundamental importance here. Certainly the timing of Bismarck's social legislation was determined by tactical considerations regarding his anti-socialist laws, but his genuine concern for social problems considerably antedates this; regulation and absorption of social grievances had always been a characteristic feature of the Prussian state, as much the product of *raison d'état* as of the Pietist tradition. Bismarck's social legislation and that of his successors can justifiably be considered a further step along the path of established tradition. But equally important is the fact that Prussian state socialism was part of the policy to secure, consolidate and expand the state; or as Max Weber put it, 'the national state is for us not an unedified something the elevation of which increases in equal proportion with the amount of mythology one believes it has to be shrouded with, but the organization of the power of the nation, and in that national state the ultimate yardstick – which also applies to economic considerations – is the *raison d'état*'.

Fifthly, and lastly, there is the remarkable feature that Germany's Industrial Revolution did not bring forth an independent pluralist social and economic order, but a social order in which all sections of the nation were ultimately capable of subordinating their interests to those of the state. Therefore, according to Dahrendorf, Germany's Industrial Revolution crushed the liberal principle instead of allowing it to blossom.

Germany at the beginning of the twentieth century had an economy in which much property was state-owned, in which even the private sector was state-regulated, and in which pursuit of profit as one's sole motive was subject to official censure. The state also carried out both industrial and social welfare tasks, and rather better than in other comparable countries at the time. As a contemporary observer, Thorstein Veblen, commented:

The imperial state has come into the usufruct of this industrial state without the burden of its long-term institutional consequences. Carrying over a traditional bias of Romantic loyalty, infused anew with a military patriotism by several successful wars, and irritably conscious of national power in their new-found economic efficiency, the feudalistic spirit of the population has as yet been hardly dampened by their brief experience as a modern industrial community. And borne up by its ancient tradition of prowess and dynastic aggression the Prussian imperial state has faithfully fostered this militant spirit and cultivated in the people the animus of a solidarity of achievement. Hence a pronounced retardation in the movement towards popular autonomy.

. . . Though much of this is in need of serious qualification, the conclusion is valid, namely that the Industrial Revolution in Germany did not lead to a liberal bourgeois society and that the motive power for all social, economic and political changes remained the overmighty state with its citizens as worshippers. This of course raises the question as to why Prussian citizens, German citizens, should have acquiesced in a compromise between freedom and power. Prussian militarism, teutonic aggressiveness, represent fillers in the cracks that show the lack of a valid explanation.

Why was it that Prussian society, then German society as a whole and ultimately even its socialist component, subordinated their interests to the interest of the state, thus allowing it to become the preserver of the *status quo* as well as the prime mover in any change? The consciousness of the protective power of the state, the ideology of the state community prevalent in Prussia since the early eighteenth century, transformed itself in response to the call for German unification along the lines of the Romantic concept of the nation into an ideology of a national community. Prussia was an essentially artificial creation, intrinsically insecure, and in its army lay its one guarantee of survival. Both as a means of defence and as a means of consolidating the state territorially, the army decisively stamped its imprint upon Prussian society. German unification and the events which brought it about transferred the specifically Prussian problem onto Germany as a whole. In the interest of national security it was the object of government, as well as the desire of large parts of the German middle class, to absorb social and economic conflicts and to achieve a synthesis.

In terms of political developments a comparison is often made with Great Britain, France and the United States of America. Germany did not experience the revolutions that are said to have shaped the development of these nations, and Prussia in particular is alleged to have exercised an influence that prevented the feudal society from developing into a democratic one. Yet it can be argued that the Puritan Revolution in England did not produce a democratic society, that that revolution – if revolution it was – enjoyed little popularity in England. In France revolution was made by a small minority and ended in a compromise between the aristocracy and the *haute bourgeoisie* which led to a division of the nation noticeable to this day, while in America the conservative character of the revolution is its most outstanding feature. A reading of the Federalist Papers will supply quick confirmation. Until well into the nineteenth century it was the ideas (in different guises) of Alexander Hamilton and John Adams that prevailed, not those of Jefferson, let alone of Sam Adams and Tom Paine.

That the ideals of the French Revolution, particularly the concept of human rights, 'came in the supply trains of an army of invasion', was hardly conducive to their recommendation. One tends to forget that enlightened absolutism brought benefits to its subjects which were the envy of many contemporaries abroad, and even a hundred years later Richard Cobden considered Prussia as a highly efficient, well-administered state which did more for its population than any other. Where is the need for revolution from below when reform is carried out from above? Schiller's and Goethe's contemporary Friedrich Daniel Schubart, himself the victim of absolutist practice of the worst kind and a fervent supporter of the French Revolution exclaimed: 'Not from France, and not from England has true toleration come into Germany. Luther brought the liberty of thought, Frederick [the Great] and Joseph [II] were the pillars of toleration.' And Goethe in 1824 in his conversations with Eckermann stated:

Revolutions are quite impossible so long as governments are always just and aware of what is going on in order that they can introduce necessary improvements and not resist until what is necessary is forced upon them from below. Enlightened despotism never occurred in France, while however great its faults in retrospect its practice in Prussia and under Joseph II in Austria served as an example to many contemporaries that was worthy of emulation. Napoleon placed between the busts of Washington and Mirabeau that of Frederick the Great. Frederick became a literary cult figure in a play that drew the crowds as did no other play in Paris in the revolutionary year of 1789. Indeed within the context of the eighteenth century, German progress made through enlightened absolutism was ultimately the cause of German political underdevelopment, when that development is compared with that of the nations to its west.

Bismarck had worked and aimed towards a synthesis of society and state, but had only partially succeeded. Still moulded by traditions of sobriety and rationality he approached problems by trying to achieve that which was possible. But in the end he himself no longer understood the age in which he lived. Politics to him was at best a very complex business, and with the intrusion of the masses it became virtually uncontrollable. His attempts to stem the tide were the fundamental reason for his downfall.

His departure marked the end of Prussia as idea and ethos. *De facto* it had ended in 1871. The old Prussian nobility, its social position rooted in the land and the army, found itself confronted by a new age; agriculture confronted the machines of the age of steam. The simple code of honour and duty to the state were no longer sufficient to cope with the complexity of the industrial age. Power acquired by sudden riches threatened to displace the old ruling class. The estate-owner was no match for the captain of industry. Bleichröder's clientèle provides ample evidence of the extent to which the scions of the old Prussian families, Bismarck included, succumbed to the temptations of wealth. What remained of the old Prussia were the external trappings, military parades, marching and counter-marching, the whip-cracking tone of the barracks square, uniforms and sabre rattling. The death of William I in 1888 was the beginning of the end of an era. Considering the determining influence of German liberalism in the policies of his successor Emperor Frederick III, there is nothing to suggest that had he not suffered from the fatal disease of which he died 100 days after his accession, his policy would not have been devoid of the new imperialist features which characterize late nineteenth-century German nationalism. While Bismarck was at the helm of state the prophets of irrationalism had their say but they were held at bay, away from politcal influence. During the reign of the last Hohenzollern King and last German Emperor, William II, shifts of policy occurred which abandoned the paths carefully trodden by Bismarck and moved into a realm of greater risk and danger without being very clear in their aim. William II was more of a German than a Prussian; that he was also half an Englishman, inheriting from his mother a boundless degree of tactlessness of which he himself was never aware throughout his life, did not help matters either.

Prussia had fused into Germany and not Germany into Prussia. Germany's confidence in her strength and the power of her state had not slowly matured but suddenly ripened into over-confidence. The period up to the First World War is one marked by a constant awareness of weakness, when German doubts about the solidity of the foundations of their new state were ever-present. Prussian policy had at long last been replaced by German policy; the ideas of 1848 had finally won supremacy.

Notes

1. The industrial tariffs reduced Germany's share of the export market to Russia from 24 per cent in 1875 to 5 per cent in 1885.
2. Stoecker was a chaplain at the Prussian court.

Chapter 14

The end of Prussia

Prussia had been a state which did not rest on the concept of the *Volk*, a concept in its original meaning derived from Herder's postulate that *state* and *nation* should be conterminous, that ethnic as well as cultural origins predestined such a unit to statehood since it represented not an artificial but a natural, organically developed community. Prussia was an artificial creation, the product of the dynasty and its servants, as was the Hapsburg Empire. But unlike that Empire, throughout most of its history it was a purely German state untroubled by the problems of national minorities. These did not arise until the final phases of its history when the German national idea gained predominance and thus gave further strength and motiviation to the forces of the national *risorgimento* that had affected eastern central, south-eastern and southern Europe throughout the nineteenth century. Particularly the Poles made it quite clear in 1871 that whilst they did not mind being subjects of the Prussian crown they adamantly refused to be German citizens.

Prussia had been the first state on German soil whose endeavours, at least since the reign of Frederick William I, had been directed towards the state rather than the dynasty. The concept of state provided unity and the force of integration over a patchwork of territories of vastly different traditions, economic social and political development. It was not the product of dynastic marriages or deaths. It could last only as long as in every one of its subjects or citizens the concept of state exercised its dominant influence. Why this concept exercised such an integrating force is a question difficult if not impossible to answer. After all, it has nothing to offer other than rigorous demands. From its monarchs downwards it did not reward pious intentions, only efforts and accomplishments. It never pretended to be or tried to become a democratic state. Its pride lay in being an authoritarian state, marked by its hierarchic structure. The totalitarian state whose origins are of a democratic character was alien to Prussia, as the Prussian substance was alien to totalitarianism. In its methods it had always been revolutionary, but in its nature it was and remained conservative.

However, the essentially German character of Prussia was a source of both its innate strengths and weaknesses. On the one hand it caused Prussia to exercise a magnetism which attracted many who saw in it the only German state capable of reforging the German nation into a politically relevant unit, into the Reich. But because it was comprised of such differing elements as Westphalians, Lithuanians, Frisians, Pomeranians, Brandenburgers, East Prussians and Poles, none of whom had to sacrifice their own identity in order to be Prussians, the common link which Prussia represented broke asunder after German reunification. Unlike the Bavarians, for instance, 'the Prussians' did not represent an ethnic group whose consciousness had developed over almost 2,000 years of common history. Therefore, the concept of Germany was bound to dilute that of Prussia once Germany was politically unified again. From that moment onwards the integrating force which Prussia had exercised over its constituent parts was bound to be severely weakened. As Bismarck once put it: 'As Prussians we had and still have a particular national feeling, originally a branch of that great German one. Basically it had no more justification than the specific patriotism of the German states. As far as I was concerned it was self-evident that I felt deeply this Prussian consciousness in which I had grown up, but as soon as I became convinced that Prussian national feeling was the anvil on which to forge together the others, I gave up pursuing one-sided Prussian aims.'

But the pursuit of German aims was bound to affect the spiritual substance of Prussia, especially in an age of world-wide imperialism, and this substance was increasingly diluted until finally it was almost submerged. This process was not recognized either in Germany or by the rest of the world. 'The Prussian heritage' became a synonym for German policy pursuing aims that bore little or no resemblance to the traditional Prussian *raison d'état*, and for the resulting collisions with powers no less acquisitive than the newly emerged German national state (the only difference being that these powers had already acquired territories while whatever Germany could gain would be at their expense).

'The idea of Prussia' became a romanticized vehicle of German nationalism, in that form supplying ample ammunition to its critics inside and outside the Empire of Bismarck and William II. In terms of domestic policy it became synonymous with the economic interests of the land-owners east of the Elbe, the Prussian Conservatives and their opposition to the advance of an industrial society and the demand for greater democratization. Yet, the Conservatives represented only one component of Prussia. If Prussia was the heartland of conservatism in Germany, it was also the heartland of Germany's Social Democracy. By 1912 the Social Democrats were the largest single party represented in the *Reichstag* and the largest socialist party in the world, renowned for their organization and 'Prussian' discipline. To the world outside, judging mainly on the basis of surface appearances, it was all too easy to see in Germany an enlarged Prussia and nothing else, to find a common thread linking Frederick the Great to Bismarck and to William II and later even to Hitler, to refer to German's foreign policy as one of typical 'Prussian expansionism', conveniently forgetting that, strictly speaking,

Prussia in its entire history had conducted only two aggressive wars, that of 1740 and that of 1866.

Prussia was identified as that part of Germany untouched by the civilizing Roman influence, therefore barbaric to its very core, a product of the east ideally suited to Lutheranism and the subservience to secular powers that it preached. Again, such an identification is misleading, neglecting as it does the strong intellectual currents coming from the west, especially that of Calvinism from the Netherlands and France, producing a stoic ethos, a sense of duty rejecting 'the romanesque Baroque as hollow vanity devoid of efficiency'. But then efficiency is a quality often appreciated but never loved, especially when that efficiency is deployed in the service of the state and not that of private enterprise; service to the ultimate, to death. It belonged to the standard introductory speeches delivered to 10-year-old boys entering the Prussian cadet institutes: 'Gentlemen! You have chosen the most beautiful profession there is on this earth. Before your eyes you have the highest aim there can be. Here we teach you to reach that aim. You are here to learn that which gives your life its ultimate meaning. You are here in order to learn how to die.' And whatever may be said against Prussia and the Prussians, no one can say that they did not know how to die well on the battlefields of Europe or Hitler's gallows.

But death in the service of the state as an educational aim was bound to be an anathema to a world and a world order that believed and believes itself to be liberal, a society in which death as a subject has become one of the great taboos. Inevitably it was bound to be seen as a threat, especially when, as during William II's Empire, German foreign policy was lacking in firm, concrete objectives and, since at the time no one could believe that, was felt to be threatening everywhere as Sir Eyre Crowe's memorandum of 1907 so strikingly illustrates.

Prussia did not cease to exist with the abdication of William II in 1918 and the proclamation of the German Republic (a republic whose constitutional assembly had been careful to play down any reference to the *Republik* in the Weimar constitution). The surprising thing is that it was non-Prussians, men like Friedrich Ebert from the Palatinate, or the Generals Reinhardt and Groener from Württemberg, who were the most anxious to preserve Prussia and frequently invoked the old Prussian virtues.

Although in the Weimar Republic Prussia's influence in the politics of the Reich was diminished, it was not eliminated. In the *Reichsrat*, that chamber in which the lands of the republic were represented, Prussia, although still the largest German state had no more influence than any of the others. Moreover the *Reichsrat* could not initiate any legislation. What marks the history of Prussia during the Weimar Republic is its great stability compared with that of the republic as a whole. Between 1920 and 1932 Prussia's government was headed by the Social Democrat Otto Braun and consisted of representatives of those parties which had also led the original Weimar coalition (Social

Democrats, Liberals and the Centre Party), joined between 1921 and 1925 by a representative of Stresemann's German People's Party. During almost the same period, 1919 to 1933, the Weimar Republic had 20 governments. This stability allowed Prussia to carry out a process of democratization in its administrative apparatus, and civil servants opposing this process could be removed quickly, something virtually impossible in the civil service of the Reich. Prussia could keep under control the extremes of both left and right, producing in its administration a synthesis between the old Prussian and the new democratic forces.

When Field-Marshal von Hindenburg succeeded the dead Ebert in 1925 it seemed that with the arch-Junker at the helm of state the forces of reaction had triumphed, a feeling which ignored the fact that Ludendorff had been defeated in that presidential election. On the whole, Hindenburg was more loyal towards the republic than was to be expected of a man of his background. When elected again in 1932, he was ultimately also the candidate of the moderate left, opposed to the Austrian Hitler, the candidate of the extreme right. It is difficult to find among the Weimar politicians one who could have defended the republic, then already in its death throes, more energetically and successfully than the Kaiser's erstwhile field-marshal. His election did not dig the grave of the republic; the parliamentarians of the republic were unwittingly already busy doing this themselves. Given a functioning parliamentary democracy – which the Weimar Republic was not – and given less severe external pressures than those to which the republic was subjected, Hindenburg could well have been the bridge between the forces of tradition and those of democracy.

Hindenburg did not set out to destroy the constitution, but once the *Reichstag* began to fail in its function as legislator as well as that of an instrument for integrating the political will, it created a power vacuum which constitutionally could only be filled by the presidency. He has often been accused of lack of political judgement, of old age impeding his mental faculties. If that were true, then he still manifested a greater reserve and scepticism towards Hitler than did most of his younger contemporaries. Without the obstacle called Hindenburg Hitler would have been at the seat of power rather earlier than was ultimately the case. In the last two years of the republic it was Hindenburg's constant endeavour to return to a government supported by a parliamentary majority. That he wanted that majority to consist of centre-to-right parties (excluding Hitler) rather than a left-wing coalition (in fact an impossibility because the Communists hated the 'Social Fascists', as they called the Social Democrats, more than they feared Hitler) shows his own personal political inclination but does not demonstrate any design to subvert the constitution. The one alternative open to the republic to prevent Hitler coming to power was military dictatorship. General von Schleicher appears to have thought of this. Hindenburg thwarted the scheme, remaining true to the letter of the constitution. Because the president refused to take or sanction an unconstitutional step, the Weimar Republic, already on its deathbed, finally expired. But the president preserved his scepticism of Hitler to the last and tried his utmost to keep the most powerful instrument of the executive, the army, out of his hands. That, following the advice of his son and Papen and appointing Blomberg as *Reichswehr* minister he had appointed a man who sympathized with Hitler, the last president of the republic did not know. Once Hitler was in power the old man, like the rest of the Conservatives who believed that they could tame and contain Hitler, was taken in. Still that last law passed by the *Reichstag* of the republic, the Enabling Act giving Hitler extraordinary dictatorial powers, was passed by a two-third's majority, which would still have been a two-third's majority had all the members of the opposition been present. But it was not a presidential decree. If the concept of guilt has any meaning in history, then in Hindenburg's case it would apply only to his sanctioning of Hitler's June purge of 1934, a little more than a month before the old man's death.

Hitler's policy of *Gleichschaltung* had, as far as Prussia was concerned, already been anticipated during the chancellorship of Franz von Papen when, on 20 July 1932 after the Prussian government had lost its majority in the Prussian diet, the Braun government carried on as a caretaker government. Papen, under the pretext of preserving law and order, had it forcibly dismissed and subjected Prussia to the government of a Reich commissioner. On exactly the same date, 12 years later, it was representatives of the Prussian nobility who formed the core of the conspiracy against Hitler and who risked the last attempt upon the dictator's life. The conspiracy failed, and in retrospect was bound to have failed, one important reason among many being the equation made by the Allies between 'Prussianism' and National Socialism. Their failure was almost tantamount to the liquidation of a former ruling class. 'Rarely has a social class succeeded in making its "exit from history" more impressively.' (Joachim Fest)

But the history of Prussia had, to all appearances, already ended long before that. Yet in order to make quite sure, the Allied Control Council, on 25 February 1947, thought it necessary to promulgate its Law No. 46 which formally dissolved the state of Prussia. States can be dissolved by law; not so their underlying ethos which can be resurrected at any time and place. Two years later the renowned anti-militarist writer Arnold Zweig wrote: 'Since about 1860 a tradition formed itself from which a human type emerged that continually ran towards its own destruction. If we can change this type, turning away from the craft of war towards a positive, creative craft, we shall save it and do the cause of peace a service . . . But in order to be able to do that, we shall have to X-ray war right to its skeleton.' Perhaps this has been done and success has been achieved, the answer being the 'economic miracle' in Germany, West and East. The famous Prussian names that are left are no longer found in the armed forces but in the management of industry, or in political parties on whose banners the cause of social reform is writ large, while in East Germany the Prussian virtues are driven home incessantly with Saxon accents to a population that has never had the opportunity to test the alternatives.

In East Germany the complete negation of the Prussian legacy has given way to a process of slow integration of that legacy into its historical consciousness. Instead of destroying its architectural remnants, they are now being restored. Even the equestrian statue of Frederick the Great, formerly in Berlin's *Unter den Linden*, now graces the park of Sanssouci. True, the Garrison Church at Potsdam has gone forever, and the coffins of Frederick William I and his son have found a new place of rest in the chapel of the Hohenzollern castle near Hechingen. There they lie side by side under the worn and tattered flags of some of Prussia's most famous regiments. A 'refuge of the outlawed, waiting for their return', as Pierre Gaxotte has put it. Perhaps.

The name of Prussia is still highly evocative, eliciting a range of responses from the affirmative to the negative, but rarely without great emotional intensity. As times move on and generation succeeds generation, these emotions will simmer down; what will remain is a historical memory of a state and its ethos to which Shakespeare's words might very well be used as an epitaph:

> Beat thou the drum, that it speak mournfully;
> Trail your steel pikes. Though in this city he
> has widowed and unchilded many a one,
> Which to this hour bewail the injury,
> Yet he shall have a noble memory.

Bibliography

*Selected as important works
†Works relevant to more than one chapter

Chapter 1

*H. **Aubin**, 'The lands east of the Elbe and German colonisation eastwards', *Cambridge Economic History*, vol. i, Cambridge 1941.

*M. **Biskup**, 'Polish research on the history of the Teutonic Order State Organisation in Prussia 1949–1959', *Acta Poloniae Historica* 3

*A. B. **Boswell**, 'The Teutonic Order', in *Cambridge Medieval History*, vol. vii, Cambridge 1932.

E. **Capspar**, *Hermann von Salza und die Gruendung des Deutschordensstaates in Preussen*, Tuebingen 1924.

*_Deutsche Ostssiedlung im Mittellealter und Neuzeit_, Cologne 1971.

G. **Gause**, *Deutsch-slavische Schicksalsgemeinschaft. Abriss einer Geschichte Ostdeutschlands und seiner Nachbarlaender*, London 1972

*K. **Gorski**, 'The Teutonic Order in Prussia', *Medievalia et Humanistica*, 17, 1966.

R. **ten Haaf**, *Kurze Bibliographie zur Geschichte des deutschen Ordens*, Kitzingen 1949.

†Otto **Hintze**, *Die Hohenzollern und ihr Werk*, Berlin 1915.

W. **Hubatsch**, 'Kreuzritterstaat und Hohenzollernmönarchie', in *Zur Frage der Fortdauer des Deutschen Ordens in Preussen* (Festschrift fuer Hans Rothfels), ed. by W. Conze, Duesseldorf 1951.

M. **Perlbach**, 'Die Statuten des Deutschen Ordens' (1890): *Spritores rerum Prussicarum* (5 vols., 1861–74, reprint 1965), vol. vi, 1968.

D. **Seward**, *The Monks of War. The Military Religious Orders*, London 1972.

*H. v. **Treitschke**, 'Das deutsche Ordensland Preussen', in *Historische und Politische Aufsaetze*, vol. ii, Leipzig 1913. English transl., *The Origins of Prussianisms*, London 1942.)

P. **Marian Tummler**, *Der Deutsche Orden im Werden, Wachsen und Wirken bis 1400*, Vienna 1955.

J. **Voigt**, *Geschichte des des Deutschen Ritterordens in seinen zwoelf Balleien in Deutschland* (2 vols), Berlin 1857–59.

*R. **Wenskus**, *Das Ordensland Preussen als Territorialstaat des 14. Jahrhunderts*, Sigmaringen 1970.

Chapter 2

*F. L. **Carsten**, 'Medieval democracy in the Brandenburg towns and its defeat in the fifteenth Century'. *Transactions of the Royal Historical Society*, 4th Series, XXV/1943.

* 'The origins of the Junkers', *English Historical Review*, LXII/1947.

† *The Origins of Prussia*, Oxford 1954.

* *Princes and Parliaments in Germany*, London 1959.

F. Delius, *Die Reformation des Kurfuersten Joachim II. im Jahre 1539,* (Theologia Viatorum V), Berlin 1954.
E. Fidicin, *Die Territorien der Mark Brandenburg* (4 vols), Berlin 1857-64.
U. Stutz, *Johann Sigismund von Brandenburg und das Reformationsrecht,* Berlin 1922.
H. Wischhoefer, *Die ostpreussischen Staende im letzten Jahrzehnt vor dem Regierungs-antritt des Grossen Kurfuersten,* Goettingen 1958.
L. Zscharnack, *Das Werk Martin Luthers in der Mark Brandenburg von Joachim I, bis zum Grossen Kurfuersten,* Berlin 1917.

Chapter 3

F. L. Carsten, 'The Great Elector and the foundation of Hohenzollern despotism', *English Historical Review,* LXV. 1950.
K. Breysig, *Geschichte der Brandenburgischen Finanzen 1640-1697,* Leipzig 1895.
†**H. Delbrueck,** *Geschichte der Kriegskunst,* vol. iv, Berlin 1962 (reprint).
H. Erbe, *Die Hugenotten in Deutschland,* Essen 1937.
F. Flaskamp, *Die Religions-und Kirchenpolitik des Grossen Kurfuersten nach ihren persoenlichen Bedingungen,* Bonn 1925.
*****R. Hatton,** *Europe in the Age of Louis XIV,* London 1969.
* *Louis XIV and his World,* London 1972.
* (ed.), *Louis XIV and Europe,* London 1976.
v. Meinardus (ed.), *Protokolle und Relationen des brandenburgischen Geheimen Rates aus der Zeit des Grossen Kurfuersten Friedrich Wilhelm* (7 vols), 1640-1660, Leipzig 1889-1919.
G. Oestreich, *Der brandenburgisch-preussische Geheime Rat am Regierungsantritt des Grossen Kurfuersten bis zur Neuordnung im Jahre 1651,* Wuerzburg 1937.
*****E. Opgenoorth,** *Friedrich Wilhelm. Der Grosse Kurfuerst von Brandenburg, vol. i 1620-1660,* Goettingen 1971.
H. v. Peterdorff, *Der Grosse Kurfuerst,* Berlin 1939.
M. Phillipson, *Der Grosse Kurfuerst Friedrich Wilhelm von Brandenburg* (3 vols), Berlin 1897-1903.
F. Schevill, *The Great Elector,* Chicago 1947.
W. v. Unger, *Feldmarschall Derfflinger,* Berlin 1896.
Urkunden und Aktenstuecke zur Geschichte der inneren Politik Kurfuerst Friedrich Wilhelm von Brandenburg (3 vols), Berlin 1895-1915.
A. Waddington, *Le grand Electeur Fréderic Guillaume de Brandenburg, Sa Politique extérieure 1640-1688,* Paris 1908.

Chapter 4

A. Berney, *Koenig Friederich I. und das Habsburg, 1701-1707,* Munich 1927.
J. v. Besser, *Preussische Croenungsgeschichte,* Coelln an der Spree 1712, reprint Berlin 1901.
*****K. Deppermann,** *Der Hallesche Pietismus und der Preussiche Staat unter Friedrich III,* Goettingen 1961.
†**C. Hinrichs,** *Preussen als Historisches Problem,* Berlin 1964.
L. v. Ranke, *Zwoelf Buecher preussischer Geschichte* (3 vols), Berlin 1930.
Th. Schieder, *Die preussische Koenigskroenung von 1701 und die polnische Ideenge-schichte,* Koenigsberg 1935.
H. J. Schoeps, *Preussen, Geschichte eines Staates,* Berlin 1966.

Chapter 5

*Acta Borrussica, Denkmaeler der preussischen Staatsverwaltung im 18. Jahrhundert, Pruussische Akademic der Wissenschaften in Berlin, vols I–VI. n.d.

*O. **Buesch**, *Militaersystem und Sozialleben im alten Preussen*, Berlin 1962.

G. A. **Craig**, *The Politics of the Prussian Army*, Oxford 1955.

K. **Demeter**, *The Prussian Officer Corps*, London 1968.

*W. L. **Dorn**, 'The Prussian bureaucracy in the Eighteenth century', *Political Science Quarterly*, XLVI, 1931.

*R. A. **Dorwart**, *The Administrative Reforms of Frederick William of Prussia*, Cambridge, Mass. 1953.

J. G. **Droysen**, *Geschichte der preussischen Politik*, Leipzig 1872.

R. **Ergang**, *The Potsdam Fuehrer*, New York 1941.

S. B. **Fay**, *The Rise of Brandenburg–Prussia to 1786*, New York 1937.

F. **Foerster**, *Friedrich Wilhelm I Koenig von Preussen* (3 vols), Potsdam 1834.

E. v. **Frauenholz** (ed.) *Entwicklungsgeschichte des preussischen Heerwesens*, vol. iv Munich 1940.

† Th. **Fuchs**, *Geschichte des europaeischen Kriegswesens* (3 vols), Munich 1972.

*C. **Hinrichs**, *Der Kronprinzenprozess*, Hamburg 1936.

*   *Friedrich Wilhem I*, Darmstadt 1968 (reprint).

†   *Preussentum und Pietismus*, Goettingen 1971.

J. **Klepper**, *Der Vater*, Stuttgart 1957.

   (ed.), *In tormentis pinxit. Briefe und Bilder Friedrich Wilhelm I*, Stuttgart 1938.

G. **Kuentze** (ed.), *Die politischen Testamente der Hohenzollern*, Leipzig/Berlin 1919.

*C. A. **Macartney**, (ed.), *The Habsburg and Hohenzollern Dynasties in the Seventeenth and Eighteenth Centuries*, London 1970.

G. **Rhode**, *Brandenburg–Preussen und die Protestanten in Polen 1640–1740: Ein Jahrhundert preussischer Schutzpolitik fuer eine unterdrueckte Minderheit*, Leipzig 1941.

† H. **Rosenberg**, *Bureaucracy, Aristocracy and Autocracy: The Prussian Experience 1660–1815*, Boston 1966.

† G. **Schmoller**, *Umrisse und Untersuchungen zur Verfassungs-Veraltungs-und Wirtschaftsgeschichte besonders des preussischen Staates im 17. und 18. Jahrhundert*, Berlin 1921.

*L. D. **White** (ed.), *The Civil Service in the Modern State. A Collection of Documents*, Chicago 1930.

Chapter 6

*W. H. **Bruford**, *Germany in the Eighteenth Century*, Cambridge 1935.

W. **Bussmann**, 'Friedrich der Grosse im Wandel des europaeischen Urteils', in *Deutschland und Europa. Fesschrift fuer Hans Rothfels*, Duesseldorf 1951.

H. **Butterfield**, *Man on his Past*, Boston 1960.

W. **Dilthey**, 'Friedrich der Grosse und die deutsche Aufklaerung', in *Gesammelte Schriften*, vol. III, Berlin 1927.

J. G. **Droysen**, M. **Duncker**, and G. B. **Volz** (eds), *Politische Correspondenz Friedrichs des Grossen* (45 vols), Berlin 1870–1938.

Ch. **Duffy**, *The Army of Frederick the Great*, Newton Abbot 1974.

C. W. **Eldon**, *England's Subsidy Policy towards the Continent during the Seven Years' War*, Philadelphia 1938.

*P. **Gaxotte**, *Frederick the Great*, London 1941.

G. P. **Gooch**, *Frederick the Great*, London 1947.

*W. O. **Henderson**, *The State and the Industrial Revolution in Prussia 1740–1870*, Liverpool 1958.

*   *Studies in the Economic Policy of Frederick the Great*, London 1963.

sia

schwoerung gegen das internationale Proletariat, Berlin

ndrecht und Klassenkampf, Berlin 1960.
Revolution, London 1962.
1875, London 1975.
assungsgeschichte seit 1789 (3 vols), Stuttgart 1963.
die deutsche Revolution, Berlin 1913.
ion of the Intellectuals, Oxford 1944.
von 1815 bis 1849, Berlin 1967.
tion von 1848, Berlin 1970.
olution, Munich 1972.
iedrich Wilhelm IV, Berlin 1900.
ssene Briefe und Aufzeichnungen zur Geschichte der Jahre
gart 1922.
lm IV Briefwechsel mit Bunsen, Saemmtliche Werke, vols.

f 1848: a Social History, Princeton 1953.
sche Protestantismus vor der sozialen Frage 1815-1871,

aat und sein Verhaeltnis zu Deismus und Judentum, Berlin

olitisches Prinzip, Berlin 1863.
Die Politik und Taktik der 'Neuen Rheinischen Zeitung'
h-demokratischen Revolution in Deutschland, Berlin 1971.
deutschen Revolution 1848-1849 (2 vols), Stuttgart 1922,
1848: Chapters of German History, London 1940.
ssen. Von den Anfaengen bis zur Reichsgruendung, Berlin

inheitsbewegung, Berlin 1968.

and Political Conflict in Prussia 1858-1864, Nebraska 1954.
1848/49 bis 1963, Munich 1963.
und Erinnerungen (3 vols), Stuttgart 1898-1921.
den, Briefe, Gespraeche, Friedrichsruher Ausgabe, Berlin

Weg zur Grossmacht, Cologne 1966.
sgruendungszeit, Cologne 1968.
and the Hohenzollern Candidature for the Spanish Throne,

sche Wirtschaftsgeschichte, Cologne 1966.
Geheimes Kriegstagebuch 1870/71, Bonn 1954.
n 1815-1864, London 1963.
mic Development of France and Germany, Cambridge 1951.
ie Arbeiterbewegung in der nationalen Bewegung, Stuttgart

and Society in Germany, London 1967.
ution of Modern Germany, London 1908.
kreich und die spanische Thronkandidatur der Hohenzollern

er, Im Widerstreit um die Reichsgruendung, Berlin 1970.
German Empire, London 1950.
erfassungsgeschichte der Neuzeit, Stuttgart 1961.
casca, Das Ende des alten Europa, Vienna 1968.
for Supremacy in Germany 1859-1866, London 1935.
ck Problem, Cologne 1971.

O. **Hintze**, 'Friedrich der Grosse und die preussische Justizreform des 18. Jahrhunderts', in *Recht und Wirtschaft*, vol. I, 1912.
D. B. **Horn**, *Frederick the Great and the Rise of Prussia*, London 1964.
*W. **Hubatsch**, *Frederick the Great: Absolutism and Administration*, London 1975.
† S. **Isaacsohn**, *Geschichte des preussischen Beamtenthums* (3 vols), Berlin 1874-84.
*H. C. **Johnson**, *Frederick the Great and His Officials*, Yale 1975.
H. **Kaplan**, *The First Partition of Poland*, Boston 1962.
R. **Koser**, *Geschichte Friedrichs des Grossen* (4 vols), Berlin 1921.
*F. **Meinecke**, *Machiavellism*, New Haven 1957.
*P. **Paret** (ed.), *Frederick the Great. A profile*, London 1972.
J. D. E. **Preuss** (ed.), *Oeuvres de Frederic le Grand* (30 vols), Berlin 1846-57.
G. **Ritter**, *Frederick the Great*, Berkeley 1968.
† *The Sword and the Sceptre*, vol. I and II, Coral Gables, Florida, 1970.
E. **Simon**, *The Making of Frederick the Great*, London 1963.
*M. **Schlenke**, *England und das friederizianische Preussen 1740-1763*, Freiburg 1963.
S. **Skalweit**, *Frankreich und Friedrich der Grosse. Der Aufstieg Preussens in der oeffentlichen Meinung des Ancien Regime*, Goettingen 1952.
'Friedrich der Grosse und der Aufstieg Preussens', in *Die Europaeer und ihre Geschichte*, ed. L. Reinisch, Munich 1961.
*H. **Weill**, *Frederick the Great and Samuel Cocceji: A Study in the Reform of the Prussian Judicial Administration 1745-1755*, Madison, Wisc., 1961.

Chapter 7

*C. **Brinton**, *A Decade of Revolution 1789-1799*, New York 1934.
* H. **Brunschwig**, *La crise de l'état prussien à la fin du XVIIIe siècle et la genèse de la mentalité romantique*, Paris 1947.
H. **Conrad**, *Die geistigen Grundlagen des Allgemeinen Landrechts fuer die preussischen Staaten von 1794*, Cologne 1958.
K. **Epstein**, *The Genesis of German Conservatism*, Princeton 1966.
K. D. **Erdmann**, *Die Umgestaltung Deutschlands im Zeitalter der Franzoesischen Revolution und Napoleons 1786-1815*, Stuttgart 1952.
*L. **Gershoy**, *From Despotism to Revolution 1763-1789*, New York 1944.
*G. P. **Gooch**, *Germany and the French Revolution*, London 1965.
K. **Griewank**, 'Hardenberg und die preussische Politik 1804-1806', *Forschungen zur Brandenburgischen und Preussischen Geschichte*, XLVII, 1935.
O. **Hintze**, 'Preussische Reformbestrebungen von 1806', in *Gesammelte Abhandlungen III*, Leipzig 1943.
W. **Hubatsch**, *Eckpfeiler Europas. Probleme des Preussenlandes in geschichtlicher Sicht*, Heidelberg 1953.
H. v. **Kleist**, *Saemmtliche Werke und Briefe*, Munich 1964.
*R. **Koselleck**, 'Staat und Gesellschaft in Preussen 1815-1848', in *Staat und Gesellschaft im deutschen Vormaerz*, Stuttgart 1962.
*P. **Lahnstein** (ed.), *Report einer 'guten alten Zeit' Zeugnisse und Berichte 1750-1805*, Munich 1977.
O. v. **Lettow-Vorbeck**, *Der Krieg von 1806 und 1807* (4 vols), Berlin 1891-96.
*H. **Möller**, *Anfklärung in Preussen*, Berlin 1974.
E. **Ruppel-Kuhfuss**, *Das Generaldirektorium unter der Regierung Friedrich Wilhelm II*, Wuerzburg 1937.
H. J. **Schoeps**, *Aus den Jahren preussischer Not und Erneuerung, Tagebuecher und Briefe der Gebrueder Gerlach und ihres Kreises 1805-1820*, Berlin 1963.
*A. **Sorel**, *Europe and the French Revolution. The Political Traditions of the Old Régime*, eds A. Cobban and J. W. Hunt, London 1969.
C. G. **Svarez**, *Vortraege ueber Recht und Staat von 1791*, ed. H. Conrad and G. Kleinheyer, Cologne 1966.
*A. de **Tocqueville**, *L'ancien régime et la revolution*, Paris 1952.

Chapters 8 and 9

*E. N. Anderson, *Nationalism and the Cultural Crisis in Prussia*, Princeton 1939.
R. Aris, *Political Thought in Germany 1789–1815*, London 1936.
*H. Butterfield, *The System of Peace. Tactics of Napoleon 1806–1808*, Cambridge 1929.
H. Delbrueck, *Das Leben des GFM Neithardt von Gneisenau* (2 vols), Berlin 1920.
H. Diwald, *Ernst Moritz Arndt – Das Entstehen des deutschen Nationalbewusstseins*, C. F. v. Siemensstiftung, Munich 1971.
J. G. Droysen, *Das Leben des GFM Graf Yorck von Wartenburg* (2 vols), Berlin 1913.
J. Droz, *L'Allemagne et al revolution française*, Paris 1949.
*H. C. Engelbrecht, *Johann Gottlieb Fichte: A Study of his Political Writings with Special Reference to his Nationalism*, New York 1933.
*J. G. Fichte, *Addresses to the German Nation*, New York 1968.
G. S. Ford, *Hanover and Prussia 1795–1903. A Study in Neutrality*, New York 1903.
Stein and the Era of Reforms in Prussia, Princeton 1922.
I. Freund, *Die Emanzipation der Juden in Preussen* (2 vols), Berlin 1912.
† P. Hassel, *Joseph Maria von Radowitz*, Berlin 1905.
C. J. H. Hayes, *The Historical Evolution of Modern Nationalism*, New York 1931.
H. Heitzer, *Insurrektionen zwischen Weser und Elbe*, Berlin 1959.
†O. Hintze, *Historical Essays of Otto Hintze*, ed. Felix Gilbert, Oxford 1975.
R. Ibbeken, *Preussen 1807–1813*, Berlin 1970.
S. A. Kaehler, *Wilhelm von Humboldt und der Staat*, Munich 1927.
*E. Kehr, 'Zur Genesis der preussischen Buerokratie und des Rechtsstaats', in *Der Primat der Innenpolitik*, ed. H. U. Wehler, Berlin 1965.
*G. F. Knapp, *Die Bauernbefreiung und der Ursprung des Landarbeiter in den aelteren Teiler Preussens* (2 vols), Berlin 1927.
*H. Kohn, *Prelude to Nation States. The French and German Experience 1789–1815*, New York 1967.
M. Lehmann, *Scharnhorst* (2 vols), Leipzig 1886–87.
F. Lenz, *Agrarlehre und Agrarpolitik der deutschen Romantik*, Berlin 1912.
E. Longford, *Wellington. The Years of the Sword*, London 1969.
*G. Mann, *Friedrich von Gentz*, Berlin 1972.
F. Meinecke, *Leben des GFM von Boyen* (2 vols), Stuttgart 1896–99.
Das Zeitalter der deutschen Erhebung 1795–1815, Bielefeld 1913.
Cosmopolitanism and the National State, Princeton 1970.
*S. Neumann, *Die Stufen des preussischen Konservatismus: Ein Beitrag zum Statts-und Gesellschaftsbild Deutschlands im 19. Jahrhundert*, Berlin 1930.
† P. Paret, *Yorck and the Era of Prussian Reform 1807–1815*, Princeton 1966.
† *Clausewitz and the State*, Oxford 1976.
R. Parkinson, *Hussar General: The Life of Blücher*, London 1975.
Clausewitz, London 1970.
R. C. Raack, *The Fall of Stein*, Cambridge, Mass. 1965.
G. Ritter, *Stein, eine politische Biographie*, Stuttgart 1931.
*H. Roessler, *Graf Johann Philipp Stadion. Napoleons Deutscher Gegenspieler* (2 vols), Vienna 1966.
†F. Schnabel, *Deutsche Geschichte im neunzehnten Jahrhundert*, 8 vols (paperback ed.) Freiburg 1964.
*J. R. Seeley, *Life and Times of Stein* (3 vols), Cambridge 1878.
F. C. Sell, *Die Tragoedie des deutschen Liberalismus*, Stuttgart 1953.
*W. O. Shanahan, *Prussian Military Reforms 1786–1813*, New York 1945.
*W. M. Simon, *The Failure of the Prussian Reform Movement*, New York 1971.
*H. Stuebig, *Armee und Nation. Die paedagogisch-politischen Motive der preussichen Heeresreform 1907–1914*, Frankfurt 1971.
*P. R. Sweet, *Friedrich von Gentz: Defender of the Old Order*, Madison, Wisc. 1941.
†H. v. Treitschke, *History of Germany in the 19th Century* (7 vols), New York 1915–19.
H. Ulman, *Geschichte der Befreiungskriege*, (2 vols), Munich 1914.
W. v. Unger, *Bluecher* (2 vols), Berlin 1907–8.

C. K. Webster, *The [...]*
Reconstruction of [...]
The Foreign Policy o[...]
London 1934.
P. Wentzcke, *Geschichte [...]*
R. Wohlfeil, *Spanien un[...]*
E. W. Zeeden, *Harden[...]*
1807–1812, Berlin 19[...]
J. Ziekursch, *Hundert Ja[...]*
bis zum Abschluss a[...]

Chapter 10

E. N. Anderson, 'German[...]
History of Ideas, 194[...]
W. v. Eisenhardt-Rothe a[...]
deutschen Zollverein[...]
W. Foerst, (ed.), *Das Rhe[...]*
E. Foerster, *Die Entste[...]*
Friedrich Wilhelm II[...]
*T. E. Hamerow, *Resto[...]*
Princeton 1958.
*W. O. Henderson, *The Z[...]*
W. Kosch, *Die deutsche Li[...]*
1925.
*R. Koselleck, *Preussen z[...]*
G. R. Mason, *From Gotts[...]*
J. H. Pirenne, *La Sainte A[...]*
P. Rassow (ed.), *Deutsche [...]*
G. de Ruggiero, *The Histo[...]*
H. G. Schenck, *The Aftern[...]*
H. Schneider, *Der preussis[...]*
H. J. Schoeps, *Die Ehre P[...]*
Das andere Preussen, Be[...]
*H. v. Srbik, *Metternich*, ([...]
† *Deutsche Einheit* (4 vol[...]
*W. Treue, *Wirtschaftszu[...]*
Stuttgart 1937.
V. Valentin, *Das Hambac[...]*
L. A. Willoughby, *The Ron[...]*

Chapter 11

L. Bergstraesser, *Geschichte [...]*
H. Bleiber, *Zwischen Refor[...]*
Bauern und Landarbeite[...]
L. Dehie, *Friedrich Wilhelm [...]*
*F. Eyck, *The Frankfurt Pa[...]*
F. Fejtö (ed.), *The Opening [...]*
L. v. Gerlach, *Denkwuerdigk[...]*
Geschichte der deutschen [...]
Marxismus-Leninismus [...]
*B. Gloger, *Als Ruebezahl s[...]*
1961.

R. Herrnstadt, *Die ers[...]*
1958.
H. J. Heuer, *Allgemein[...]*
*E. Hobsbawm, *The A[...]*
* *The Age of Capital [...]*
*E. R. Huber, *Deutsch[...]*
*F. Meinecke, *Radowi[...]*
*L. B. Namier, *1848 Re[...]*
*K. Obermann, *Deutsc[...]*
(ed.), *Maenner der R[...]*
(ed.), *Flugblaetter de[...]*
H. v. Petersdorff, *Koen[...]*
J. M. v. Radowitz, *Nac[...]*
1848–1853 (2 vols), [...]
L. v. Ranke, *Friedrich [...]*
49–50, n.d.
P. Robertson, *Revoluti[...]*
W. O. Shanahan, *Der [...]*
Munich 1962.
F. J. Stahl, *Der christli[...]*
1847.
Der Protestantismus [...]
J. Strey and G. Wink[...]
waehrend der buerg[...]
*V. Valentin, *Geschicht[...]*
abridged English tr[...]
†G. Vogler/K. Vetter, [...]
1974.
*E. Zechlin, *Die deutsc[...]*

Chapters 12 and [...]

*E. N. Anderson, *The S[...]*
F. Balser, *Sozialdemok[...]*
O. v. Bismarck, *Gedank[...]*
Politische Schriften, [...]
1924–32.
*H. Boehme, *Deutschla[...]*
(ed.), *Probleme der R[...]*
*G. Bonnin (ed.), *Bisma[...]*
London 1957.
*K. E. Born, *Moderne [...]*
P. Bronsart v. Schellend[...]
W. Carr, *Schleswig-Hol[...]*
*J. H. Clapham, *The Ec[...]*
W. Conze and D. Groh[...]
1966.
R. Dahrendorf, *Democr[...]*
*W. E. Dawson, *The Ev[...]*
*J. Dittrich, *Bismarck, F[...]*
Munich 1962.
E. Engeleberg and R. W[...]
E. Eyck, *Bismarck and [...]*
*E. Forsthoff, *Deutsche [...]*
E. Franzel, *1866 Il mon[...]*
H. Friedjung, *The Strug[...]*
*L. Gall (ed.), *Das Bism[...]*

*A. Gerschenkron, *Bread and Democracy in Germany*, New York 1943.

O. Hauser, *Preussische Staatsraison und nationaler Gedanke*, Neumuenster 1960.

H. Heffter, *Die deutsche Selbstverwaltung im 19. Jahrhundert*, Stuttgart 1950.

*A. Hillgruber, *Bismarcks Aussenpolitik*, Freiburg 1972.

*M. Howard, *The Franco-Prussian War*, London 1961.

*E. Kehr, 'Das soziale System der Reaktion in Preussen unter dem Ministerium Putkamer', in *Primat der Innenpolitik* ed. H.-U. Wehler, Berlin 1965.

* 'Zur Genese des Koeniglich-Preussischen Reserveoffiziers', in *Der Primat der Innenpolitik* ed. H.-U. Wehler, Berlin 1965.

E. Kessel, *Moltke*, Stuttgart 1957.

W. L. Langer, 'Red Rag and Gallic Bull', in *Festschrift fuer Egmont Zechlin*, Hamburg 1961.

G. Masur, *Imperial Berlin*, London 1971.

A. O. Meyer, *Bismarck*, Stuttgart 1949.

W. Mommsen, *Deutsche Parteiprogramme*, Munich 1960.

W. E. Mosse, *The European Powers and the German Question 1848-1871*, Cambridge 1958.

L. v. Muralt, *Bismarck's Verantwortlichkeit*, Frankfurt 1955.

*S. Na'man, *Lassalle*, Hanover 1970.

*Th. Nipperdey, *Die Organisation der deutschen Parteien vor 1918*, Duesseldorf 1961.

H. Oncken, *Lassalle. Eine Biographie*, Munich 1965.

*O. Pflanze, *Bismarck and the Development of Germany*, vol. I, Princeton 1963.

*N. v. Preradovich, *Die Führungsschichten in Österreich und Preussen 1804 bis 1918*, Wiesbaden 1955.

*R. W. Reichard, *Crippled from Birth. German Social Democracy 1844-1870*, Iowa 1969.

*G. A. Rein, *Die Revolution in der Politik Bismarcks*, Goettingen 1957.

L. Reiners, *Bismarck* (2 vols), Munich 1957/58.

*W. Richter, *Bismarck*, London 1962.

G. Ritter, *Die preussischen Konservativen und Bismarck's Politik 1858-1876*, Heidelberg 1913.

Das deutsche Problem, Munich 1962.

D. G. Rohr, *The Origins of Social Liberalism in Germany*, Chicago 1966.

H. Rosenberg, *Grosse Depression und Bismarckzeit. Wirtschaftsablauf, Gesellschaft und Politik in Mitteleuropa*, Berlin 1967.

*H. Rothfels, *Bismarck, der Osten und das Reich*, Stuttgart 1960.

Bismarck, Stuttgart 1970.

*Th. Schieder and E. Deuerlein (eds), *Reichsgruendung 1870/71*, Stuttgart 1970.

W. Schuessler, *Bismarck's Kampf um Sueddeutschland 1867*, Berlin 1929.

H. v. Seybel, *Die Gruendung des deutschen Reiches durch Wilhelm I*, (7 vols), Munich 1889-94.

*L. D. Steefel, *Bismarck, the Hohenzollern Candidature and the Origins of the Franco-German War of 1870*, Cambridge, Mass. 1962.

*F. Stern, *Gold and Iron*, London 1977.

*M. Stuermer (ed.) *Das kaiserliche Deutschland*, Duesseldorf 1970.

A. J. P. Taylor, *The Struggle for Supremacy in Europe 1848-1918*, Oxford 1954.

* *Bismarck. The Man and the Statesman*, London 1955.

Th. Veblen, *Imperial Germany and the Industrial Revolution*, Ann Arbor 1966.

*L. Walker Muncy, *The Junker in the Prussian Administration*, New York 1970.

*H.-U. Wehler (ed.) *Moderne deutsche Sozialgeschichte*, Cologne 1966.

H. A. Winkler, *Preussischer Liberalismus und deutscher Nationalstaat*, Tuebingen 1964.

E. Zechlin, *Schwarz-Rot-Gold und Schwarz-Weiss-Rot in Geschichte und Gegenwart*, Berlin 1926.

* *Bismarck und die Grundlagen der deutschen Grossmacht*, Darmstadt 1960.

Chapter 14

*M. **Balfour,** *The Kaiser and his Times*, London 1964.
*K. D. **Bracher,** *Die Auflaesung der Weimarer Republik*, Villingen 1960.
O. **Braun,** *Von Weimar zu Hitler* 1947.
E. v. **Salomon,** *Die Kadetten*, Hamburg 1959.
*H.-U. **Wehler,** *Krisenherde des Kaiserreiches 1871-1918.* Goettingen 1970.
  Sozialdemokratie und Nationalstaat, Goettingen 1971.
  Das deutsche Kaiserreich 1871-1918, Göttingen 1973.

Genealogical tables and maps

Table 1   The rise of the Hohenzollerns in Brandenburg-Prussia in the 16th and
17th centuries

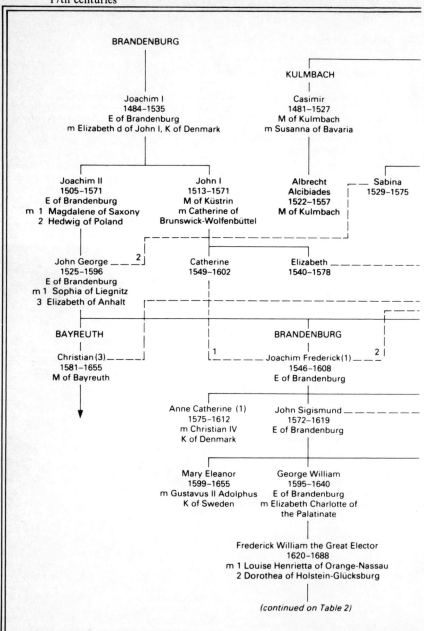

(continued on Table 2)

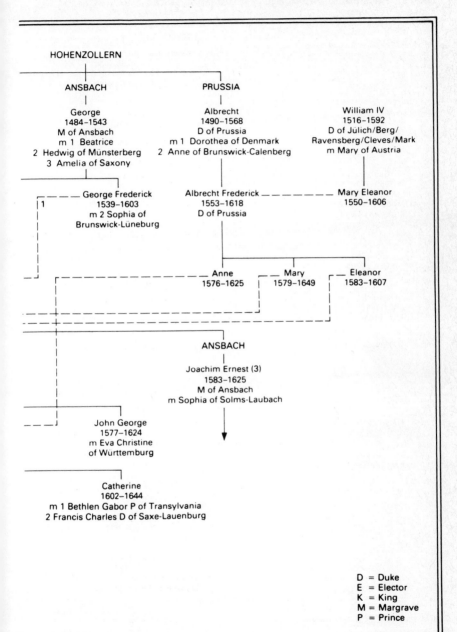

HOHENZOLLERN

ANSBACH

PRUSSIA

George
1484–1543
M of Ansbach
m 1 Beatrice
2 Hedwig of Münsterberg
3 Amelia of Saxony

Albrecht
1490–1568
D of Prussia
m 1 Dorothea of Denmark
2 Anne of Brunswick-Calenberg

William IV
1516–1592
D of Jülich/Berg/
Ravensberg/Cleves/Mark
m Mary of Austria

George Frederick
1539–1603
m 2 Sophia of
Brunswick-Lüneburg

Albrecht Frederick
1553–1618
D of Prussia

Mary Eleanor
1550–1606

Anne
1576–1625

Mary
1579–1649

Eleanor
1583–1607

ANSBACH

Joachim Ernest (3)
1583–1625
M of Ansbach
m Sophia of Solms-Laubach

John George
1577–1624
m Eva Christine
of Württemburg

Catherine
1602–1644
m 1 Bethlen Gabor P of Transylvania
2 Francis Charles D of Saxe-Lauenburg

D = Duke
E = Elector
K = King
M = Margrave
P = Prince

Table 2   The Hohenzollern dynasty after the Great Elector

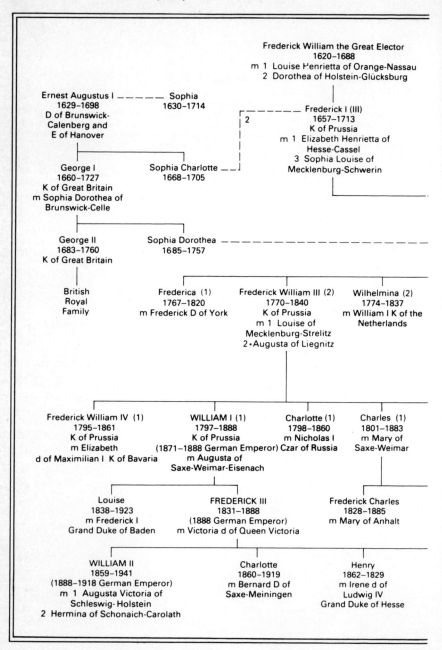

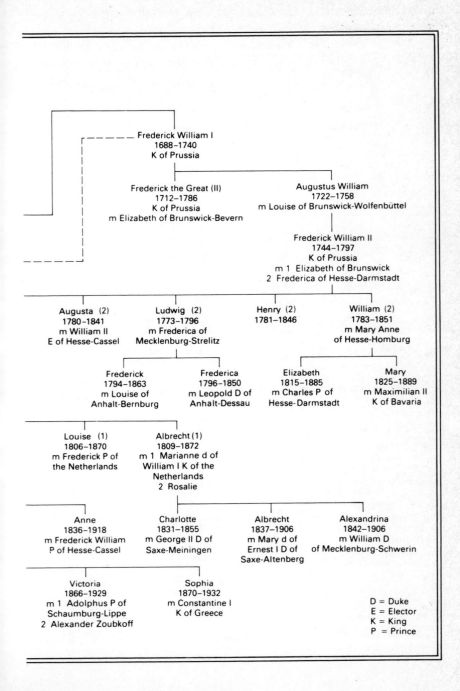

Frederick William I
1688–1740
K of Prussia

Frederick the Great (II)
1712–1786
K of Prussia
m Elizabeth of Brunswick-Bevern

Augustus William
1722–1758
m Louise of Brunswick-Wolfenbüttel

Frederick William II
1744–1797
K of Prussia
m 1 Elizabeth of Brunswick
2 Frederica of Hesse-Darmstadt

Augusta (2)
1780–1841
m William II
E of Hesse-Cassel

Ludwig (2)
1773–1796
m Frederica of
Mecklenburg-Strelitz

Henry (2)
1781–1846

William (2)
1783–1851
m Mary Anne
of Hesse-Homburg

Frederick
1794–1863
m Louise of
Anhalt-Bernburg

Frederica
1796–1850
m Leopold D of
Anhalt-Dessau

Elizabeth
1815–1885
m Charles P of
Hesse-Darmstadt

Mary
1825–1889
m Maximilian II
K of Bavaria

Louise (1)
1806–1870
m Frederick P of
the Netherlands

Albrecht (1)
1809–1872
m 1 Marianne d of
William I K of the
Netherlands
2 Rosalie

Anne
1836–1918
m Frederick William
P of Hesse-Cassel

Charlotte
1831–1855
m George II D of
Saxe-Meiningen

Albrecht
1837–1906
m Mary d of
Ernest I D of
Saxe-Altenberg

Alexandrina
1842–1906
m William D
of Mecklenburg-Schwerin

Victoria
1866–1929
m 1 Adolphus P of
Schaumburg-Lippe
2 Alexander Zoubkoff

Sophia
1870–1932
m Constantine I
K of Greece

D = Duke
E = Elector
K = King
P = Prince

Map 1 Northern Germany and Scandinavia in the later Middle Ages

O. **Hintze**, 'Friedrich der Grosse und die preussische Justizreform des 18. Jahrhunderts', in *Recht und Wirtschaft*, vol. I, 1912.

D. B. **Horn**, *Frederick the Great and the Rise of Prussia*, London 1964.

*W. **Hubatsch**, *Frederick the Great: Absolutism and Administration*, London 1975.

† S. **Isaacsohn**, *Geschichte des preussischen Beamtenthums* (3 vols), Berlin 1874–84.

*H. C. **Johnson**, *Frederick the Great and His Officials*, Yale 1975.

H. **Kaplan**, *The First Partition of Poland*, Boston 1962.

R. **Koser**, *Geschichte Friedrichs des Grossen* (4 vols), Berlin 1921.

*F. **Meinecke**, *Machiavellism*, New Haven 1957.

*P. **Paret** (ed.), *Frederick the Great. A profile*, London 1972.

J. D. E. **Preuss** (ed.), *Oeuvres de Frederic le Grand* (30 vols), Berlin 1846–57.

G. **Ritter**, *Frederick the Great*, Berkeley 1968.

† *The Sword and the Sceptre*, vol. I and II, Coral Gables, Florida, 1970.

E. **Simon**, *The Making of Frederick the Great*, London 1963.

*M. **Schlenke**, *England und das friederizianische Preussen 1740–1763*, Freiburg 1963.

S. **Skalweit**, *Frankreich und Friedrich der Grosse. Der Aufstieg Preussens in der oeffentlichen Meinung des Ancien Regime*, Goettingen 1952.

'Friedrich der Grosse und der Aufstieg Preussens', in *Die Europaeer und ihre Geschichte*, ed. L. Reinisch, Munich 1961.

*H. **Weill**, *Frederick the Great and Samuel Cocceji: A Study in the Reform of the Prussian Judicial Administration 1745–1755*, Madison, Wisc., 1961.

Chapter 7

*C. **Brinton**, *A Decade of Revolution 1789–1799*, New York 1934.

* H. **Brunschwig**, *La crise de l'état prussien à la fin du XVIIIe siècle et la genèse de la mentalité romantique*, Paris 1947.

H. **Conrad**, *Die geistigen Grundlagen des Allgemeinen Landrechts fuer die preussischen Staaten von 1794*, Cologne 1958.

K. **Epstein**, *The Genesis of German Conservatism*, Princeton 1966.

K. D. **Erdmann**, *Die Umgestaltung Deutschlands im Zeitalter der Franzoesischen Revolution und Napoleons 1786–1815*, Stuttgart 1952.

*L. **Gershoy**, *From Despotism to Revolution 1763–1789*, New York 1944.

*G. P. **Gooch**, *Germany and the French Revolution*, London 1965.

K. **Griewank**, 'Hardenberg und die preussische Politik 1804–1806', *Forschungen zur Brandenburgischen und Preussischen Geschichte*, XLVII, 1935.

O. **Hintze**, 'Preussische Reformbestrebungen von 1806', in *Gesammelte Abhandlungen III*, Leipzig 1943.

W. **Hubatsch**, *Eckpfeiler Europas. Probleme des Preussenlandes in geschichtlicher Sicht*, Heidelberg 1953.

H. v. **Kleist**, *Saemmtliche Werke und Briefe*, Munich 1964.

*R. **Koselleck**, 'Staat und Gesellschaft in Preussen 1815–1848', in *Staat und Gesellschaft im deutschen Vormaerz*, Stuttgart 1962.

*P. **Lahnstein** (ed.), *Report einer 'guten alten Zeit' Zeugnisse und Berichte 1750–1805*, Munich 1977.

O. v. **Lettow-Vorbeck**, *Der Krieg von 1806 und 1807* (4 vols), Berlin 1891–96.

*H. **Möller**, *Anfklärung in Preussen*, Berlin 1974.

E. **Ruppel-Kuhfuss**, *Das Generaldirektorium unter der Regierung Friedrich Wilhelm II*, Wuerzburg 1937.

H. J. **Schoeps**, *Aus den Jahren preussischer Not und Erneuerung, Tagebuecher und Briefe der Gebrueder Gerlach und ihres Kreises 1805–1820*, Berlin 1963.

*A. **Sorel**, *Europe and the French Revolution. The Political Traditions of the Old Régime*, eds A. Cobban and J. W. Hunt, London 1969.

C. G. **Svarez**, *Vortraege ueber Recht und Staat von 1791*, ed. H. Conrad and G. Kleinheyer, Cologne 1966.

*A. de **Tocqueville**, *L'ancien régime et la revolution*, Paris 1952.

Chapters 8 and 9

**E. N. Anderson, *Nationalism and the Cultural Crisis in Prussia*, Princeton 1939.

R. Aris, *Political Thought in Germany 1789-1815*, London 1936.

*H. Butterfield, *The System of Peace. Tactics of Napoleon 1806-1808*, Cambridge 1929.

H. Delbrueck, *Das Leben des GFM Neithardt von Gneisenau* (2 vols), Berlin 1920.

H. Diwald, *Ernst Moritz Arndt – Das Entstehen des deutschen Nationalbewusstseins*, C. F. v. Siemensstiftung, Munich 1971.

J. G. Droysen, *Das Leben des GFM Graf Yorck von Wartenburg* (2 vols), Berlin 1913.

J. Droz, *L'Allemagne et al revolution française*, Paris 1949.

*H. C. Engelbrecht, *Johann Gottlieb Fichte: A Study of his Political Writings with Special Reference to his Nationalism*, New York 1933.

*J. G. Fichte, *Addresses to the German Nation*, New York 1968.

G. S. Ford, *Hanover and Prussia 1795-1903. A Study in Neutrality*, New York 1903.

Stein and the Era of Reforms in Prussia, Princeton 1922.

I. Freund, *Die Emanzipation der Juden in Preussen* (2 vols), Berlin 1912.

† P. Hassel, *Joseph Maria von Radowitz*, Berlin 1905.

C. J. H. Hayes, *The Historical Evolution of Modern Nationalism*, New York 1931.

H. Heitzer, *Insurrektionen zwischen Weser und Elbe*, Berlin 1959.

†O. Hintze, *Historical Essays of Otto Hintze*, ed. Felix Gilbert, Oxford 1975.

R. Ibbeken, *Preussen 1807-1813*, Berlin 1970.

S. A. Kaehler, *Wilhelm von Humboldt und der Staat*, Munich 1927.

*E. Kehr, 'Zur Genesis der preussischen Buerokratie und des Rechtstaats', in *Der Primat der Innenpolitik*, ed. H. U. Wehler, Berlin 1965.

*G. F. Knapp, *Die Bauernbefreiung und der Ursprung des Landarbeiter in den aelteren Teiler Preussens* (2 vols), Berlin 1927.

*H. Kohn, *Prelude to Nation States. The French and German Experience 1789-1815*, New York 1967.

M. Lehmann, *Scharnhorst* (2 vols), Leipzig 1886-87.

F. Lenz, *Agrarlehre und Agrarpolitik der deutschen Romantik*, Berlin 1912.

E. Longford, *Wellington. The Years of the Sword*, London 1969.

*G. Mann, *Friedrich von Gentz*, Berlin 1972.

F. Meinecke, *Leben des GFM von Boyen* (2 vols), Stuttgart 1896-99.

Das Zeitalter der deutschen Erhebung 1795-1815, Bielefeld 1913.

Cosmopolitanism and the National State, Princeton 1970.

*S. Neumann, *Die Stufen des preussischen Konservatismus: Ein Beitrag zum Statts-und Gesellschaftsbild Deutschlands im 19. Jahrhundert*, Berlin 1930.

† P. Paret, *Yorck and the Era of Prussian Reform 1807-1815*, Princeton 1966.

†   *Clausewitz and the State*, Oxford 1976.

R. Parkinson, *Hussar General: The Life of Blücher*, London 1975.

Clausewitz, London 1970.

R. C. Raack, *The Fall of Stein*, Cambridge, Mass. 1965.

G. Ritter, *Stein, eine politische Biographie*, Stuttgart 1931.

*H. Roessler, *Graf Johann Philipp Stadion. Napoleons Deutscher Gegenspieler* (2 vols), Vienna 1966.

†F. Schnabel, *Deutsche Geschichte im neunzehnten Jahrhundert*, 8 vols (paperback ed.) Freiburg 1964.

*J. R. Seeley, *Life and Times of Stein* (3 vols), Cambridge 1878.

F. C. Sell, *Die Tragoedie des deutschen Liberalismus*, Stuttgart 1953.

*W. O. Shanahan, *Prussian Military Reforms 1786-1813*, New York 1945.

*W. M. Simon, *The Failure of the Prussian Reform Movement*, New York 1971.

*H. Stuebig, *Armee und Nation. Die paedagogish-politischen Motive der preussichen Heeresreform 1907-1914*, Frankfurt 1971.

*P. R. Sweet, *Friedrich von Gentz: Defender of the Old Order*, Madison, Wisc. 1941.

†H. v. Treitschke, *History of Germany in the 19th Century* (7 vols), New York 1915-19.

H. Ulman, *Geschichte der Befreiungskriege*, (2 vols), Munich 1914.

W. v. Unger, *Bluecher* (2 vols), Berlin 1907-8.

C. K. **Webster,** *The Foreign Policy of Castlereagh 1812–1815. Britain and the Reconstruction of Europe,* London 1931.
The Foreign Policy of Castlereagh 1815–1822. Britain and the European Alliance, London 1934.
P. **Wentzcke,** *Geschichte der deutschen Burschenschaft,* vol. I, Heidelberg 1919.
R. **Wohlfeil,** *Spanien und die deutsche Erhebung,* Wiesbaden 1965.
E. W. **Zeeden,** *Hardenberg und der Gedanke einer Volksvertretung in Preussen 1807–1812,* Berlin 1940.
J. **Ziekursch,** *Hundert Jahre schlesischer Agrargeschichte: Vom Hubertusburger Frieden bis zum Abschluss der Bauernbefreiung,* Breslau 1915.

Chapter 10

*E. N. **Anderson,** 'German romanticism as an ideology of cultural crisis', *Journal of the History of Ideas,* 1941.
W. v. **Eisenhardt-Rothe** and A. **Ritthaler,** (eds), *Vorgeschichte und Begruendung des deutschen Zollvereins 1815–1834,* (3 vols), Berlin 1934.
W. **Foerst,** (ed.), *Das Rheinland in preussischer Zeit,* Cologne 1965.
E. **Foerster,** *Die Entstehung des preussischen Landeskirche unter der Regierung Friedrich Wilhelm III,* (2 vols), Tuebingen 1905–7.
*T. E. **Hamerow,** *Restoration Revolution and Reaction in Germany 1815–1871,* Princeton 1958.
*W. O. **Henderson,** *The Zollverein,* Cambridge 1938.
W. **Kosch,** *Die deutsche Literatur im Spiegel der nationalen Entwicklung,* vol. I, Munich 1925.
*R. **Koselleck,** *Preussen zwischen Reform und Revolution,* Stuttgart 1967.
G. R. **Mason,** *From Gottsched to Hebbel,* London 1962.
J. H. **Pirenne,** *La Sainte Alliance,* Paris 1946.
P. **Rassow** (ed.), *Deutsche Geschichte im Ueberblick,* Stuttgart 1953.
G. de **Ruggiero,** *The History of European Liberalism,* Oxford 1927.
H. G. **Schenck,** *The Aftermath of the Napoleonic Wars,* London 1947.
H. **Schneider,** *Der preussische Staatsrat 1817–1918,* Munich 1952.
H. J. **Schoeps,** *Die Ehre Preussens,* Berlin 1951.
Das andere Preussen, Berlin 1952.
*H. v. **Srbik,** *Metternich,* (3 vols), Munich 1957.
† *Deutsche Einheit* (4 vols), Darmstadt 1963.
*W. **Treue,** *Wirtschaftszustaender und Wirtschaftspolitik in Preussen 1815–1825,* Stuttgart 1937.
V. **Valentin,** *Das Hambacher Nationalfest,* Berlin 1932.
L. A. **Willoughby,** *The Romantic Movement in Germany,* Oxford 1930.

Chapter 11

L. **Bergstraesser,** *Geschichte der politischen Parteien in Deutschland,* Munich 1960.
H. **Bleiber,** *Zwischen Reform und Revolution. Lage und Kaempfe der schlesischen Bauern und Landarbeiter im Vormaerz 1840–1847,* Berlin 1966.
L. **Dehie,** *Friedrich Wilhelm IV ein Baukuenster der Romantik,* Munich 1961.
*F. **Eyck,** *The Frankfurt Parliament 1848–49,* London 1968.
F. **Fejtö** (ed.), *The Opening of an Era 1848,* London (n.d.).
L. v. **Gerlach,** *Denkwuerdigkeiten aus seinem Leben* (2 vols), Berlin 1891–92.
Geschichte der deutschen Arbeiterbewegung, vol. I, pub. by the Institut fuer Marxismus-Leninismus beim ZK der SED, Berlin 1966.
*B. **Gloger,** *Als Ruebezahl schlief. Vom Aufstand der schlesischen Weber 1844,* Berlin 1961.

R. Herrnstadt, *Die erste Verschwoerung gegen das internationale Proletariat,* Berlin 1958.

H. J. Heuer, *Allgemeines Landrecht und Klassenkampf,* Berlin 1960.

*****E. Hobsbawm,** *The Age of Revolution,* London 1962.

***** *The Age of Capital 1848–1875,* London 1975.

*****E. R. Huber,** *Deutsche Verfassungsgeschichte seit 1789* (3 vols), Stuttgart 1963.

*****F. Meinecke,** *Radowitz und die deutsche Revolution,* Berlin 1913.

*****L. B. Namier,** *1848 Revolution of the Intellectuals,* Oxford 1944.

*****K. Obermann,** *Deutschland von 1815 bis 1849,* Berlin 1967.

(ed.), *Maenner der Revolution von 1848,* Berlin 1970.

(ed.), *Flugblaetter der Revolution,* Munich 1972.

H. v. Petersdorff, *Koenig Friedrich Wilhelm IV,* Berlin 1900.

J. M. v. Radowitz, *Nachgelassene Briefe und Aufzeichnungen zur Geschichte der Jahre 1848–1853* (2 vols), Stuttgart 1922.

L. v. Ranke, *Friedrich Wilhelm IV Briefwechsel mit Bunsen, Saemmtliche Werke,* vols. 49–50, n.d.

P. Robertson, *Revolutions of 1848: a Social History,* Princeton 1953.

W. O. Shanahan, *Der deutsche Protestantismus vor der sozialen Frage 1815–1871,* Munich 1962.

F. J. Stahl, *Der christliche Staat und sein Verhaeltnis zu Deismus und Judentum,* Berlin 1847.

Der Protestantismus als politisches Prinzip, Berlin 1863.

J. Strey and **G. Winkler,** *Die Politik und Taktik der 'Neuen Rheinischen Zeitung' waehrend der buergerlich-demokratischen Revolution in Deutschland,* Berlin 1971.

*****V. Valentin,** *Geschichte der deutschen Revolution 1848–1849* (2 vols), Stuttgart 1922, abridged English trans. *1848: Chapters of German History,* London 1940.

†**G. Vogler/K. Vetter,** *Preussen. Von den Anfaengen bis zur Reichsgruendung,* Berlin 1974.

*****E. Zechlin,** *Die deutsche Einheitsbewegung,* Berlin 1968.

Chapters 12 and 13

*****E. N. Anderson,** *The Social and Political Conflict in Prussia 1858–1864,* Nebraska 1954.

F. Balser, *Sozialdemokratie 1848/49 bis 1963,* Munich 1963.

O. v. Bismarck, *Gedanken und Erinnerungen* (3 vols), Stuttgart 1898–1921.

Politische Schriften, Reden, Briefe, Gespraeche, Friedrichsruher Ausgabe, Berlin 1924–32.

*****H. Boehme,** *Deutschlands Weg zur Grossmacht,* Cologne 1966.

(ed.), *Probleme der Reichsgruendungszeit,* Cologne 1968.

*****G. Bonnin** (ed.), *Bismarck and the Hohenzollern Candidature for the Spanish Throne,* London 1957.

*****K. E. Born,** *Moderne deutsche Wirtschaftsgeschichte,* Cologne 1966.

P. Bronsart v. Schellendorf, *Geheimes Kriegstagebuch 1870/71,* Bonn 1954.

W. Carr, *Schleswig-Holstein 1815–1864,* London 1963.

*****J. H. Clapham,** *The Economic Development of France and Germany,* Cambridge 1951.

W. Conze and **D. Groh,** *Die Arbeiterbewegung in der nationalen Bewegung,* Stuttgart 1966.

R. Dahrendorf, *Democracy and Society in Germany,* London 1967.

*****W. E. Dawson,** *The Evolution of Modern Germany,* London 1908.

*****J. Dittrich,** *Bismarck, Frankreich und die spanische Thronkandidatur der Hohenzollern,* Munich 1962.

E. Engeleberg and **R. Weber,** *Im Widerstreit um die Reichsgruendung,* Berlin 1970.

E. Eyck, *Bismarck and the German Empire,* London 1950.

*****E. Forsthoff,** *Deutsche Verfassungsgeschichte der Neuzeit,* Stuttgart 1961.

E. Franzel, *1866 Il monde casca, Das Ende des alten Europa,* Vienna 1968.

H. Friedjung, *The Struggle for Supremacy in Germany 1859–1866,* London 1935.

*****L. Gall** (ed.), *Das Bismarck Problem,* Cologne 1971.

*A. Gerschenkron, *Bread and Democracy in Germany*, New York 1943.
O. Hauser, *Preussische Staatsraison und nationaler Gedanke*, Neumuenster 1960.
H. Heffter, *Die deutsche Selbstverwaltung im 19. Jahrhundert*, Stuttgart 1950.
*A. Hillgruber, *Bismarcks Aussenpolitik*, Freiburg 1972.
*M. Howard, *The Franco-Prussian War*, London 1961.
*E. Kehr, 'Das soziale System der Reaktion in Preussen unter dem Ministerium Putkamer', in *Primat der Innenpolitik* ed. H.-U. Wehler, Berlin 1965.
* 'Zur Genese des Koeniglich-Preussischen Reserveoffiziers', in *Der Primat der Innenpolitik* ed. H.-U. Wehler, Berlin 1965.
E. Kessel, *Moltke*, Stuttgart 1957.
W. L. Langer, 'Red Rag and Gallic Bull', in *Festschrift fuer Egmont Zechlin*, Hamburg 1961.
G. Masur, *Imperial Berlin*, London 1971.
A. O. Meyer, *Bismarck*, Stuttgart 1949.
W. Mommsen, *Deutsche Parteiprogramme*, Munich 1960.
W. E. Mosse, *The European Powers and the German Question 1848-1871*, Cambridge 1958.
L. v. Muralt, *Bismarck's Verantwortlichkeit*, Frankfurt 1955.
*S. Na'man, *Lassalle*, Hanover 1970.
*Th. Nipperdey, *Die Organisation der deutschen Parteien vor 1918*, Duesseldorf 1961.
H. Oncken, *Lassalle. Eine Biographie*, Munich 1965.
*O. Pflanze, *Bismarck and the Development of Germany*, vol. I, Princeton 1963.
*N. v. Preradovich, *Die Führungsschichten in Österreich und Preussen 1804 bis 1918*, Wiesbaden 1955.
*R. W. Reichard, *Crippled from Birth. German Social Democracy 1844-1870*, Iowa 1969.
*G. A. Rein, *Die Revolution in der Politik Bismarcks*, Goettingen 1957.
L. Reiners, *Bismarck* (2 vols), Munich 1957/58.
*W. Richter, *Bismarck*, London 1962.
G. Ritter, *Die preussischen Konservativen und Bismarck's Politik 1858-1876*, Heidelberg 1913.
Das deutsche Problem, Munich 1962.
D. G. Rohr, *The Origins of Social Liberalism in Germany*, Chicago 1966.
H. Rosenberg, *Grosse Depression und Bismarckzeit. Wirtschaftsablauf, Gesellschaft und Politik in Mitteleuropa*, Berlin 1967.
*H. Rothfels, *Bismarck, der Osten und das Reich*, Stuttgart 1960.
Bismarck, Stuttgart 1970.
*Th. Schieder and E. Deuerlein (eds), *Reichsgruendung 1870/71*, Stuttgart 1970.
W. Schuessler, *Bismarck's Kampf um Sueddeutschland 1867*, Berlin 1929.
H. v. Seybel, *Die Gruendung des deutschen Reiches durch Wilhelm I*, (7 vols), Munich 1889-94.
*L. D. Steefel, *Bismarck, the Hohenzollern Candidature and the Origins of the Franco-German War of 1870*, Cambridge, Mass. 1962.
*F. Stern, *Gold and Iron*, London 1977.
*M. Stuermer (ed.) *Das kaiserliche Deutschland*, Duesseldorf 1970.
A. J. P. Taylor, *The Struggle for Supremacy in Europe 1848-1918*, Oxford 1954.
* *Bismarck. The Man and the Statesman*, London 1955.
Th. Veblen, *Imperial Germany and the Industrial Revolution*, Ann Arbor 1966.
*L. Walker Muncy, *The Junker in the Prussian Administration*, New York 1970.
*H.-U. Wehler (ed.) *Moderne deutsche Sozialgeschichte*, Cologne 1966.
H. A. Winkler, *Preussischer Liberalismus und deutscher Nationalstaat*, Tuebingen 1964.
E. Zechlin, *Schwarz-Rot-Gold und Schwarz-Weiss-Rot in Geschichte und Gegenwart*, Berlin 1926.
* *Bismarck und die Grundlagen der deutschen Grossmacht*, Darmstadt 1960.

Chapter 14

*M. Balfour, *The Kaiser and his Times*, London 1964.
*K. D. Bracher, *Die Auflaesung der Weimarer Republik*, Villingen 1960.
O. Braun, *Von Weimar zu Hitler* 1947.
E. v. Salomon, *Die Kadetten*, Hamburg 1959.
*H.-U. Wehler, *Krisenherde des Kaiserreiches 1871-1918*. Goettingen 1970.
  Sozialdemokratie und Nationalstaat, Goettingen 1971.
  Das deutsche Kaiserreich 1871-1918, Göttingen 1973.

Table 1   The rise of the Hohenzollerns in Brandenburg-Prussia in the 16th and 17th centuries

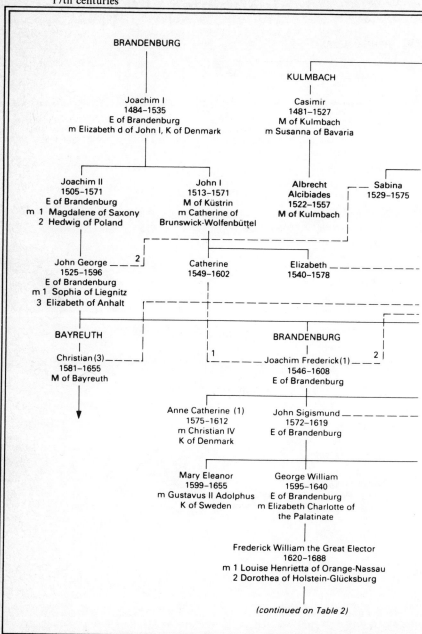

(continued on Table 2)

Genealogical tables and maps

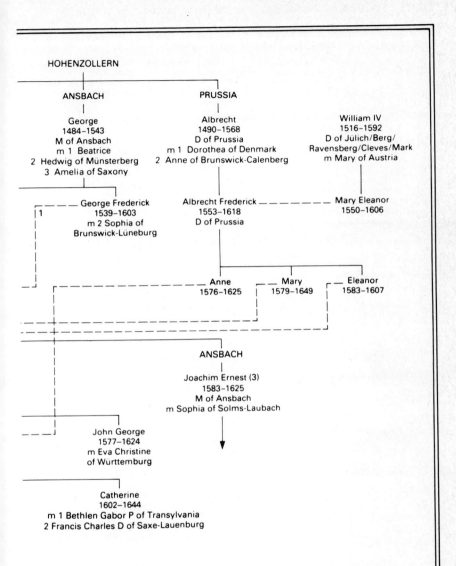

HOHENZOLLERN

ANSBACH

George
1484–1543
M of Ansbach
m 1 Beatrice
2 Hedwig of Münsterberg
3 Amelia of Saxony

PRUSSIA

Albrecht
1490–1568
D of Prussia
m 1 Dorothea of Denmark
2 Anne of Brunswick-Calenberg

William IV
1516–1592
D of Jülich/Berg/
Ravensberg/Cleves/Mark
m Mary of Austria

George Frederick
1539–1603
m 2 Sophia of
Brunswick-Lüneburg

1

Albrecht Frederick
1553–1618
D of Prussia

Mary Eleanor
1550–1606

Anne
1576–1625

Mary
1579–1649

Eleanor
1583–1607

ANSBACH

Joachim Ernest (3)
1583–1625
M of Ansbach
m Sophia of Solms-Laubach

John George
1577–1624
m Eva Christine
of Württemburg

Catherine
1602–1644
m 1 Bethlen Gabor P of Transylvania
2 Francis Charles D of Saxe-Lauenburg

D = Duke
E = Elector
K = King
M = Margrave
P = Prince

Table 2 The Hohenzollern dynasty after the Great Elector

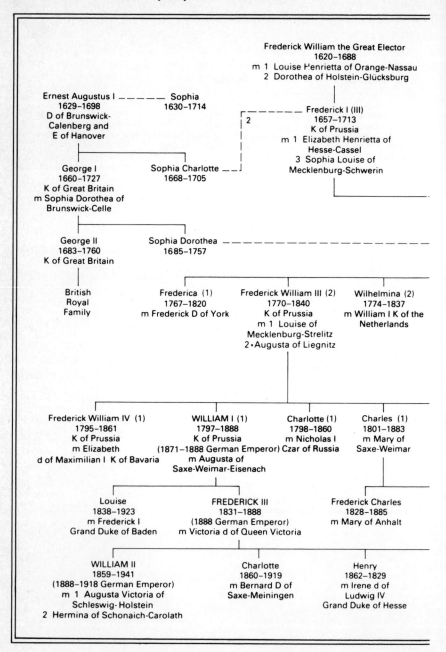

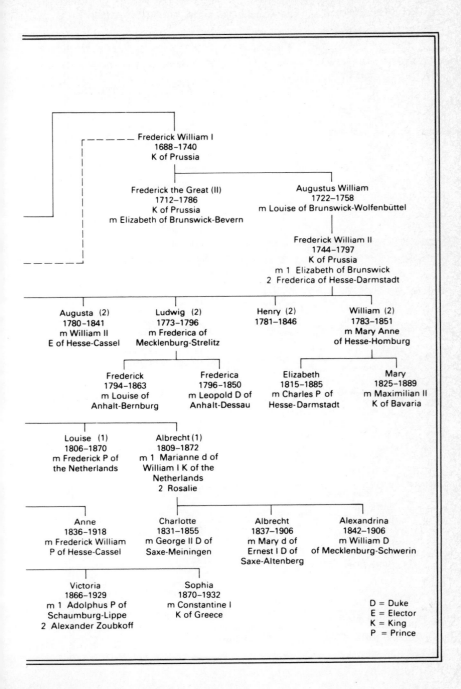

Frederick William I
1688–1740
K of Prussia

Frederick the Great (II)
1712–1786
K of Prussia
m Elizabeth of Brunswick-Bevern

Augustus William
1722–1758
m Louise of Brunswick-Wolfenbüttel

Frederick William II
1744–1797
K of Prussia
m 1 Elizabeth of Brunswick
2 Frederica of Hesse-Darmstadt

Augusta (2)
1780–1841
m William II
E of Hesse-Cassel

Ludwig (2)
1773–1796
m Frederica of
Mecklenburg-Strelitz

Henry (2)
1781–1846

William (2)
1783–1851
m Mary Anne
of Hesse-Homburg

Frederick
1794–1863
m Louise of
Anhalt-Bernburg

Frederica
1796–1850
m Leopold D of
Anhalt-Dessau

Elizabeth
1815–1885
m Charles P of
Hesse-Darmstadt

Mary
1825–1889
m Maximilian II
K of Bavaria

Louise (1)
1806–1870
m Frederick P of
the Netherlands

Albrecht (1)
1809–1872
m 1 Marianne d of
William I K of the
Netherlands
2 Rosalie

Anne
1836–1918
m Frederick William
P of Hesse-Cassel

Charlotte
1831–1855
m George II D of
Saxe-Meiningen

Albrecht
1837–1906
m Mary d of
Ernest I D of
Saxe-Altenberg

Alexandrina
1842–1906
m William D
of Mecklenburg-Schwerin

Victoria
1866–1929
m 1 Adolphus P of
Schaumburg-Lippe
2 Alexander Zoubkoff

Sophia
1870–1932
m Constantine I
K of Greece

D = Duke
E = Elector
K = King
P = Prince

Map 1 Northern Germany and Scandinavia in the later Middle Ages

Nidaros
(Trondheim)

S W E D E N

FINLAND

N O R W A Y

Bergen

Oslo

Uppsala

Gulf of Finland

Stavanger

Stockholm

North Sea

Vadstena

Visby

GOTLAND

Kalmar

Baltic Sea

JUTLAND

The Sound

D E N M A R K

SCANIA

BORNHOLM

Copenhagen

Lund

Falsterbo

SCHLESWIG

RUGEN

HOLSTEIN   Stralsund

TEUTONIC
ORDER

Lübeck

Rostock

POMERANIA

Danzig

Marienburg

Hamburg

Wismar

Stettin

Tannenberg

Bremen

Luneburg

MECKLENBURG

BRANDENBURG

BRUNSWICK

Elbe

Berlin

POLAND

Utrecht

Osnabrück

Magdeburg

Frankfurt-a-d-Oder

SILESIA

Warsaw

CLEVES

Münster

WESTPHALIA

SAXONY

Dortmund

Paderborn

THURINGIA

JULICH

BERG   HESSE

Leipzig

Aachen

Cologne

Erfurt

Meissen

R. Oder

Breslau

Fulda

WETTIN LANDS

R. Rhine

FRANCONIA

Trier

Frankfurt-am-Main

BOHEMIA

Luxemburg

Mainz

PALATINATE

Prague

Metz

WURTTEMBURG

UPPER PALATINATE

Nuremberg

LORRAINE

Stuttgart

SWABIA

Regensburg

Ingolstadt

ALSACE

Strasbourg

R. Danube

Ulm

Augsburg

Vienna

Basel

Ravensburg

Munich

Innsbruck

Salzburg

SWISS
CONFEDERATION

TIROL

Brenner Pass

AUSTRIA

Brixen

0   100 mls

0   100 km

- - -   Approximate
- - -   frontiers

Map 2 The lands of the Teutonic Order at their greatest extent, beginning of the 15th century

Map 3   The expansion of Brandenburg-Prussia during the reign of the Great Elector, 1640–1688

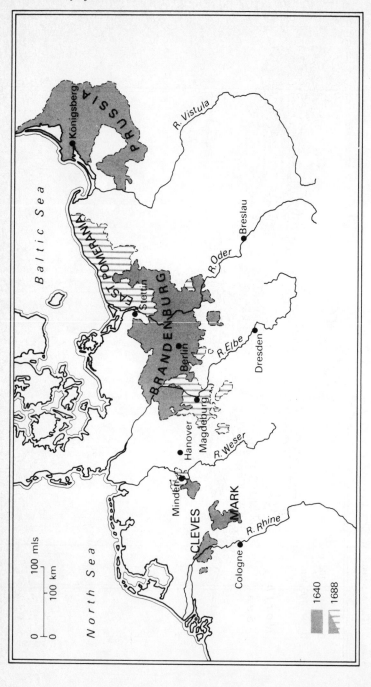

Baltic Sea

North Sea

R. Vistula

Königsberg

PRUSSIA

EAST POMERANIA

Stettin

Breslau

R. Oder

BRANDENBURG

Berlin

R. Elbe

Dresden

Magdeburg

Hanover

R. Weser

Minden

CLEVES

MARK

R. Rhine

Cologne

0   100 mls
0   100 km

1640
1688

Map 4 The expansion of Brandenburg-Prussia in the 18th century

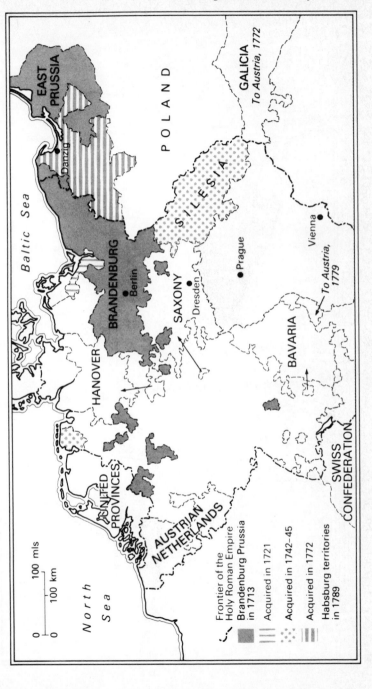

Map 5   Prussia 1806–1812

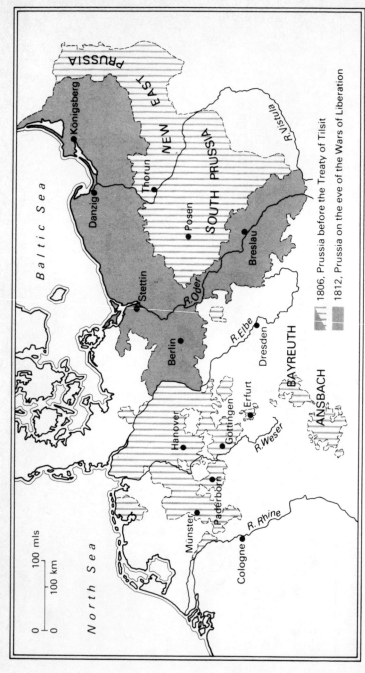

1806, Prussia before the Treaty of Tilsit

1812, Prussia on the eve of the Wars of Liberation

PRUSSIA

NEW EAST

SOUTH PRUSSIA

R. Vistula

Königsberg

Thorun

Posen

Breslau

Danzig

Baltic Sea

Stettin

R. Oder

Berlin

R. Elbe

Dresden

BAYREUTH

ANSBACH

Erfurt

Göttingen

Hanover

R. Weser

Paderborn

Münster

Cologne

R. Rhine

North Sea

0   100 mls

0   100 km

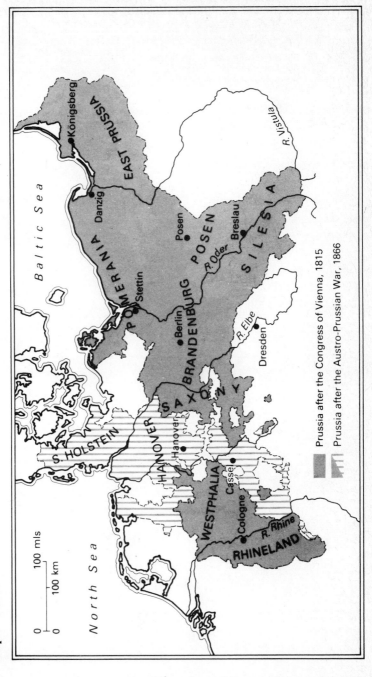

Map 6 Prussia 1815–1866

Baltic Sea

North Sea

Königsberg

EAST PRUSSIA

R. Vistula

Danzig

Posen

Breslau

POSEN

SILESIA

POMERANIA

R. Oder

Stettin

BRANDENBURG

Berlin

R. Elbe

Dresden

SAXONY

HANOVER

S. HOLSTEIN

Hanover

WESTPHALIA

Cassel

Cologne

R. Rhine

RHINELAND

Prussia after the Congress of Vienna, 1815

Prussia after the Austro-Prussian War, 1866

0   100 mls

0   100 km

Map 7   Prussia and the unification of Germany, 1871

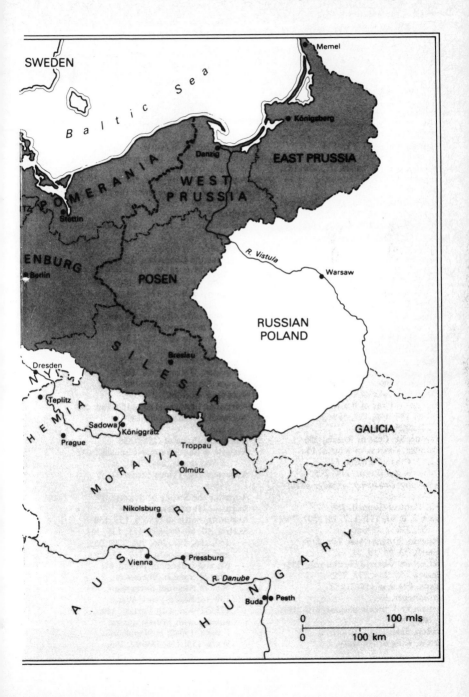

Index